1995

Buddhist Thought and Asian Civilization

Herbert V. Guenther

Buddhist Thought and Asian Civilization

Essays in Honor of Herbert V. Guenther on His Sixtieth Birthday

Edited by

Leslie S. Kawamura
and
Keith Scott

DHARMA PUBLISHING

 For information address:
Dharma Publishing, 5856 Doyle St.,
Emeryville, California 94608

ISBN: 0-913546-51-8
Library of Congress Catalog Card Number: 77-71194

Typeset in Fototronic Plantin and Garamond and
Printed by Dharma Press, Emeryville, California

9 8 7 6 5 4 3 2 1

Contents

Foreword

Dr. Guenther has been a very dear friend since we first began working together in India, over fifteen years ago. At that time he was in charge of the Department of Buddhist Philosophy and Tibetan Studies at the Sanskrit University in Varanasi. The Indian Government had asked him to develop a program of Tibetan Studies entailing the preservation of 'lost' Sanskrit works that had been preserved in the Tibetan, a program that called for Dr. Guenther to work closely with Tibetan scholars. When we began working together I found that Dr. Guenther was as interested in what the 'living spirit' of Buddhism had to offer as I was in helping to make it available. Since that time, Dr. Guenther and I have been of one mind in the concern for the preservation of the Tibetan Buddhist tradition. We both had come to the realization that in order to preserve this tradition in these troubled times, it was important that it be made available to the peoples of the West in as pure a form as possible.

My appreciation of Dr. Guenther's work has continued to grow as we have worked together over the years. I do not think that it is wrong to say that he has become the leading figure in the translation of Tibetan texts into English. Yet he is not simply a scholar—he is a 'thinker', who has made his quest for knowledge a quest for 'lived' meaning, rather than for accumulated facts. He has taken care that his translations should never fall into the trap of the 'mechanical', but rather that they should communicate an interpretive understanding of the original author's meaning. Dr. Guenther's depth of knowledge and appreciation for Western as well as Eastern philosophies has given him the unique ability to lay a solid foundation for the transmission of the vast scope of Buddhism to a Western audience. Through his efforts, a few important texts, such as Klong-chen rab-'byams-pa's trilogy, *Kindly Bent to Ease Us*, are now available, and we hope to work together on others in the future. Dr. Guenther's contributions to continuing the 'living spirit' of ancient Buddhist thought and tradition cannot be over-emphasized.

I am grateful that Dr. Kawamura, in putting together this collection in honor of Dr. Guenther, has given me the opportunity to express my deep regard and respect for Herbert Guenther—for both the man and his work. Such a person, with tireless energy and dedication to his task, is very rare. Thus, I am happy that Dharma Publishing could help make this volume available in his honor.

TARTHANG TULKU RINPOCHE

Preface

DR. HERBERT V. GUENTHER was born on March 17, 1917 in Bremen, Germany, the only son of Mr. and Mrs. Reinhold Guenther. Because he showed a great interest in the Orient from an early age his father encouraged him to pursue studies in this field. To this end he began the study of the Chinese language when he was nine. By the time he graduated from high school, in 1936, he had learned the Sanskrit language as well.

After graduation he went to Munich for further study, earning the Ph.D. degree in 1939. Four years later he received the degree Dr. Phil. Habil. in Vienna. From this beginning, Dr. Guenther went on to become one of the leading Buddhist scholars of our time. Amongst the most influential of his European mentors were Professor W. Geiger, a specialist in Pali and Sinhalese, and Professor W. Wuest —both of Munich. In Vienna, Professor W. Havers was his main teacher. During this time his considerable aptitude for languages manifested itself. In addition to Pali, Sinhalese, Sanskrit, Tibetan, Chinese, Japanese, English, German, Russian, and Hindi, there were those languages he studied 'for enjoyment'—Hebrew, Greek, Latin, Arabic, Spanish, and Italian.

After having taught at Vienna University, 1943–1950, Dr. Guenther journeyed to India, where he lived and taught for the next fourteen years. He was at Lucknow University from 1950–1958, and then went to the Sanskrit University in Varanasi, where he was Head of the Department of Comparative Philosophy and Buddhist Studies from 1958–1963. The following year was spent at the International School of America. The personal and intellectual encounters he had in India and the Himalayan region were to leave a lasting mark, for he was fortunate in studying with many prominent Tibetan and Mongolian lamas. Among encounters of special note were those with the following teachers: His Holiness the Dalai Lama; Khri-byang Blo-bzang Ye-shes Rin-po-che, tutor to His Holiness; the Incarnate Lama Ka-thog dbon sprul-sku; the Incarnate Lama Dar-mdo sprul-sku Thub-bstan lhun-grub legs-bzang of 'Bras sprungs Blo-gsal-gling rgyal-rong and Abbot of Budhgaya; the Incarnate Lama Tarthang Tulku (Dar-thang sprul-sku), formerly of Golog Monastery in Tibet and the Sanskrit University in Varanasi, and presently Head Lama of the Tibetan Nyingma Meditation Center and Nyingma Institute in Berkeley; Lama Dam-chos rin-chen; Guru brTul-zhugs gling-pa; gNas-nang dPa'-bo Rin-po-che of Darjeeling; dGe-bshes Ngag-dbang Nyi-ma of sGo-mang sgrva tshang; dGe-bshes bsTan-'dzin rgyal mtshan; and the Mongolian Dalama Sog-po Ta-bla-ma rNam-rgyal rDo-rje.

In 1964 Dr. Guenther left India to assume the position which he presently holds of Professor and Head of the Department of Far Eastern Studies at the University of Saskatchewan, Saskatoon, Canada. Throughout his career he has been encouraged and sustained by his wife, Dr. Ilse (née Rossrucker) Guenther, whom he married in 1944 in Vienna. The Guenthers have two daughters: Mrs. Edith Kimball, now of Stockton, California—a former recipient of the Woodrow Wilson Fellowship and Master of Arts from the University of Saskatchewan; and Miss Nora Guenther, who presently studies music at Brandon University, in Brandon, Manitoba. The Guenther family has, for many years, enjoyed musical performance—Dr. Guenther is a flutist, Mrs. Guenther plays the piano, and Nora Guenther plays the viola.

It has been a great honor for us to serve as editors of this volume marking the sixtieth birthday of Herbert V. Guenther. Our task has been a pleasure thanks to the co-operation and contributions of eminent scholars throughout the world. This volume could not have been realized without their generous energies and efforts. Special mention must be made of the gracious grant which was provided through the *President's Publication Fund*, University of Saskatchewan, Saskatoon, Canada.

Respect and appreciation must be expressed to Tarthang Tulku, Rinpoche, Head Lama of the Tibetan Nyingma Meditation Center and the Nyingma Institute, in Berkeley, who made the production of this volume possible through the facilities and staff of Dharma Publishing and Press.

LESLIE KAWAMURA
KEITH SCOTT

Herbert V. Guenther's Publications

BOOKS

1. *Das Seelenproblem im Alteren Buddhismus*, Curt Weller, Konstanz, 1949.
2. *Yuganaddha—The Tantric Way of Life*, Chowkhamba Sanskrit Series, Vol. 3, Benares, 1952.
3. *Der Buddha und Seine Lehre*, Rascher & Co., Zurich, 1956.
4. *Philosophy and Psychology in the Abhidharma*, Buddha Vihara, Lucknow, 1957. Revised at Shambhala, Berkeley, 1974. Motilal Banarsidass.
5. *Sgam-po-pa—The Jewel Ornament of Liberation*, Rider & Co., London, 1959; Berkeley, 1971. Paperback: London, 1970; Berkeley, 1971. Translated into Italian, 1976.
6. *The Life and Teaching of Naropa*, Claredon Press, Oxford 1963. Paperback 1971, Oxford University Press. Translated into Italian, 1976.
7. *Tibetan Buddhism without Mystification*, E. J. Brill, Leiden, 1966.
8. *Treasures on the Tibetan Middle Way*, Shambhala, Berkeley, 1971.
9. *The Royal Song of Saraha*, University of Washington Press, Seattle, 1969.
10. *Buddhist Philosophy in Theory and Practice*, Penguin, Baltimore, 1972.
11. *The Tantric View of Life*, Shambhala, Berkeley and London, 1972.
12. *Tantra als Lebens-Anschauung*, Otto Wilhelm, Barth Verlag, München, 1974.
13. *The Dawn of Tantra* (co-author Chögyam Trungpa), Shambhala, Berkeley, 1975.

14. *La Concezione Tantrica della Vita*, Casa Editrice Astrolabio-Ubaldini Editore, Roma, 1975.
15. *Mind in Buddhist Psychology* (co-author Leslie S. Kawamura), Dharma Publishing, Emeryville, 1975.
16. *Kindly Bent to Ease Us, Part One: Mind*, Dharma Publishing, Emeryville, 1975.
17. *Kindly Bent to Ease Us, Part Two: Meditation*, Dharma Publishing, Emeryville, 1976.
18. *Kindly Bent to Ease Us, Part Three: Wonderment*, Dharma Publishing, Emeryville, 1976.
19. *Tibetan Buddhism in Western Perspective*, Dharma Publishing, Emeryville, 1977.
20. *La Mente nella Psicologia Buddhista*, Casa Editrice Astrolabio-Ubaldini Editore, Roma, 1977.

ARTICLES

1. "Das Sidat Samgarava, eine Grammatik des Klassischen Sinhalesisch" (*ZDMG*, 1942).
2. "Über das 'ka'-Suffix im Sinhalesischen und die Einheimische Genuslehre" (*ZDMG*, 1943).
3. "Die Buddhistische Kosmogonie" (*ZDMG*, 1944).
4. "Die Sinhalesische Sandesa-Dichtung des vierzehnten und fünfzehnten Jahrhunderts" (*WZKM*, 1946).
5. "Der Mahanagakula-Sandesa" (*WZKM*, 1946).
6. "Einige Überlieferungsgeschichtliche Bemerkungen zum Dutthagamani-Epos" (*WZKM*, 1946).
7. "Ceylon im fünfzehnten Jahrhundert" (*WZKM*, 1946).
8. "Die Verwandtschaftsverhaltnisse der Sinhalesischen Könige im fünfzehnten und sechzehnten Jahrhundert" (*WZKM*, 1947).
9. "Das Geistesleben der Naturvölker und Indische Welt Anschauung" (*Archiv für Völkerkunde*, 1947).
10. "Noun Inflexion in Old Sinhalese" (Journal *J.A.S.*, 1949).
11. "The Conditional Mood in Sinhalese" (*JAOS*, Vol. 69, 1949).
12. "Der Begriff des Leeren im Altindoarischen" (*KZ*, 1950).
13. "Gabe und Geber" (*KZ*, 1951).
14. "The Bodhisattva's Realm of Knowledge" (*Stepping Stones*, Vol. 1/7, 1951).

15. "Excerpts from the Gandavyuha Sutra, II" (*Stepping Stones*, Vol. 1/8, 1950–51).
16. "In Praise of Bodhicitta" (*Stepping Stones*, Vol. 1/8).
17. "Friends in the Good Life" (*Stepping Stones*, Vol. 1/9–10).
18. "The Diamond of Omniscience" (*Stepping Stones*, Vol. 2/2).
19. "The Jewel of Buddhahood" (*Stepping Stones*, Vol. 2/4).
20. "The Origin and Spirit of Vajrayana" (*Stepping Stones*, Vol. 2/7–8).
21. "Our Position in Life" (*Stepping Stones*, Vol. 2/7–8).
22. "Ahankara and Selflessness" (*Stepping Stones*, Vol. 6/8).
23. "The Psychology of the Three Kāyas" (*Uttara Bharati*, Vol. 2/1, 1955).
24. "Refuge" (*Mahabodhi*, Vol. 63, 1955).
25. "Mantrayana and Sahajayana" (*2500 Years of Buddhism*, Government of India, 1956).
26. "How to Listen to Dharma" (*Mahabodhi*, Vol. 64, 1956).
27. "Mantrayana aur Sahayana" (in Hindi, *Bauddh-dharm ke 2500 varsh*, Delhi, 1956).
28. "The Concept of Mind in Buddhist Tantrism" (*Journal of Oriental Studies*, Vol. 3, pp. 261 ff., 1956).
29. "Equanimity" (*Mahabodhi*, Vol. 66, 1958).
30. "The Philosophical Background of Buddhist Tantrism" (*Journal of Oriental Studies*, Vol. 5, pp. 45 ff., 1959-60).
31. "Levels of Understanding in Buddhism" (*Journal of the American Oriental Society*, Vol. 78/1, pp. 19 ff., 1958).
32. "Three Essentials" (*Middle Way*, pp. 99 ff., 1961).
33. Introduction to *A New Tibeto-Mongol Pantheon*, Raghu Vira and Lokesh Chandra, New Delhi, pp. 5 ff., 1961).
34. "Religion and Everyday Life" (*Middle Way*, pp. 194 ff., 1962).
35. "Indian Buddhist Thought in Tibetan Perspective–Infinite Transcendence versus Finiteness" (*History of Religions*, Vol. 3, pp. 83 ff., 1963).
36. "Saraha's Song of Human Action" (*Middle Way*, pp. 95 ff., 1965).
37. "Art and Thought in the Eastern World" (Saskatchewan Society for Education through Art, *Art Journal*, pp. 11 ff., 1965).
38. "Some Aspects of Tibetan Religious Thought" (*History of Religions*, Vol. 6, pp. 70 ff., 1966).
39. "Mentalism and Beyond in Buddhist Philosophy" (*JAOS*, Vol. 86, pp. 288 ff., 1966).
40. "Le Maître Spirituel en Tibet" (*Hermes*, Paris, pp. 226 ff., 1966–67).
41. "An Introduction to Tibetan Buddhism" (*The Tibet Society Newsletter*, Vol. 1/7, 1967).

42. "The Concept of Freedom in Cross-Cultural Perspective" (*Saskatchewan History Teachers' Association Newsletter*, Vol. 5/1, pp. 23-24, 1968).
43. "Tantra and Revelation" (*History of Religions*, Vol. 7/4, pp. 279-301, May, 1968).
44. "The Spiritual Guide as Mystical Experience" (*The R.M. Bucke Memorial Society Newsletter-Review*, Vol. 3/1, pp. 22-26, Spring, 1968).
45. "Guilt and Purification in Buddhist Tantrism" (*Proceedings of the Eleventh International Congress of the International Association for the History of Religions*, Vol. 2, pp. 152-53, Leiden, 1968).
46. "Tantra—Meaningful Existence" (*Maitreya*, Vol. 1, pp. 20-24, 1969).
47. "Mind, Space, and Aesthetic Awareness" (*Anjali*, pp. 152-154, Paradeniya, 1970).
48. "Absolute Perfection" (*Crystal Mirror*, Vol. 1, pp. 31-38, Dharma Publishing, Emeryville, California, 1971).
49. "Buddhist Metaphysics and Existential Meditation" (*Sciences Religieuses Studies in Religion*, Vol. 1/4, pp. 291-297, 1972).
50. "The Path and the Goal" (*The American Theosophist*, Vol. 60/5, pp. 110-116, 1972).
51. "On Spiritual Discipline" (*Maitreya*, Vol. 3, pp. 29-34, Shambhala, 1972).
52. "Fact and Fiction in the Experience of Being" (*Crystal Mirror*, Vol. 2, pp. 44-51, Dharma Publishing, 1972).
53. "Saṁvṛti and Paramārtha in Yogācāra According to Tibetan Sources" (*Two Truths in Buddhism and Vedanta*, edited by M. Sprung, pp. 89-97, D. Reidel Publishing Company, Dordrecht, Holland, 1973).
54. Foreword to *Calm and Clear*, by Lama Mipham (Dharma Publishing, 1973).
55. "The Male-Female Polarity in Oriental and Western Thought" (*Maitreya*, V. 4, pp. 51-63, Shambhala, 1973).
56. "The Teacher and Student" (*Maitreya*, Vol. 5, pp. 39-51, Shambhala, 1974).
57. "Buddhist Sacred Literature" (Fifteenth Edition of *Encyclopaedia Britannica*, pp. 431-441, Helen Hemingway Benton Publishers, 1974).
58. "Buddhist Mysticism" (Fifteenth Edition of *Encyclopaedia Britannica*, pp. 414-418, Helen Hemingway Benton Publishers, 1974).
59. "The Development of Tibetan Art" (*Sacred Art of Tibet*, second edition, pp. 9-13, Dharma Publishing, 1974).
60. "Early Forms of Tibetan Buddhism" (*Crystal Mirror*, Vol. 3, pp. 80-92, Dharma Publishing, 1974).

61. Foreword to *An Introduction to Tantric Buddhism*, by Shashi Bhushan Dasgupta, Shambhala.
62. "Mahamudra—The Method of Self-Actualization" (*The Tibet Journal*, Vol. 1, pp. 5-23, 1975).
63. "The Natural Freedom of Mind" (*Crystal Mirror*, Vol. 4, pp. 113-146, Dharma Publishing, 1975).
64. "Three Paths with a Single Goal" (*Gesar*, Vol. 2/4, pp. 9-10, Dharma Publishing, 1975).
65. Conversations with Herbert Guenther (*Gesar*, Vol. 3/1, pp. 10-11, Dharma Publishing, 1975).
66. "Toward an Experience of Being Through Psychological Purification" in (*A Study of Kleśa—A Study of Impurity and its Purification in Oriental Religions*, edited by Genjun W. Sasaki, pp. 478-493, Shimizukobundo Ltd., Tokyo, 1975).
67. "A Journey Through Life: Five Stages on the Buddhist Path" (*Gesar*, Vol. 3/2, pp. 6-11, Dharma Publishing, 1975).
68. "The Road to Growth—the Buddhist 'Way' " (*Gesar*, Vol. 3/3, pp. 6-9, Dharma Publishing, 1976).
69. "Trikāya in Buddhist Philosophy—Tibetan and Chinese *Hua Yen* Interpretation" (forthcoming in *Murti Festschrift*), Dharma Publishing, 1977.

BOOK REVIEWS

1. Christmas Humphreys, *Buddhism* (*Stepping Stones*, Vol. 2/3, 1951).
2. Edward Conze, *Buddhism—Its Essence and Development* (*Stepping Stones*, Vol. 2/9, 1951).
3. Alfanso Ferrari, *Mk'yen brtse's Guide to the Holy Places of Central Tibet* (*Journal of Oriental Studies*, Vol. 5, (1959-60).
4. D. L. Snellgrove, *The Hevajra Tantra* (*Journal of Oriental Studies*, Vol. 5, 1959-60).
5. Giuseppi Tucci, *Minor Buddhist Texts, Part II* (*Journal of Oriental Studies*, Vol. 5, 1959-60).
6. Agehananda Bharati, *The Tantric Tradition* (*JAOS*, Vol. 87/2, 1967).
7. Winston L. King, *A Thousand Lives Away* (*JAOS*, Vol. 87/2, 1967).
8. Lu K'uan Yu (Charles Luk), trans., *The Surangama Sutra* (*The R. M. Bucke Memorial Society Newsletter-Review*, Vol. 2/2, 1967).
9. Tsepon, W. D. Shakabpa, *Tibet: A Political History* (*American Historical Review*, 1968).

10. David L. Snellgrove, *Four Lamas of Dolpo: Tibetan Biographies*, Vol. 1. Introduction and Translation (*American Historical Review*, 1968).
11. Guy Richard Welbon, *The Buddhist Nirvana and Its Western Interpreters* (*Journal of Asian Studies*, Vol. 28/2, 1969).
12. Henri Arvon, *L'Atheisme*, "Que sais-je?" No. 1291 (*Journal of the History of Philosophy*, Vol. 7/1, 1969).
13. Ferdinand D. Lessing and Alex Wayman, *Mkhas grub rje's Fundamentals of the Buddhist Tantras* (*Indo-Iranian Journal*, Vol. 8/1, 1971).
14. Vidya Dehajia, *Early Buddhist Rock Temples*, ed. D. Strong (*Pacific Affairs*, Vol. 45/3, 1972).
15. R. A. Stein, *Tibetan Civilization* (*Pacific Affairs*, Vol. 46/1, 1972).

Bhartṛhari versus Śaṅkara on the Overcoming of Error

Harold G. Coward

INTRODUCTION

In traditional Indian thought Śaṅkara's Advaita Vedānta and Bhartṛhari's Grammarian philosophy of language are both absolutistic monisms in which error or ignorance (*avidyā*) plays the important function of obstructing the real from view. Professor K. A. Subramania Iyer, in his recent book entitled *Bhartṛhari*, explains Bhartṛhari's theory of error as analogous to Śaṅkara's analysis of the rope snake illusion.[1] However, as this paper will demonstrate, a careful study of the function of *avidyā* in the two theories evidences no basis for this analogy. Whereas Śaṅkara describes the error as being transcended via a single negation, Bhartṛhari holds that the error is overcome positively by increasingly clear cognition of the whole (*sphoṭa*) which the succeeding perceptions reveal. Whereas the overcoming of error for Śaṅkara takes a negative form, for Bhartṛhari it is positive. We will examine the supporting arguments behind these two opposing viewpoints in detail. By way of conclusion and practical application it will be suggested that Bhartṛhari's theory of error provides a better basis for understanding both esthetic experience and the realization of freedom (*mokṣa*).

THE ARGUMENT

Much of Bhartṛhari's thinking on the overcoming of error appears in his *Vākyapadīya*, Chapter 1, as is concisely summarized by Maṇḍana Miśra in his *Sphoṭasiddhi*. To grasp Bhartṛhari's argument it is helpful to know something of the larger content of which it is a part. Bhartṛhari develops his theory of language by maintaining that the *sphoṭa* (the meaning-whole) is something over and above the uttered or written letters. The individual letters are alterable (malleable by variations such as accent, speed of delivery, etc.) and when uttered serve only to manifest that changeless *sphoṭa* which exists within the speaker and is potentially present within every hearer. The letters themselves do not convey meaning: it is the *sphoṭa*, once manifested, which conveys it. Between the *sphoṭa* and its word-meaning aspect the relationship is that between expression and the thing or meaning expressed. This is a natural relationship which is indestructible and beginningless. Convention only serves to bring it out. Bhartṛhari emphasizes that the *sphoṭa* is an entity which is within each person. All of us have the capacity to instinctively feel its existence within, and ultimately to directly perceive it with the mind. The contention that the *sphoṭa* may be directly perceived, and is not merely a thing which is inferred, is one of the key points of the *sphoṭa* theory,[2] and provides the main point of argument with Śaṅkara on the overcoming of error. This is clearly seen if Bhartṛhari's analysis of the process of hearing is analyzed.

The process by which the *sphoṭa* is cognized is summarized by Maṇḍana in his commentary on *Sūtra* 18 of the *Sphoṭasiddhi* as follows:

> Each sound individually reveals the whole *sphoṭa*. Nor do the other sounds thus become useless because there is a difference in the revelation. It is like this: All the previous sounds bring about in the listener, whose mind is free from any particular residual impression [*saṃskāra*], cognitions in which the word figures vaguely and which sow seeds in the form of residual impressions capable of producing a later clear cognition of the word. The last sound produces a clear cognition in which figures, as it were, clearly the image of the *sphoṭa* caused by all the seeds in the form of residual impressions left by the vague cognitions of the previous sounds.[3]

Maṇḍana offers the analogy of a jeweler who assesses the genuineness of a precious stone. His continuous gaze is really a series of cognitions, each of which perceives the genuineness of the stone but with increasing clarity. Each cognition leaves its *saṃskāra* or common memory trace. The last cognition, helped by the *saṃskāra* of the previous one, fully perceives the genuineness of the stone. But for the *saṃskāras* of the intervening cognitions, there would be no difference between the last one and the first one. An important point is that the jeweler is described as 'expert', meaning that before beginning the examination he already had the image of a precious stone ingrained in his subconscious, and it was this image (like the inhering *sphoṭa*) which was revealed to the jeweler's mind by his series of partial (and since partial, also erroneous) perceptions.

The *Vṛtti* on Bhartṛhari's *Vākyapadīya* I:89 and Maṇḍana's comment on *Sūtra* 19 of the *Sphoṭasiddhi* state that the final clear perception of the *sphoṭa* is achieved through a series of errors. The analogy is offered of how from a distance one (at least in India) may mistake a tree for an elephant. But if one keeps looking at it, the tree is ultimately recognized in its true form. In this situation the truth has been arrived at through a series of errors. The sense organ (in this case the eye) has been in contact with the tree throughout. The errors of perception have had the tree as their object, but the cognitions produced by the eye have had an elephant as their form. When, however, the final or true cognition takes place, it has the form of the tree itself and is one with its object. But this true cognition has been arrived at by going through the series of erroneous perceptions that preceded it. Now this change from error to true perception cannot be explained by factors such as change in distance, since simply standing in the same spot and gazing with intense concentration often produces the described result. According to Maṇḍana, "It is the previous cognitions (having tree as the object and the form of the elephant) leaving progressively clearer residual impressions, which become the cause of the clear perception of the tree."[4] There could have been no erroneous cognition of an elephant had the tree been there as an object for the sense organ to come into contact with in the first place. The error, therefore, may be described as misapprehension or vague perception.

In Bhartṛhari's theory of language, the *sphoṭa* is similarly said to be the object of the cognition of each of the letters, yet it first appears in the form of a letter. However, through cognition of the subsequent letters the *sphoṭa* is seen with increasing clarity, until with the uttering of the final letter the form of all the letters becomes identical with that of the *sphoṭa*. Here the letters are seen in a position which at first glance seems parallel to the snake in the famous rope-snake illusion of the Advaita Vedāntins. The perception of the rope as snake is error, but it is through the negating of the erroneous snake-perception that the true rope-perception is finally realized. And were it not for the prior existence of the rope, the erroneous perception would have lacked the necessary ground for its phenomenal existence. Similarly, in this case, the letters are seen as dependent upon the *sphoṭa* for their phenomenal existence, but that existence is regarded as the means by which the noumenal *sphoṭa* may be perceived.

This apparent parallelism, however, does not hold up under closer analysis. Advaita theory provides for only true or false cognitions and allows no progressive approximation to the real,[5] as is the case in a series of erroneous *sphoṭa* perceptions. Whereas the Advaitin describes his error as being transcended via a single negation (e.g., as when it is realized "this is not snake"), the Grammarian holds that his error (e.g., the vagueness of the perception of the whole in the first letter) is overcome positively by the increasingly clear perception of the *sphoṭa* which the succeeding letters reveal.

This analysis of how error is overcome would seem to give further weight to Gaurinath Sastri's suggestion that in some ways the doctrine of reflection (*ābhāsa*) of the Kashmir Trika writers may provide the closest parallel to *sphoṭa* theory.[6] In the Kashmir Trika view consciousness (*caitanya*) is the only reality, and all external manifestation is held to be a reflection on consciousness as on a mirror. Error, in this view, occurs not because the initial perception has no existence but because its reflection of the object captures or includes only a part of its totality and adds other material (*saṃskāra*s) taken from the old stock of memory. This error is transcended positively as the form of the reflection is progressively purified of memory material until it perfectly reflects the object. This perfect reflection, which is true knowledge, is further described as a union of the subjective and objective aspects of consciousness—a return to the oneness which is its essential nature.[7] This brief glance at the Kashmir *ābhāsa* theory may provide a helpful parallel supporting the *sphoṭa* view of the way in which the manifest letters erroneously but positively approximate their true object, the *sphoṭa* itself.

Maṇḍana has an explanation of the paradox of how the indivisible *sphoṭa* appears as single letters and the letters as the parts of the partless *sphoṭa*. He says it is the sounds that resemble one another which are the cause of both the error and the final correct cognition of the *sphoṭa*. If, for the manifestation of two different word-*sphoṭa*s, one has to make similar movements of the vocal organs, the letters produced by these movements appear to be parts of both of the indivisible words.[8] This is an error which is fostered by the construction of such artificial devices as alphabet letters or word syllables, usually for teaching purposes. It is precisely because of this kind of confusion, says Maṇḍana, that sentences, words, and letters appear to have parts whereas in reality they have none.[9] The obverse of this applies to the *sphoṭa*. From the phenomenal viewpoint the *sphoṭa* 'cow', for example, may appear to possess qualities such as accent, speed, loudness, time, place, and person in its utterance. That these are qualities of the phenomenal sounds and not the noumenal *sphoṭa* is what makes possible the common recognition of the word 'cow' in spite of its diversity of utterance. From the *sphoṭa* viewpoint, it is this noumenal grounding or basis that makes possible such things as the translation of thought from one phenomenal language to another.

Maṇḍana offers the example of a picture. He points out that in our cognition of a picture, although we may be aware of the different parts and colors, the picture is perceived as a whole which is over and above its parts.[10] Similarly, when we perceive a piece of cloth our cognition is of the cloth as a whole and is quite distinct from the particular threads and colors involved.[11]

In both of these examples there is a necessary perception of the parts prior to the perception of the whole. This aspect is brought out clearly by Bhartṛhari who describes the painter as going through three stages when he paints a picture: "When a painter wishes to paint a figure having parts like that of a man, he first sees it gradually in a sequence, then as the object of a single cognition, and then paints it on cloth or on a wall in sequence."[12] So also the hearer of a word perceives the word in a sequence of letters which manifest in him the whole word as the object of a single cognition. As a speaker, however, he utters the whole word in its differentiated appearance as a sequence of letters. It is in this context that the perception of the many letters, before the final perception of the unitary *sphoṭa*, is described as error, illusion, or appearance. But it is a unique kind of error in that it has a fixed sequence and form, it ultimately leads to the perception of the truth, and is thus regarded as a universal error.[13] The chief cause of this universal error is described as *avidyā* or the limitation of the individual self-consciousness. A characteristic of this *avidyā* is that it provides no other means for cognizing the *sphoṭa*, except the letters. That is why all individual selves universally experience the same error with regard to speech, but it is an error which ultimately leads to cognition of truth. It is only through this error or appearance of differentiation that the individual *sphoṭa* comes within the range of worldly usage so that we ordinary mortals have a way of comprehending it.[14]

With the above understanding of Bhartṛhari's *sphoṭa* theory, we are now able to observe its significant difference from Śaṅkara's view of error. As we saw, the Advaitin usually describes his error as being transcended via negation (e.g., as when it is said "this is not snake"); and the Grammarian holds that his error (e.g., the vagueness of the perception of the whole in the first letter) is overcome positively by the increasingly clear cognition of the *sphoṭa* which the succeeding letters reveal.[15] And the final clear cognition is a case of perfect perception or *pratibhā*—a flash of intuition revealing the *sphoṭa* or whole word.[16]

At a more mundane level of psychological functioning, however, the positive process of perfecting the perception is described by Iyer as follows:

> [The final] clear cognition is a case of perception. The previous cognitions also had the *sphoṭa* as their object, but the cognition of it was vague and that is why they had the form of the sounds. . . . But when the final cognition reveals the *sphoṭa* in all its clarity and distinctness, it no longer has the form of sounds. The error has given place to truth. Such a cognition can only be perception. The object and forms of the cognition are now identical.[17]

This conformity between the object and the form of the cognition is referred to by Bhartṛhari as a certain 'fitness' (*yogatā*) between the sounds and the *sphoṭa* which results in the clear manifestation of the word.[18] The perfect perception in which there is identity between the object (i.e., the *sphoṭa*) and the form of its cognition (i.e., the letters or sounds) is a special kind of perception which, the modern reader must realize, is held to be a function of the mind[19] rather than of the external sense. The designation of the final cognition of the *sphoṭa* as a case of *perception* rather than *inference* has important logical implications.[20]

Maṇḍana makes the point clearly:

> The revelation (of an object) clearly or vaguely is confined to direct perception. In the case of the other means of knowledge there is either apprehension (of the object) or none at all.[21]

According to almost all schools of Indian philosophy, the valid means of knowledge (*pramāṇa*s), other than perception, either reveal the object completely or do not reveal it at all. There can be increasing clarity of revelation only in the case of perception. This is most important for *sphoṭa* theory in its contention that error due to vagueness of perception of the initial letters may be gradually and positively overcome, as described above. It is also crucial for *sphoṭa* theory in its contention that the existence of the *sphoṭa* is not a postulation, as the Mīmāṃsakas maintain, but is proven by direct perception.

Śaṅkara, in his commentary on *Brahma-Sūtra* I.3.28, argues against Bhartṛhari's notion that the *sphoṭa* is directly perceived. According to Śaṅkara, only the individual letters of a word are perceived, and these are combined through the inferential activity of the mind into a word aggregate.[22] Since the psychological process is one of inference rather than perception, there can be no question of degrees of cognition. The inference *pramāṇa* is an all-or-nothing process. The error, if it is to be overcome, must be completely replaced all at once by a new inferential construction of the mind or a super-conscious intuition of Brahman. Thus the position of Bhartṛhari (that the overcoming of error is a process of perception admitting of degrees of positive approximation) is not analogous to the position of Śaṅkara (that the overcoming of error is a process of negative inference admitting of no degrees).

If the evidence is indeed so clear-cut, why did Professor Iyer advance the suggestion of an analogy in the first place? He did so on the basis of his observation that many ancient commentaries on the *Vākyapadīya* interpret Bhartṛhari's thought as *vivartavāda*.[23] And he suggests that Bhartṛhari himself admits a parallel between his position and that of Vedānta, for he openly refers to the followers of *Trayyanta* (i.e., Vedānta) and seems to consider himself one of them. Also, the *Vṛtti*, which Iyer holds to be Bhartṛhari's, frequently uses terms such as *avidyā* and *vivarta*—terms prominently associated with Śaṅkara's Vedānta. Finally, Iyer cites Helārāja as being "very conscious of the distinction between *pariṇāma* and *vivarta* and emphasizes on more than one occasion that Bhartṛhari held *vivarta* and not *pariṇāma*."[24]

However, the force of these observations is negated by Gaurinath Sastri's clear demonstration that Helārāja was an exponent of Advaita and sought to reinterpret Bhartṛhari from the standpoint of Śaṅkara's notion of *vivarta* as 'false appearance'. Sastri concludes that Bhartṛhari was not familiar with the technical differences between the terms *vivarta* and *pariṇāma*, as developed subsequently by Advaita scholars.[25] Thus the grounds cited by Iyer for an analogy between Bhartṛhari and Śaṅkara are seen to be open to serious questioning. And when the above analysis of the different psychological processes in the overcoming of error (i.e., perception for Bhartṛhari, inference for Śaṅkara) is included in the debate, there seems little ground left upon which to base the claim of analogy.

SUMMARY

Let us briefly recapitulate Bhartṛhari's position. For Bhartṛhari, the *sphoṭa* is like a two-sided coin. On the one side is the meaning-whole—an eternal 'given' inherent in consciousness—of which the other side, the spoken letters, are the external manifestation. Bhartṛhari generally describes one's cognition of the *sphoṭa* from the hearer's perspective. A child learning a word, or an adult on first hearing a word, usually at first cognizes the *sphoṭa* erroneously. Having failed to grasp the whole *sphoṭa*, the listener asks, "What did you say?" Through a series of erroneous cognitions, in response to the repeated vocalizations of the word sounds, there arises a progressively clearer cognition of the whole *sphoṭa* and its two-sided aspects which Bhartṛhari describes as a case of *pratibhā*—a special perception or flash of intuition.[26] It is not logical or inferential in nature, nor is it capable of being directly described to others. The spoken letters used in attempting to describe this *pratibhā* to someone else can do no more than evoke in the other person the conditions which will allow the *sphoṭa* (already present in his consciousness) to be revealed in the listener's own *pratibhā* experience.

Since this final *pratibhā* of the *sphoṭa* is held to be a case of perception, various perceptual analogies were offered as examples. When from a distance a tree is vaguely cognized, the cognition may take the form of an elephant. When finally, through repeated effort, it is recognized as a tree, the cognition is clearly a case of perception. Or when the expert jeweler finally sees the genuineness of a precious stone after a continuous gaze at it which is comprised of a series of comparatively vague cognitions of it, this is an example of perception. Bhartṛhari claims that means of knowledge other than perception (e.g., inference) either reveal the object or do not reveal it at all. It is perception only when the object (in this case the word-meaning) is at first seen vaguely and then more and more clearly. While this is the process experienced by ordinary men, Bhartṛhari, along with most other Indian philosophers, allows that the great *ṛṣis* are able to cognize the complete unitary *sphoṭa* directly, without having to go through the process of repeated perception and error-correction.

Our analysis has shown that for Śaṅkara there is only true or false cognition; and error is overcome by a single negation of the false inference which simultaneously completely reveals the real. Bhartṛhari, by contrast, analyzes the overcoming of error as a progressive approximation to the real. While the first perception may be quite vague, the second will be less so, the third will be increasingly clear, and the final perception of the real in all its wholeness. For Śaṅkara the process is a single all-or-nothing negation; for Bhartṛhari it is a series of perceptions with an increasingly positive approximation to the real. This significant difference, plus the doubtful validity of the arguments offered by Professor Iyer, refutes his interpretation of Bhartṛhari as analogous to Śaṅkara.

APPLICATION TO ESTHETICS

Bhartṛhari's understanding of error and its function seems to fit well with esthetic experience. Take, for example, the experience of 'love', which Bhartṛhari would call a *sphoṭa*. Although the meaning of the word 'love' may ultimately be experienced as unitary, the verbalization and communication of that insightful knowledge may well require the employment of a variety of evocative poetic expressions. For example, in Shakespeare's sonnet:

> Let me not to the marriage of true minds
> Admit impediments. Love is not love
> Which alters when it alteration finds,
> Or bends with the remover to remove:
> O, No! it is an ever-fixèd mark,
> That looks on tempests, and is never shaken;
> It is the star to every wandering bark,
> Whose worth's unknown, although his height be taken.
> Love's not Time's fool, though rosy lips and cheeks
> Within his bending sickle's compass come;
> Love alters not with his brief hours and weeks,
> But bears it out e'en to the edge of doom.
> If this be error and upon me prov'd
> I never writ, nor no man ever lov'd.[27]

In this sonnet Shakespeare, through the use of his poetic imagination, composes a variety of expressions which when uttered manifest in the listener's mind an intuitive perception of the word-symbol 'love' and its meaning. Different people reading the sonnet may experience the manifestation of unitary word-meaning differently. For some it may come as a sudden flash of intuition, emerging fully developed. Others may experience a gradual and progressive revelation through repeated exposure to his evocative poetic phrases. According to Bhartṛhari's theory, the word-*sphoṭa* 'love' is a 'given', unitary and eternal in nature. However, as evidenced in literature, religion, and marital relations, such 'givens' require many imperfect or erroneous expressions before their meaning is fully grasped or intuitively realized.

In Indian esthetics the philosophical analysis of language in terms of *sphoṭa* theory seems to have been assumed as a basic premise. At the hands of scholars such as Abhinavagupta, Bhartṛhari's notion of word-sound or *dhvani* developed into the concept of *rasa* or poetic bliss.[28] While Śaṅkara's construct of the overcoming of error may fit the 'love at first sight' situation, Bhartṛhari's has the advantage not only of being applicable in this realm (e.g., as when the first letter completely reveals the entire *sphoṭa*) but in the realm of gradually-emerging, progressive esthetic experience.

APPLICATION TO MOKṢA

In Śaṅkara's theory, the realization of *mokṣa* would be a sudden realization experience requiring a radical change in the way the universe is experienced. One's experience would suddenly 'flip-over' from *māyā* (worldly illusion) to Brahman as the ground or essence of all. This would approximate what William James has called "the sick soul conversion experience."[29] For Bhartṛhari the realization of *mokṣa*, like the esthetic experience, would most likely be the result of a gradual change. The *karma* of the obscuring *avidyā* is continuously 'burnt up' through yogic meditation and chant. This discipline is described in the *vṛtti* on *Vākyapadīya* 1:123 which Iyer translates as follows:

> . . . taking his stand on the essence of the Word lying beyond the activity of breath (*prāṇa*), resting in one's self with all sequence eliminated. After having purified speech and after having rested it on the mind, after having broken its bonds and made it error-free, after having reached the inner light, he with his knots cut, becomes united with the Supreme Light.[30]

The removal of error through gradual purifying of *vāk* or speech results in the spiritual realization of *mokṣa*.

While not denying the interpretation of Śaṅkara as fitting for certain cases, these sample applications suggest that a great deal of human experience can be understood by applying Bhartṛhari's view of how error is overcome.

NOTES

1. K. A. Subramania Iyer, *Bhartṛhari*. Poona: Deccan College, 1969, p. 163.

2. *Sphoṭasiddhi of Maṇḍana Miśra*, translated by K. A. Subramania Iyer. Poona: Deccan College, 1966, p. 10.

3. *Ibid.*, *Sūtra* 18, p. 44.

4. *Ibid.*, *Sūtra* 19. Similar arguments are offered to show how the progressively clearer perception cannot be attributed to defects of the senses or memory through resemblance (p. 49).

5. T. M. P. Mahadevan, *The Philosophy of Advaita*. Madrass: Ganesh & Co., 1969, p. 62.

6. Gaurinath Sastri, *The Philosophy of Word and Meaning*. Calcutta: Sanskrit College, 1959, p. 50.

7. K. C. Pandey, *Abhinavagupta*. Varanasi: Chowkhamba Sanskrit Series, 2nd ed., 1963. The *ābhāsa* theory is summarized on pp. 400–427.

8. *Sphoṭasiddhi*, *op. cit.*, *Sūtra* 20, pp. 51–52; and *Vākyapadīya* I:88, "*Vṛtti*."

9. *Ibid.*

10. *Ibid.*, *Sūtra* 24, p. 64. See also K. A. S. Iyer's article, "The Conception of *Guṇa* Among the Vaiyyākaraṇas," in which he makes clear that from the *sphoṭa* viewpoint whatever distinction of degree or part is made in an object must be done through a *guṇa* (quality or particular). For the Grammarians it is the *guṇa* and never the universal which serves to express degrees in objects. *New Indian Antiquary*, Vol. 6, pp. 121–130.

It should also be noted that of the many possible ways of interpreting the universal, Bhartṛhari prefers the following. A movement like lifting the hand consists of a series of movements. As these movements are transitory, they cannot coexist and form a whole of which they would be the parts and in which the universal of the movement of lifting the hand would inhere. Now such a universal is more specific than the wider universal of movement in general. Although it inheres in each moment of movement, it is not capable of being cognized in movements alone due to too much similarity between moments of lifting and those of the moments of other movements such as turning the hand. The moments of each movement are the result of a special effort to make that movement and they are the substrata of the universal of that movement. But that universal cannot be cognized until a series of moments has been cognized. One or two moments of movement are not enough, but after a series of moments is cognized the cognition of the universal inherent in each moment becomes clear. Lifting, for example, may be identified and other movements such as turning excluded. The process is similar in the manifestation of *sphoṭas*. Each is manifested by a series of special efforts to utter letters. One or two utterances of the series are not enough to eliminate other words with similar sounds. But as the complete series of letters is cognized, the cognition of the *sphoṭa* or universal of the particular word is clearly perceived, and meaningful usage of it in speech becomes possible. *Vākyapadīya* II:20-21 as interpreted by K. A. S. Iyer in *Bhartṛhari, op. cit.*, pp. 168-169.

11. *Ibid.*

12. *Vākyapadīya, op. cit.*, I:52, p. 59.

13. If one moves beyond Sanskrit itself and into the world of languages, I would take the 'universal error' to refer to the necessity of going from the differentiated letters ('error') to the whole *sphoṭa* (meaning or ultimate reality). The fixed sequence and form of differentiation for a particular word-*sphoṭa* would only be a constant error within each language (such as Sanskrit).

14. *Vākyapadīya, op. cit.*, I:85, p. 86.

15. *Sphoṭasiddhi, op. cit., Sūtra* 22, p. 58-59.

16. Gopinath Kaviraj, "The Doctrine of Pratibhā in Indian Philosophy," *Annals of the Bhandarkar Oriental Research Institute*, 1924, pp. 1-18 and 113-132.

17. *Sphoṭasiddhi, op. cit.*, "Introduction," p. 26.

18. *Vākyapadīya, op. cit.*, I:78-I:84, pp. 81-85. Among the analogies offered to explain the process, Bhartṛhari's favorite seems to be that the sounds leave impression-seeds (*saṃskāra, bhāvanā* or *bīja*) which, as they mature in the mind, are conducive to an increasingly clear perception of the *sphoṭa* to which they finally offer a perfect 'fitness' or identity. A literal rendering of *yogatā* could be 'to fit in a frame'—the 'fit' of the 'matured' series of letters into the 'frame' of the *sphoṭa*. See also *Vṛtti* on *Vākyapadīya*, III:1:8, p. 12.

19. The phrase "function of the mind" here is intended to indicate that *pratibhā* is not a function of the ordinary senses (of the *buddhi* stage of consciousness), but is characteristic of the pre-*buddhi* or *śabdatattva* stage.

20. It should be clearly understood here that perfect perception of *pratibhā*, however valid in itself, remains outside the realm of *pramāṇa* (which is characterized by sensory perception and *discursive* cognition). With regard to language, therefore, it is *sphoṭa* when manifested as speech that is *pramāṇa* (and not *sphoṭa* at the unified level of *pratibhā*). The point made above, however, still stands. The cognition of *sphoṭa* at the level of either *śabda pramāṇa* or *pratibhā* is via direct perception rather than inference.

21. *Sphoṭasiddhi, op. cit.*, *Sūtra* 23, p. 60.

22. The *Vedānta-Sūtras* with Śaṅkara's commentary, translated by George Thibaut. Delhi: Motilal Banarsidass, 1968, Part 1, p. 210.

23. *Bhartṛhari, op. cit.*, pp. 131-135.

24. *Ibid.*, p. 135.

25. *The Philosophy of Word and Meaning, op. cit.*, pp. 57-58.

26. *Vākyapadīya Cantos 1 and 2*, translated by K. Raghavan Pillai. Delhi: Motilal Banarsidass, 1971, II:143-145.

27. William Shakespeare, *The Works of William Shakespeare*. London: Frederick Warne and Co., 1893, Sonnet #116, p. 1110.

28. For a convincing demonstration of this contention, see Tarapada Chakrabarti, *Indian Aesthetics and the Science of Language*. Calcutta: Sanskrit Pustak Bhandar, 1971.

29. William James, *Varieties of Religious Experience*. New York: Mentor Books, 1958.

30. *Bhartṛhari, op. cit.*, p. 145.

BIBLIOGRAPHY

Primary Sources

Sphoṭasiddhi of Maṇḍana Miśra, translated by K. A. Subramania Iyer. Poona: Deccan College, 1966.

The Vākyapadīya of Bhartṛhari with the Vṛtti, translated by K. A. Subramania Iyer. Poona: Deccan College, Chapter 1, 1965, Chapter 3, Part 1, 1971.

The Vākyapadīya Cantos 1 and 2, translated by K. Raghavan Pillai. Delhi: Motilal Banarsidass, 1971.

The Vedānta-Sūtras, with commentary by Śaṅkara, translated by G. Thibaut, Parts 1 and 2. Delhi: Motilal Banarsidass, 1968.

Secondary Sources

Chatterjee, S., *The Nyāya Theory of Knowledge*. Calcutta: University of Calcutta, 1965.

Iyer, K. A. Subramania, *Bhartṛhari*. Poona: Deccan College, 1969.

Iyer, K. A. S., "The Conception of *Guṇa* Among the Vaiyyākaraṇas." *New Indian Antiquary*, Vol. 6, pp. 121-130.

James, William, *The Varieties of Religious Experience*. New York: Mentor Books, 1958.

Kaviraj, Gopinath, "The Doctrine of *Pratibhā* in Indian Philosophy," *Annals of the Bhandarkar Oriental Research Institute*, pp. 1-18 and 113-132, 1924.

Mahadevan, T. M. P., *The Philosophy of Advaita*. Madras: Ganesh & Co., 1969.

Murti, T. R. V., "Some Comments on the Philosophy of Language in the Indian Context," *Journal of Indian Philosophy*, Vol. 2, pp. 321-331, 1974.

Pandey, K. C., *Abhinavagupta*. Varanasi: Chowkhamba Sanskrit Series Office, 1963.

Sastri, Gaurinath, *The Philosophy of Word and Meaning*. Calcutta: Sanskrit College, 1959.

Sinha, Jadunath, *Indian Psychology: Cognition*. Calcutta: Sinha Publishing House, 1958.

Tsong-kha-pa and His Relation to Atīśa and Padmasambhava

Eva K. Dargyay

THE DEVELOPMENT OF BUDDHISM in Tibet is divided into two periods. The first period of dissemination (*snga-dar*) was initiated by such great Indian masters as Śāntarakṣita, Padmasambhava, Kamalaśīla, Vairocana, and others. Śāntarakṣita, one of the first and most famous Indian scholars to visit Tibet, entered the country in the second half of the eighth century. However, he met with such severe obstacles while attempting to teach the Buddha-dharma to the inhabitants that finally he was forced to leave. The Bon religion, which already prevailed in Tibet at that time, emphasized ritual observances both to please benevolent demons and to avert the dangerous and evil influences of numerous other demons and ghosts that inhabited the mountains, rocks, trees, lakes, and soil. The teachings of the Buddhist Mādhyamika system, whose tenets Śāntarakṣita tried to establish, belonged to another level of man's thinking. Both Bon and Buddhism at that point failed to communicate constructively. Śāntarakṣita was unable to convince the Tibetan ruling class of the superb maturity of Buddhist thought, and the adherents of Bon worried that their gods and demons would be angered by a new foreign religion. Every misfortune was considered an evil omen of the now malevolent deities. In the end Śāntarakṣita was forced to compete against sorcerers and magicians, and he lost the first round. Thereafter, on his recommendation, the great Tantric master Padmasambhava was invited to Tibet to promulgate the Buddha-dharma. King Khri-srong lde'u-bstan (755–797 A.D.) sent his minister sBa gSal-snang to India to meet Padmasambhava and to pass on to him the royal invitation.

Padmasambhava, the Lotus-Born, entered this world near the delta of the Indus. The Elder Indrabhūti, King of Uḍḍiyāna, (today the Swat valley), adopted Padmasambhava as his son. King Indrabhūti was himself an outstanding Tantric master, and he educated Padmasambhava accordingly. Padmasambhava soon displayed the full range of parapsychic phenomena known as the Tantric *siddhi*. He was a pre-eminent master of the Tantric path and was also thoroughly aware of the faint-heartedness of human nature. When he came to Tibet he discovered successfully how to make Buddhist teachings welcome to a people paralyzed by fear of angering their deities.

Tibetan historical sources differ about Padmasambhava's role in Tibet. The rNying-ma-pa tradition emphasizes the fact that Padmasambhava stayed for several years in Tibet, during which time he founded chapels, built bSam-yas (the first Tibetan monastery), and tirelessly taught his Tibetan disciples the Tantric mysteries. According to the rNying-ma-pas, he brought a large number of Buddhist texts—especially Tantras—to Tibet. These were translated from Sanskrit and Chinese into Tibetan by Vairocana, Jñānaśrīmitra, and other pandits. Later Tibetan schools differ in their views of these Tantras, which have come down to us today as the *rNying-ma'i rgyud-'bum* (The Hundred-Thousand Tantras of the Old Ones).[1]

Sum-pa mkhan-po (1704–1788), an adherent of the dGe-lugs-pa School, questioned whether the main doctrines promulgated by the rNying-ma-pas were authentic teachings of the Buddha. He was critical of the *theg-pa-rim-pa dgu* (The Vehicle of the Nine Stages), the typical rNying-ma Tantras, and the doctrine of the *gter-ma* (concealed treasures). Sum-pa mkhan-po quotes Rin-chen bzang-po (958–1055), who confesses in his *Chos-dang-chos-min-rnam-'byed* that all attempts to track down the Sanskrit originals of the rNying-ma Tantras have been in vain. Further, he quotes Chag Lo-tsa-ba, who claimed that the *rDzogs-chen* texts were composed by Zur and gNubs, *i.e.*, by men in whose hearts the evil rGyal-po demons dwelled.[2] Sum-pa mkhan-po charged Ka-ru-'dzin, a native of Nepal, with defamation and imposture, saying he disguised himself in Padmasambhava's Chinese coat (*ber*). Thus, Sum-pa mkhan-po suggests that most of the doctrines which the rNying-ma-pa claim as Padmasambhava's were in truth evil machinations of an imposter. So much for Sum-pa mkhan-po's arguments against the authenticity of the rNying-ma-pa School.

One point of agreement among the various schools of Tibetan Buddhism is the fact that Buddhist spirituality declined after King gLang-dar-ma persecuted the followers of the Buddha-dharma. This decadence was well documented in a letter written by King Byang-chub-'od. He and other kings and patrons of Western Tibet strove ardently to revive Buddhism, and its revival, called the later period of dissemination (*phyi-dar*) by Tibetan tradition, began at the dawn of the second millenium.

Initiators were eminent scholars such as Rin-chen bzang-po, rNgog Lo-tsa-ba, Atīśa, Mar-pa, and others. The first impulse came from Kashmir, a stronghold of Buddhist learning in those days. King Ye-shes-'od invited Atīśa, one of the most learned Buddhist masters, to Western Tibet. Atīśa was born of a noble family in Za-hor, a petty principality in Bengal.[3] He studied at the famous Buddhist university of Nālandā. He was taught the Buddha-dharma by the most outstanding Buddhist masters of those days: Dharmakīrti, Dharmarakṣita, Śānti-pā, Nā-ro-pā, and Avadhūti-pā. Thus, he became well-trained in the ethical-philosophical systems of both the Sūtras and the Tantras. As he often had realizations of Tārā, he was indebted throughout his life to her cult. He was well-travelled, having visited the Buddhist centers of Indo-China and the most prominent monastic universities in India. There are indications that he was in Northern India, and tried to escape, during the time of the Mohammedan invasions of Mahmud Ghaznavi.

In 1042 A.D. Atīśa, more than sixty years of age, arrived in mNga'-ris (Western Tibet), where he stayed for three years. His activities covered a wide range of interest. He engaged himself in teaching his noble patrons and the Tibetan disciples, in guiding

Rin-chen-bzang-po to a more profound understanding of the Dharma, and in demonstrating a straight and indisputable path to deliverance. For this purpose he composed his famous *Bodhi-patha-pradīpa* (The Lamp for the Path to Enlightenment), which became the paragon for the later *lam-rim* literature. Atīśa stressed a synoptic view of the several Buddhist ways; he showed the Tibetans how to practice the three Methods (Hīnayāna, Mahāyāna, and Tantrayāna) at once, thus initiating a new mode of thinking in Tibet. From that time on, the Tibetans sought to practice the vows of the Bodhisattva Path as well as those of the Vajrayāna. Thus, the ethics and philosophy of the Sūtras became inextricably intertwined with the mysticism and rituals of the Tantras. This gave Tibetan Buddhism its unique aspect, differentiating it from the Buddhist tradition in other countries.

Tsong-kha-pa, the well-known founder of the dGe-lugs-pa School, brought this view of Buddhist practice to perfection. He settled the interpretation of the Sūtras as well as that of the Tantras through his thorough mastery of the principles of Buddhist philosophy and logic. Even the most sublime realms of meditation had to be permanently checked by spiritual and intellectual investigation. The Tibetan traditions extol him as the 'One who has accomplished both the Tantras and the Sūtra systems'. In his teachings, Tsong-kha-pa relied heavily on the bKa'-gdams-pa School which was founded by Atīśa and his disciple 'Brom-ston. For Tsong-kha-pa and his disciples it was obligatory to keep the monastic pledges of the *vināya*. During the lifetime of Tsong-kha-pa (1357–1419), most of the other schools as well as their hierarchs were involved in political quarrels. As the dGe-lugs-pa did not participate in those quarrels they soon came to enjoy a high reputation. Well-known innovations introduced by Tsong-kha-pa are the Great Prayer (*smon-lam chen-mo*) and the monastic debates. The Great Prayer is celebrated a few days after the Tibetan New Year, and the monastic debates were considered excellent training in preventing one's mind from becoming deluded during meditation.

Each of these three eminent masters of Tibetan Buddhism founded a tradition of his own which later evolved into a distinct school. These religious schools allied themselves to political powers and became involved in political bickerings, monastery against monastery. These rivalries have been discussed by G. Tucci and other scholars.[4] In addition to dealing with the political tension there was the task of tracing the lineage of Buddhism from the time of the Tantric masters, Padmasambhava and Atīśa, up to Tsong-kha-pa's time. The greatest problem, however, was how to integrate the different and diversified teachings of these three noble men. How did the Tibetans see the relations between their most famous masters and their schools?

Within the dGe-lugs-pa *chos-'byung* literature—the description of the rise of the Dharma as seen by the school of Tsong-kha-pa—there are several prophecies ascribed to the ancient *Maṇi-bka'-bum* and *bKa'-thang-sde-lnga* and other works of the rNying-ma-pa School. Most of these reference works were *gter-ma* (concealed and revealed books) that were held in high esteem in the rNying-ma-pa School,[5] but there were also prophecies quoted from the *Mañjuśrīmūla-tantra* and other texts. After the *Vaiḍūrya-ser-po*[6] (the famous description of the rise of the dGe-lugs-pa School) was composed by sDe-srid Sangs-rgyas-rgya-mtsho in 1698, these prophecies constituted a regular part of every biography of Tsong-kha-pa as well as of each dGe-lugs-pa *chos-'byung*.[7] It is not the aim of this paper to authenticate these prophecies or to investigate their age. They are utilized here to document how the dGe-lugs-pa valued their relation to other Buddhist sects, particularly that of the rNying-ma-pa. We will limit our source of substantiation to the *Vaiḍūrya-ser-po* and complement it with some excerpts from Tsong-kha-pa's biography by Dar-han mKhan-sprul bLo-bzang phrin-las, which was written in the nineteenth century.

PROPHECIES FROM ANCIENT RNYING-MA TEXTS RELATING TO TSONG-KHA-PA

THE *RGYAL-PO-BKA'-BUM*[8]

> [At the end of time] will come a Bhikṣu, endowed with the enlightened mind (*bodhicitta*), who will accomplish the very essence of the Teaching. This Bhikṣu will achieve the Tantras and unfold noble

and incomprehensible qualities. Many noble ones will venerate him. Afterwards, the particular reverence will even increase. This noble and great person, who will have a grasp of the Tantra, will be born as dGe-slong (*bhikṣu*) Byang-sems in the east. This great yogi, sNying-po-mtha'-brten ('Relying on the Utmost Essence') will change the face of Jo-bo and venerate him deeply. All those who will venerate him deeply will be noble ones and *bhikṣus*. For this reason, they all should be venerated. Why are they called 'noble ones'? They are noble beings because of their achievements for the Buddhas. When noble beings arise in this way, the appropriate community, the word of the Buddha, and the real figure of the Teacher will exist, and there will also be that excellent mountain. About this prophesy, there are several ancient explanations. Though in ancient times, this prophesy was interpreted in several different ways, if it is to be taken as a prophesy relating to sGam-po Tshul-khrims-snying-po, it would clearly indicate the following: It would refer to the normal lifetime of Tsong-kha-pha and to his birthplace, Tsong-kha.[9] What is called 'East' denotes the country. The name sNying-po-mtha'-brten denotes Tsong-kha-pa's monastic name, Kun-dga'-snying-po. 'To change the face . . .'—although this sentence is slightly incomplete—the phrases, 'the real figure of the Teacher' and 'and also changing the face he venerated him deeply' denote that Tsong-kha-pa changed the appearance of Jo-bo into the shape of his *sambhoga-kaya*.[10] 'The great achievements' denote, for instance, the esteemed *puja* during the first month (*i.e.* the great *smon-lam* festival).

THE *PADMA-THANG-YIG*

The next prophecy is said to belong to the *Padma-thang-yig*, the famous hagiography of Padmasambhava:[11]

> At the holy monastery of dGa'-ldan, the best of the sages, who knows the meaning of the Sūtras as well as that of the Tantras [and who is] the embodiment of Vajradhara, will open the doors of the pronouncements of the secret words.[12] He will be like a pilot, a guide for all beings, showing them the way to liberation. He will be born as a human being whose name will be composed of *blo* (mind) and *bzang* (pure).[13] His secret name will be Las-rab rdo-rje bde-ba rtsal.

THE *PADMA-BKA'-CHEMS*[14]

> The embodiment of Mañjuśrī, the master of the disciples and the teaching, who commands the teachings of the Tantras and the Sūtras, will be called bLo-bzang grags-pa. After eight human generations, he will teach the secret words (the meaning of the Tantras) in detail. When he departs from this life, he will come to Maitreya's realm. Those who grasp his tradition will realize Buddhahood within a single lifetime. During this long aeon, *rang-byung*, they will become Arhats without any doubt.

The *Vaiḍurya-ser-po* quotes further prophecies from the *rGyal-po bka'-thang*, Ratna-gling-pa's *sPyi-lung chen-mo*, and rDo-rje gling-pa's *gTer-yig.*[15] The last two, the prophecy of Chos-rje mgon-po rin-chen-pa (the same as the one cited by Guru Chos-dbang [1212–1270] in his *gTer-yig*), and the story of the vision realized by Grub-chen Nyi-zla-sangs-rgyas,[16] were identical. dGe-bshes Ngag-dbang-nyi-ma cited almost the same prophecies in his *Chos-byung lung-rigs sgron-me.*[17] There were also other prophecies of Tsong-kha-pa traced in some of the most prominent Buddhist texts: the *kriyā-tantra* of the *Mañjuśrī-mūla-tantra,*[18] *Mahāyānasūtralaṃkāra,*[19] and the Chinese version of the *Laṅkāvatāra-sūtra.*[20]

VARIOUS PROPHECIES IDENTIFYING TSONG-KHA-PA WITH ATĪŚA AND PADMASAMBHAVA

A second group of prophecies styles Tsong-kha-pa as an incarnation of Atīśa. Chapter 26 of the *'Brom-gyis-'bul-mo-che mdzad-pa*, found in the voluminous *bKa'-gdams glegs-bam pha-chos*, is the main exposition of the bKa'-gdams-pa School. Here is its prophecy, transmitted in the *Vaiḍūrya-ser-po.*[21]

> [Atīśa's incarnation] will be a noble one. Sometimes he will be a real *bhikṣu*. He will protect this country. Sometimes he will come in the shape of a child, sometimes in the shape of a poor beggar, sometimes in the shape of an animal, like a bird or a dog. Sometimes he will find his shape in the melody of a prayer or in the letter of a mantra. In any case, he will be a famous *bhikṣu*. As long as the Buddha-Law exists, he will

> always return. Those who follow his tradition will be equal to him. Hundreds of people will meditate at this place; they will aspire to be propitious to the three kinds of beings while this law-abiding one (the *bhikṣu*) will bless them. As he will feel little remorse concerning the teaching (*lta-ba*), he will be provoked by the demons of sensuous charm. His concentration will be robbed by hate and lust. However, because he will be blessed as an incarnate being, he will become an object of veneration by all beings up to the gods. To venerate him will certainly be appropriate. In a word, at first there will be only four monks, but at the end there will be two and one-half thousand who will become the best object of veneration. This real son of Śākyamuni will be endowed with the three tenets of training[22] and will become the patron of all beings. Around him countless monks will assemble from all directions under the heavens. Generally, the worthy ones will proceed to the ten directions, and nobody will be able to degrade them as they are like the outer oceans which can never be filled even by a hundred rivers.

Further, it is said in the same book:

> At last the flickering Doctrine will be kindled by one having the name Grags-pa. He will be a noble object to be venerated, as he will act for the benefit and luck of many beings.

Further on in the *Vaiḍūrya-ser-po*[23] the author quotes from the Stories of the Previous Births of dKon-cog-'bangs (*dKon-cog-'bangs-kyi skye-rabs*). In the course of these stories references are made to Bla-ma Dri-ma-tsho-skyes-rdo-rje, one of the previous existences of Atīśa. Dri-ma-mtsho-skyes-rdo-rje's prophecy is interspersed with the author's own commentary:

> Bla-ma Dri-ma-mtsho-skyes-rdo-rje spoke the following sentences in a manner similar to the language of the country of Uḍḍiyāna:
>
> "I shall also go to this place to subdue gods and demons." This refers to Ācārya Padmasambhava, who subdued gods and demons.
>
> "One incarnated being will go to India." This refers to Jo-bo-rje Dīpaṃkara (Atīśa), the incarnation of Dri-med Bla-ma.
>
> "One incarnation will go to the midland of Nepal." This refers to the Pandit of Nepal, Padmavajra, a previous existence of dGe-'dun-'grub.
>
> "One incarnation will go to the lowlands of mDo-Khams." Thus, it is prophesied that the mild patron, the great Bla-ma Tsong-kha-pa

Blo-bzang-gras-pa, will be born in the country of Tsong-kha in mDo-smad.

In the voluminous biography of Tsong-kha-pa, composed by Dar-han mKhan-sprul Blo-bzang-phrin-las, there is a reference to the sayings of dGe-'dun-rgya-mtsho[24] which reads as follows:

> Relying on these arguments (the prophecy of bLa-ma Dri-med-mtsho-skyes-rdo-rje), the all-knowing dGe-'dun-rgya-mtsho (the second Dalai Lama) also says, "I venerate Padmasambhava, the master of Siddhas and Vidyādharas; the venerable Dīpaṃkara (Atīśa), the chief ornament of the end of time; and the glorious bLo-bzang-grags-pa, who is equal to Vajradhara—all who are merely different shapes of a single actor. In this way these persons are spiritually interwoven with one another."

In summarizing the contents of these prophecies we find that, in the Tibetan tradition, these exalted promulgators of the Buddha-Law in Tibet—Padmasambhava, Atīśa, and Tsong-kha-pa—were interlaced with one another in a unique spiritual relationship (*thugs-rgyud gcig par*).[25] As all three were not simply human beings but manifestations of the supreme compassion embodied in the Buddhas and the Great Bodhisattvas, they were seen as the same actor playing different roles.

When certain Westerners busy themselves in the activity of labeling Tsong-kha-pa as a reformer of Buddhism in Tibet like Luther in Europe, we can conclude that this is not in concordance with the Tibetan tradition. It is more than curious to observe in some of the Western literature the attempt to condemn Padmasambhava as a mere sorcerer and build up Atīśa and Tsong-kha-pa as righteous monk-scholars according to European ideals of the nineteenth century.[26] The history of religions becomes mere self-adulation if it does not go to the sources of native traditions. The West must acknowledge that the relationship among the various Buddhist schools in Tibet was very different from that among the Christian denominations in Europe. In this light, individual masters and founders of these three Tibetan Schools did not preach different teachings: rather, they demonstrated different methods for realizing a single goal—Buddhahood.

NOTES

1. Dilgo Kyentze Rinpoche, ed., The *rNying-ma'i rgyud-'bum, Tantras of the Nyingmapa Tradition*, 34 volumes, 1973–74. Further, see G. Tucci, *Die Religionen Tibets und der Mongolei*, Tucci-Heissig, pp. 28 and 53, 1970.

2. Sum-pa-mkhan-po, *dPag-bsam-ljon-bzang*, Vols. 1 and 2, S. Das, ed., p. 392, line 1 ff., 1908.

3. A. Chattopadhyaya, *Atīśa and Tibet*, p. 56 ff., 1967.

4. G. Tucci, Tucci-Heissig, *op. cit.*, p. 54 ff.; G. Tucci, *Tibetan Painted Scrolls*, Vol. 1, p. 39 ff., 1949.

5. G. Tucci, Tucci-Heissig, *op. cit.*, p. 52 ff.; E. Neumaier, "Einige Aspekte der gTer-ma Literature," in *Zeitschrift der Deutschen Morgenländischen Gesellschaft*, Suppl. 1, Part 3, p. 849 ff., 1969; E. Dargyay, *The Rise of Esoteric Buddhism in Tibet*, p. 62 ff., 1977.

6. Lokesh Candra, ed., *Vaiḍūrya-ṣer-po*, A history of the dGe-lugs-pa Monasteries of Tibet, Parts 1 and 2, *Śatapiṭaka Series*, 1960.

7. See 'Jam-dbyangs-bshad-pa 'Jigs-med-dbang-po, "dGe-lugs-pa chos-byung," *Collected Works of dKon-mchog 'Jigs-med-dbang-po, the Second 'Jam-dbyangs-bzhad-pa*, Vol. 5. *Gedan Sungrab Minyam Gyunphel Series*, No. 25, pp. 538–553, 1971. "Tsong-kha-pa's Biography," Vol. 2, *The Collected Works of Cha-har dGe-bshes bLo-bzang-tshul-khrims*, Chatring Jansar Tenzin, ed., 1971. This work was analyzed by R. Kaschewsky in *Das Leben des Lamistischen Heiligen Tsong-kha-pa bLo-bzang-grags-pa*, 1967. Dar-han mKhan-sprul bLo-bzang-phrin-las, *'Jam-mgon-chos-kyi-rgyal-po Tsong-kha-pa chen-po'i rnam-thar thub-bstan mdzes-pa'i rgyan-gcig ngo-mtshar nor-bu'i phreng-ba*, Gurudeva, ed., 1967. dGe-bshes Ngag-dbang-nyi-ma, *Chos-'byung-lung-rigs-sgron-me*, 1966.

8. The quotation used is from the *Vaiḍūrya-ser-po*, Part 1, L. Chandra, ed., p. 50, line 14 ff., 1960. The title of the *rGyal-po-bka'-'bum* is usually cited as *Ma-ṇi-bka'-'bum* or *rGyal-po Srong-bstan-sgam-po'i bKa'-'bum*. See A. Vostrikov, *Tibetan Historical Literature*, p. 52 ff., 1970.

9. Throughout the *Vaiḍūrya-ser-po*, the name of the native country of Tsong-kha-pa is spelled 'bTsong-kha' instead of the more common 'Tsong-kha'. So also the surname of bLo-bzang-grags-pa is spelled 'bTsong-kha-pa' instead of 'Tsong-kha-pa'. But I have rendered both names in the more common way as 'Tsong-kha' and 'Tsong-kha-pa'.

10. One of the most admired deeds of Tsong-kha-pa was the changing of the famous Buddha figure called 'Jo-bo' in the main temple of Lha-sa, the Jo-khang. Originally, the statue, which was brought from Nepal to Tibet by the Nepalese wife of King Srong-bstan-sgam-po in the eighth century, showed the Buddha in the common shape of Śākyamuni. But Tsong-kha-pa

adorned this figure with jewelry typical for the figures of Bodhisattvas. For that reason the author of the text refers to Jo-bo as a figure of the *sambhoga-kāya*. For a definition of this term see H. V. Guenther, *Kindly Bent to Ease Us, Part One*, 1975, p. 11 ff., and 223 ff.

11. The quotation used is from the *Vaiḍurya-ser-po*, Part 1, p. 51, lines 9–12; for the *Padma-thang-yig*, see A. Vostrikov, *op. cit.*, p. 32 ff.

12. *Gsang-sngags* denotes *mantra* as well as the Vajrayāna doctrines.

13. This indicates Tsong-kha-pa's name, bLo-bzang-grags-pa.

14. The quotation here is from the *Vaiḍūrya-ser-po*, Part 1, p. 51, lines 12–15; for the *Padma-bka'-chems* (Padamsambhava's Testament) see A. Vostrikov, *op. cit.*, p. 33 ff.

15. Page 51, lines 15–20; for the *rGyal-po-bka'-thang* see A. Vostrikov, *op. cit.*, p. 49 ff.; for Ratna-gling-pa see E. Dargyay, *op. cit.*, p. 144 ff.; for rDo-rje-gling-pa's *gTer-yig* see E. Dargyay, *op. cit.*, p. 140; for Guru Chos-dbang's *gTer-yig* see E. Dargyay, *op. cit.*, p. 108.

16. *Vaiḍurya-ser-po*, Part 1, p. 51 ff.

17. Page 55 ff., 1966.

18. *Vaiḍurya-ser-po*, Part 1, p. 49 ff.

19. *Op. cit.*, p. 50.

20. *Collected Works of dKon-mchog 'Jigs-med-dbang-phyug—the Second 'Jam-dbyangs-bzhad-pa*, Vol. 5, p. 541, line 4, 1971; and dGe-bshes Ngag-dbang-nyi-ma's *Chos-'byung-lungs-rigs-sgron-me*, p. 53, 1966.

21. Page 52, line 6 ff.

22. See Jaeschke, *Tibetan-English Dictionary*, p. 594 ff., 1949.

23. Page 53, line 3 ff.

24. *'Jam-mgon-chos-kyi-rgyal-po Tsong-kha-pa-chen-po'i rnam-thar thub-bstan mdzes-pa'i rgyan-gcig ngo-mtshar nor-bu'i phreng-ba*, with preface by Yonzin Trijang Rinpoche; p. 45, line 9, India, 1967.

25. Blo-bzang phrin-las, *Tsong-kha-pa rnam-thar* (see N. 23), p. 47, line 8.

26. See, for instance, G. Schulemann, *Die Geschichte der Dalai Lamas*, pp. 40, 46, and 55, 1911; H. Hoffmann, *Die Religionen Tibets*, pp. 46 and 165, 1956.

The *Bodhisattvāvadānakalpalatā* and the *Ṣaḍdantāvadāna*

J. W. de Jong

THE *Bodhisattvāvadānakalpalatā*[1] was published in the *Bibliotheca Indica* in two volumes. Sarat Chandra Das and Paṇḍit Hari Mohan Vidyābhūshaṇa edited the first five fascicles of Volume 1 (Calcutta, 1888-1895, pp. xlii + 1-442) and the first five fascicles of Volume 2 (Calcutta, 1890-1897, pp. 1-480). After a long interval, publication was resumed by Das in 1906, and with Satis Chandra Vidyābhūṣaṇa he edited the remaining fascicles of both volumes (Vol. I, Fascicles 6-13, pp. 443-1171, Calcutta, 1906-1913; Vol. II, Fascicles 6-11, pp. 481-1093 +13 pp., Calcutta, 1910-1913). In 1959 P. L. Vaidya reprinted the Sanskrit text in Volumes 22 and 23 of *The Buddhist Sanskrit Texts*.

Das's edition is based upon a Tibetan blockprint which contains both the Sanskrit text in Tibetan transliteration and the Tibetan translation. According to him this blockprint consists of 620 folios and was printed in 1662-1663.[2] In editing the *Bodhisattvāvadāna-kalpalatā*, Das has done some rearrangement of the text. In the Peking edition of the Tanjur the *Bodhisattvāvadānakalpalatā* occupies Vol. 93 of the *Mdo-'grel.*[3] Story 107 ends on page 346a1. Then follows Somendra's introduction to the last tale composed by himself: 346al-347b2 (=Das Vol. 2, pp. 1008-1015). This tale occupies ff. 347b2–357a7 (= Das Vol. 2, pp. 1016–1087). Then follows Somadeva's introduction to the *Bodhisattvāvadānakalpalatā*: ff. 357a8–358a6. This introduction has been published by Das on pp. xxiv–xxix of his introduction. The table of contents of the *Bodhisattvāvadānakalpalatā* occupies ff. 358a6–360a5 (cf. Das, Introduction, pp. xxx–xli). This table contains 42 verses and not 43. The 43d verse in Das's edition is the first of the four verses of the colophon for which see Das, Vol. 2, pp. 1088–1091 (= Tibetan translation, ff. 360a5–360b3). This colophon is followed in the Peking edition of the Tibetan translation by the colophon of the translation, ff. 360b4–361a8). The first lines of this colophon (ff. 360b4–6) are also found in the colophon of the blockprint used by Das (cf. Vol. 2, p. 1092, lines 1–7 of the Tibetan text). The same blockprint also contains a lengthy text edited with separate pagination (pp. 1–13) by Das at the beginning of Fascicle 11 of Volume 2. According to Das this text contains the "concluding remarks of the last Tibetan editor."

In the Tibetan translation the tenth *pallava* is called *Mngal-las 'byung-ba*. However, the Tibetan blockprint used by Das does not contain the Sanskrit text of this *pallava*. For this reason Das has relegated it to the end of Volume 1 (pp. 1165–1171). Moreover, Das has changed the numbers of *Pallava*s 11–49 to 10–48. Consequently, there is no *Pallava* 49 in his edition. This rearrangement of the *pallava*s agrees with the table of contents, which lists as the tenth *pallava* the story of Sundarīnanda. According to this table the forty-ninth story is the *Ṣaḍdantāvadāna*, text and translation, which are lacking in the Tibetan blockprint and in the Peking edition of the Tibetan translation. It is obvious that in the text used by the Tibetan translators one story was missing. According to Satis Chandra Vidyābhūṣaṇa (Vol. 1, p. 1171, footnote) the *Mngal-las 'byung-ba* was evidently an interpolation introduced to make up the auspicious total of 108 *pallava*s. Tucci speculates that the forty-ninth *pallava*, the *Ṣaḍdantāvadāna*, was lacking in the text on which the Tibetan translation was based and that, for this reason, the editors of the Tibetan translation compiled the *Mngal-las 'byung-ba*.[4] Tucci does not explain why the editors have filled the gap caused by the absence of the forty-ninth story by adding a story after the ninth with the consequence that Stories 10–48 had to be renumbered 11–49.

The *Mngal-las 'byung-ba*, 'The coming forth from the womb', is a sermon preached by the Buddha to Ānanda near Campā on conception, birth, and the miseries of human life. Vidyābhūṣaṇa reconstructs the Sanskrit title as *Garbhakrāntyavadāna*, but Tucci prefers *Garbhāvakrānti*. A *Garbhāvakrānti-sūtra* is quoted in the *Abhidharmakośabhāṣya* and the *Yogācārabhūmi* (ed. V. Bhattacharya, Calcutta, 1957, p. 27.5). The *Abhidharmakośavyākhyā* (ed. U. Wogihara, Tokyo, 1932–1936, p. 67.1) refers to the *Garbhāvakrānti-sūtra*, but the *Abhidharmakośabhāṣya* omits the word *sūtra*. Cf. *Abhidharmakośabhāsya* (ed. P. Pradhan, Patna, 1967, p. 24.10): *ṣaḍdhātur iyaṃ puruṣa iti garbhāvakrāntau*. The Tibetan translation of the *bhāṣya* renders *Garbhāvakrānti* with *Mngal-du 'jug-pa*. The *Mngal-du 'byung-ba* is not identical with the text quoted in the *Abhidharmakośabhāṣya* and other texts. A reconstructed Sanskrit title would not be *Garbhāvakrānti* but *Garbhotpatti*. As to the *Garbhāvakrānti-sūtra*, La Vallée Poussin refers to Chapter 11 of the *Vinayasaṃyuktakavastu* (Nanjio 1121, Taishō 1451), to Chapter 14 of the *Ratnakūṭa* (Nanjio 23.14, Taishō 310.14), and to the *Dhātuvibhaṅgasutta* in the *Majjhima-nikāya* (No. 140).[5] Moreover, he adds that the *Garbhāvakrāntisūtra* is one of the sources of the *Pitāputrasamāgama* which is quoted in the *Śikṣāsamuccaya*, the *Bodhicaryāvatāra*, and the *Madhyamakāvatāra*. However, he has not checked whether the quotations of the *Garbhāvakrāntisūtra* in the *Abhidharmakośabhāṣya* can be traced in the texts mentioned by him. He mentions only Chapter 14 of the *Ratnakūṭa*, but both the Chinese and Tibetan translations of the *Ratnakūṭa* contain two texts, entitled *Garbhāvakrāntinirdeśa*. According to the Peking edition of the Kanjur, the full Sanskrit titles are *Āyuṣmannandagarbhāvakrāntinirdeśa* and *Nandagarbhāvakrāntinirdeśa*.[6]

Pelliot has pointed out that the Chinese translation of the *Ratnakūṭa* contains two translations (Taishō 310.13 and 310.14) which correspond to Sūtras 13 and 14 of the Tibetan version of the *Ratnakūṭa*.[7] However, in Taishō 310.13 the Buddha is questioned by Ānanda; in the corresponding Tibetan text the Buddha addresses himself not to Ānanda but to Nanda. Pelliot remarks that in an older Chinese translation by Dharmarakṣa (Taishō 317) Nanda figures in the beginning but is later replaced by Ānanda. Marcelle Lalou has pointed out that the Tibetan text was translated by Chos-grub from the Chinese translation by Bodhiruci (Taishō 310.13).[8] Pelliot had already advanced the hypothesis that this text was translated from the Chinese and that the translator had substituted the name Nanda for Ānanda.[9] A careful comparison of both texts will be required in order to show whether this is the only substantial difference between the two texts.

As concerns Sūtra 14 of *Ratnakūṭa*, the situation is more complicated. Pelliot had pointed out that Chapters 11 and 12 of the Vinaya of the Mūlasarvāstivādin[10] are absolutely identical with Chapter 14 of the Chinese *Ratnakūṭa*. The *Vinayakṣudrakavastu* was translated by I-tsing, and in compiling the Chinese *Ratnakūṭa* Bodhiruci therefore must have made use of I-tsing's translation of Chapters 11 and 12. The Tibetan translation of the *Vinayakṣudrakavastu* contains, according to Csoma's analysis (folios 202–248 of Volume 10 of the Narthang edition of the *Vinaya*) instructions to Nanda on the conditions of existence in the womb and on the gradual formation of the human body.[11] Pelliot concluded that probably this sūtra too had been translated from the Chinese. Sakurabe Bunkyō arrived at the same conclusion in his study of the *Ratnakūṭa*.[12]

Marcelle Lalou, however, compared the Tibetan translation of Chapters 11 and 12 of the *Vinayakṣudrakavastu* with *Sūtras* 13 and 14 of the Tibetan *Ratnakūṭa* and showed that the text of *Sūtra* 13 is different from that of *Sūtra* 14 and that the latter is not identical with the text of the *Vinayakṣudrakavastu*. This conclusion, though, does not exclude the possibility that *Sūtra* 14 of the Tibetan *Ratnakūṭa* was translated from I-tsing's version of Chapters 11 and 12 of the *Vinayakṣudrakavastu*. It is quite possible that I-tsing's translation of these two chapters is not completely identical with the Tibetan translation of the same chapters. A final solution will require a close comparison of the Chinese and Tibetan versions of Sūtras 13 and 14 of the *Ratnakūṭa* with the Chinese and Tibetan versions of Chapters 11 and 12 of the *Vinayakṣudrakavastu*.

In *Sūtra* 14 of the Tibetan *Ratnakūṭa*, Buddha is first at Kapilavastu and then goes to Śrāvasti. From Śrāvasti he goes to Campā, and it is here on the banks of the pond of the *ṛṣi* Garga that he teaches Nanda the *Garbhāvakrāntisūtra*. In Chapter 11 of the *Vinayakṣu-*

drakavastu Buddha teaches the *Garbhāvakrāntisūtra* to Nanda at exactly the same place.[13] The *Vinaya* of the Mūlasarvāstivādin was well-known to the Tibetans. The fact that Buddha taught a *Garbhāvakrāntisūtra* to Nanda on the banks of the Pond of Garga[14] must have been in the minds of the compilers of the *Mngal-las 'byung-ba*, which is also set on the banks of a lotus-pond near Campā. Although they substituted Ānanda for Nanda they must have been aware of the fact that a *Garbhāvakrāntisūtra* is found in the Buddhist canon in connection with the story of Nanda. This is certainly the reason why the *Mngal-las 'byung-ba* is placed in the Tibetan translation of the *Bodhisattvāvadānakalpalatā* before the story of Nanda, which is No. 11 in the Tibetan translation and No. 10 in Das's edition.

In the Sanskrit text of the table of contents of the *Bodhisattvāvadānakalpalatā* no mention is made of the *Mngal-las 'byung-ba*. However, in the Peking and Cone editions of the Tibetan translation the title of this text has been mentioned in an additional *pāda* of Verse 4: *gang-zhig dpal-sbas la bstan dang / / me-skyes skal-ldan du* (Peking: *dus*) *gsung dang / / mngal-nas 'byung-ba bstan-pa dang / / gang-zhig dga'-bo'i mdzes-ma la / / chags-pa dag ni 'bad-pas bsal* (Peking: *gsal*) / /. It is obvious that this *pāda* has been added later in order to account for the presence of the *Mngal-las 'byung-ba*.

The *Ṣaḍdantāvadāna* is mentioned in both the Sanskrit text and the Tibetan translation of the table of contents. In his detailed bibliography on the *Ṣaḍdantajātaka*, Lamotte indicates that the *Ṣaḍdantāvadāna* is not found in the Paris manuscripts of the *Bodhisattvāvadānakalpalatā*. However, he points out that the two Cambridge manuscripts, Add. 1306 and Add. 913, contain this *avadāna*.[15] Add. 1306 is a manuscript written in A.D. 1302.[16] According to Somendra's introduction the *Bodhisattvāvadānakalpalatā* was completed in the twenty-seventh year, i.e., 1051–1052. The Cambridge manuscript is therefore written 250 years after the completion of the work. Bendall has described the manuscript in detail.[17] Leaves 1–174 are missing, and the manuscript begins with the last word, *sahiṣṇavaḥ*, of Verse 7 of Tale 42, *Paṇḍitāvadāna*. Bendall remarks that in the manuscript Tales 41–48 are numbered 42–49. He has changed the numbering according to the metrical table of contents. However, the numbering of the manuscripts agrees entirely with that of the Tibetan translation of the *Bodhisattvāvadānakalpalatā* in which Tale 42 is the *Paṇḍitāvadāna*. In Das's edition this is Tale 41, wrongly called *Kapilāvadāna*. The table of contents also gives the name *Paṇḍita*. If we keep the numbering of the tales as found in Add. 1306, Tale 49 (*Hastakāvadāna*) ends on f. 198b. Tale 50 (*Daśakarmaplutyavadāna*) begins on f. 199b: *namo buddhāya / ye helocchita-*.

However, this manuscript contains seven extra leaves numbered 199-205. Bendall has given them the numbers 199*-205*. The *Ṣaḍdantāvadāna* begins on the last line of f. 198b and occupies the leaves 199*-205*. It is obvious that the scribe completed the first part of the *Bodhisattvāvadānakalpalatā* (Tales 1-49) on f. 198b and continued with the second part on f. 199b. According to Bendall the scribe had by accident omitted this tale and copied it in afterwards. Bendall's conclusion was certainly justified because the table of contents lists the *Ṣaḍdantāvadāna* as the Tale 49. However, with the publication of Das's edition it has become evident that the *Ṣaḍdantāvadāna* was missing in the Sanskrit text translated in Tibet. It must also have been missing in the manuscript used by the scribe of Add. 1306, Mañjuśrībhadrasudhi. When copying the table of contents Mañjuśrībhadrasudhi must have made the same discovery as Bendall, i.e., that the *Ṣaḍdantāvadāna* is listed as Tale 49.

In order to supply this missing tale the scribe made use of another collection of tales which contains a recension of the *Ṣaḍdantāvadāna*: the *Kalpadrumāvadānamālā*. Both the Paris and Cambridge manuscripts contain the text of the *Ṣaḍdantāvadāna*.[18] In the *Kalpadrumāvadānamālā* the tale is comprised of 198 verses. They are followed by several additional verses of a moralistic nature which do not belong to the story itself, and which need not be considered. The scribe of the *Bodhisattvāvadānakalpalatā* did not use all 198 verses. He reproduced 110 verses without any alteration and added eight others, most of which were made from *pādas* of verses of the *Kalpadrumāvadānamālā* recension of the story.

Feer[19] has studied the *Kalpadrumāvadānamālā* recension of the *Ṣaḍdanta* story together with other recensions. However, in order to show how the scribe of the *Bodhisattvāvadānakalpalatā* made use of the *Kalpadrumāvadānamālā* recension, it is necessary to give a summary and to indicate the *Kalpadrumāvadānamālā* verse-numbers.

Verses 1–4: Introduction. Aśoka asks Upagupta to tell another tale.

5: A good man is purified by the fire of a bad man (*durjanāgni*) just as a jewel shines after having been polished by a whetstone.

6–11: Buddha teaches the law at the Garga Pond near Campā.

12–31: Devadatta warns the *kṣapaṇakas* against the Buddha.

32–37: His words provoke different reactions among them.

38–58: A *kṣapaṇaka* says that he knows a way to destroy the reputation of the Buddha. He asks Cañāmānavikā to simulate pregnancy and to accuse the Buddha of having made her pregnant. She fastens a wooden bowl under her garment.

59–88: Cañcāmānavikā goes to the Buddha and accuses him of having made her pregnant and of having abandoned her. Thc Buddha is unperturbed but the gods are greatly upset. Śakra creates two rats who cut the cord which holds the wooden bowl. Crying "I am burnt," Cañcāmānavikā disappears in the flames of Hell.

89–94: The Buddha explains that she has been guilty of a grave sin in a previous existence.

95–123: The Elephant King Ṣaḍdanta lived happily in the Himālayas with his two wives, Bhadrā and Subhadrā. Once he played with Subhadrā in the lotus pond Mandākinī. Bhadrā became jealous and decided to take revenge. She went to the forest where the *muni*s live and took upon herself a fast in eight parts. She expressed the wish to be reborn as a queen and to obtain a seat of pleasure (*krīḍāsana*) made from the tusks of Ṣaḍdanta. She killed herself by throwing herself from a mountain, and was reborn as the daughter of the minister Khaṇḍita (mistake for Paṇḍita ?) of King Brahmadatta in Kāśi.

The king married her. She asked him for a seat made from the tusks of Ṣaḍdanta. The king summoned an old hunter, who tried to dissuade him from killing Ṣaḍdanta because he was a Bodhisattva.

124–143: The old hunter persuaded the king, but Bhadrā insisted on her wish. The king summoned another hunter, who declared himself willing to kill Ṣaḍdanta.

144–161: Dressed in a yellow robe, the hunter was seen by Subhadrā. She told the king [Ṣaḍdanta] that she was frightened, but the king explained that she had nothing to fear from someone who wears a yellow robe. He had just spoken these words when the hunter pierced him with a poisoned arrow. Subhadrā fainted, but Ṣaḍdanta consoled her and asked the hunter why he wanted to kill him.

162–165: The hunter explained that Queen Bhadrā desired a seat made from his tusks.

166–184: Ṣaḍdanta arrived at the conclusion that he must give his tusks to the hunter, because it was impossible to disappoint someone who came with a request. He broke off his tusks against a mountain. Five hundred elephants arrived, but Ṣaḍdanta protected the hunter with his chest and sent him back with his tusks.

185–189: The hunter brought the tusks to the king, who recompensed him with gold. He sent him back to his own house. Suddenly both his hands were cut off and fell on the ground.

190: Bhadrā mounted the seat made from the tusks. Saying "I am burnt," she fell into Hell.

191–192: Brahmadatta's kingdom was destroyed by terrible plagues.

193–198: The *dramatis personnae* are identified. Ṣaḍdanta = the Buddha; Bhadrā = Cañcāmānavikā; the hunter = Devadatta' the other elephants = monks. There are two verses on the evil behaviour of women. In the last verse the Buddha proclaims that one must speak the truth, refrain from inflicting injuries, and concentrate on śānti.

The scribe of the *Bodhisattvāvadānakalpalatā* took from the *Kalpadrumāvadānamālā* recension the following verses: 5, 59-123, 144-161, 166-184, 190, and 193-198. In order to fill the lacunae he added five verses (A-E) between Verse 5 and Verse 59, one verse (F) between Verses 123 and 144, one verse (G) between Verses 161 and 166, and one verse (H) between Verses 190 and 193. A-B: The Buddha preaches the law at the Garga Pond near Campā. C-E: The jealous *kṣapaṇaka*s say, "You must destroy the lustre (*dīpti*) of the Buddha by saying that you have been made pregnant by him." The young woman simulates a pregnancy by means of a wooden bowl. F: A second hunter declares himself willing to kill Ṣaḍdanta. G: The hunter says that Queen Bhadrā wants to have a seat made from Ṣaḍdanta's tusks. H: The hunter loses his hands, and Brahmadatta's kingdom is destroyed by excessive rains.

It is obvious that the scribe of the *Bodhisattvāvadānakalpalatā* was more interested in the story of the past concerning Ṣaḍdanta than in the story of the present relating to Cañcāmānavikā. Through the omission of Verses 6-58, nothing is said of the role played by Devadatta, although identification of Devadatta with the hunter (Verse 194) has been maintained. Moreover, verses C-E do not explain why the *kṣapaṇaka*s are jealous nor the identity of the young woman whom they ask to simulate pregnancy. It is equally obvious that the scribe of the *Bodhisattvāvadānakalpalatā* has made use of the *Kalpadrumāvadānamālā*. In a long note added to the English translation of his article on the *Ṣaḍdanta-jātaka*, "*Essai de classement chronologique des diverses versions du Ṣaḍdanta-jâtaka*" (*Mélanges d'Indianisme*, Paris, 1911, pp. 231-248) Foucher writes that "The author of the latter collection [*Kalpadrumāvadānamālā*] restricted himself to reproducing, without however (in any way) informing the reader of the fact, the work of Kshemendra, except that on two points he has lengthened the narrative of his predecessor, which in his opinion was too much abbreviated."[20]

I hope to be able to publish shortly the text of the *Kalpadrumāvadānamālā* recension of the *Ṣaḍdantāvadāna* including the eight verses added by the scribe of the *Bodhisattvāvadānakalpalatā*. It will then become absolutely clear that Foucher was wrong in assuming that the *Kalpadrumāvadānamālā* recension is based upon the

Bodhisattvāvadānakalpalatā recension. It is not possible to prove that the scribe of Manuscript Add. 1306, Mañjuśrībhadrasudhi, himself took the *Ṣaḍdantāvadāna* from a manuscript of the *Kalpadrumāvadānamālā*, but the similarity of the script in the *Ṣaḍdantāvadāna* to that in other parts of the manuscript of the *Bodhisattvāvadānakalpalatā* makes this supposition highly probable.

The fact that the *Ṣaḍdantāvadāna* is listed in the table of contents as the forty-ninth *avadāna* obliges us to assume that originally the text contained this story. It was, however, already missing in the copy which was translated in Tibet in the second half of the thirteenth century.[21] It is difficult to find a satisfactory explanation for the disappearance of the *Ṣaḍdantāvadāna*. This is not the only problem connected with the *Bodhisattvāvadānakalpalatā*. It was completed by Kṣemendra in 1052, but he did not compose Tale 108. This is surprising in view of the fact that he was still living in 1066 (when he wrote the *Daśāvatāracarita*).[22] Somendra does not explain why his father, after having composed 107 tales, did not complete his work by writing the 108th. If it had been Kṣemendra's wish that his son fulfill this task, one would expect Somendra to have mentioned this.

NOTES

1. The *Bodhisattvāvadānakalpalatā* is often referred to as *Avadānakalpalatā*. However, according to all the colophons and the Tibetan translation the title is *Bodhisattvāvadānakalpalatā*.

2. A copy of the same blockprint edition is listed in *A Catalogue of the Tohoku University Collection of Tibetan Works on Buddhism* (Sendai, 1953), p. 521, No. 7034, but I have not been able to consult it. In the Cone Tanjur the *Bodhisattvāvadānakalpalatā* occupies two volumes (Vols. 91-92: *Khri-shing*). The Cone edition contains both the Sanskrit text and the Tibetan translation. I have not been able to consult the Derge edition, but it also probably contains the Sanskrit text, though this is not mentioned in the catalogue of the Tohoku University: *A Complete Catalogue of the Tibetan Buddhist Canons* (Sendai, 1934), pp. 633-634, No. 4155. In the Narthang Tanjur the *Bodhisattvāvadānakalpalatā* occupies only one volume. Cf. Mibu Taishun, *A Comparative List of the Tibetan Tripiṭaka of the Narthang Edition* (Tokyo, 1967), p. 98, No. 3646, Vol. Ge, ff. 1-328. It would appear that the Peking and Narthang editions contain only the Tibetan translation, while the Derge and Cone editions contain both text and translation.

3. Cf. P. Cordier, *Catalogue du fonds tibétain de la Bibliothèque Nationale*, Troisième Partie (Paris, 1915), pp. 419-421.

4. *Tibetan Painted Scrolls*, Vol. 2 (Rome, 1949), p. 613, n. 118.

5. *L'Abhidharmakośa de Vasubandhu*, Vol. 1 (Paris-Louvain, 1923), p. 49, n. 2.

6. *A Comparative Analytical Catalogue of the Kanjur Division of the Tibetan Tripiṭaka* (Kyoto, 1930-1932), p. 238.

7. "Notes à propos d'un catalogue du *Kanjur*," in *Journal Asiatique*, 1914, Vol. 2, p. 123.

8. "La version tibétaine du *Ratnakūṭa*", in *Journal Asiatique*, 1927, Vol. 2, pp. 240, 245.

9. *Op. cit.*, p. 126, No. 1.

10. Pelliot refers to Chapters 11 and 12 of the *Vinayakṣudrakavastu*, the same text which La Vallée Poussin refers to as the *Vinayasamyuktakavastu*. Cf. Taishō, Vol. 24, No. 1451, pp. 251a-263a.

11. Pelliot, *op. cit.*, p. 125.

12. "Chibetto-yaku Daihōshakukyō no kenkyū," *Ōtani Gakuhō*, Vol. 11 (1930), p. 550. In his analysis of this article Serge Elisséef says wrongly that Sakurabe tried to prove that the whole Tibetan *Ratnakūṭa* had been translated from the Chinese. See *Bibliographie Bouddhique*, Vol. 2 (Paris, 1931), p. 37, No. 110). Sakurabe observed that Chapters 7, 13, and 40 were translated from the Chinese by Chos-grub and suggested that Chapters 11, 14, 17, and 20 must also have been translated from the Chinese.

13. For the Tibetan version see Lalou, *op. cit.*, p. 242. For the Chinese version see Taishō, Vol. 24, No. 1451, p. 253a17-21.

14. In the Sanskrit text of the *Mūlasarvāstivādavinaya* the name of the pond is Gargā. Cf. Edgerton, *Buddhist Hybrid Sanskrit Dictionary*, p. 210. In Pāli texts the Gaggarā Pond is named after Queen Gaggarā.

15. Ét. Lamotte, *Le Traité de la Grande Vertu de Sagesse*, Tome 2 (Louvain, 1949), p. 716, n. 1. According to Bendall Add. 913 is a copy of a copy, more or less direct, of Add. 1306.

16. According to Petech the date mentioned in the colophon is Sunday, April 8th, 1302. Cf. L. Petech, *Mediaeval History of Nepal* (Roma, 1958), p. 98.

17. C. Bendall, *Catalogue of the Buddhist Sanskrit Manuscripts in the University Library, Cambridge* (Cambridge, 1883), pp. 41-43.

18. Cf. Bendall, *op. cit.*, p. 131, Add. 1590; also J. Filliozat, *Catalogue du fonds sanscrit*, Fascicule 1 (Paris, 1941), pp. 14-15. For other manuscripts see Seiren Matsunami, *A Catalogue of the Sanskrit Manuscripts in the Tokyo University Library* (Tokyo, 1965), pp. 230-231.

19. "Le Chaddanta-Jātaka," *Journal Asiatique*, 1895, Part 1, pp. 31-85 and 189-223.

20. A. Foucher, "The Six-Tusked Elephant," *Beginnings of Buddhist Art* (Paris-London, 1917), p. 204, n. 1.

21. The *Bodhisattvāvadānakalpalatā* was translated by Lakṣmīkara and the Master fron Ṣhong rDo-rje rgyal-mtshan, at the instigation of 'Phags-pa and the Regent Śākya bzang-po. According to Cordier (*op. cit.*, p. 420) the translation was probably made in the year 1272 A.D. The colophon of the Peking edition does not mention a date, and it is not clear from which source Cordier took the date 1272. From the names mentioned in the colophon it is possible to deduce that the translation was made in the period 1260 to 1280.

22. Cf. Oscar Botto, *Il Poeta Kṣemendra e il suo Daśāvatāracarita* (Torino, 1951), p. 9.

H. V. Guenther as Interpreter of the Tantric View of Life

Lama Anagarika Govinda

When the first knowledge of the Tantras penetrated the Western world such indignation was aroused that the average Sanskrit scholar, (brought up under the ideals of the Victorian era) tried to dismiss them as a degenerate form of religious tradition not worthy of serious attention. Anybody who tried to recognize the important role which the Tantras played for more than a millennium in the religious life of India and Tibet or who endeavored to justify basic ideas of Tantrism by demonstrating their general human validity was suspected of favoring immorality or libertine views. A scholar was expected to remain personally aloof from the subject of his research in order to maintain 'subjective objectivity'. And consequently, any form of personal involvement or conviction, which led to a scholar identifying himself with the doctrines under study, was considered suspect and unscholarly.

Under those conditions, it was a courageous undertaking when Dr. Guenther, in 1952, published his *Yuganaddha* and tried to interpret the Tantric view of life in the light of modern psychology. He showed the value of the Tantras, not only in their historical and cultural setting, but also in relation to our present times and in the general context of human nature and spiritual experience. Thus, his book represented an entirely new approach to the problems, ideology, and practice.

Almost twenty-five years have passed since the first publication of his book, and during this time the Tantras, which until then had been hardly more than the happy hunting ground of a few specialists, have become one of the most discussed—though still widely misunderstood—branches of Eastern knowledge. Nowadays, the danger of Tantric doctine arousing inimical criticism has turned into its opposite—the danger that the Tantric symbolism of the *conjunctio oppositorum* in the man-woman relationship is misunderstood and hailed as an endorsement and encouragement of the modern obsession with sex and its indiscriminate satisfaction. The misunderstanding goes so far that the average Westerner equates Tantra with 'sex-indulgence', or an exaltation of sex as the main factor of human life through which final liberation can be attained. This kind of wishful thinking is as far from the truth as mistaking the sacrament of marriage for an encouragement of sensuality and sex-indulgence.

"When certain scholars speak of an 'eroticized' form of Buddhism, blowing the trumpets of righteous indignation, they merely advertize their ignorance of the symbol-language."[1] A symbol has meaning only in a complete system of interrelated concepts and archetypal experiences or mental images, against the background of a stabilized tradition or within the framework of an all-embracing organic conception of the world. It is this universal and mutual relationship of all existential forms and configurations and of all forces of nature which is expressed in the word 'Tantra'. This word is derived from the concept of weaving, hinting at the interwovenness of all things and actions, as well as at the continuity of cause and effect in individual, spiritual, and traditional development, which like a thread weaves its way through the infinite fabric of the universe in space and time.

In the words of Guru Gampopa (Milarepa's famous disciple), the Buddhist Tantras represent "a philosophy comprehensive enough to embrace the whole of knowledge, a system of meditation which will produce the power of concentrating the mind upon anything whatsoever, and an art of living which will enable one to utilize each activity (of body, speech, and mind) as an aid on the path to liberation." Thus the Buddhist Tantras are concerned with the totality of life in all its aspects, without allowing any separate function to dominate the rest and to upset the balance of our vital forces. All our actions derive their meaning and justification only from their relationship to the whole. This applies to sex as much as to our intellectual life, to our physical as well as to our spiritual existence. Just as the intellect can become a hindrance to the development of our psychic qualities and spiritual growth, sex can become a stumbling-block on the way of self-realization, if it usurps a position out of proportion to its natural function or the rest of our faculties.

At the same time, we must remember that none of the constituents that make up our psycho-physical existence can be neglected or suppressed without impairing the subtle balance of forces, on which the completeness of life and the full realization of our inborn nature (*sahaja*) depends. Thus, the recognition of sex, as one of the vital factors of human existence, does not constitute an undue emphasis on sex, but rather that unprejudiced acceptance of a fact that is as universal as the force of gravitation. Spiritual life does not consist of the suppression of certain forces and faculties, but of their harmonization and transformation from the level of blind egocentric drives to the level of a fully-awakened and conscious cooperation of all our forces and faculties, in accordance with the laws of the universe in which we live. The Tantras would say we are then in harmony with the universe that lives within us, because "We have an inkling of the fact that we are not altogether compressed within the dimensions of the cosmos created by the genius of our scientists, that we extend somewhere else, into a world which, although enclosed within ourselves, stretches beyond space and time. Such, indeed, is our universe. Why then, shall we not realize it?"[2]

Here we approach the central meaning of the Tantras—the realization of the universe within ourselves, the experience of universality within the individual and through individuality, the *conjunctio oppositorum* on the highest level. This is possible, because the individual is not merely a part and product of the universe, but "a point in which the whole universe has condensed, as it were, when the allegedly lowliest physical needs take on a cosmic character, to say nothing of the mental activities which, after all, cannot be dealt with as something apart."[3] In other words, "Man is not moulded on reality–he is not a copy of something antecedently given and wholly independent of man, but that he is rather the mould in which reality first expresses itself."[4]

The *Guhyasamāja-Tantra* points out that the five constituents (*skandha*) of the human personality–corporality (form), feeling, perception, volition, and consciousness (in its intuitive, reflective, and coordinating capacity)–represent potentially the qualities of the five Dhyāni-Buddhas, who, therefore, are not remote metaphysical ideas or divinities, but psychic realities. They constitute the completeness of Buddhahood–perfect enlightenment–in which the individual awakens to the wholeness and universality of his true nature. Therefore, even our passions and imperfections are the seeds from which the noblest qualities of the Enlightened Ones can spring, provided we do not arrest our spiritual growth by trying to cling or to hold on to the objects of our sense-experience or to the illusions, limitations, and dogmas of our intellect.

We suffer through our errors and our passion, but through suffering we mature and grow. A person incapable of passion is incapable of 'com-passion', and without compassion we remain enclosed in the hard shell of egocentricity. Compassion is the widening, liberating force of our mind and soul which converts knowledge into wisdom, which transcends the limits of narrow selfhood by participation and by overcoming the subject-object attitude of intellectual knowlege, replacing it by identification or integration of subject and object. It is this transcendental knowledge (*prajñā*), which can never be separated from compassion (*karuṇā*), upon which the Tantric view of life is based. Therefore, the aim of the Buddhist Tantra is not power (*shakti*), but transcendental knowledge or wisdom, which is not used as an instrument of power, but of happiness and supreme bliss, shared by all who desire it. "Any victory over the delusion in a single mind, any realization of being the whole, is a step toward its attainment."[5] It is for this reason that the concept of *shakti* (used in the Hindu Tantras) has been replaced by the concept of *prajñā* (or its synonyms) in the Buddhist Tantras. This is of the greatest importance, because it reveals the fundamental attitude of Buddhism, which is not interested in power but in *knowledge*. The Buddhist does not want to control the world or his fellow-beings; he wants to understand them, as well as himself. By understanding others we create harmony and make communication possible; through communication we are able to share with others whatever we have gained in love and wisdom, as much as we are able to share others' joys and sufferings.

In order to achieve this kind of knowledge and participation we have to go to the very roots of life and human relationship. According to the Tantric view of life, we have to begin, not with abstract intellectual ideas or theories of how the world should be, but with the recognition of where we ourselves stand *now*—our immediate present reality, the plane on which we actually live. The saying, "Man is the mold in which reality expresses itself" means we have to consider the fact that the human being in concrete form presents itself as either man or woman, *i.e.*, partially under an aspect of this reality which, though it is embedded in the human psyche, expresses itself through the predominance of one pole or another. This creates a feeling of insufficiency or incompleteness; and since man's inherent urge is directed toward completeness he will be drawn toward the opposite pole in an endeavor to attain it.

This is the basis of all man-woman relationships, which begin as biological urges on the physical plane, but find true fulfillment only in the complete self-surrender of both sides. In this union neither the male nor the female qualities dominate, but complement each other in the creation of a higher unity. Here all individual limitations are transcended and the primordial state of universal oneness is recreated, resulting in the experience of highest bliss (*mahā-sukha*). At that moment we are liberated from the self-created prisons of our egos. "Liberation is not clinging to one of the contraries. It is not the isolation of an allegedly immortal soul from the mortal human body, but is the transfiguration of the whole man."[6]

Unless the *whole* human being is engaged in this transfiguration, *i.e.*, on *all* planes of consciousness from the physical to the highest spiritual one, union will only be a temporary, if not merely mometary, achievement. "The essential fact is to experience this basic unity and never to lose it again. *This lasting experience can certainly not be achieved by the satisfaction of a sudden biological urge.* The realization and the experience of the basic unity is very *like* sexual fulfillment.

Therefore, *sexuality is to be understood as a picture or a symbol, but not as a reality per se.*"[7]

The union of man and woman is certainly the strongest and most universal symbol of the harmonious and creative unity of two opposites, of a relationship which involves more than the mere physical aspect and which therefore is 'creative' in more than a physical way. This has to be clearly understood in order to avoid the current misunderstanding that the Tantras promulgate the sexual act *per se* as a means to liberation. Whether it is a means or a hindrance to liberation depends on the inner attitudes of the individuals concerned, on their motivations and levels of spiritual awareness. Only profound love can achieve complete self-surrender, the precondition of perfect unification or creative integration. If, however, there is no other motive than the relief of sexual tension, all that can be achieved is momentary release and physical satisfaction without any lasting value.

The lasting value of creative integration and spiritual awareness can only be attained by the *sādhaka*, the practitioner of internal yoga, a psycho-physical training (*sādhana*) pertaining to the highest level of Tantric teaching—the *Anuttara-yoga-tantra*s. Tantras like the *Guhyasamāja* and the *Hevajra*, with their highly symbolic language, were not meant for the general public, but only for initiated *sādhaka*s who had gone through a strict discipline of meditative practices and who knew the secret of the yogic process of the union of male and female constituents within their own beings, symbolized by the sexual union of 'yogi' and 'yoginī'.[8]

The mere fact that these Tantras were taught even in exclusively celibate monasteries in Tibet and were practiced and held in highest regard by the greatest yogis and the most austere hermits, such as Milarepa, should suffice to expose the silliness of certain modern interpreters and their misguided followers, who use the Tantras as a pretext or a shield for unrestricted sexual indulgence and a denial of fundamental ethical values. "The description of a psychological process of integration in the symbol of a love relationship, which has misled many an uninformed person into believing that Mantrayāna is an 'erotic' form of Buddhism (a conception as absurd as the assumption that Christian mysticism in the Middle Ages was an eroticized

Christianity) has been prompted by the fact that 'those who first set out on the path of the Mantrayāna belong to a sensuous and sensual world and are, moreover, apt to seek enlightenment merely by making their passion for the charms of their female fellow-beings the path to it.'[9] *Therefore, one hunts in vain for concrete 'sex practices' in any one of the four Tantras*."[10]

Only people who have a thorough knowledge of the Tantric view of life and its various aspects on the physiological, psychological, and spiritual plane, as well as a general knowledge of its cultural and historical background, which conditioned its terminology, can gain by the study of Tantric literature. It is for this reason that I appreciate Dr. Guenther's frank discussion of the various aspects of Yuganaddha. Armed with a thorough knowledge not only of Sanskrit and Tibetan, but also of modern psychology and philosophy, he certainly is well-qualified to speak on this profound subject. Moreover the fact that he spent many years in India teaching these subjects in various universities and living in close contact with the Tibetan communities in India, and intermittently also living in the remote Tibetan-inhabited regions of the inner Himalayas, has given him a deeper insight into the vital aspects of Tantric tradition than mere book-knowledge could ever have done. His many valuable works published over the years speak for themselves. They are the works of a dedicated scholar who is not only deeply and personally involved in the subject of his research but who is equally alive to the problems of our own time.

NOTES

1. H. V. Guenther, *Treasures On the Tibetan Middle Way*, Berkeley: Shambhala, 1969, p. 39.
2. H. V. Guenther, *Yuganaddha—The Tantric Way of Life*, Benares: Chowkhamba Sanskrit Series, Vol. 3, 1952, p. 137.
3. *Ibid.*, p. 162.
4. *Ibid.*, p. 95.
5. *Ibid.*, p. 186.
6. *Ibid.*, p. 23.
7. *Ibid.*, p. 44; italics are mine.

8. In this connection, refer to the chapter "The Polarity of the Male and Female Principles in the Symbolic Language of the Vajrayāna" in my book, *Foundation of Tibetan Mysticism*, London: Rider, Fourth Edition, 1969.

9. *The Collected Works of Tsong-kha-pa*, Tashilhunpo Edition, III 38b.

10. H. V. Guenther, *Treasures On The Tibetan Middle Way*, p. 66; italics mine.

The Sautrāntika Background of the *Apoha* Theory

Massaki Hattori

Speculations concerning the meaning of words started in India in the fairly early days. The views of some Vaiyākaraṇas are referred to in the *Mahābhāṣya* of Patañjali, which dates back to the second century B.C., and the discussions among the early Mīmāṃsakas, which must have extended for a long span of time, are reflected in Śabarasvāmin's commentary on the *Mīmāṃsāsūtra*. In the classical period, the problem of meaning was a common concern of philosophical schools and there were frequent disputes among the upholders of different theories.

Unlike the other schools, the Bauddhas denied that a word has a direct reference to any real entity whether specific or universal. They maintained that the function of a word is nothing other than *anyāpoha*, i.e., the differentiation of an object from other things.

The theory of *anyāpoha* was first expounded by Dignāga. He made a sharp distinction between the particular (*svalakṣaṇa*), which is real and directly perceived, and the universal (*sāmānyalakṣaṇa*), which is mentally constructed. The particular is an indivisible unity of various aspects and as such has nothing in common with any other thing. The black cow standing here is totally different from the white cow lying there. The word 'cow', which is applied indiscriminately to any cow, cannot be held to refer directly to a particular one. If it were to refer to *this* black cow, it could not be applied to *that* white cow. The object referred to by the word 'cow' is the universal, which is mentally constructed through the process of differentiating the object from other things. On perceiving the particular which is endowed with dewlap, horns, a hump on the back, and so forth, one understands that it is not a non-cow, because one knows that a non-cow (e.g., a horse, an elephant, or the like) is not endowed with these attributes. Accordingly, he differentiates the directly perceived object from the non-cow and consequently forms the concept 'cow'. The cow thus conceived is not a real entity, but it is 'cow in general' which has no objective reality. It is this conceptually constructed 'cow in general' that is referred to by the word 'cow'. With this careful analysis of the process of conceptual construction, Dignāga stated that a word denotes its own object by means of *anyāpoha*, or that a word expresses the object qualified (*viśiṣṭa*) by *anyāpoha*.

With a view to making some observations on the trends of philosophical thinking concerning meaning, which are assumed to have provided a background for the formulation of the theory of *anyāpoha*, I will direct my attention to the following three aspects of that theory. The first is that the function of a word lies not in the direct reference to the object but in the differentiation of the object from other things (*apoha*).[1] The second aspect is that *apoha* is similar in nature to the universal, which is recognized as 'real' by the Naiyāyikas and other realists. The universal is one (*eka*) although it exists within many specific entities; it is eternal (*nitya*) because it is inherent in each entity existing at any time, and it occurs as an undivided whole in each individual entity (*pratyekaparisamāpti*). All these characteristic features apply to *apoha*.[2] The third aspect is that *apoha* is not a real entity like the universal of the realists. It is a product of conceptual construction and has no objective reality.

THE CONCEPT OF DIFFERENTIATION

The view that a word functions to differentiate the object from other things is known to have been held by Vyāḍi, a pre-Patañjali

Vaiyākaraṇa. Among the early Vaiyākaraṇas there was a divergence of opinion regarding the meaning of a word and that of a sentence. Vyāḍi, who held that the meaning of a word is any specific entity (*dravya*) of a class, set forth the view that the meaning of a sentence consists in the differentiation (*bheda*) of each specific entity from the others in the same class. On the other hand, it was maintained by Vājapyāyana that a word refers directly to a universal (*jāti*), and that the meaning of a sentence is nothing other than the relation (*saṃsarga*) of the universals which are denoted by different words in the sentence. These two views are often contrasted with each other in the works of the Vaiyākaraṇas and the Mīmāṃsakas of the later period.[3] It can be noted that the concept of differentiation (*bheda*) formed by Vyāḍi has a close affinity to the Bauddha concept of *apoha*. According to Vyāḍi the word 'cow' (*go-*) in the sentence "Here is a white cow" (*atra śuklā gauḥ*) refers to any cow regardless of its color, and the word 'white' (*śukla-*) which is syntactically connected with 'cow' functions to differentiate the white cow from the cows of any other color. In the same way, the word 'white' means anything that is white; and the word 'cow' connected with it functions to differentiate the white cow from the other white things.

It has been observed by Kunjunni Rāja that the Bauddha theory of *apoha* was foreshadowed in Vyāḍi's view of 'differentiation'.[4] Of the above-mentioned three aspects that characterize the *apoha* theory, the first may be traced back to the *bheda* theory of Vyāḍi, but there is an essential difference between the two theories that should not be overlooked. Vyāḍi admits that a single word has direct reference to a specific entity which is real. The function of differentiating the object from other things is attributed by him to the word in a sentence but not to the word unrelated to other words. However, the Bauddhas attribute the same function unconditionally to any single word. For the Bauddhas the word is an indicator of the concept which is mentally constructed, and the differentiation of the object from the other things is the process of this mental construction. Any single concept is formed through this process, and therefore any word that stands for the concept has this function. The Bauddha view of the function of the word is thus grounded on the scrutiny of the nature of the concept.

THE CONCEPT OF THE UNIVERSAL

The view represented by Vājapyāyana, that a word refers to a universal, is also maintained by the later Vaiyākaraṇas and by the Mīmāṃsakas. Among the upholders of this view special attention is to be directed to Bhartṛhari, a pre-Dignāga grammarian-philosopher, because he puts forward his arguments with the terms that are in the same terminology employed by the Bauddhas. The view that the universal existing in many similar specifics constitutes the object of a word necessarily implies that, when a word is applied to the object, the specificity of the object is disregarded. In other words, the cognition derived from a word is not concerned with the difference among specifics. This point is discussed in detail by Bhartṛhari in the *Vākyapadīya* III. 1: *jātisamuddeśa*. The idea that verbal cognition ignores the specificity of the object is expressed by the Bauddhas with the term *bhedāgraha*, i.e., the non-apprehension of the difference (among specifics). This term is almost synonymous to *apoha* for them, since *apoha* is commonly attributed to many specific entities which are totally different from one another. Worth noting is that Bhartṛhari uses the term *bhedāpoha* in the course of his discussion on the cognition of the universal.

> *sakṛtpravṛttāv ekatvam āvṛttau sadṛśātmatām*
> *bhinnātmikānāṃ vyaktīnāṃ* bhedāpohāt *prapadyate*[5]
>
> The specific entities, which are essentially different [from one another], are [cognized as] identical when they occur [in the cognition] simultaneously, and [as] resembling [each other] when they occur [in the cognition] in succession, because the difference [among them] is neglected.

It is through neglecting the difference among specifics that one has the consciousness of resemblance or of identity in respect to them. The consciousness of resemblance presupposes plurality of objects, but the consciousness of identity proves the existence of the universal within different specifics.

A similar expression is found in the *Vākyapadīya* III.1.96, in which Bhartṛhari explains the cognition of the universal in accordance with the Sāṃkhya and the Vedānta views.

yadā bhedān parityajya *buddhyaika iva gṛhyate*
vyaktyātmaiva tadā tatra buddhir ekā pravartate

When that which is of the nature of the manifestation [of the ultimate cause] is grasped by the mind, through discarding its particularities, as if [it were] identical [with the other manifestations], there arises in respect to it the single cognition [that takes the universal for its object].

According to the Sāṃkhyas, phenomenal entities are modifications (*vikāra, pariṇāma*) of primary matter (*prakṛti*), and are, for the Vedāntins, unreal manifestations (*vivarta*) of the ultimate reality which is the highest universal (*mahāsāmānya*). Therefore, by ignoring the distinctive attributes of particular phenomenal entities one obtains the cognition that remains uniform in respect to any object.

In view of the fact that Dignāga was much influenced by Bhartṛhari in the formulation of his philosophical thoughts,[6] it is possible to assume that he derived the idea of *apoha* from this grammarian-philosopher. However, unlike the Bauddhas, Bhartṛhari firmly maintains that the universal has objective reality. He is acquainted with the view held by the Bauddha idealists that identity is subjectively ascribed to different objects on the basis of the identity of ideas,[7] but he docs not endorse it—he insists that there are universals existing in cognitions, in words, and in objects.

jñānaśabdārthaviṣayā viśeṣā ye vyavasthitāḥ
teṣāṃ duravadhāratvāt jñānādyekatvadarśanam[8]

Since the specificities existing in the cognitions, in the words, and in the objects are difficult to discern, the [different] cognitions, etc., are recognized as identical.

In spite of the difference between the cognition of a black cow and that of a white cow, between the word 'cow' uttered by Devadatta and that uttered by Yajñadatta, or between this black cow and that white cow, both are conceived as identical because the difference is very subtle. This observation does not lead Bhartṛhari to the idealist standpoint. He does not admit that such cognition of identity is merely subjective, because, according to him, the cognition is never brought to consciousness by itself without any object. He says, "Just as the light is not illuminated by another light, even so the form of cognition is not apprehended by another cognition."[9] The conclusion to be drawn from this argument is that there is an external basis for recognizing the identity of the cognitions, of the words, or of the objects; namely, the universal. Thus it is possible to trace the second aspect of the *apoha* theory in Bhartṛhari's arguments; but the third aspect seems to have a different origin.

THE CONCEPT OF NOMINAL EXISTENCE

The thought that the universal to which a word refers is merely the concept constructed mentally is a special characteristic of the Bauddhas; and this thought constitutes an important aspect of the *apoha* theory. Among the Bauddhas, the Sautrāntikas are known to have developed the idea of 'nominal existence' (*prajñapti-sat*)—that which is conventionally assumed to exist but has no objective reality. All the *dharmas* classed as *cittaviprayuktāḥ saṃskārāḥ* by the Vaibhāṣikas are regarded as 'nominal existences' by the Sautrāntikas.[10] The universal (*sabhāgatā*)[11] is on the Vaibhāṣika list of the *cittaviprayuktasaṃskāras*. Vasubandhu denies, from the Sautrāntika standpoint, its reality, and states that it is of ideated nature.[12] It seems likely that Dignāga is indebted to this Sautrāntika view of the universal for the formulation of his *apoha* theory.

In the *Pramāṇavārttika* III (*pratyakṣa*) 231 ff., Dharmakīrti gives an exposition of Dignāga's idea as expressed in the *Pramāṇasamuccaya* I.5: "The substratum (*dharmin*) possessing many properties cannot be cognized in all its aspects by the sense."[13] It is distinctly stated therein by Dharmakīrti that a thing comes to be cognized as possessing such and such properties according to how it is differentiated from other things.[14] By the sense-organ a thing is perceived as it is, i.e., as an indivisible whole. It is by the mind that the thing is split into substratum (*dharmin*) and properties (*dharma*) and comes to be cognized as possessing certain properties. Dharmakīrti is concerned in the above explanation with this process of the operation of the mind. The particular thing directly perceived is cognized as possessing 'cowness' when differentiated by the mind from other animals. It is cognized as possessing whiteness when differentiated from other colors. In the same way, as many properties are assigned to the same thing as there are mental acts of differentiating it from other things. By cognizing the thing as possessing a certain property there arises a concept in respect to it. The concepts 'cow', 'white', and the like, are thus produced mentally through the process of differentiation described. The concept 'cow', therefore, is not indicative of any real entity. It simply denotes 'difference' from other animals commonly attributed through the operation of the mind to many different cows. It is a universal as it unifies many specific entities, but there is no 'real' external basis for it.

The *apoha* theory is treated by Dharmakīrti in great detail in the *Pramāṇavārttika* I (*svārthānumāna*) 40 ff.[15] The thought that the word stands for the concept which is formed through the differentiation of the directly perceived object from other things is clearly presented there. According to him there would be no need for conceptual and verbal cognitions if the concept and the word had direct reference to the object, because the object is thoroughly cognized by means of the sense-perception. It is for the purpose of removing the false notions which might be imposed upon the directly perceived object that the object is conceptualized and verbally expressed. Therefore, as many concepts and words are applied to the object as there are false notions imposed upon it. Since the object itself is an indivisible whole, the aspects of the object to which these concepts and words refer are unreal. If it were assumed that the concept and the word were correlative to the real thing, there would be the absurdity that all concepts are identical and all words are synonymous.[16]

The same idea that forms the basis of Dharmakīrti's arguments is found expressed by Dignāga in the *Pramāṇasamuccaya* V.12:

> *bahudhāpy abhidheyasya na śabdāt sarvathā gatiḥ*
> *svasaṃbandhānurūpyeṇa vyavacchedārthakāry asau*
>
> Although the thing to be denoted [by the word] is of manifold aspect, it is not apprehended in all its aspects by means of the word. It (the word) has the effect of excluding [the other things] in accordance with its own relation [to the thing].

This may explain why many words are applied to a single object. They are not synonymous with each other because each word has its own meaning, denoting only one aspect of the object through excluding those things which do not have that aspect. In all likelihood Dignāga framed this thought on the basis of the Sautrāntika theory of nominal existence.

Dignāga composed a short treatise dealing with the Sautrāntika theory of nominal existence: the *Upādāyaprajñaptiprakaraṇa*.[17] In this treatise nominal existence is classified in three categories: whole (*samūha*), continuant (*saṃtāna*), and particular states or aspects (*avasthāviśeṣa*).[18] A body, for example, which does not exist apart from hands, feet, and so forth, is conventionally assumed to exist as a *whole*. A person, who is really a series of the momentary existences of all of the different stages of life, is conventionally assumed to exist as a *continuant*. The third category deserves special notice. A material element (*rūpa*), for example, can be described as evanescent (*anitya*), perceptible (*sanidarśana*), impenetrable (*sapratigha*), and so forth. In reality such things as evanescence do not exist, but they are conventionally assumed to exist as *aspects* of the material element. Here it is seen that Sautrāntika philosophy scrutinized the fact that different concepts are applied to a single object.

The description of material elements as perceptible or impenetrable suggests that the concept of differentiation may also have been germinated by Sautrāntika theory. In the *Abhidharmakośabhāṣya* there is a section in which Vasubandhu classifies the eighteen *dhātus* (the six senses, their respective objects, and cognitions resulting from the contact of senses and objects) first into the perceptible (*sanidarśana*) and the imperceptible (*anidarśana*), then into the impenetrable (*sapratigha*) and the penetrable (*apratigha*), and then into other pairs of triplets of categories.[19] That a material element is perceptible means, therefore, that it is not classed as imperceptible. In other words it is described as perceptible by differentiation from the imperceptible. In the same way it is described as impenetrable by differentiating it from the penetrable. Needless to say it was by denying the permanence of phenomenal existence that the Bauddhas arrived at the doctrine that all *dharma*s are evanescent. The thought that constitutes the core of *apoha* theory is thus traceable to the Sautrāntika view that the *aspects* of a thing are nominal existences.

No direct mention is made by Dignāga of the Sautrāntika theory of nominal existence in his elucidation of *apoha* theory in the

Pramāṇasamuccaya. However, in his *Svavṛtti* on the *Pramāṇavārttika* I. 137-142 Dharmakīrti refers to the whole, continuant, and aspectual types of nominal existence. He explains that a number of different things which have the power of producing the same effect are grouped together through the act of differentiating them from those which do not have that power, and that a word is framed conventionally by the designation of things thus grouped, although there is no real universal that unifies these things. One may coin, for example, the term *yara* or *śasa* just to designate 'cause of visual cognition'. The various components of visual cognition such as eye, color, light, and attention are designated equally by this term although the individual components have nothing in common. They simply have the same power of producing visual cognition; and in that respect they are differentiated from those things which have no such power and are grouped together by a single designation.

In the same way, the word 'pot' is applied to the *wholes*—which do not exist apart from the conglomerations of atoms—because the power of carrying water is commonly attributed to them; and the word 'rice' is applied to many continuants, whose existence is merely assumed in dependence on the number of momentary existences. In some cases objects are equally describable by several words (perceptible, impenetrable, etc.); and they are grouped together by these *aspects*, being differentiated from those which do not have the same aspects.[20]

The thought that many wholes and many continuants are unified through differentiation is not traced in the Sautrāntika theory as presented in the *Upādyāyaprajñaptiprakaraṇa*. It is understood that Dharmakīrti applies the theory of differentiation to the Sautrāntika concepts of *whole* and *continuant* with the aid of his original thought that different entities can be grouped together because of their 'power of producing the same effect'. Regarding the concept of *aspect*, he explains simply that many objects are unified by common aspects through differentiation from those which do not have the same aspects. However, his view in the *Pramāṇavārttika* I. 50-51 is that differentiation is the process through which each aspect is attributed to the object. As observed earlier this view had its roots in Sautrāntika theory found in the *Upādāyaprajñaptiprakaraṇa*. It is of special note that the examples of aspects given by Dharmakīrti, i.e., perceptibility and impenetrability, are identical with those mentioned by the Sautrāntikas.

The above-mentioned portion of Dharmakīrti's *Svavṛtti* on the *Pramāṇavārttika* is summarized with slight modifications by Śāntarakṣita in the *Tattvasaṃgraha*, kk. 1033–42. The fact that an individual object can be described by many words is treated there as the subject. Śāntarakṣita gives the explanation that a number of functions are attributed to an individual object in accordance with the multiplicity of mental acts involved in differentiating it from others dissimilar to it in view of a certain function. As an example he offers the fact that a material element (*rūpa*) is described as 'perceptible' and 'impenetrable'.[21] Here is seen clear exposition based on the *apoha* theory of the Sautrāntika view that the aspects of a thing are nominal existences.

Various theories might have influenced Dignāga in the philosophical scrutiny of the problem of meaning, but it was in all likelihood the Sautrāntika theory of nominal existence that provided him with the background for the formulation of the *apoha* theory.

NOTES

1. There are a variety of terms employed to mean the 'differentiation of *x* from non-*x*': *anyâpoha, -vyāvṛtti, -nivṛtti, atad-*, etc. I use the term *apoha* in this technical sense without taking into account in this paper the later modifications of its meaning.

2. *Pramāṇasamuccaya*, V, k. 36d: *jātidharmavyavasthitiḥ. Ibid., Vṛtti: sarvatrābhedād āśrayasyānucchedāt kṛtsnārthaparisamāpteś ca yathākramaṃ jātidharmā ekatva[nityatva]pratyekaparisamāptilakṣaṇā apoha evāvatiṣṭhante* ... For the sources of the Sanskrit fragments of the *Pramāṇasamuccaya*, V, see M. Hattori, "A Study of the Chapter on *Apoha* of the *Mīmāṃsāślokavārttika* (II)" (in Japanese), *Memoirs of the Faculty of Letters, Kyoto University*, No. 15 (1975), pp. 1–63, Appendix.

3. Cf. Kunjunni Rāja, *Indian Theories of Meaning*, The Adyar Library Series, Vol. 91, Adyar: 1963, p. 191, n. 1.

4. *Ibid.*, p. 193.

5. *Vākyapadīya*, III. 1. 98.

6. Cf. E. Frauwallner, 'Dignāga, sein Werk und seine Entwicklung," *WZKSO* III (1959), pp. 83–164.

7. *Vākyapadīya*, III. 1. 99: *anupravṛtteti yathābhinnā buddhiḥ pratīyate / artho vyāvṛttarūpo 'pi tathā tattvena gṛhyate //* "When an idea which is different [from another] is understood as conforming [to the latter], then the object which is differentiated [from another] is apprehended as identical [with the latter]."

8. *Vākyapadīya*, III. 1. 101.

9. *Ibid.*, III. 1. 104: *yathā jyotiḥ prakāśena nānyenābhiprakāśyate / jñānākāras tathānyena na jñānenopagṛhyate //*

10. Cf. *Abhidharmakośabhāṣya* (edited by P. Pradhan, Patna: 1967), Chap. II.

11. *Sabhāgatā* is a dharma which makes a group of living beings resemble each other. The similarity of *sabhāgatā* to the *sāmānya* of the Vaiśeṣikas is pointed out by the opponent of the Vaibhāṣikas, cf. *Abhidharmakośabhāṣya*, p. 68.4-5: *Vaiśeṣikās caivaṃ dyotitā bhavanti. teṣāṃ hy eṣa siddhāntaḥ: sāmānyapadārtho nāmāsti yataḥ sāmānyapratyayotpattir atulyaprakāreṣv- iti.*

12. *Ibid.*, p. 68.6-9: *asty eṣā tu sabhāgatā sūtre vacanād iti Vaibhāṣikāḥ. uktaṃ hi bhagavatā "sa ced itthaṃ tvam āgacchati manusyāṇāṃ sabhāgatām" iti. uktam etan na tūktam dravyāntaram iti. kā tarhi sā. ta eva hi tathābhūtāḥ saṃskārā yeṣu manusyādiprajñaptiḥ śālyādiṣu sabhāgatāvat.*

13. *Pramāṇasamuccaya*, I, k. 5ab: *dharmiṇo 'nekarupasya nendriyāt sarvathā gatiḥ* / Cf. M. Hattori, *Dignāga, On Perception*, HOS 47, Cambridge, Mass.: 1968, p. 91, n. 1.43.

14. *Pramāṇavārttika*, III. 231: *sarvato vinivṛttasya vinivṛttir yato yataḥ / tadbhedonnītabhedā sā dharmiṇo 'nekarūpatā //*

15. Cf. E. Frauwallner, "Beiträge zur Apohalehre, I. Dharmakīrti," *WZKM* 39 (1932), pp. 247-285; 40 (1933), pp. 51-94: Übersetzung; *ibid.* 42 (1935), pp. 93-102: Zusammenfassung.

16. *Pramāṇavārttika*, I. 50-51: *yāvanto 'ṃśasamāropas tannirāse veniścayāḥ / tāvanta eva śabdāś ca tena te bhinnagocarāḥ // anyathaikena śabdena vyāpta ekatra vastuni / buddhyā vā nānyaviṣaya iti paryāyatā bhavet //*

17. Taisho ed. of the Chinese Tripitaka, No. 1622 (vol. 31). The Sanskrit title was reconstructed from the Chinese by Frauwallner, cf. *WZKSO* III, p. 121. H. Kitagawa made an abridged English translation of this treatise, see *Indo-koten-ronrigaku no Kenkyu–Jinnano Taikei*–(A Study of Indian Classical Logic–Dignāga's System–), Tokyo: Suzuki Research Foundation, 1965, Appendix A, II: A Study of a Short Philosophical Treatise ascribed to Dignāga (pp. 430-439).

18. Cf. Kitagawa, *op. cit.*, p. 432. Kitagawa failed to give the Sanskrit for 'tsung-chü', though he rightly thought that it was not '*avayavin*'. The term '*samūha*' is found in Dharmakīrti's *Svavṛtti* on the *Pramāṇavārttika* cited below in n. 20.

19. *Abhidharmakośabhāṣya*, p. 18.24ff.: *ye punar ime aṣṭādaśa dhātava uktās teṣāṃ kati sanidarśanāḥ katy anidarśanāḥ.* sanidarśana eko 'tra rūpaṃ (I. 29a–b). *sa hi śakyate nidarśayitum idam ihāmutreti. uktaṃ bhavaty anidarśanāḥ śeṣā iti. kati sapratighāḥ katy apratighāḥ.* sapratighā daśa rūpiṇaḥ (I. 29b–c). *ya ete rūpaskandhasaṃgṛhītā daśa dhātava uktās te sapratighāḥ. . . .*

20. R. Gnoli, *The Pramāṇavārttikam of Dharmakīrti, The First Chapter with the Autocommentary*, Serie Orientale Roma XXIII, Roma: IsMEO, 1960, pp. 67–68: *yathā cakṣūrūpālokamanaskāreṣu . . . kecit sāṃketikīṃ śrutiṃ niveśayet yaro rūpavijñānahetuḥ śaso veti. . . . na cātrānugāmi kiṃcid rūpam asti. kevalaṃ tadarthatayā te bhāvā 'tadarthebhyo bhinnā iti bheda evaiṣām abhedaḥ. evaṃjātīyāś ca sarve samūhasaṃtānāvasthāviśeṣaśabdāḥ. ye samastāḥ kiṃcid ekaṃ kāryaṃ kurvanti teṣāṃ tatra viśeṣābhāvād apārthikā viśeṣa codaneti sakṛt sarveṣāṃ niyojanārtham ekaṁ ayaṃ lokaḥ śabdaṃ teṣu niyuṅkte ghaṭa iti. . . . ye 'pi pṛthak samastā vā kvacid upayujyante ta avasthāviśeṣavācibhiḥ sakṛd eva śabdaiḥ pratyayārthaṃ khyāpyante sanidarśanāḥ sapratighā veti tadanyebhyo bhedasāmānyena. . . .*

21. *Tattvasaṃgraha* (Bauddha Bharati Ser., 1), kk. 1038–39: *tathānekārthakāritvād eko naika ivocyate / atatkāryaparāvṛttibāhulyaparikalpitaḥ // yathā sapratighaṃ rūpaṃ sanidarśanam ity api / . . .*

The Abhidharma on the 'Four Aids to Penetration'

Leon Hurvitz

THIS IS TO BE YET another contribution to the study of the impact of the notion of salvation on the early Chinese Buddhists. It was preceded by a paper on the 'four stations of mindfulness' (*catvāri smṛtyupasthānāni, ssu nien ch'u, ssu nien chu*) in which the point of departure was an *Abhidharma* text surviving only in Chinese, under the title of *A-p'i-t'an hsin lun*.[1] In both that text and the *Abhidharma-kośa*, the 'four stations of mindfulness' are followed by 'four aids to penetration' (*catvāri nirvedhabhāgīyāni kuśalamūlāni, ssu chüeh tse fen, ssu chüeh ting fen*). This is complicated by an almost lateral statement that the group of four is the last of three groups of 'wholesome roots', the first two being *puṇya*° and *mokṣabhāgīya*, having to do, respectively, with merit and deliverance. What Fa-sheng has to say about them should be postponed until a closer study has been made of the *Abhidharmamahāvibhāṣā*, which is really the cardinal source for this tradition. As a preliminary to that, however, it seems advisable to proceed from the relatively known to the relatively unknown. While the *Abhidharmamahāvibhāṣā* survives in only one version—that of Hsüan-tsang without any commentary, the text of the *Kośa* is available in the original Sanskrit as well as in two Chinese translations, Paramārtha's and Hsüan-tsang's, the later being a superb edition with much commentary. There is also an excellent translation of the *Kośa* into French, one that made use of all available aids.[2] Finally, there survives in Sanskrit (and in Tibetan translation) a Sanskrit commentary, a work of Yaśomitra entitled *Sphuṭārthā* (hereinafter to be referred to as the *Vyākhyā*). The present paper shall consider first the *kārikās*, then the *Bhāṣya* (in Sanskrit and/or Chinese, as the need may be), and also, occasionally, the *Mahāvibhāṣā*.

In V. V. Gokhale's edition of the *kārikās*, the pertinent verses are numbered 18-26 in Chapter 6, while in Swami Dwarikadas Shastri's (svāmī Dvārikādāsaśāstrī's) edition of the combined text of the *Bhāṣya* and the *Sphuṭārthā* the verses are numbered 17-25 (Vol. 3, pp. 907-922). Paramārtha's translation of the same passage of text will be found in T29.271b-273b; Hsüan-tsang's in T29.119b-121b. In Saeki's Kyokuga annotated text (*Kandō Abidatsumakusha ron*), the passage in question is located in 23.3a-10b. First to the verses, as given in Gokhale but observing Swami Dwarikadas's numeration, which is the same as that of La Vallée Poussin (vi. 163-179).

tata uṣmagatotpattis tac catuḥsatyagocaram/
ṣoḍaśākāram ūṣmabhyo mūrdhānas te 'pi tādṛśāḥ//17//
ubhayākaraṇaṃ dharmeṇānyair api tu vardhanam/
tebhyaḥ kṣāntir dvidhā tadvat kṣāntyā dharmeṇa vardhanam//18//
kāmāptaduḥkhaviṣayā tv adhimātrā kṣaṇaṃ ca sā/
tathāgradharmāḥ sarve tu pañcaskandhā vināptibhiḥ//19//
iti nirvedhabhāgīyaṃ caturdhā bhāvanāmayam/
anāgamyāntaradhyānabhūmikaṃ dve tv adho 'pi vā//20//
kāmāśrayāṇy agradharmān dvyāśrayān labhate 'ṅganā/
bhūmityāgāt tyajaty āryas tāny anāryas tu mṛtyunā//21//
ādye dve parihāṇyā ca maulais tatraiva satyadṛk/
apūrvāptir vihīneṣu hānī dve asamanvitiḥ/22/
mūrdhalābhī na mūlacchit kṣāntilābhy anapāyagaḥ/
śiṣyagotrād vivartya dve buddhaḥ syāt trīṇy apītaraḥ//23//
ābodheḥ sarvam ekatra dhyāne 'ntye śāstṛkhaḍgayoḥ/
prāk tebhyo mokṣabhāgīyaṃ kṣipraṃ mokṣas tribhir bhavaiḥ//24//
śrutacintāmayaṃ trīṇi karmāṇy ākṣipyate triṣu/
laukikebhyo 'gradharmebhyo dharmakṣāntir anāsravā//25//

We now reproduce La Vallée Poussin's translation, which we give in prose form.

(Placé dans le *dharmasmṛtyupasthāna* d'objet mêlé, mettant ensemble le corps, la sensation, etc., il les voit sous le quadruple aspect d'impermanent, de douloureux, de vide, de non-moi). De là, naît le chaud, qui a pour objet les quatre vérités, qui a seize aspects. Du chaud, les sommets, qui lui sont pareils. C'est par le *dharma* que ces deux "impriment." Par les autres aussi ils grandissent. De cela, la patience (*kṣānti*). Deux sont comme ci-dessus. Toute entière, elle grandit par le *dharma*. Forte, elle a pour objet la douleur du Kāmadhātu. Elle est d'un moment. De même, les *dharma*s suprêmes. Toutes comportent les cinq *skandha*s, à l'exclusion des possessions. C'est le quadruple *nirvedhabhāgīya*. (Ces quatre *nirvedhabhāgīya*s, tous) naissent du recueillement. Leur terre est l'*anāgamya*, l'intermédiaire, les *dhyāna*s. Ou bien, deux sont aussi de la terre inférieure. (Tous les quatre) appartiennent à des êtres du Kāma. La femme obtient les *dharma*s suprêmes destinés à se trouver dans corps féminin et masculin. L'Ārya les perd en perdant la terre; le non-Ārya, par la mort. Il perd aussi les deux premiers par chute. Lorsqu'ils appartiennent aux *dhyāna*s fondamentaux, vue des vérités dès cette vie. Perdus, ils sont acquis nouveaux. Les deux pertes sont non-possession. Celui qui a atteint les têtes ne coupe pas les racines. Celui qui obtient la patience ne va pas aux mauvaises destinées. On peut retirer deux *nirvedhabhāgīya*s de la famille des Śrāvakas, et devenir Bouddha. On peut retirer trois, et devenir l'autre. Le Maître et le Rhinocéros vont jusqu'à la Bodhi, en une séance, en s'appuyant sur le dernier *dhyāna*. (Arrive-t-il que le préparatif, *prayoga*, des *nirvedhabhāgīya*s et la production des *nirvedhabhāgīya*s aient lieu dans une même existence? Cela n'est pas possible. Nécessairement, il faut produire,) avant, les *mokṣabhāgīya*s. Le plus rapide obtient la délivrance en trois existences. (L'école admet, *Vibhāṣā* 7.15, que les *mokṣabhāgīya*s) procédent d'audition et de réflexion (non pas de recueillement. Combien de sortes d'actes peuvent être *mokṣabhāgīya*?). Les trois actes, projetés parmi les hommes. Des suprêmes *dharma*s mondains procède une "patience," une *dharmakṣānti* qui est pure.[3]

From here we proceed to the *Bhāṣya*. As indicated above, the basic text shall be in the Sanskrit, with references to Yaśomitra, Paramārtha, Hsüan-tsang, and Louis de La Vallée Poussin as appropriate.

To introduce the subject Hsüan-tsang asks a rhetorical question: namely, which 'wholesome roots' (*shan ken*, *kuśalamūlāni*) the practitioner cultivates when he has traversed the 'four stations of mindfulness'. Kyokuga, in his commentary, quotes *Mahāvibhāṣā* 7.12b[4] to the following effect: "One who exercises 'warmth' (*nuan chia hsing che, ūṣmagataprayogam*) first views, in terms both of common and of peculiar characteristics (*i tzu hsiang kung hsiang, svasāmānyalakṣaṇaiḥ*?), the eighteen *dhātu*s, next the twelve *āyatana*s, the five *skandha*s, the four *smṛtyupasthāna*s, the four truths in their sixteen aspects (*catvāry āryasatyāni ṣoḍaśākāraiḥ*). When hearing and cogitation (*wen ssu, śruticetane*) are complete and perfect, the practitioner launches a cultivation of wisdom (*hsiu hui, prajñābhāvanā*? or is it a 'realization of gnosis', *jñānabhāvanā*?) whose name is 'warmth'." After giving further references to the *Mahāvibhāṣā* for commentary on the 'four aids to penetration', Kyokuga refers his reader to charts to be found on the page inserted between 23.4 and 23.5.[5]

Hsüan-tsang's question is then answered by the first three *ślokas*, which occur consecutively in his version followed by the *Bhāṣya*, while in the Sanskrit the latter interrupts the verses. The purport of vi.17 is as follows: When the practitioner has achieved the station of *dharma*-mindfulness in which he contemplates body, sensation, thought, and *dharma* together, seeing them under four aspects—those of impermanence, woe, emptiness, and non-self or absence of self, depending on the interpretation (*anityato duḥkhataḥ śūnyato 'nātmataś ca*)—then, in due course, comes what is known as 'warmth' (*uṣmagata, ūṣmagata*), so called because it is the first harbinger of the 'noble path' that consumes the passions (*kleśa*) as if with fire. This 'warmth', like the 'summits' or 'heads' (*mūrdhan*) that follow it, has as its object the 'four noble truths', each of which has four aspects.[6] The 'heads' are so called because they are the highest form of spiritual achievement from which one may still backslide. The difference between them and 'warmth' is, so to speak, quantitative, not qualitative. In the words of the original, 'utkṛśṭataratvāt tu nāmāntaram (see Dwarikadas 908), is rendered by La Vallée Poussin (vi.164) as "Ils reçoivent un autre nom en raison de leur excellence."

As already mentioned, there can be both progress and regression from the 'summits', a thought expressed by the *Bhāṣya* in the words *calakuśalamūrdhatvāt mūrdhānaḥ* (p. 908), rendered by La Vallée Poussin (vi. 164) as "Ils sont nommés 'sommets' ou 'têtes', parce qu'ils sont la plus élevée ou la tête des racines de bien non fixes . . ." The *Vyākhyā* glosses the word 'summits' by saying that it is used much as in worldly speech, as in the expression that a person is at the 'summit of his glory' (*mūrdhagatā khalv asya śrīr iti*). It proceeds to say that of the 'four aids to penetration' two are unstable (*cala*), namely 'warmth' and 'summits'—the former a lesser ('soft') 'root of wholesomeness' (*mṛdu kuśalamūlam*), the latter a greater one (literally 'beyond measure', *adhimātraṃ kuśalamūlam*). The remaining two are stable (*acala*), having the same mutual relationship as the first two. Finally, the 'summit' implies the possibility of motion forward or backward, just as one can jump upward or fall down from a treetop. *Vibhāṣā* 6, as quoted in Kyokuga 23.4a, says the same thing about the character of the 'four aids to penetration'.

Verse 18 proceeds to say that the two states just mentioned, 'warmth' and 'summits' or 'heads', are inaugurated by the last of the 'four stations of mindfulness', that of *dharma*, and enhanced by the first three. 'Warmth' and 'summits' are expressed in Sanskrit by the nouns *ākaraṇa* and *vardhana*, rendered by La Vallée Poussin as 'imprimer' and 'grandir' respectively. 'Warmth' is glossed in the *Bhāṣya* as *vinyasana*, in the *Vyākhyā* as *upanipātana* and *pravartana*. *Vinyasana* is rendered by La Vallée Poussin (*ibid.*) as 'application'. Paramārtha uses *an hsiang* ('placer l'aspect') in the verse, *an li* ('set securely') in the *Bhāṣya*. Kyokuga (*ibid.*) notes that the 'four aids to penetration' 'follow' (*shun*) the path of vision (*chien tao, darśanamārga*), within which the only station of mindfulness is that of *dharma*, which is why only mindfulness of *dharma* is possible at first, while the other three are possible later. Another opinion is that, while the separate view of the 'aids to penetration' makes change of station impossible, this is not true of the general view. This, according to the same source, explains why only the mindfulness of *dharma* functions at first and the remaining three later. Perhaps the most lucid explanation is given in La Vallée Poussin vi. 164, note 4:

> C'est par le *dharmasmṛtyupasthāna*, c'est en considérant les *dharmas* que l'ascète, au début des stades de chaud et de têtes, voit les *upādānaskandhas* comme impermanents, douloureux, etc. Il imprime sur les vérités—c'est-à-dire sur les *upādānaskandhas* effets (*duḥkha*),

> sur les *upādānaskandhas* causes (*samudaya*), sur la destruction (*nirodha-nirvāṇa*), sur le chemin (*mārga*)–les caractères ou aspects (*ākāra*) qui leur conviennent. C'est le *vinyasana* ou *ākaraṇa* des aspects.

There follows a statement whose relevance I fail to see. The Sanskrit of the *Bhāṣya* and the *Vyākhyā*, La Vallée Poussin's French version, and both Chinese versions state unanimously that, as the practitioner progresses, he puts his former 'wholesome roots' out of his mind because he attaches no great importance to them. Nowhere is it specified, however, which roots are meant; nor is any connection made between this statement and what precedes or follows.

The final statement about the 'summits' is that they are of three degrees: slight ('soft', *mṛdu*), middle (*madhya*), and strong ('beyond measure', *adhimātra*). A direct consequence of the last degree is the aid to penetration called 'patience' (*kṣānti*), itself manifest in three degrees. The *Bhāṣya* glosses the word *kṣānti* in two words, *adhimātra-satyakṣamaṇād aparihāṇitaḥ*, meaning that patience is immune to all possibility of diminution because of the delight it takes in supreme truth.[7] It is both like and unlike its two predecessors in that it is inaugurated and enhanced by *dharmasmṛtyupasthāna* and not by any of the other three states.

It might not be out of place here to recall what the *kārikā* has to say about 'patience'. "De cela, la patience (*kṣānti*) . . . Forte, elle a pour objet la douleur du Kāmadhātu. Elle est d'un moment." The first sentence is glossed in La Vallée Poussin vi. 166 as follows: "La patience forte, joignant les *agradharmas* . . . a seulement pour objet la douleur . . . du domaine du Kāma." This renders *agradharma-śleṣād asau* (*kṣāntiḥ*) *kamāvacaraduḥkhâlambanaiva* (p. 909). This is explained by the Vyākhyā in terms that might be paraphrased as follows:

> The 'supreme (worldly) *dharmas*' (which follow 'patience' directly), by virtue of their close association (literally 'embrace', *śleṣa*) with the path of vision (*i.e.*, the fifteen *abhisamayas*, which, in turn, follow the 'supreme worldly *dharmas*'), have the nature of the stage of the mindfulness of *dharma*. Because these 'supreme worldly *dharmas*', whose focus is nothing other than the truth of suffering within the framework of the

> 'sphere of desire' (*kāmāvacaratvaduḥkhasatya*), follow immediately upon 'patience', the latter two have their focus upon the same truth, the similarity being due to the close connection.

The *Bhāṣya* goes on to say that this very fact is proof that the first two 'aids to penetration' have their focus on the truth of suffering on the level of all three spheres.[8]

Just before the final statement in *ardhaśloka* 19a, *kṣaṇaṃ ca sā*, "Elle est d'un moment . . . ," there is a statement that seems to mean the following (though, as shall be pointed out, there is some disagreement and considerable commentary on its meaning):

> When the practitioner, having each of the sixteen aspects of the 'four noble truths' as his object, diminishes the obstacles that beset the spheres of 'form' and 'formlessness', and when by doing so he brings the objects of his contemplation down to the truth of suffering, in terms of thc 'sphere of desire', for two consecutive moments (*dvābhyāṃ kṣaṇābhyām*), this constitutes 'middle patience' (*madhyā kṣāntiḥ*). When this has been reduced to a single moment, the 'patience' is strong (literally, 'exceeding measure', *tad adhimātreti*).

The two Chinese versions as well as La Vallée Poussin, based on Hsüan-tsang, say essentially the same thing though in somewhat different ways. (See Kyokuga 23.4b, La Vallée Poussin vi. 166, T29.271c. Kyokuga mentions that he has written an article on the subject but does not say where it is to be found.)

The original says: *yadā kila rūpārupyapratipakṣādīnām ekaika-satyākārālambanāpahrāsena yāvat kāmāvacaram eva dvābhyāṃ kṣaṇābhyāṃ manasi karoti eṣā sarvaiva madhyā kṣāntiḥ/ yadaikam eva kṣaṇaṃ tad adhimātreti/* The *Vyākhyā* version can be found on pages 910 and 911 in the Dwarikadas edition. In a somewhat abridged paraphrase, it would read:

> *rūpārūpyapratipakṣādīnām* means not what is indicated in the translation above but rather the first three of the four truths in terms of the spheres of 'form' and 'formlessness', in addition to the obstacles that beset the 'sphere of desire'. What has to be diminished is each of the aspects of the 'four truths', then the truths themselves as objects. Everything from that point onward is 'middle patience'. It begins with the 'knowledge by analogy' (*anvayajñāna*), knowledge on the part of a

> denizen of the 'sphere of desire' but bearing on the two upper spheres of the fourth noble truth in terms of its four aspects.[9] Successively he omits the aspects one at a time till he has disposed of the fourth noble truth altogether. He then does the same for the third, second, and first on the level of the two higher spheres; next the obstacle that besets the 'sphere of desire'; then the fourth, third, and second truths on that level. Down to the first truth, he considers that in terms of all four aspects, then three, finally two, after which he has achieved 'middle patience'. In the fourth moment (*kṣaṇa*), his object is the 'supreme worldly *dharma*s'.

Another view is that the idea is not to eliminate first the aspects and then the objects, but rather to eliminate the aspects *as* objects.

The latter half of the *Vyākhyā* I now give for what it is worth; I confess there are places in which I do not follow it, particularly where it resorts to mathematical calculation. 'Middle patience' is described as consisting of 1,900 moments (*ekānnaviṃśatikṣaṇaśataṃ madhyā kṣāntir iti varṇayanti/*). If, however, the objects are diminished before the aspects, too many moments of thought creep in, which is not logical (*ākārāpahrāsake hy ālambanāpahrāse sati atibahavaś cittakṣaṇā visarpanti/ na caitan nyāyyam/*). The abandonment of aspects makes no sense as long as the truths themselves continue to exist, since it is only the abandonment of the aspects that makes possible the abandonment of the truths. There are two kinds of truths, concentrated and unconcentrated.[10] If each of these has four aspects, the total is thirty-two, according to one view. When the practitioner contemplates, in its four aspects, the truth of suffering on the level of the 'sphere of desire', then directs the same attention to the obstacles that beset the two upper spheres, that is what characterizes 'soft', *i.e.*, slight, patience (*mṛdvī kṣāntiḥ*). To contemplate the truth of suffering on the level of the 'sphere of desire' is to contemplate, on the same level, the counteragents to deed-formations (*saṃskārāṇāṃ pratipakṣam*). When the practitioner finishes with the latter on the level of the two upper spheres, he has undertaken 'middle patience' (*madhyā kṣāntir ārabdhā*). From that point on the number of moments of thought left is twenty-eight. When the above obstacles have been dealt with on the level of the two upper spheres, there are twenty moments of thought left. When the same has been done on the level of the 'sphere of desire', there remain sixteen. When the origin of suffering has been disposed of on the level of the two upper spheres, there remain twelve; when on the level of the 'sphere of desire', eight. When suffering has been abandoned on the two upper spheres, four moments of thought remain. The practitioner then contemplates, in its four aspects, the truth of suffering on the level of the 'sphere of desire'.

The practice flowing from this is of two kinds, depending on whether the practitioner is motivated by false views (*dṛṣṭicarita*) or by greed (*tṛṣṇācarita*). The former is also of two kinds, depending upon whether it is motivated by a view of the self (*ātmadṛṣṭicarita*) or by a view of what belongs to the self (*ātmīyadṛṣṭicarita*). The person motivated by the first view achieves certainty (*niyāmam avakrāmati?*) by viewing the aspect of non-self, the other by viewing the aspect of emptiness. The person motivated by greed is also of two sorts, depending on whether his underlying motive is conceit (*asmimāna*) or sloth (*kausīdya*). Conceit resorts to the view of impermanence, sloth to that of woe. The one motivated by his view of self views the 'truth of woe' on the level of the 'sphere of desire' in terms of three aspects, omitting the first, then the second, then the third, and finally viewing the 'truth of woe' in terms of his direct experience on the level of the 'sphere of desire' and of conjecture in terms of the two upper spheres. This is 'middle patience', consisting of 1,900 moments of thought (*sic*). The one motivated by the view of what belongs to himself regards two aspects, that of emptiness and that of non-self, which is his form of 'middle patience'. 'Strong patience' ('beyond measure') consists of a single moment, and is bound to the view of one of four aspects: woe, impermanence, emptiness, or non-self. The commentary concludes by saying that the practitioner begins by viewing the obstacles to salvation throughout the 'triple sphere' and then concentrates on the 'sphere of desire' since it is the abode of woe *par excellence.*

Next in turn come the 'supreme worldly *dharmas*', which, like 'strong patience', bear on the truth of woe in the 'sphere of desire' and, like it, are momentary. They are 'supreme' in the sense that they are as far as one can go in religious development and still be in the world; 'worldly' in the same sense. They lead the practitioner out of the world by the sheer force of their virtue, since they are not a 'like cause' (*sabhāgahetu*) for the path of vision (*darśanamārga*) that follows them.

With this the description of the individual aids to enlightenment is concluded. What follow are some general observations. To begin with, all four aids, being of a piece with the station of the 'mindfulness of *dharma*', are said to be of the nature of wisdom (*prajñātmakā ucyante*). They consist of all five *skandhas* (and, adds the *Bhāṣya*, of their concomitants), with the exception of 'possessions' (*vināptibhiḥ*), the last being so because the superior man (*ārya*) would otherwise have to achieve a double realization: that of the aids themselves and that of their possession.[11]

The time relationships of the four aids can best be seen by consulting one of the diagrams. These aids are called the 'four aids to penetration' (*iti nirvedhabhāgīyaṃ caturdhā*). An etymological explanation of the word *nirvedhabhāgīya*: the *niḥ* is alleged to mean *niścita* (certain), while the root *vidh* is said to signify 'distinction' (*vibhāga*). Thus *nirvedhabhāgīya* signifies a noble path by resort to which first doubt is abandoned, then reality discerned in the formula, "This is woe; . . . this is the path (that leads to the suppression of woe)." The verse goes on to say that the composite of aids to penetration consists of 'realization' (*bhāvanā*); the *Bhāṣya* adds that this excludes what has been learned (literally 'heard', *śruta*) and the products of discursive thinking (*cintā*). The four aids are found in the stage preceding (*anāgamya*) and 'trances' (*dhyāna*) of the 'sphere of form', in the stage intermediate between the first and second (*dhyānāntara*) and in all four of the 'trances' proper. In the view of a certain Ghoṣaka, the *Bhāṣya* concludes, the first two aids are found in the 'sphere of desire' as well.

There are some divergences between the two Chinese versions and the original, but the most striking one is the passage in Hsüantsang's translation (verse 23.5b, *Bhāṣya* 23.6b), not present in the original or in Paramārtha's version—nor, surprisingly enough, in La Vallée Poussin—in which one sees ascribed to the venerable Ghoṣaka the following view: The 'four aids to penetration' are based on the six grounds just mentioned and a seventh, the 'sphere of desire'. The practitioner is reborn, whether as man or as god, in any of nine places (the 'sphere of desire', any of the four god-worlds in the 'sphere of form', or any of the four in the 'sphere of formlessness') with the exception of Uttarakuru (the continent to the north of Sumeru; our own continent, Jambudvīpa, being to the south).[12]

The *Kośa* goes on to say that the scene of the 'four aids to penetration' is the 'sphere of desire'. The reason for this, says the *Vyākhyā*, is that only there does the comprehension of the 'four noble truths' (*satyābhisamaya*) take place, there being no 'path of view' (*dṛkpatha*) in the upper spheres since there is not enough emotional agitation (*asaṃvegāt*) in either of them to stimulate it.[13] Three of the four (the first three, according to the *Vyākhyā*) originate only among human beings, and that only on three of the four continents centering on Mount Sumeru (all, as indicated above, with the exception of Uttarakuru), but they can originate in both sexes. The fourth, that of the 'supreme worldly *dharma*s', is achieved by gods alone.[14]

Ardhaśloka 21a concludes with the statement that a woman can attain the 'supreme worldly *dharma*s' in either sex, while the *Bhāṣya* says a man can attain them only in masculine form. The *Vyākhyā* comments that a woman who attains them as a woman will be reincarnated as a man, while a man will remain a man. The *Bhāṣya* states that there is not sufficient reason for a man to be reborn as a woman under these circumstances (*strītvasyāpratisaṃkhyānirodhalābhāt*), while the *Vyākhyā* maintains that one who has attained the 'supreme worldly *dharma*s' inevitably and immediately goes on to the 'path of view', from which women are excluded.

Ardhaśloka 21b says that a superior person (*ārya*) loses his 'aids to penetration' through the loss of his 'ground' (*bhūmityāgāt*) while others lose theirs through death. The *Bhāṣya* states that, when an *ārya* abandons a certain *bhūmi*, he abandons the 'aids to penetration' on that level but not otherwise, and that this refers to passage from one *bhūmi* to another. The *Vyākhyā* goes on to say that *bhūmi* refers to the specific *dhyāna*s of the two upper spheres, and that passage from one *bhūmi* to another is contrasted with 'detachment' (*bhūmisaṃcāra* as opposed to *vairāgya*).[15]

The ordinary person (*pṛthagjana*), on the other hand, loses his 'aids to penetration' by mere death even if he is reborn in the same sphere and on the same level. The *Vyākhyā* presents and attacks the view of Vasumitra, quoting in support the position of Saṃghabhadra, who maintains that the acquisition of the 'four aids to penetration' is possible only in the 'sphere of desire', and that an ordinary person loses them only through death.

Ardhaśloka 22a, which reads *ādye dve parihāṇyā ca maulais tatraiva satyadṛk/*, has a meaning of which I am not quite certain. Since *ardhaśloka* 21b reads *bhūmityāgāt tyajaty āryas tāny anāryas tu mṛtyunā//*, it seems proper to view everything from *bhūmityāgāt* through *ca* as a single sentence meaning "The superior person loses his 'aids to penetration' through the loss of his 'ground' while the inferior one loses his through death; the first two ('aids to penetration') can be lost through backsliding as well." (La Vallée Poussin, as will have been seen, agrees with this.) The *Bhāṣya* goes on to say that even the ordinary person does not lose the highest two aids by backsliding. The remainder of 22a is something of a philological problem. La Vallée Poussin (vi. 172.22b), not having the original, rendered it as follows from the Tibetan (*dngos gzhis de nyid la bden mthong*): "Lorsqu'ils appartiennent aux dhyānas fondamentaux, vue des vérités dès cette vie." Paramārtha says *yu pen chung chien ti*, Hsüan-tsang *i pen pi chien ti*, meaning that, on the basis of the *mūladhyānas*, the practitioner sees the 'truths' without fail (Hsüan-tsang) in terms of the particular 'ground' he occupies (Paramārtha). Thus the passage in question might be glossed *maulair dhyānais tatraiva dhyāneṣu satyadṛg bhavati yogī*, in Paramārtha's meaning. The *Bhāṣya* adds that the practitioner on the level of any of the *mauladhyāna*s, if he masters the 'four aids to penetration', views the 'four truths' in that very life without fail by virtue of the intensity of his agitation. La Vallée Poussin (*ibid.*) says, "Parce que le dégoût de l'existence . . . est très fort." Paramārtha (29.272b) agrees with him, Hsüan-tsang (Kyokuga 23.7a) with me.

Ardhaśloka 22b maintains that 'aids to penetration', once lost, must be reacquired quite as if the practitioner had never had them, whether they were lost in an upward or downward move; that there is no such thing as resuming where one left off. The *Bhāṣya* explains that, as in the case of a monastic vow (*prātimokṣasaṃvara*) once broken, resumption is impossible because of discontinuation of habit and the effort necessary for the acquisition of the 'aids to penetration'.

The *Vyākhyā* adds that since there is no prior experience, not to say habit, of the 'aids to penetration', given their association with the 'noble path' (*āryamārga*), there can be no question of their being acquired through disenchantment;[16] because of the effort required there can also be no thought of taking up where one left off. The *Bhāṣya* qualifies this by saying that the practitioner can indeed resume his course without beginning again if he meets, within the same area (*sīmā*), a teacher who can instruct him. The *Vyākhyā* specifies that the teacher must be a master of *praṇidhijñāna*; without such a teacher resumption is impossible.[17]

The next statement is that one who achieves 'warmth', even if later he loses it, is capable of *parinirvāṇa*. The *Bhāṣya* concludes with a remark about the difference between *nirvedhabhāgīya* and *mokṣabhāgīya* ('aids to deliverance'), about which more shall be said below.

Śloka 23 deals with the advantages (to use the term somewhat loosely) gained by those who have achieved one or more of the 'aids to penetration'. One who has achieved the 'summits', the second of the four aids, can never be deprived of the karmic background that will lead to eventual *nirvāṇa*. This is true even if he suffers rebirth, for a time, in one of the three lowest destinies. Such rebirth cannot happen, however, to anyone who has achieved 'patience', the third of the four aids. For the practitioner who achieves 'slight patience' (*mṛdvīṃ kṣāntim*) there will be no rebirth in those destinies. For the one who achieves the highest form of 'patience' (*adhimātrāṃ kṣāntim*) there is escape not only from these but from the following: birth from an egg (*aṇḍajayoni*), birth 'from moisture' (*saṃsvedajayoni*), birth as an *asaṃjñisattva*,[18] birth on Uttarakuru, birth as Mahābrahman, birth as a congenital eunuch (*ṣaṇḍha*), castration (*paṇḍaka*), birth as an hermaphrodite (*ubhayavyañjanāśraya*), more than seven reincarnations, and all defilements that can be eliminated by the view of the 'four noble truths' (*darśanaheyakleśa*).

It is here that the Sanskrit and the Chinese, in both translations, diverge. While an *ardhaśloka* is rendered with two Chinese feet, here 23a corresponds to the second and third feet, the first and fourth having no analog in the Sanskrit. The first and fourth, in both Chinese versions, are reproduced in close paraphrase in La Vallée Poussin vi. 173, note 2, and 175, note 1, respectively. Perhaps the thing to do first is to paraphrase the *śloka* and *Bhāṣya* as they appear in Paramārtha (29.272c) and then in Hsüan-tsang (Kyokuga 23.7b–8b).

Paramārtha. Verse: (One who achieves) 'warmth' is not subject to false teachings.[19] Commentary: One who achieves 'warmth', even if he loses it for a time, is still immune to false doctrines. That being the case, what difference is there between 'warmth' and the 'summits'? Verse: (One who attains the) 'summits' does not sever his 'wholesome roots'. Commentary: One who attains them does not sever the roots even if he backslides. This means that he may descend into one of the evil destinies and commit the most terrible of sins (without, however, losing his 'wholesome roots'). Verse: (One who achieves) 'patience' will not descend into the evil destinies. Commentary: This means that a person who loses his status by moving to another one (not by dying, which implies an upward move), thus losing his 'patience', will still never descend into one of the evil destinies. The reason for this is that he is already far removed from the defilements[20] that convey beings to the lowest destinies. The reason for this, in turn, is that one who gains 'patience' while residing among ordinary beings is completely exempt from the rebirths listed above in the comments on *śloka* 23 of the Sanskrit. This being so for those who have achieved 'mild patience', it is all the more true for those who have achieved the highest form. Verse: (One who has attained the) 'supreme worldly *dharma*s' is free of ordinary status. Commentary: One who has gained the 'wholesome root' known as 'supreme worldly *dharma*s' cannot possibly lose it, whether by change of status or by death, for there is no cause sufficient to effect such a person's rebirth as a common being (*pṛthagjana*). The reason is that without any effort the practitioner will unfailingly witness in the very next moment (*kṣaṇa*) the 'truth of woe'.

Hsüan-tsang. Verse: //(One who attains) 'warmth' shall without fail reach *nirvāṇa*./ (One who attains the) 'summits' shall never sever his 'wholesome roots'./ (One who attains) 'patience' shall not fall into an evil destiny./ (One who attains) the first ('worldly *dharma*s') shall enter (into a state where he) separates himself from birth.//[21] Commentary: The best thing to do is to reproduce La Vallée Poussin, who says it much better than I can.

> Celui qui obtient les *dharma*s suprêmes, quoiqu'il soit dans la condition de *pṛthagjana*, est néanmoins capable d'entrer dans le

> *samyaktvaniyāma*. Bien que la stance ne dise pas que ces *dharmas* ne sont pas abandonnés à la mort, cependant, du fait que, par ces *dharmas*, on entre immédiatement dans le *samyaktvanyāma*, il résulte implicitement qu'ils ne sont pas abandonnés à la mort. —Pourquoi le seul possesseur des *dharmas* suprêmes est-il capable d'entrer dans le *nyāma*?—Parce qu'il a déjà obtenu la destruction-par-absence-des-causes (*apratisaṃkhyānirodha*) de la qualité de *pṛthagjana*; parce que les *dharmas* suprêmes sont capables . . . d'expulser la qualité de *pṛthagjana*.[22]

Ardhaśloka 23b touches on the issue of the *gotra*, a major question in its own right. In the present context there are three *gotras*: those of *śrāvaka*, of *pratyekabuddha*, and of *buddha*. A *śrāvaka* who has achieved the first, or the first two, 'aids to penetration' can move into the *gotra* of a *buddha*, something not possible once he has achieved 'patience'. The reason for this, as has been seen, is that the achievement of 'patience' exempts the practitioner from rebirth in any of the three lowest destinies, something that the *bodhisattva* must undergo if he is to save the beings in those spheres. The same *śrāvaka* can move into the *pratyekagotra* upon attainment of any of the first three 'aids to penetration', but an occupant of the *pratyekagotra* or of the *buddhagotra* cannot move into another state.

Paramārtha adds (see La Vallée Poussin vi. 176, note 4), "*Le pratyekabuddhagotra* ne peut être révoqué.—Pourquoi?—La stance dit: 23 e-f. Parce qu'il ne cherche pas le bien d'autrui; changer autrement le *gotra* n'est pas nié."

Paramārtha's *Bhāṣya* (29.273a), which La Vallée Poussin (*ibid.*) abridges somewhat, states:

> *Pratyekabuddhatā* is not subject to change. Why? The reason is that the *pratyekabuddha*, as the verse says, does not seek to benefit others, a circumstance that prevents that particular change but no others. The meaning is that if a practitioner of contemplation originally took a vow of *pratyekabodhi* and then later, through religious practice, achieved the first two of the four 'wholesome roots', these could never be transformed into those of a *bodhisattva*. In other words, the practitioner in question has vowed to cultivate religious practice without concern for the benefit of anyone but himself. The other two (*śrāvaka* and *bodhisattva*) may change; the *pratyekabuddha* never, given the intensity of his resolve.

Hsüan-tsang adds nothing, but Kyokuga (23.8a-9a) has some commentary quoted from *Mahāvibhāṣā* 7:

> Each of the four 'aids to penetration' has six *gotras*, *viz.*, (1) *parihāṇadharman* (susceptible de chute), (2) *cetanādharman* (susceptible de mettre fin à son existence), (3) *anurakṣaṇādharman* (susceptible de garder),[23] (4) *sthitākampya* (celui qui, quand manquent de fortes causes de chute, même sans garder, est susceptible de ne pas bouger, c'est-à-dire de rester dans le fruit; qui, ne tombant pas, à faute d'effort, *abhiyoga*, n'est pas susceptible de progresser), (5) *prativedhanādharman* (susceptible de pénétrer sans effort chez les Inébranlables), (6) *akopyadharman* (inébranlable, non susceptible de chute). It is possible to convert the 'warmth' of the *parihāṇadharmagotra* into that of the *cetanādharmagotra*, *i.e.*, to rise one degree; likewise that of the *prativedhanādharmagotra* into that of the *akopyadharmagotra*, that of the *śrāvakagotra* into that of the *pratyekagotra* or of the *buddhagotra*, [and] that of the *pratyekogotra* into that of either of the other two. The 'warmth' of the *buddhagotra*, however, cannot be changed.[24]

Ardhaśloka 24a reads, *ābodheḥ sarvam ekatra dhyānāntye śāstṛkhaḍgayoḥ*, in which the word *dhyānāntye* is a bit puzzling. In terms of both the *Bhāṣya* (*ekatraivāsane*, p. 920) and the two Chinese translations (*i tso*, 29.273a, 23.8a), the word *antya* means 'sitting'. The Tibetan translator, apparently wishing to have the best of both worlds, renders the key phrase *mtha' stan gcig la*.[25] The grammar of the *ardhaśloka* is also a bit obscure; but the *Bhāṣya* leaves no doubt. If some verb such as *utpadyate* is understood, then as literally as possible "Up to (supreme) enlightenment (*ābodheḥ*), everything (*sarvam*) in a single sitting in meditation (*ekatra dhyānāntye*) on the part of the Teacher and of the rhinoceros(-like one, *śāstṛkhaḍgayoḥ*) is achieved." The Teacher is the Buddha, while the 'rhinoceros-like one' or, according to some, the one 'likened to the horn of a rhinoceros (*khaḍgaviṣāṇakalpa*),' is one kind of *pratyekabuddha*, the other being the *vargacārin*, 'who goes in a group.'[26] The *Bhāṣya* states that 'everything' means the 'four aids to penetration' and says also that it signifies the whole process beginning with the first station of mindfulness and culminating in supreme enlightened intuition. It adds that those who posit the existence of a *pratyekabuddha* as different from the *khaḍgaviṣāṇakalpa* say that he can, upon attainment of the first one or two of the 'four aids to penetration', exchange his *gotra* for that of a *bodhisattva*. Hsüan-tsang adds nothing, except to specify that 'in one sitting' means quite literally 'without leaving his seat'. It should be added that all versions agree that the importance of the fourth *dhyāna* in this context is due to its imperturbability, which according to the *Vyākhyā* it owes to its freedom from eight distractions.[27] All agree, finally, that the 'enlightened intuition' (*bodhi*) just mentioned consists of the gnostic insight that the defilements (*kleśa*) have perished (*kṣayajñāna*) and will never arise again (*anutpādajñāna*).

To the question of whether the 'four aids to penetration' can be achieved in the same life as the preparatory steps to them, the answer is negative. The verse states that first one must gain the 'aid to deliverance', and this takes at least three existences. The *Bhāṣya* specifies that the 'wholesome aid pertaining to deliverance' (*mokṣabhāgīyaṃ kuśalamūlam*) is gained in one incarnation, the 'aids to penetration' in the next, and the 'noble path' (*āryamārga*) in the one after that, adding that the order of sequence must be entry (*avatāra*), maturation (*paripāka*), and deliverance (*vimukti*). While the *Bhāṣya* states that three existences are the minimum (*sarvasvalpam*), the *Vyākhyā* says that one 'equipped' in his previous birth (*yas tu pūrvasmiñ janmani saṃbhṛtamokṣabhāgīyo bhavati*) with the 'aid to deliverance' can achieve the 'aids to penetration' and the 'noble path' within one incarnation.[28] As is so frequently done, the process is likened here to the one that begins with seeding and leads, in the plant world, to florescence.

Paramārtha begins with the question of whether one who has not planted the 'wholesome root' i.e., the 'aid to deliverance' in a previous life can, through great exertion (*tso kung yung*), achieve the 'aids to penetration' within one incarnation. The answer is unequivocally negative, for the former is an indispensable precondition to the latter.[29] For the rest, Paramārtha agrees with the original. Hsüan-tsang says essentially the same, which Kyokuga (23.9) explicates with many references to the *Vibhāṣā* and other sources and also with some diagrams (which we will not reproduce).

Before going on to our digest of *Mahāvibhāṣa* 7, we will cite *śloka* 25, dealing, however, only with *ardhaśloka* 25a and simply repeating in English the contents of 25b. Then we will proceed to the *puṇyabhāgīyaṃ kuśalamūlam*.

The *śloka* says that the 'aid to deliverance' is made up of what one has learned ('heard') and thought about (*śrutacintāmayam*); the *Vyākhyā* adds that this excludes 'realization', *i.e.*, meditation (*na bhāvanāmayam*). The *śloka* goes on to speak of 'three (kinds of) deeds' (*trīṇi karmāṇi*), understood to be those of body, speech, and mind. The *Bhāṣya* states that the last being a mental resolve inevitably comprises both action and speech. The illustrations are interesting from our point of view. An act leading to ultimate deliverance is the gift of alms, however slight, to a mendicant monk. Speech may lead to the same result, the receipt of instruction (since the latter involves the solicitation of instruction, then repetition from memory of sacred text). They lead to deliverance because they were performed with that goal in view. The *Vyākhyā* makes the obvious point that actions and speech spring from thought. The *ardhaśloka* concludes with the observation that *mokṣabhāgīyaṃ kuśalamūlam* is available only to humans. The *Bhāṣya* restricts even that to the three continents (exclusive of Uttarakuru), on the grounds that disgust with the world and the wisdom necessary to deal with it are confined to humans on those continents.[30]

Paramārtha (29.273b) says the same thing, except that his language in places is rather cryptic. Hsüan-tsang (Kyokuga 23.9b) has "observe the admonitions" (*i.e.*, adhere to the monastic code, *ch'ih chieh*) instead of "receive instruction." He also adds that one must be born in an age in which there is a Buddha in the world in order to achieve the above-mentioned four 'wholesome roots'. Hsüan-tsang mentions that an encounter with a *pratyekabuddha* can have the same effect.

As to *puṇyabhāgīyaṃ kuśalamūlam*, the *Kośa* has little to say about it. The first statement (p. 752 f.) is negative: *Ato mahatīṃ ta ātmanaḥ puṇyajyāniṃ kurvanti ye viparītadharmaṃ deśayanti/ kliṣṭacittā vā lābhasatkārayaśāṃsi vāñchantaḥ/*. This is rendered by La Vallée Poussin (iv. 252), "Par conséquent, ceux qui exposent le Dharma soit faussement, soit avec une pensée souillée, par le désir de gain . . . , de respects . . . , de réputation . . . , ils détruisent le grand mérite qui leur échéait." The second statement, though positive, is laconic: *puṇyabhāgīyaṃ yad iṣṭavipākam*; " 'Pertaining to merit' is anything having a desired result." The *Vyākhyā* offers two interpretations of the term *puṇyabhāgīya*, one going back to *puṇyabhāga*, the other alleging that the word is synonymous to *puṇyabhāj*. In the first interpretation *puṇyabhāgaḥ* may mean *puṇyasya bhāgah*, *i.e. puṇyasya prāptiḥ*, the 'acquisition of merit', or *iṣṭaphalaprāpti*, the 'acquisition of a desired result'; and a thing is *puṇyabhāgīya* if it conduces to *puṇyabhāga*. That accounts for the word *iṣṭavipāka* ('having a desired result'), glossed as *tatprāptyanukūla* ('in keeping with the acquisition thereof'). On the other hand, *puṇyabhāgīya* may mean 'conducive to the meritorious division', for deeds may be divided into three categories: meritorious (*puṇyo bhāgaḥ*), sinful (*apuṇyo bhāgaḥ*), and irrelevant to either, *i.e.*, over and above them (*aniñjyo bhāgaḥ*). In the second interpretation, as already indicated, *puṇyabhāgīya* is synonymous with *puṇyabhāj*, referring to something that 'partakes of merit' (*puṇyaṃ bhajata iti puṇyabhāk*).[31]

Parāmartha agrees, also maintaining that by preaching false doctrines one ruins not only one's own merit but that of others as well. By 'desirable results' Paramārtha means rebirth as man or god. Hsüan-tsang's version is much closer to the original. Kyokuga (18.19b-20a) quotes *Mahāvibhāṣā* 7 to the effect that what determines *puṇya-bhāgīya* is not so much the meritorious act itself as the intention with which the act was performed; namely, whether or not *nirvāṇa* was the goal and disgust with the world the motive.

Mahāvibhāṣā 7, beginning T27.30c, takes up a final treatment of the 'four aids to penetration' individually and collectively. The discussion begins with a verse preceded by the statement that the Venerable Sage of the West[32] summed up the 'four aids to penetration' under seventeen headings. To the extent that I have understood them, they are listed below.

1) *i ch'ü, manoviṣaya*
2) *i, āśraya*
3) *yin, hetu*
4) *so yüan, pratyaya*
5) *kuo, phala*
6) *teng liu, niṣyanda*
7) *i shu, vipāka*
8) *sheng li, atiśaya*?

9) *hsing hsiang, ākāra*
10) *erh yüan, dve ālambane*
11) *hui, jñāna?*
12) *chieh, dhātu*
13) *ting, samādhi? dhyāna?*
14) *hsün teng, vitarkādi*
15) *ken, indriya*
16) *hsin, citta*
17) *t'ui, vihāni? vivartana?*

The seventeen headings are then dealt with in seventeen question-and-answer exchanges, which I have paraphrased.

1) Q. What is the field of mental perception, where 'patience' is concerned?
   A. The totality of everything previously experienced, beginning with pious gifts (*dāna*) and ending with the 'seven skills' (*saptasthānakauśalya*, all of it directed toward the goal of deliverance.[33]
2) Q. On what base does 'warmth' rely in order to come into being?
   A. On a 'trance' appropriate to the level of the practitioner.
3) Q. What is the cause of 'warmth'?
   A. 'Wholesome roots' of the same class produced by the practitioner on his 'then' level.
4) Q. What are the conditions of 'warmth'?
   A. The 'four noble truths'.[34]
5) Q. What is the fruit of 'warmth'?
   A. The 'heads' or 'summits' are the immediate *puruṣakāra-phala.*[35]
6) Q. What is the 'outpouring' of 'warmth'?[36]
   A. The 'wholesome roots' to be produced on the 'then' level of the practitioner, being of his type.[37]
7) Q. What is the retribution of 'warmth'?
   A. The five *skandhas* in the 'sphere of form'.
8) Q. What is the superiority of 'warmth'?
   A. Its being a definite cause of the attainment of *nirvāṇa*. Some say also its not rejecting one's 'wholesome roots'.

9) Q. How many aspects does 'warmth' have?
A. The same sixteen as the 'four noble truths'.
10) Q. Does 'warmth' have as its (mental) object a name or a reality?
A. Both.
11) Q. Is 'warmth' the product of hearing, of thought, or of realization?
A. Of realization alone.
12) Q. Is 'warmth' a feature of the 'sphere of desire', of the 'sphere of form', or of the 'sphere of formlessness'?
A. Of the 'sphere of form' alone.
13) Q. Is 'warmth' concentrated (*tsai ting, samāhita*, 'recueilli') or not?
A. It is concentrated.
14) Q. Is 'warmth' characterized by both *vitarka* and *vicāra*, or by the latter alone, or by neither?
A. It can be any of the three.
15) Q. Is 'warmth' connected to the faculty of zest, or to that of gladness, or to that of evenmindedness?
A. To all three.
16) Q. Is 'warmth' characterized by one thought or by many?
A. By many.
17) Q. Is there any backsliding from 'warmth', or is there not?
A. There is.

The detailed treatment of 'warmth' being completed, there follows a rather cursory treatment of the remaining three 'aids to penetration', involving only certain of the seventeen features listed above.

The mental objects of the 'heads/summits' are described as everything from gift-giving (*dāna*) to the fruits of 'warmth'; their immediate *puruṣakāraphala* is 'patience'; their superiority is their non-abandonment of their 'wholesome roots' or, according to some, the avoidance of the five most terrible sins (*ānantaryakarmāṇi*). Everything else is considered to be the same as in the case of 'warmth.' For 'patience' the mental objects are described as everything from *dāna* to the fruits of the 'heads/summits'; its immediate *puruṣakāraphala*s are the 'supreme worldly *dharmas*'; its superiority is its avoidance of the five most terrible sins and of the descent into evil destinies or, according to some, the avoidance of clinging to the notion of self. Everything else is considered to be the same as in the case of the 'heads/summits'. As to the 'supreme worldly *dharmas*', their mental objects are everything from *dāna* to the objects of 'patience'; their fruit is the 'truth of woe'; their immediate *puruṣakāraphala* is their acquiescence in the '*dharma* of woe'; their superiority consists in their being (a) an immediate condition for the certain destiny of deliverance, (b) in possession of all four aspects of the 'truth of woe', (c) characterized by a single thought. Everything else is considered to be the same as in the case of 'patience'.

There follows (T27.31c–32a) discussion of whether a person who has already attained 'warmth' and is about to attain the 'heads/summits', but who dies at that point, has to begin again or can resume his career from the point at which death interrupted it. That is followed by discussion of whether the 'four aids to penetration' assure deliverance or not, including the question of whether the point at which the practitioner began was one of the *dhyānas* or the *dhyānāntara* (the intermediate point between the first and second *dhyānas*). Then comes discussion of particular practitioners. (This takes up the end of page 32 and all of page 33.) Specifically, the *bodhisattva* whose base is the fourth *dhyāna*, once he has produced the 'four aids to penetration', is certain of ultimate deliverance, since these along with his other qualifications are all he needs to produce the other necessary achievements beginning with contemplation of impurity (*aśubhābhāvanā*) and ending with the intuitive knowledge that his defilements, once extinguished, will never be reproduced (*anutpādajñāna*). The same is true of the lone (*khaḍgaviṣāṇakalpa*) *pratyekabuddha*, but not necessarily of the one who moves in a group (*vargacārin*) nor of the *śrāvaka*. What was said above about the *bodhisattva* means that, once equipped with the 'four aids to penetration', he can achieve final deliverance in a single sitting.

Q. Has the *bodhisattva* already, in previous incarnations, achieved the 'aids to penetration' before attaining his *bodhisattva* status? If so, what justification is there for saying that he achieves them 'in one sitting'? If he was not yet a *bodhisattva* when he achieved them, what is it that kept him immune for 91 *kalpa*s from descending into evil destinies?

A. According to one view the *bodhisattva* did achieve the 'aids to penetration' before attaining his *bodhisattva* status, and it is thanks to his 'patience' that he has contrived to avoid [such a] descent for that length of time.

Q. In that case, what is the meaning of the expression 'in a single sitting'?

A. What the *bodhisattva* has up to this point are attainments for *gotra*s below that of *bodhisattva*. Then in one sitting he gets them for his own *gotra* as well. On the other hand, there are those who say that the *bodhisattva* has not previously achieved the 'aids to penetration' because he plants all of his 'wholesome roots' at one time under the Tree of Enlightenment.

Q. That brings me back to my original question. What keeps the *bodhisattva*, for a full 91 *kalpa*s, from descent into evil destinies?

A. To avoid evil destinies the *bodhisattva* is not necessarily in need of all four 'aids to penetration'; either of the first two will do. For that matter he can achieve the same result by gift-giving, by moral discipline (*śīla*), by his knowledge (literally 'hearing'), or by thought.[38] That is to say, either of the first two is enough for a *bodhisattva* of acute faculties. One of dull faculties cannot achieve the same end short of 'patience'. On the other hand, of the triad of gift-giving, moral self-discipline, and wisdom, a *bodhisattva* can achieve all three by the mere acquisition of one. By this means he can escape an untold number of evil destinies, to say nothing of a mere three.

Those who achieve the 'aids to penetration' are of six sorts, *viz.*,

1) 'les susceptibles de chute', *parihāṇadharmāṇaḥ, t'ui fa*
2) 'les susceptibles de mettre fin à leur existence', *cetanādharmāṇaḥ, ssu fa*
3) 'les susceptibles de garder', *anurakṣaṇadharmāṇaḥ, hu fa*
4) 'les susceptibles de ne pas bouger', *sthitidharmāṇaḥ* (?), *chu fa*
5) 'les susceptibles de pénétrer', *prativedhanādharmāṇaḥ, k'an ta fa*
6) 'les inébranlables, les non susceptibles de chute', those of steadfast character, *akopyadharmāṇaḥ, pu tvng fa*[39]

It is possible to achieve either of the first two aids at the first level and to develop it to the second level or to go from the fifth level to the sixth level. It is also possible to achieve either of the two aids from the level of *śrāvakagotra* to that of *pratyekabuddhagotra* or *vice versa*; but once one has achieved either of the first two aids within the *buddhagotra* one cannot move.[40] When one comes to 'patience', that of the *śrāvakagotra* can be exchanged for that of the *pratyekabuddhagotra*; but neither can be developed into 'patience' within the *buddhagotra*, since 'patience' excludes rebirth in an evil destiny, something that a *bodhisattva* must undergo if he is to save others. Nor can 'patience' within the *pratyekabuddhagotra* be exchanged for that of the *śrāvakagotra*, since 'patience' cannot recede.

The 'aids to penetration' come into being only within the 'sphere of desire'.[41] They are possible among gods, but it is among men that they must originate, elsewhere than on Uttarakuru, to be carried on thence, whether among men or among gods. To achieve the 'aids to penetration' one must have a superior body and a superior resolve to separate oneself from the world.[42] The evil destinies lack the former, gods the latter. Only men have both. The inhabitants of the 'spheres of form and formlessness', having no certainty of deliverance, are also incapable of achieving the 'aids to penetration'. Certainty of deliverance (*samyaktvaniyāma*) requires both gnosis and acquiescence (*jñānakṣanti*), and acquiescence is lacking in those two spheres.[43] To achieve certainty of deliverance one must have two kinds of knowledge, direct and by analogy, of which only the analogous is possible in the two upper spheres.[44] Finally, in order to achieve certainty of deliverance one must have both a superior base and the sensation of woe; and woe is missing in the two upper spheres.[45]

There follows in 27.33c–34a discussion of the sex of one who achieves the 'aids to penetration'. Attainment is possible for members of both sexes; but a person of either sex who, having 'taken possession'[46] of any of the first three aids is then reborn as a woman without realizing[47] that aid, cannot then realize it in feminine form but must await further rebirth as a man. Any of the three achieved in a female body may furnish a cause (*yin*, *hetu*) for further achievement in a body of either sex; but one achieved in a male body can be a motivating force only for a similar achievement in another male body, because a superior cause cannot produce an inferior effect (*kuo*, *pha-*

la). One can, on the other hand, achieve all three of the first aids and still be reborn as a woman, but not the fourth, because it is momentary (*kṣaṇika*). After achieving either of the first two, for that one matter, one can be reborn a 'castrate' or eunuch (*ṣaṇḍhapaṇḍaka*), or an hermaphrodite. This is not possible after the achievement of 'patience', because any of the above three, while undeniably human (*manuṣya*), is, so to speak, an inferior destiny (*durgati*).

There follows a brief exchange on the 'abandonment of class membership' (presumably *nikāyasabhāgatāvihāni*) of an ordinary person (*pṛthagjana*) who has attained 'patience'.

Q. Describe, if you will, the effort to realize 'warmth' (*ūṣmagata-bhāvanāprayoga*?).

A. In sum, it is characterized by three gnoses born of knowledge (of Scripture, literally 'hearing', *śruti*), of thought (*cintā*), and of realization (*bhāvanā*, *i.e.*, meditation).

Q. What is meant by the first of these three?

A. The cultivator of insight (*hsiu kuan hsing che, vipaśyanābhāvayitṛ*?) may meet an enlightened teacher who will give him a summary explanation of the *dharma* encapsulated in the 'eighteen spheres' (*dhātu*), the 'twelve entries' (*āyatana*), the 'five masses' (*skandha*), etc. Or the practitioner may himself read and commit to memory Scripture (*sūtra*), monastic code (*vinaya*), and patrology (*abhidharma*), then say to himself, 'This literature is very extensive. If I carry it about in my memory, I shall grow tired. In sum, however, it comes down to 'eighteen spheres', 'twelve entries', and 'five masses'." Thinking thus, he will examine the 'eighteen spheres', seeing a threefold division into name (*ming, vyañjana*), peculiar marks (*tzu hsiang, svalakṣaṇa*), and common marks (*kung hsiang, sāmānya-lakṣaṇa*). By 'name' are meant the conventional names of the 'eighteen spheres'—everything from the sphere of vision (*cakṣurdhātu*) to the sphere of mental cognition (*manovijñānadhātu*). The 'peculiar marks' are the marks of the spheres themselves. The 'common marks' are the sixteen aspects of the 'four noble truths'.

By resorting to the methods just described, the practitioner achieves both gnosis (*jñāna*) and calm (*śamatha*). He proceeds to reduce the 'eighteen spheres' to 'twelve entries', which he again views in terms of name, peculiar marks, and common marks. He tells himself that the 'eighteen spheres' can be further reduced by viewing the whole complex in terms of 'five masses' and the unconditioned *dharmas*. The same is done with the 'twelve entries'.[48]

The practitioner tells himself that the *skandhas* are all, in fact, *asaṃskṛta*, which leads him into the stations of mindfulness: (1) *rūpa* corresponding to (1′) *kāya*; (2) *vedanā* to (2′) itself; (3) *saṃjñā*; (4) *saṃskārāḥ* and the *asaṃskṛtas* to (4′) *dharma*; (5) *vijñāna* to (3′) *citta*. Then the practitioner applies the same threefold division as before (names, peculiar marks, common marks), leading to the 'four noble truths'. He makes the distinction between the constituted (conditioned) *dharmas* and their fruits corresponding to the 'truth of woe'. He distinguishes between causes and their effects (fruits) corresponding to the 'truth of the origin of woe'. He relates intentional suppression (*pratisaṃkhyānirodha*) of *dharmas* (*i.e.*, *nirvāṇa*) to the 'truth of the suppression of woe'. He relates the counteragents (*pratipakṣa*) to the conditioned *dharmas* corresponding to the 'truth of the way' to the 'suppression of woe'. Then again he makes a division by name, peculiar marks, and common marks. When his understanding of the 'sphere of desire' is complete, the practitioner applies it to the two upper spheres. This completes gnosis on the basis of what is 'heard'. Thought and meditation follow meditation consisting of the 'four aids to penetration'. These lead to the 'path of vision' (*darśanamārga*), which leads to the path of realization' (*bhāvanāmārga*), which leads to the 'path of the adepts' (literally 'of them who have nothing more to learn', *aśaikṣamārga*). That completes the planting of the 'wholesome roots'.

The next passage (from 27.34c to the end of the roll) deals with the three groups of 'wholesome roots', of which the 'four aids to penetration' are the third and last. The first group, the 'aids to merit' (*puṇyabhāgīya, shun fu fen*), 'plants the seeds for rebirth as man or god' (*chung shen jen sheng t'ien chung tzu, manuṣyadevajātibījāny avaropayati*?). The term 'man' refers specifically to a human being of great wealth and many dependents, handsome of face and form, even a universal monarch (*cakravartirāja*). The term 'god' means a god in any of the three spheres, one of wondrous efficacy, in the best instance Indra, a Mārarāja, or Brahmarāja; one of imposing might, holding sway over many.

The second group, the 'aids to deliverance' (*mokṣabhāgīya, shun chieh t'o fen*), 'plants the seeds of certain deliverance' (*chung chüeh ting chieh t'o chung tzu, niyatamokṣabījāny avaropayati*?), which means that, thanks to them, *parinirvāṇa* is a certainty.

To come back to the first group (*mokṣabhāgīya*), one can say specifically that its members are (1) of the nature of deeds of body, speech, and mind, but principally of mind; (2) situated on the ground of mind (*manas*), but not on that of the five senses; (3) attainable through effort, because they are associated with the 'sphere of desire';[49] (4) made up of what one has learned (literally 'heard', *wen, śruta*) and thought; (5) of Kāmadhātu origin, and at that only among humans elsewhere than on Uttarakuru; (6) to be found only when there is a Buddha in the world (although some say that one can plant these 'wholesome seeds' upon meeting a *pratyekabuddha*); (7) attainable by both sexes; (8) achievable by gift-giving, by moral self-discipline, or by hearing the doctrine preached by an 'adept'.[50] In the last category there must be a superior aspiration (*i yao, adhyāśaya*) as well as the desire for extinction (*hsin ch'iu nieh-p'an, nirvāṇaparyeṣaṇā*?) and a break with birth and death (*yen pei sheng ssu, saṃsāravisaṃyoga*?).

From the planting of these 'wholesome roots' until the attainment of deliverance, the shortest time-lapse is three lifetimes. One may achieve the first two sets of 'wholesome roots' and never attain the 'aids to penetration' at all, or achieve the aids without attaining certainty of deliverance. The 'aids to penetration', as do the 'aids to deliverance', have six kinds of practitioners (from '*les susceptibles de chute*' to '*les inébranlables*'). The comments following that list of six are as applicable to the 'aids to deliverance' as they are to the 'aids to penetration'.

NOTES

1. The paper on the 'four stations of mindfulness' will appear in a collection of studies dedicated to the memory of Richard Robinson, to be published by the University of Wisconsin. As to the *A-p'i-t'an hsin lun* itself, since the original does not survive there is no reconstructing with certainty either the title or the author's name. The title will be either *Abhidharmahṛdaya* or *sāra*.

As to the author's name, which appears as 'Fa-sheng', one thinks of Dharmottara, Dharmodgata, Dharmaśreṣṭha, Dharmajit, etc. The work survives in three versions, those of Saṃghadeva and Hui-yüan, of Narendrayaśas, and of Saṃghavarman and unnamed collaborators. They are Taishō, Nos. 1550, 1551, and 1552, all contained in Vol. 28. The three translations are far from uniform.

2. The translation is, of course, that of Louis de la Vallée Poussin, based primarily on Hsüan-tsang but taking careful note of Paramārtha as well as the Tibetan translation throughout. This paper, because of its Chinese orientation and also because good Tibetan texts are not easily available, will take no account of the Tibetan version. It should be added that La Vallée Poussin had no access to the Sanskrit text though he did have the use of Yaśomitra's commentary, to be mentioned below.

3. At the end of the paper there will be a summarized restatement of the contents of *Mahāvibhāṣā* 7.

4. Cf. note 3 above.

5. At the end of the paper, along with the *Mahāvibhāṣā* summary there will be seven charts, with Kyokuga's Chinese rendered into Sanskrit.

6. Cf. La Vallée Poussin vii. 30–34.

7. The Sanskrit of the *Bhāṣya* and Hsüan-tsang's version say the same things but in different ways. La Vallée Poussin, who did not have the original, is closer to Hsüan-tsang. Also, vi. 165 note e, has much lateral information on the whole question of *kṣānti*.

8. The *Vyākhyā*'s proof of this escapes me.

9. Cf. note 6. One calls attention here to the four views governing the four aspects of the fourth noble truth, *viz.*,

a. It is (1) a road (*mārga*), because one traverses it to the goal of *nirvāṇa*; (2) reasonable (*nyāya*), in the sense that it is *yogayukta*, *i.e.*, equipped with proof (*upapattiyukta*), with means or resources (*upāyayukta*); (3) acquisition, in the sense that it enables one to acquire, to obtain *nirvāṇa* correctly (*samyakpratipādanārthena*); (4) a definitive departure (*nairyāṇika*), since it enables one to go beyond in a definitive manner (*atyantaṃ prabhavati*).

b. It is (1) a road (*mārga*), in the sense that it is opposed to the wrong path (*mithyāmārga*); (2) reasonable (*nyāya*), in the sense that it is opposed to the unreasonable; (3) acquisition (*pratipad*), in the sense that it is not in contradiction with the 'city of *nirvāṇa*' (*nirvāṇapurāvirodhanārthena*); (4) a definitive departure (*nairyāṇkaia*), in the sense that it rejects and abandons the threefold *bhava*, *i.e.*, existence in the three spheres.

c. It is (1) a road (*mārga*) in the sense that it is like a straight road; (2) reasonable (*nyāya*) in the sense that it is true; (3) acquisition (*pratipad*) in the sense that it is determined or exclusive (*pratiniyata*), *i.e.*, that one arrives at the 'goal' by that 'path' and by no other; (4) a definitive departure (*nairyāṇika*) in the sense that it leads to a definitive separation from threefold existence (*bhava*).

d. It is a counteragent to the view that (1) there is no 'path'; (2) that a certain (but in fact mistaken) path is the right one; (3) that there is another path in addition to this one; (4) that the 'path' is not protection from backsliding.

10. This is rendered *samāhitāsamāhitaduḥkhasamudayanirodhamārgaḥ*, but I do not know what it means.

11. La Vallée Poussin vi. 167, note 4, professes not to understand the reason for this. For what it is worth, Yaśomitra (p. 912) says that it is not reasonable that a superior person, having acquired the fruits of a certain exercise, should then have to concern himself with the exercise itself (*na hi prāptaprayogaphalasyāryasya prayogasaṃmukhīkaraṇaṃ nyāyyam iti*).

12. In a somewhat different form, this idea is contained in the original in the passages that follow.

13. The *Āgama*—which one is not specified—is alleged to support this proposition with the expression *idha vidhā tatra niṣṭhā*, which seems to mean that here, *i.e.*, in the 'sphere of desire', there is the discernment that characterizes the first three aids, while there, *i.e.*, in the two upper spheres, is the confirmation that characterizes the 'supreme worldly *dharmas*'.

14. To be precise, the *Bhāṣya* says *deveṣv api*, while the *Vyākhyā* glosses this as *teṣv eva ca nānyatra*. It certainly seems to me that *api* and *eva* are mutually exclusive. The *Bhāṣya* says that the first three 'aids to penetration', and they alone, are available to human beings, while all four are within the reach of the gods. The *Vyākhyā* seems to be saying that the fourth is within the reach of gods alone. Both Chinese versions say "also," but La Vallée Poussin (171) merely says, "Le quatrième peut être produit par les dieux." A crucial distinction must be made here between *utpādyate* ('être produit') and *saṃmukhībhavati* ('être actualisé'), the former being attainable by human beings with regard to the first three aids, the latter by gods also (or 'only', depending on the interpretation). The *Vyākhyā* says that the 'four aids to penetration' are not achieved on Uttarakuru because of the weakness of the faculties of the inhabitants of that continent (*Uttarakauravāṇāṃ mṛdvindriyatvāt*). It concludes by saying that a member of either sex, upon attainment of any of the first three aids, can be reborn in either sex.

15. The words "passage" and "détachement" come from La Vallée Poussin, *ibid.* The latter signifies emotional detachment, indifference, even disgust; but I am not certain of the specific connotation here.

16. The word is *vairāgyalābhya*, and it seems to mean that disgust with things the way they are is not, in and of itself, sufficient motivation to launch one into something else, even something previously experienced, if one has lost the habit of it.

17. The easiest way to explicatc *praṇidhijñāna* is to treat it along with '*araṇājñāna*', as is done in La Vallée Poussin vii. 87 ff., where one reads:

36. L'*araṇā* est savior d'ordre mondain; du domaine du quatrième *dhyāna*; produit par un homme qui est un Inébranlable. Elle porte sur les passions (*raṇa*) du domaine du Kāmadhātu, futures, ayant un objet réel.

Elle est uniquement savoir d'ordre mondain, *saṃvṛtijñāna*—comme il résulte de son objet. Elle a pour point d'appui le quatrième *dhyāna*, qui est le meilleur des chemins aisés . . . Elle est produite par les *arhat*s inébranlables (*akopyadharman*, . . .) et non par les autres: car ceux-ci ne sont pas capables de supprimer radicalement . . . leurs propres passions —ils sont en effet sujets à la chute—a plus forte raison ne peuvent-ils arrêter les passions d'autrui, du Kāmadhātu, futures, "ayant un objet réel" . . . : "Puissent les passions d'autrui ne pas naître à mon sujet!" Les passions *savastuka* sont *rāga*, *dveṣa*, etc., qui sont abandonnées par la méditation . . .

Telle est l'*araṇā* . . .

Comme l'*araṇā*, le *praṇidhijñāna*, "savoir résultant de résolution," est, de sa nature, savoir d'ordre mondain; comme l'*araṇā*, il a pour point d'appui le quatrième *dhyāna*, il se produit dans la série d'un Inébranlable, il est médité par un être de destinée humaine. Mais, à la différence de l'*araṇā*, il porte sur tous les *dharma*s . . .

18. Cf. La Vallée Poussin ii. 201: "Le recueillement d'inconscience est le recueillement dans lequel l'ascète est inconscient (*asaṃjñināṃ samāpattiḥ*), ou le recueillement exempt de conscience."

19. La Vallée Poussin vi. 173, note 2: "Celui qui a obtenu la chaleur, qui en tombe, dans cet état, il ne prend pas un faux enseignement." On the basis of the word for 'false teaching', '*hsieh chiao*', and of its resemblance to the word '*hsieh chiao t'u*', appearing in the *Mahāvyutpatti* for *pāṣaṇḍika*, La Vallée Poussin cites the latter. It should be noted that the Chinese of the *Mahāvyutpatti* is far from standard. The implication is obvious, however: 'warmth' will keep one from the worst of the reincarnations, since these are due, in the final analysis, to the acceptance of false doctrines.

20. "Defilements" renders as '*huo*', whose conventional meaning is 'doubt, uncertainty', hence, 'going astray, error'. It corresponds, however, as nearly as can be determined, to *kleśa* in this context.

21. La Vallée Poussin vi.175, note 1, renders this "Les *dharma*s suprêmes entrent dans le nyāma."

22. Cf. La Vallée Poussin vi. 180: "Qu'est-ce en effet que le *samyaktva*? Le Sūtra dit que c'est Le *nirvāṇa*.—A l'endroit du *samyaktva*, le *niyama* (ou détermination absolue) c'est ce qu'on appelle *niyāma* et encore *nyāma*." *Ibid.* pp. 180 ff., note 6, there is much valuable and interesting information on the words *niyama*, *niyāma*, and *nyāma*.

23. Cf. La Vallée Poussin vi.253, note 1, commenting on Kyokuga 25.2a.

Hiuan-tsang: Le *parihāṇadharman*, rencontrant de faibles causes de chute, tombe de ce qu'il a acquis; non pas le *cetanādharman*. Le *cetanādharman*, craignant de tomber, toujours pense à mettre fin à son existence. L'*anurakṣaṇādharman* garde ce qu'il a acquis.

24. There is apparently a difference between the *Kośa* and the *Vibhāṣā* on whether the *pratyekabuddha* can change his *gotra*. There is further commentary, *ibid.*, indicating that there was virtually total disagreement among scholars on these and kindred points. A chart from Kyokuga 23.8a is reproduced at the end of this paper, with the Chinese rendered again into Sanskrit.

25. Quoted in La Vallée Poussin vi. 177, note 1.

26. For more on the *pratyekabuddha*, cf. Ōchō Enichi, *Hokke Shisō*, pp. 376-388. The study, by Fujita Kōtatsu, has appeared in English translation in the *Journal of Indian Philosophy*, Vol. 3 (1975), pp. 79-166. The *pratyekabuddha* constitutes only one part of the study, which comprises pp. 352-405 in the original Japanese.

27. The key word in the *bhāṣya* is *āniñjyapaṭusamādhitvāt*, which the *Vyākhyā* glosses as follows: *aṣṭāpakṣālamuktatvād āniñjyaḥ samādhiḥ/ ata eva paṭur uttaptatīkṣṇendriyatvād vā*. The concentration of the fourth *dhyāna* is imperturbable because it is free of eight disturbances. It is 'sharp' (*paṭu*) for the same reason, or else because of the keenness of the practitioner's faculties. The 'eight disturbances' (if that indeed is the meaning of *apakṣāla*, a word of uncertain etymology) to contemplation are (1) *vitarka* (see below), (2) *vicāra* (see below), (3) *sukha* (weal), (4) *duḥkha* (woe), (5) *saumanasya* (good disposition), (6) *daurmanasya* (poor disposition), (7) *āśvāsa* (inhalation), (8) *praśvāsa* (exhalation). On *vitarka* and *vicāra*, cf. La Vallée Poussin ii.175, note 2:

> Le *vitarka* et le *vicāra* existent, non pas simultanément, mais successivement (*paryāyeṇa*). Quelle est la différence du *vitarka* et du *vicāra*? Les anciens maîtres disent: "Qu'est-ce que le *vitarka*?—Un entretien mental (*manojalpa*) d'enquête (*paryeṣaka*), qui a pour point d'appui la volition (*cetanā*) ou la connaissance spéculative (*prajñā*) suivant qu'il ne comporte pas ou comporte déduction (*abhyūha*). C'est l'état grossier de la pensée.—Qu'est-ce que le *vicāra*?—Un entretien mental d'appréciation, de jugement (*pratyavekṣaka*), qui a pour point d'appui la volition . . . ." D'après cette théorie, le *vitarka* et le *vicāra* constituent deux complexes psychologiques presque identiques: ils diffèrent en ceci que le premier comporte 'enquête' et le second 'jugement'. Quelques-uns donnent un exemple. En présence de nombreux pots, quelqu'un les tâte pour savoir lequel est bien cuit, lequel est mou: cette enquête (*ūha*) est le *vitarka*; à la fin, cette personne arrive à une conclusion: "Il y en a tel nombre de chaque catégorie:" c'est le *vicāra*.
>
> La *Vyākhyā*, ad i. 33, cite le *Pañcaskandhaka* de Vasubandhu, très proche de l'opinion des anciens maîtres:
>
> vitarkaḥ katamaḥ/ paryeṣako manojalpaś cetanāprajñāviśeṣaḥ/

yā cittasyaudārikatā// vicāraḥ katamaḥ/ pratyavekṣako manojalpaś cetanāprajñāviśeṣaḥ/ yā cittasya sūkṣmatā//

La *Vyākhyā* ajoute: *anabhyūhāvasthāyāṃ prajñeti vyavasthāpyate/* . . .

28. I fail to understand this, unless here as in some other places the *Bhāṣya* and the *Vyākhyā* are in disagreement. La Vallée Poussin (vi.178, note 4) does not seem to solve the problem:

Lorsque la production des *nirvedhabhāgīyas* a lieu dans l'existence qui suit immédiatement la plantation des *mokṣabhāgīyas*, le chemin ne peut être produit dans la même existence que les *nirvedhabhāgīyas*. "Mais celui qui a pris des *mokṣabhāgīyas* dans une existence antérieure, peut, dans la même existence, produire les *nirvedhabhāgīyas* et le Chemin."

29. Cf. 29.273a, 11.19-21. The answer, on 1.21, is mispunctuated. The Taishō version being given above, my version is below.

Wei yu ju tz'u i. pu pi ting. wu ju tz'u i.

Wei yu ju tz'u i pu. pi ting wu ju tz'u i.

The negative particle is thus not *pu* but *fou*.

30. *Ardhaśloka* 25b says that from the 'supreme worldly *dharmas*' one proceeds to an 'acquiescence in *dharma*' (*dharmakṣānti*) that is free of outflows. That, however, is beyond the scope of the present study.

31. It might not be out of place to mention that the same passage defines *mokṣabhāgīya* by saying it is that "upon the emergence of which (the practitioner) is destined without fail for perfect extinction (*parinirvāṇa*)." It goes on to say that the 'wholesome root' belongs to anyone who experiences horripilation or tears when he hears explanations of the miseries of *saṃsāra*, of the qualities of *nirvāṇa*. The *Vyākhyā* comments on that term, *mutatis mutandis*, much the way it did on *puṇyabhāgīya*, saying that *mokṣabhāga* is to be counterposed to *saṃsārabhāga*.

32. *Hsi fang tsun che* presumably stands for something like *āryapāścātya*, but whom it represents is not clear apart from the likelihood that the person in question was a Gāndhārī.

33. Cf. *Vyākhyā* ad *Kośa* vi. 34 (Dwarikadas 940):

kathaṃ ca bhikṣavo bhikṣuh saptasthānakuśalo bhavati/ rūpaṃ yathābhūtaṃ prajānāti rūpasamudayaṃ rūpanirodhaṃ rūpanirodhagāminīṃ pratipadaṃ rūpasyāsvādam ādīnavaṃ niḥsaraṇaṃ yathābhūtaṃ prajānāti/evaṃ vedanāṃ saṃjñām saṃskārān vijñānaṃ yathābhūtam prajānāti/ vijñānasamudayaṃ vistareṇa yāvan niḥsaraṇaṃ yathābhūtaṃ prajānātīti/

The above, given in the *Vyākhyā* as the words of the Buddha in one of the Scriptures (but I have no idea which), means that some monks are adept in respect of seven things: namely, the *skandha* in question, its mode of origination, the fact that it can be suppressed, the road to such suppression, the satisfactions associated with it, the griefs, and the manner of self-extrication from it. (I fail to see the distinction between *pratipad* and *niḥsaraṇa*, unless the latter refers to the awareness of escape from the *skandha* once it has taken place.) Cf. also La Vallée Poussin vi. 202, note 1, where one reads, "On peut comparer, d'assez loin, *Saṃyutta* iii. 160–1."

34. There are several problems. First, in standard Chinese Buddhist terminology, *ālambana* and *pratyaya* are both rendered as *yüan*. To distinguish them, the former is sometimes rendered *so yüan*. In the context of the list of seventeen headings, however, *so yüan* clearly means *pratyaya*, not *ālambana*. But what is meant when it is said that the 'four noble truths' are *ūṣmagatapratyaya*? I take it to mean quite literally that the existence of woe and its causes, of the possibility of its removal and of a way to effect that removal, is the secondary cause that makes 'warmth' possible.

35. There are five 'fruits' (*pañca phalāni*), *i.e.*, five types of effect according to the *Abhidharma* doctrine of dependent origination (*pratītyasamutpāda*). *Puruṣakāraphala* (*shih yung kuo*) is, first of all, the product of *sahabhūhetu* (*chü yu yin*) and *saṃprayuktakahetu* (*hsiang ying yin*), the former being interacting causes, the latter coexisting causes. (The comparison is to the members of a caravan, who are *sahabhū* in the sense that they must cooperate, *saṃprayuktaka* in the sense that they share the same way of life.) For what it is worth, here are some additional observations, drawn from La Vallée Poussin ii. 289.

> Le fruit du *sahabhūhetu* . . . et du *saṃprayuktakahetu* . . . s'appelle *pauruṣa*, viril, c'est-à-dire: fruit du *puruṣakāra*, fruit de l'activité virile.
>
> Le *puruṣakāra*, activité virile, n'est pas distinct de l'homme même (*puruṣabhāva*), car l'acte n'est pas distinct de ce qui accomplit l'acte. Le fruit de l'activité virile (*puruṣakāraphala*) peut donc être nommé fruit viril (*pauruṣa*).
>
> Que faut-il entendre par 'activité virile'?
>
> L'activité . . . d'un *dharma* est nommée son activité virile (*puruṣakāra*), parce qu'elle est semblable à l'activité d'un homme (*puruṣa*) . . .

36. 'Outpouring' is rendered *teng liu*, the standard equivalent of *niṣyanda*. *Niṣyandaphala* is one of the five fruits. It is the product of *sabhāgahetu* and *sarvatragahetu*, both of which require explanation.

a. *sabhāgahetu* 'cause pareille'. A man is equipped with various *dharma*s, some wholesome, some unwholesome, of which the former perish while the latter thrive. Yet there survives a wholesome root, which in turn gives rise to yet another one, and thus it is that in the course of time the man will be purified. For another example, the initial embryo is the 'similar cause' of all consequent states, from the *kalala* to the *vṛddha* (ten in all). Each subsequent state is the 'similar cause' of all that follow it until one reaches the last, which is *sabhāgahetu* to none. Similarly, a *dharma* is a 'similar cause' only to one within its own sphere (desire, form, formlessness). Finally, a *darśanaheya* can be *sabhāgahetu* only to another *darśanaheya*, and so on. Also, a *dharma* can be *sabhāgahetu* only to something superior to itself, *e.g.*, *dharmajñānakṣānti* to *dharmajñāna*, *darśanamārga* to *bhāvanāmārga*, *bhāvanāmārga* to *aśaikṣamārga*, *śrutamaya* to *cintāmaya*, *cintāmaya* to *bhāvanāmaya*.

b. *sarvatragahetu*, 'cause universelle'. If a man entertains false views, then his every act, corporeal or vocal, as well as his every wish and resolution and their concrete results, has woe and ugliness as its result, given the sinful character of false views.

37. *Abhidharmakośa* 2.57a reads:

vipāko 'vyākṛto dharmaḥ sattvākhyo vyākṛtodbhavaḥ/

La Vallée Poussin's translation of the *ardhaśloka* and its *bhāṣya* (ii. 289 f.) reads:

57 a–b. La rétribution est un *dharma* non-défini, appartenant à l'être vivant, naissant tardivement d'un défini.

La rétribution (*vipāka*) est un *dharma* non-souillé-non-défini (*anivṛtāvyākṛta*).

(290) Parmi les *dharma*s non-souillés-non-définis, quelques uns appartiennent aux êtres vivants (*sattvākhya*), les autres n'appartiennent pas aux êtres vivants. Par conséquent l'auteur précise: 'appartenant aux êtres vivants', c'est-à-dire: anissant dans la série des êtres vivants.

Appartiennent aux êtres vivants des *dharma*s dits d'accroissement (*aupacayika*, venant de la nourriture, etc., . . .) et dits d'écoulement (*naiṣyandika*, provenant d'une cause qui leur est semblable, . . .). Par conséquent l'auteur précise: 'naissant tardivement de l'acte défini'.– L'acte défini est ainsi nommé parce qu'il produit rétribution; c'est l'acte mauvais (*akuśala*) et l'acte bon-impur (*kuśalasāsrava*) . . . D'un acte de cette nature naît tardivement, non pas en même temps, non pas immédiatement après, le fruit qu'on appelle 'fruit de rétribution' ou 'fruit de maturité' (*vipākaphala*). . . . le fruit de rétribution, par définition, est propre: jamais autrui ne jouit du fruit de rétribution de l'acte que j'ai accompli . . .

38. The four, in Chinese, are *shih chieh wen ssu*, which I presume to represent *dānaśīlaśruticintā*.

39. The French equivalents are taken from La Vallée Poussin vi. 253f.; the one English equivalent from Edward Conze, *Materials for a Dictionary of the Prajñāpāramitā Literature*. The *Abhidharmakośa* has *sthitākampya*, not *sthitidharman*, to be sure; but I have rendered the Chinese more literally (though possibly less correctly, and it may be *sthitākampya* here too). Also, the *Kośa* is confining its treatment to *arhat*s, while the *Mahāvibhāṣā*, as shall be seen immediately below, goes beyond.

40. I assume this means that one can move, by single steps, from the first to the sixth level elsewhere than within the *buddhagotra*. This puzzles me, since I always presumed that a Buddha has outpassed all of these steps.

41. I fail to see how this relates to Question 12, given above. I recon-

structed the original there to read *rūpadhātupratisaṃyuktāni*, here to read *kāmadhātāv evotpadyante*, but I fail to see the distinction.

42. 'Superior body' renders *sheng i shen*, which in turn may stand for *viśiṣṭāśraya*; 'superior resolve to separate oneself from the world' stands for *sheng yen li teng tso i*, which may represent something like *visaṃyogādimanasikāra*.

43. Before 'gnosis' (*jñāna*), s.c., of the 'four noble truths', can be achieved, there must be 'acquiescence' (*kṣānti*) to them, *i.e.*, unreserved willingness to accept them on faith. In the two upper spheres this is apparently unnecessary, since gnosis is direct. But see below.

44. There are four stages to the mastery of the 'four noble truths'. First is the 'acquiescence' mentioned above, then 'gnosis', *ibid.*; both have to do with the 'sphere of desire'. In that sphere the practitioner can understand the two upper spheres only by analogy (*anvaya*), but he goes through the same process, 'acquiescence', followed by 'gnosis'. As far as I am aware, however, knowledge by analogy, while bearing on the two upper spheres, is achieved in the lowest one. I wonder whether we are not dealing here with a copyist's error. For the text has just said that of the two, 'acquiescence' and 'gnosis', the former is missing in the two upper spheres. That leaves 'gnosis', which certainly appears to contradict what is being said here.

45. 'Superior base' may be rendered either *viśiṣṭāśaya* or *viśiṣṭāśraya*. The first signifies a dwelling-place, the second a body. Both are 'superior' in the 'sphere of form', while the second is presumably lacking in the 'sphere of formlessness'. The 'sensation of woe' (*k'u shou*, *duḥkhavedanā*) is, of course, missing from both spheres.

46. This represents *te*, which presumably stands for some form of '*prāpnoti*'.

47. Here the underlying word must be *bhāvayati*, but I am not certain, in this context, of the precise difference between it and *prāpnoti*.

48. This presupposes a knowledge of *dharma* theory, specifically that of the Sarvāstivāda. Briefly, there are seventy-five *dharma*s, seventy-two 'conditioned' or 'constituted' (*saṃskṛta*, *yu wei*), three 'unconditioned' or 'unconstituted' (*asaṃskṛta*, *wu wei*). The seventy-two are grouped into five 'masses' (*skandha*, *yin*, *yün*), of which only one, the first, is 'material' (*rūpa*, *se*). Another arrangement is in terms of the 'faculties' (*indriya*, *ken*), of which there are six, five of them material and one, the mind, immaterial. These faculties have, respectively, corresponding objects and senses whereby they apprehend the objects. (The 'senses' are the five senses and the act of mental cognition.)

49. I do not really understand the reasons for (2) and (3).

50. The important thing here, as is indicated in comment of some length, is the intention. It is rendered above as 'aspiration' and stands for *yi yao*, (whose presumed original is *adhyāśaya*.) For example, a mere handful of alms may be conducive to the *mokṣabhāgīyāni kuśalamūlāni*, while a feast for an entire

community of monks, if its aim is fame and wealth, will not. As to self-discipline (*śīla*), scrupulous observance of the entire *prātimokṣa* may not lead to the *mokṣabhāgīyāni kuśalamūlāni*, while one who can observe the *aṣṭāṅgasamanvāgatopavāsa* (to be explained below) may attain it. Finally, as to *śruti*, a person might achieve the *mokṣabhāgīyāni kuśalamūlāni* by reciting a single *gāthā*, while one versed in the whole *Tripiṭaka* might not.

The *aṣṭāṅgasamanvāgatopavāsa* consists of abstention for one day and one night from (1) the taking of animate life (*prāṇātipāta*), (2) the taking of anything not freely given by the possessor (*adattādāna*), (3) sexual activity (*abrahmacaryā*), (4) lying (*mṛṣāvāda*), (5) consumption of alcohol (*madyapāna*), (6) lying on high or wide beds (*uccaśayanamahāśayana*), (7) the use of garlands, perfumes, ointments, or rouge (*gandhamālyavilepanavarṇadhāraṇa*), or participation, even as a spectator or listener, in song or dance (*nṛtyagīta*), and (8) eating more than the one authorized meal of the day (*vikālabhojanā*), the said meal to be consumed between dawn and noon.

CHINESE AND JAPANESE CHARACTERS IN TEXT AND NOTES (MATHEWS' DICTIONARY NUMBERS)

A-p'i-t'an hsin lun	1-5158-6068-2735-4253
an hsiang	26-2562
an li	26-3921
chieh	632
chien tao	860-6136
ch'ih chieh	1035-627
chu fa	1337-1762
chung chüeh ting chieh t'o chung tzu	1511-1697-6393-626-6468-1511-6939
chung sheng jen sheng t'ien chung tzu	1511-5738-3097-5738-6361-1511-6939
chü yu yin	1557-7533-7407
erh yüan	1751-7741
Fa-sheng	1762-5754
Fujita Kōtatsu	6182-6362-2377-5956
Hokke shisō	1762-2217-5580-2564
Hsi fang tsun che	2460-1802-6884-263
hsiang ying yin	2562-7477-7407
hsieh chiao	2625-719
hsieh chiao t'u	2625-719-6536

hsin	2735
hsin ch'iu nieh-p'an	2727-1217-4694-4903
hsing hsiang	2754-2562
hsiu hui	2794-2333
hsiu kuan hsing che	2794-3575-2754-263
Hsüan-tsang	2881-6700
hsün teng	2744-6178
hu fa	2190-1762
hui	2333
Hui-yüan	2333-7734
huo	2403
i	2990
i ch'ü	2960-1617
i pen pi chien ti	2932-5025-5109-860-6208
i shu	3009-5895
i tso	3016-6778
i tzu hsiang kung hsiang	2932-6960-2562-3701-2562
i yao	2960-7501
k'an ta fa	3254-5956-1762
Kandō Abidatsumakusharon	3575-6137-1-5158-5956-4543-1557-5699-4253
ken	3328
k'u shou	3493-5840
kung hsiang	3701-2562
kuo	3732
ming	4524
nuan chia hsing che	4763-580-2754-263
Ōchō Enichi	2106-251-2333-3124
pu tung fa	5379-6611-1762
Saeki Kyokuga	6775-4977-2855-7222
se	5445
shan ken	5657-3328
sheng i shen	5754-3009-5718
sheng li	5754-3867
sheng yen li teng tso i	5754-7387-3902-6178-6780-2960
shih chieh wen ssu	5768-632-7142-5580

shih yung kuo	5776-7567-3732
shun	5935
shun chieh t'o fen	5935-626-6468-1851
shun fu fen	5935-1978-1851
so yüan	5465-7741
ssu chüeh ting fen	5598-1697-6393-1851
ssu chüeh tse fen	5598-1697-276-1851
ssu fa	5580-1762
ssu nien chu	5598-4716-1337
ssu nien ch'u	5598-4716-1407
Taishō	5943-351
te	6161
teng liu	6178-4080
ting	6393
tsai ting	6657-6393
tso kung yung	6780-3698-7567
t'ui	6568
t'ui fa	6568-1762
tzu hsiang	6960-2562
wei yu ju tz'u i pu pi ting wu ju tz'u i	7059-7533-3137-6972-3002-5379-5109-6393-7180-3137-6972-3002
wen	7142
wen ssu	7142-5580
wu wei	7180-7059
yen pei sheng ssu	7387-4989-5738-5589
yin (*hetu*)	7407
yin (*skandha*)	7444
yu pen chung chien ti	7513-5025-1504-860-6208
yu wei	7533-7059
yüan	7741
yün	7770

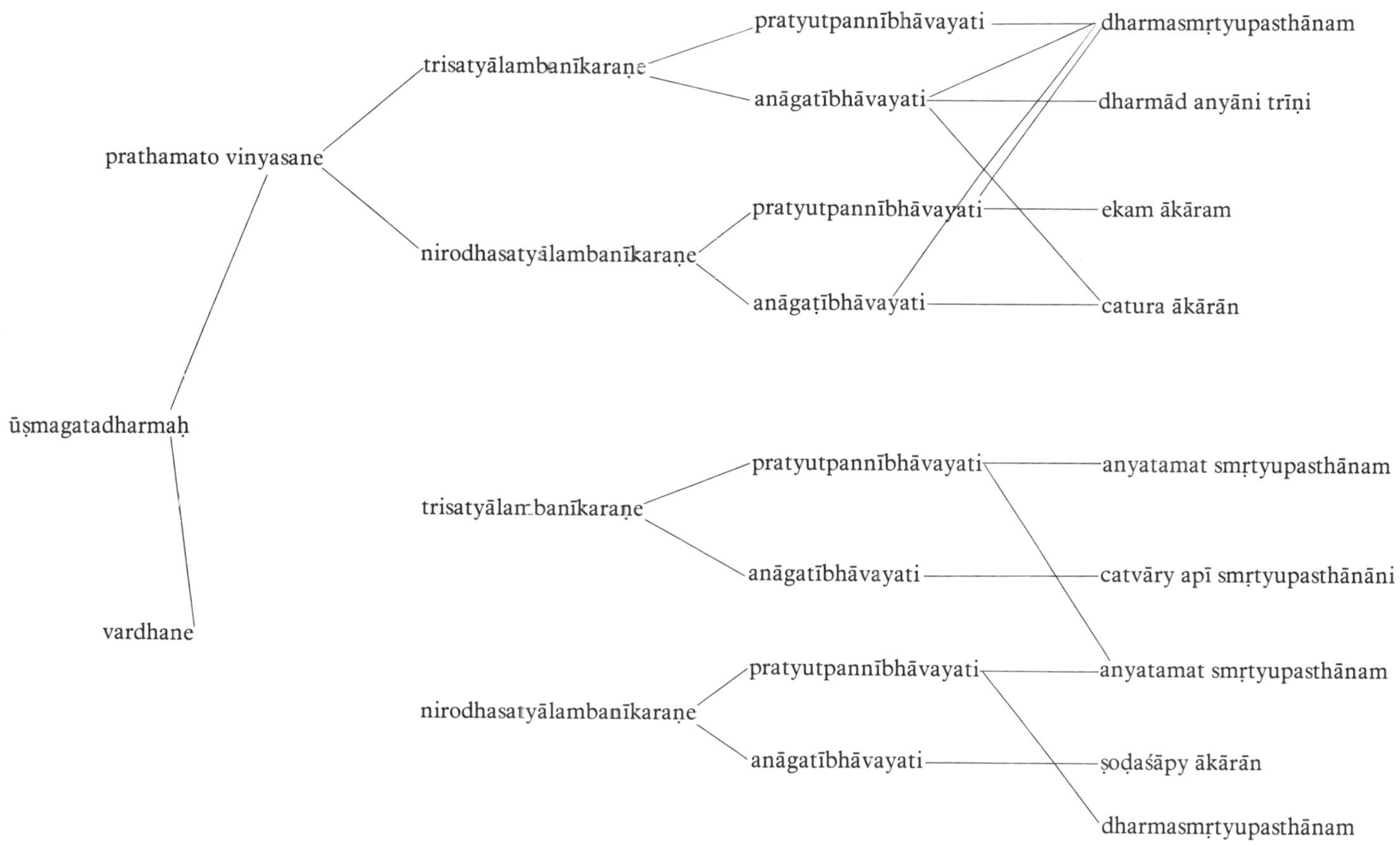
ūṣmagatadharmaḥ
prathamato vinyasane
trisatyālambanīkaraṇe
pratyutpannībhāvayati
dharmasmṛtyupasthānam
anāgatībhāvayati
dharmād anyāni trīṇi
nirodhasatyālambanīkaraṇe
pratyutpannībhāvayati
ekam ākāram
anāgaṭībhāvayati
catura ākārān
vardhane
trisatyālambanīkaraṇe
pratyutpannībhāvayati
anyatamat smṛtyupasthānam
anāgatībhāvayati
catvāry apī smṛtyupasthānāni
nirodhasatyālambanīkaraṇe
pratyutpannībhāvayati
anyatamat smṛtyupasthānam
anāgatībhāvayati
ṣoḍaśāpy ākārān
dharmasmṛtyupasthānam

- mūrdhadharmaḥ
  - prathamato vinyasane — catuḥsatyālambanīkaraṇe
    - pratyutpannībhāvayati
      - dharmasmṛtyupasthānam
      - anyatamam ākāram
    - anāgatībhāvayati
      - catvāry api smṛtyupasthānāni
      - ṣoḍaśāpy ākārān
  - vardhane
    - trisatyālambanīkaraṇe
      - pratyutpannībhāvayati
        - anyatamat smṛtyupasthānam
        - anyatamam ākāram
      - anāgatībhāvayati
        - catvāry api smṛtyupasthānāni
        - ṣoḍaśāpy ākārān
    - nirodhasatyālambanīkaraṇe
      - pratyutpannībhāvayati
        - dharmasmṛtyupasthānam
        - anyatamam ākāram
      - anāgatībhāvayati
        - catvāry api smṛtyupasthānāni
        - ṣoḍaśāpy ākārān

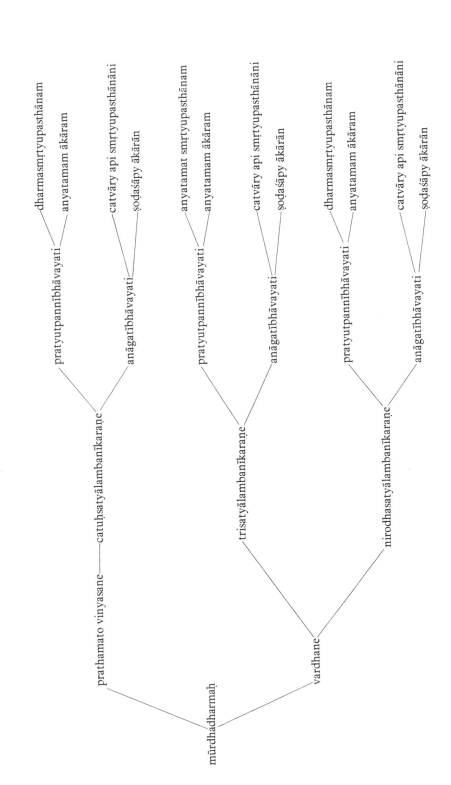

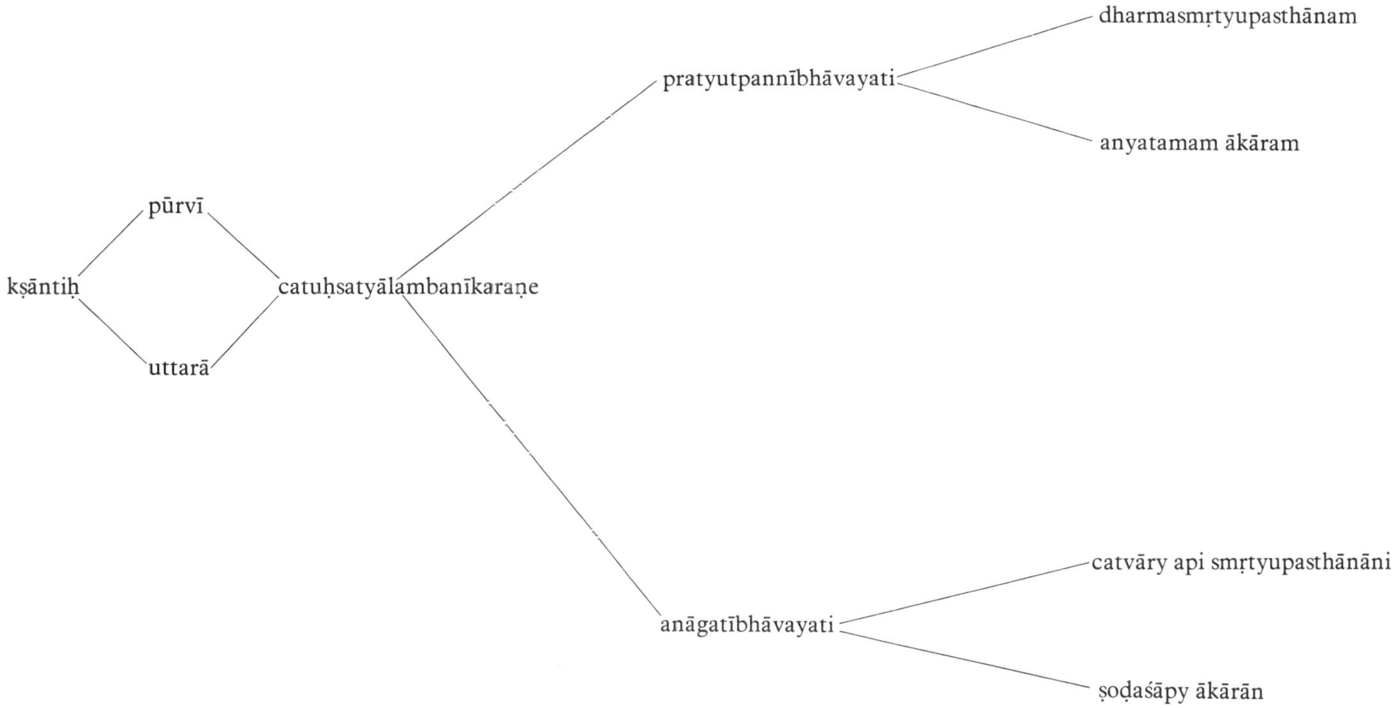
kṣāntiḥ
pūrvī
uttarā
catuḥsatyālambanīkaraṇe
pratyutpannībhāvayati
dharmasmṛtyupasthānam
anyatamam ākāram
anāgatībhāvayati
catvāry api smṛtyupasthānāni
ṣoḍaśāpy ākārān

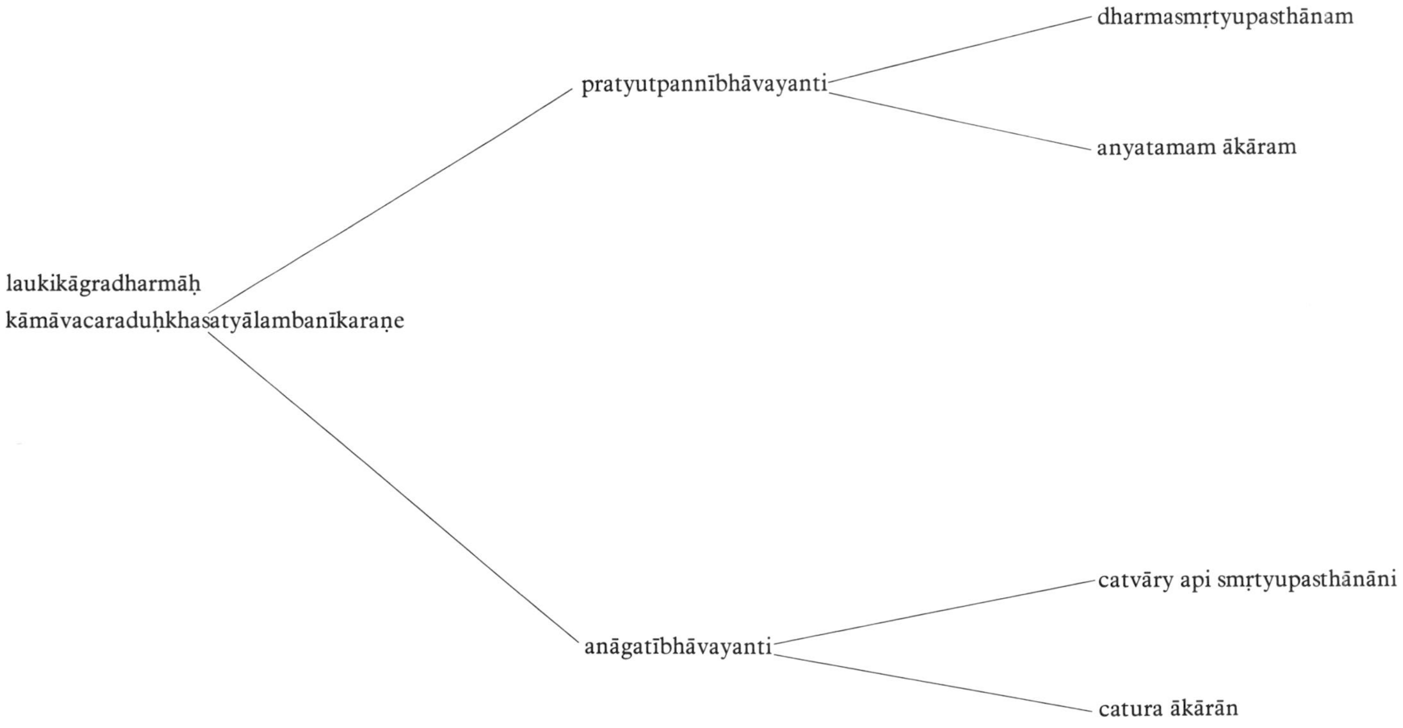
laukikāgradharmāḥ
kāmāvacaraduḥkhasatyālambanīkaraṇe
pratyutpannībhāvayanti
dharmasmṛtyupasthānam
anyatamam ākāram
anāgatībhāvayanti
catvāry api smṛtyupasthānāni
catura ākārān

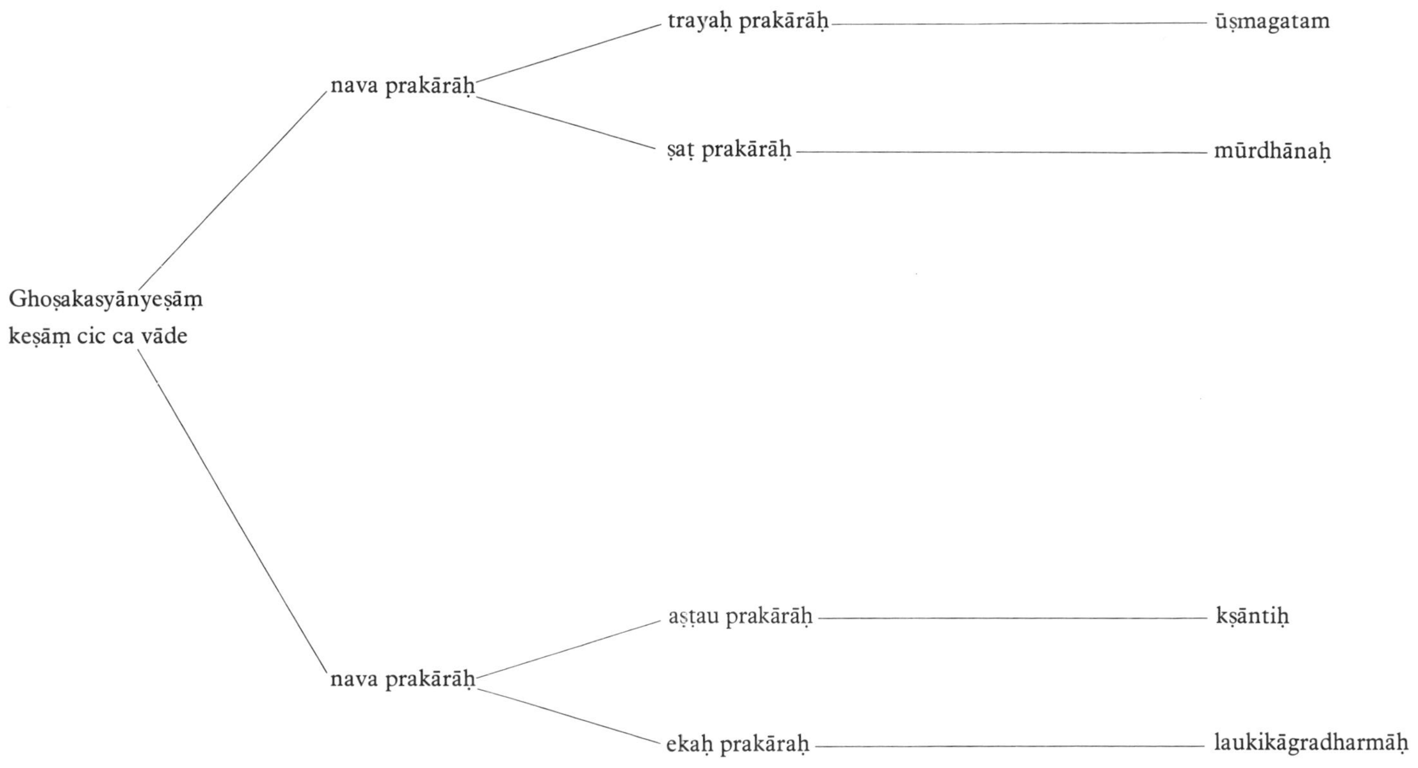
Ghoṣakasyānyeṣāṃ keṣāṃ cic ca vāde
nava prakārāḥ
trayaḥ prakārāḥ
ūṣmagatam
ṣaṭ prakārāḥ
mūrdhānaḥ
nava prakārāḥ
aṣṭau prakārāḥ
kṣāntiḥ
ekaḥ prakāraḥ
laukikāgradharmāḥ

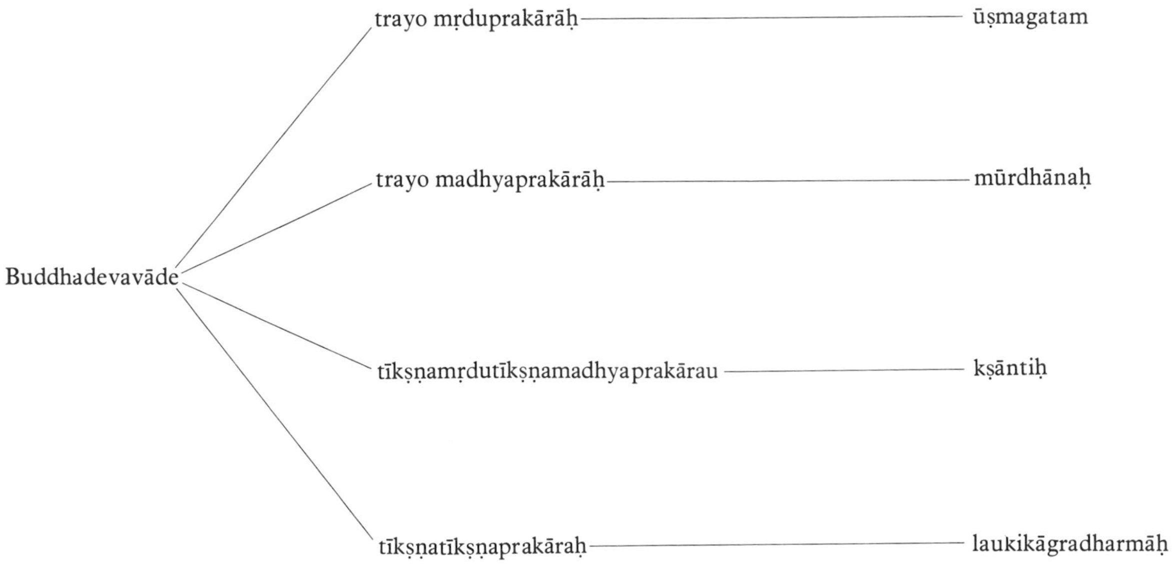
Buddhadevavāde
trayo mṛduprakārāḥ
ūṣmagatam
trayo madhyaprakārāḥ
mūrdhānaḥ
tīkṣṇamṛdutīkṣṇamadhyaprakārau
kṣāntiḥ
tīkṣṇatīkṣṇaprakāraḥ
laukikāgradharmāḥ

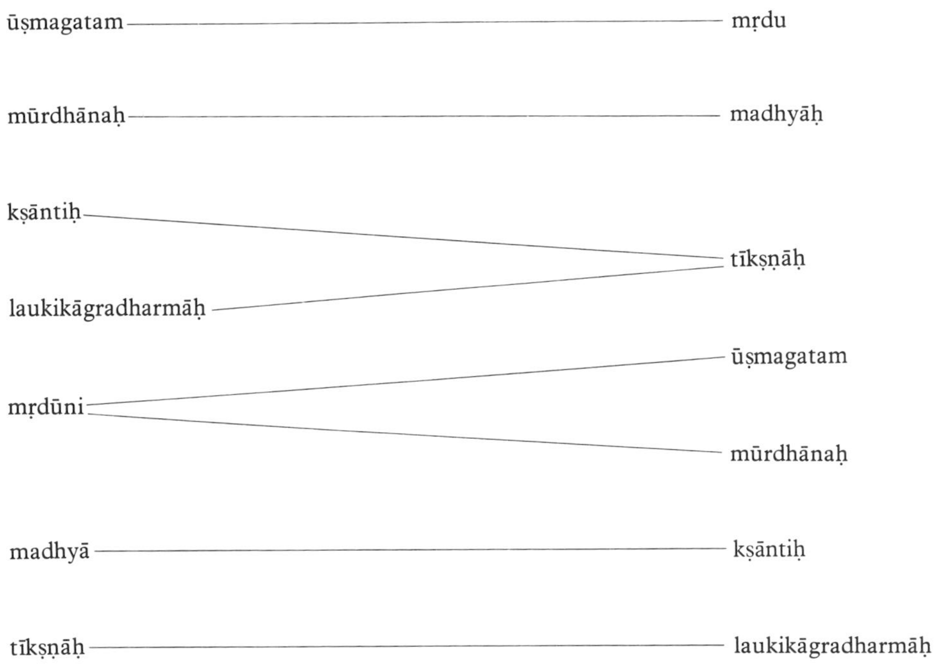

ūṣmagatam
mṛdu
mūrdhānaḥ
madhyāḥ
kṣāntiḥ
tīkṣṇāḥ
laukikāgradharmāḥ
ūṣmagatam
mṛdūni
mūrdhānaḥ
madhyā
kṣāntiḥ
tīkṣṇāḥ
laukikāgradharmāḥ

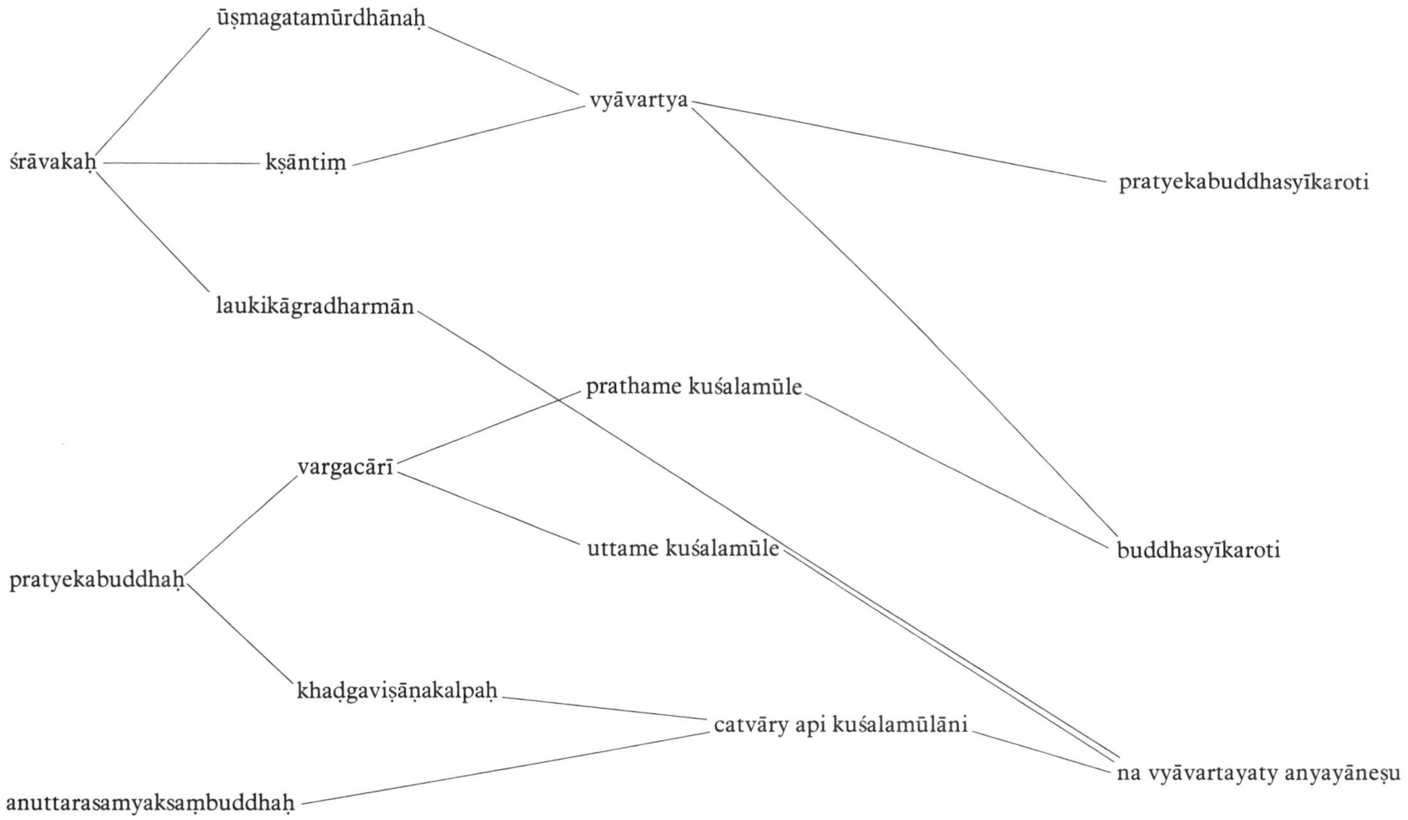
ūṣmagatamūrdhānaḥ
vyāvartya
śrāvakaḥ
kṣāntiṃ
pratyekabuddhasyīkaroti
laukikāgradharmān
prathame kuśalamūle
vargacārī
uttame kuśalamūle
buddhasyīkaroti
pratyekabuddhaḥ
khaḍgaviṣāṇakalpaḥ
catvāry api kuśalamūlāni
na vyāvartayaty anyayāneṣu
anuttarasamyaksaṃbuddhaḥ

On Chos-grub's Translation of the *Chieh-shên-mi-ching-shu*

Shōju Inaba

HSÜAN-TSANG, (600–664 A.D.) translated the *Saṁdhi-nirmocana-sūtra* into Chinese. One of his disciples, Yüan-ts'e (613–696 A.D.), from Hsin-lo in Korea, wrote a commentary on the translation, the *Chieh-shen-mi-ching-shu*. It is included in the *Manji Dai-nippon zoku-zō-kyō* (*ZZ*. 134–4 . . . 35–1). Another of Hsüan-tsang's disciples, K'uei-chi of Tz'u-en Monastery (632–682 A.D.), and his school were regarded as the orthodox line of the Fa-hsiang teaching, which once flourished and is even now much studied in China and Japan. The School of Yüan'ts'e of Hsi-ming Monastery was considered unorthodox and has now died out. Consequently Yüan-ts'e's commentary has not been widely read. The original text had ten volumes, of which the beginning of the eighth volume and the entire tenth volume are not extant.

In the Tibetan Tripiṭaka, however, Chos-grub's Tibetan translation of this commentary exists in its entirety (Ōtani Catalogue No. 5517; Tōhoku Catalogue No. 4016).

I

Our first questions deal with the circumstances under which the commentary came to be translated into Tibetan and included in the Tibetan Tripiṭaka.

Among the materials discovered in Tun-huang are the writings by T'an-k'uang and Fa-ch'êng. The former, probably born in Ho-hsi, came from Ch'ang-an where he studied at the Hsi-ming Monastery. He propagated Yüan-ts'ê's teachings in the districts surrounding Tun-huang till his death about 788 A.D.[1] In these districts T'an-k'uang's thought and writings seemed to have been studied even after his death. K'uei-chi's teachings, however, do not seem to have been handed down there.

Fa-ch'eng is rightly thought to be the Chos-grub mentioned in the Tibetan Tripiṭaka as a *lo-tsā-ba*, a translator.

When and where did Fa-ch'eng (Chos-grub) translate this commentary? His translations are many, but almost all of them were made when he lived in Hsiu-to Monastery in Kan-chou Province. The year-periods *jen-hsu* (842 A.D.) and *ping-yin* (846 A.D.) are found inscribed in the works he translated at this monastery. 'Hsiu-to Monastery', which means 'Sūtra Monastery', seems to have been a center for sūtra translations. From this we may surmise that during the same general period Fa-ch'eng (Chos-grub) undertook the translation of this commentary at this monastery.[2]

In the colophon of the Tibetan translation of the commentary, we find the following description:

> *Dpal lha-bstan-po'i bka'-lung-gis / shu-chen-gyi lo-tsā-ba dge-slong 'gos chos-grub-kyis rgya'i dpe-las bsgyur cing shus-te gtan-la phab-pa / /*
>
> (At Śrīdevarāja's command Shu-chen-gyi *lo-tsā-ba* (translator) bhikṣu 'gros Chos-grub translated, revised, and published this.)

Since at this time Kan-chou was governed by Tibet, the name Śrīdevarāja probably indicates the Tibetan King Khri-srong-lde-brtsan, Ral-pa-can (who reigned 815-841 A.D.), a warm supporter of Buddhism. It could not refer to the succeeding King Glang Darma (who reigned 841-846 A.D.), for he engaged in the suppression of Buddhism. King Ral-pa-can appointed Chos-grub as Tibetan Translator of Buddhist Texts (Ta-fan-kuo ta-te san-ts'ang fa-shih) and had him translate in the Hsui-to Monastery. Probably Chos-grub was ordered to translate from the Chinese texts extant only in Chinese translation. T'an-k'uang, as we have said, was an introducer of Yüan-ts'e's teachings and may well have brought this commentary to

Kan-chou. Whether he did or not, we may assume that it was being read there. It is thus natural that Chos-grub, ordered to translate the Chinese texts into Tibetan by King Ral-pa-chen, chose and translated this commentary by a Chinese author, and further that it came to be included in the Tibetan Tripiṭaka in the manner of his translation.

II

This commentary, as in *ZZ*, is thought to have consisted originally of ten volumes. In the *Chin-ling-k'o-ching-ch'u* edition (1922) the nine extant volumes are divided into thirty-four, and in the Tibetan translation the full ten-volume edition is divided into seventy-five *bam-po* (chapters). However, there is no relationship between the two.

Since only the Tibetan translation exists in its entirety, what is required is to restore the full text into Chinese by supplying the missing portions in Chinese equivalents as close as possible to those found in Yüan-ts'e's original text.

Initially I extracted a number of words from the existing texts and put them on cards with their Tibetan equivalents. Buddhist idiomatic terms in the original Chinese commentary were rendered into Tibetan equivalents used in the Tibetan texts, which were translated from Sanskrit. But further examination showed that Chos-grub translated terms which were particular to the Chinese texts, e.g.:

> *hui-shih* into *go-shing bshad-pa*
> *wu-chieh-che* into *go-shing rtogs-pa*

and in the case of proper nouns

> *Chen-ti san-ts'ang* into *slob-dpon yang-dag bden pa*
> (this should have read Don-dam-pa, for the Sanskrit name is Paramārtha)
>
> *Sheng-lun* into *mchog-tu smra-ba*
> (this should have read *Bye-brag-pa*, for the Sanskrit name is Vāiśeṣika)
>
> *P'u-t'i-liu-chih* into *Bo-de-le'u-ci*
> (this may be a transliteration from the Chinese)

As can be seen from the above examples, Chos-grub translated these terms and proper nouns literally from the Chinese. The Tibetan translations of Buddhist texts from the Sanskrit and the Chinese are originally very literal, so literal that we sometimes come upon strange words which do not match the Sanskrit terms. But this literal translation makes it possible to ascertain the original Sanskrit from a Tibetan translation. It is also possible to reconstruct the original Chinese text from Chos-grub's translation. There are, however, difficulties. Chinese has a rich vocabulary with many synonyms. For example, the Chinese words *jih*, *yün*, *yen*, and *wei* are used very often, and it is not possible to discover which was used in any given case. We cannot get a text exactly identical to Yüan-ts'e's original. We are, however, fortunate that Yüan'ts'e quoted frequently from the sūtras and śāstras, quotations which are found in the Chinese Tripiṭaka, so that I think it possible to reconstruct from Chos-grub's translation a very close approximation of the original.

Two points should be given attention. The first is that Chos-grub translated the Chinese text of the *Chieh-shen-mi ching* very literally (Hsüan-tsang's translation) into Tibetan, but we can still find some portions in which he instead followed the Tibetan text translated from the Sanskrit (Ōtani No. 774; Tōhoku No. 106). Moreover, his Tibetan translation of Yüan-ts'e's quotations from the *Yü-ch'ieh-shi-ti-lun* is very similar to the Tibetan texts translated from Sanskrit (Ōtani Nos. 5536–5543; Tōhoku Nos. 4035–4042); Chos-grub's words and sentence-order are very close to those of the latter. This seems to be related to the fact that Chos-grub delivered many lectures on the *Yü-ch'ieh-lun* in Tun-huang. In his translation, he followed the verses in the Tibetan translation from Sanskrit (Ōtani No. 5556; Tōhoku No. 4055), passing over Hsüan-tsang's Chinese translation of the *Wei-shih-san-shih-sung* in the *Ch'eng-wei-shih-lun*, which is often quoted by Yüan-ts'e. Nevertheless, the translation of the quotations from the sūtras and śāstras are rendered into Tibetan from the Chinese literally, without any reference to the Tibetan text originating from the Sanskrit. We must therefore be attentive to the fact that Chos-grub's translations are not always literal.

The second point to make note of is that Chos-grub's interpretations of the original Chinese text of the commentary are faulty in a few places. It may be speculated that Chos-grub sometimes misinterpreted the significance of the original text or misjudged the ending of a quotation.[3] We must pay close attention to this when we restore the original text.

With these two points in mind, I used the Tibetan translation of the parts which were lost and endeavored to restore Yüan-ts'e's commentary as closely as possible in accordance with Yüan-ts'e's Chinese. This work was completed and made public in 1971.[4]

III

When one compares the existing Chinese text with the Tibetan translation, one can observe the following:

I. Parts of the Chinese text are not found in the Tibetan translation.
   1. The Tibetan text sometimes has a laucuna because the Chinese text is too complicated. Yüan-ts'e quoted very often from *sūtra*s and *śāstra*s, but Chos-grub did not render the quotations into Tibetan when they were too long. When he left something out he did so sometimes without noting it and sometimes with the phrase *mangs-kyi dogs-nas 'dir ma brjod-do* ("omitted because too complicated").
   2. There is omission of parts which give philological interpretations and comparisons with other Chinese translations. Chos-grub omitted explanations of Sanskrit and Chinese words because they would be unnecessary in the Tibetan.
   3. There is omission of volume numbers of Chinese *sūtra*s quoted in the commentary. For Tibetans, volume numbers of the Chinese Tripiṭaka are unnecessary.
   4. There is omission of unnecessary parenthetical notes.

These omissions may be found in the missing portions of the text. We cannot restore omissions belonging to 1, 2, and 4 above. It is, however, possible to restore those in 3. I supplied the volume numbers of the Chinese Tripiṭaka where they could be ascertained.

II. Parts of the Tibetan translation are not found in the Chinese text.
   1. The missing portions comprise part of the beginning of the eighth volume and the entire tenth volume.
   2. There are great differences between the explanation of

the corresponding Tibetan translation (Ōtani No. 5517, 39.24b, 1.1 through 40a, 1.3) and that of the sentence *So-ch'üan-tsung . . . . . hsien-so-i-wei* in the first volume of the Chinese text (*Chin-ling-k'o-ching-ch'u* edition 24a through 28a). The explanation in the Chinese text is short, while there is a long one in the Tibetan translation.

3. Descriptions found only in the Tibetan translation are few.

There is a question concerning II.1 above. Is the long description, found only in the Tibetan translation, really the work of Yüan-ts'e?

I have published a restored version of this part of the Tibetan translation, which includes a comparison of the existing Chinese text and supplementary notes.[5]

Only the Tibetan translation has a detailed explanation of the '84,000 Teachings' (*pa-wan-szu-ch'ien fa-men*). Yüan-ts'e wrote about this in *Jen-wang-ching-shu* (T. No. 1708, 33:384a) stating:

> Yen pa-wan-szu-ch'ien che . . . kuang ju *Shen-mi-chi*

If the *Shen-mi-chi* in this description refers to this commentary, we must understand that it denotes the description found only in the Tibetan translation. Therefore, we may assume that the long explanation in the Tibetan translation is what Yüan-ts'e wrote. There are thus some indications that the Tibetan translation is better than the Chinese text.

The sentence in the first volume found only in the Tibetan translation is authentic. The sentence in the existing Chinese text, however, seems to be only fragmentary when compared with the Tibetan, perhaps because the text in this part of the first volume represents a later editor's attempt to restore a corrupt text. If so, it is possible that the first volume, in reality, is not complete and that some parts were dropped in the transmission.

IV

What influence did Chos-grub's Tibetan translation exert on Tibetan Buddhism? Tsong-kha-pa (1357–1419 A.D.), the great Tibetan reformer, in his work *Yid dang kun-gzhi'i dka'-ba'i gnas rgya-cher 'grel-pa legs par bshad-pa'i rgya-mtsho* (*The Complete Works of Tsong-kha-pa*, Ōtani Nos. 6149, 10124; Tōhoku, No. 5414) gives an explanation of the theory of the nine kinds of consciousness, quoted from Yüan-ts'e's commentary, which states that according to Paramārtha's theory there are nine kinds of consciousness (*amala-vijñāna* being the ninth). Yüan-ts'e refuted this theory. Tsong-kha-pa did also, but his refutation was different than Yüan-ts'e's. It can therefore be said that when Tsong-kha-pa quotes from Yüan-ts'e's commentary he is very critical of it.[6]

In *Tsong-kha-pa's Complete Works* we find the *Drang-ba dang nges-pa'i don rnam-par phye'ba'i bstan-bcos legs-bshad snying-po shes-bya-ba* (Ōtani Nos. 6142, 10103; Tōhoku, No. 6396; Tōkyo Nos. 41, 42). In this work Tsong-kha-pa takes up the theory of the 'three periods of the Buddha's teaching', criticizes the theory of the *tri-svabhāva* ('the theory of the three natures'), and concludes with a reference to the viewpoint of the Mādhyamika. The theories of the 'three periods of the Buddha's teaching' and the 'three natures' are expounded in the *Saṃdhinirmocana-sūtra*. Tsong-kha-pa's discussion on these theories seems to follow Yüan-ts'e's commentary. Although he refers to this commentary only as a reference book, the fact that he read it is itself very interesting.

After Tsong-kha-pa's death several books appeared which seem to be based on or are similar to his two books mentioned above. They appear to be related, even if indirectly, to Yüan-ts'e's commentary.

It is worth remembering that the teachings of Yüan-ts'e, which did not flourish in China or in Japan, enjoyed great success when transmitted to Tibet. Chos-grub's Tibetan translation played a great role in this.

NOTES

1. Daishun Ueyama, "T'an-k'uang and Buddhist Studies at Tunhuang" in *The Tōhō Gakuhō, Journal of Oriental Studies*, Kyoto, Number 35, 1964.
2. Daishun Ueyama, "A Study of the Life and Works of Fa-ch'eng ('go Chos-grub), a Translator of the Buddhist Texts at Tunhuang under Tibetan Rule, Part I" in *The Tōhō Gakuhō*, Kyoto, Number 38, pp. 153–155, 1967.
3. Shōju Inaba, "Yüan-ts'e of Hsi-ming Monastery and His School, in Shunjō Nogami, *Ancient Copies of Buddhist Scriptures Discovered in the Tun-huang Caves, Vol. 2*, Ōtani University, Kyōto, p. 116, 1972.

4. Shōju Inaba, "Restoration of Yüan-ts'e's *Chieh-shen-mi-ching-shu* through its Tibetan Counterpart—an attempt at Retranslating Its Lost Parts in Tibetan Translation Back into Chinese," in *The Annual Report of Research of Ōtani University*, No. 24, 1971.

5. Shōju Inaba, *A Study of the Lost Parts in Yüan-ts'e's Chieh-shen mi-ching-shu*, Mimeograph, Kyōto, pp. 1-14 and pp. 79-83, 1949. This text is scheduled for reissue with the author's corrections.

6. Gadjin Nagao, "Idealistic School of Buddhism (*vijñāna-vāda*) Preserved in Tibet" in *Journal of Indian and Buddhist Studies*, Vol. 2, No. 1, Tokyo, 1953.

I sincerely thank Mr. Hiromichi Ichihashi, M.A., for his kind assistance in translating this paper into English.

CHINESE AND JAPANESE CHARACTERS (MATHEWS' DICTIONARY NUMBERS)

Ch'ang-an	213-26
Chen-ti san-ts'ang	297-6208-5415-6718
Ch'eng-wei-shih-lun	379-7064-5825-4253
Chieh-shen-mi-ching(*-shu*)	626-5719-4464-1123-(-5861)
Chin-ling-k'o-ching-ch'u	1057-4067-3322-1123-1407
Fa-ch'eng	1762-379
Ho-hsi	2111-2460
Hsi-ming	2460-4534
hsien-so-i-wei	2692-5465-2990-7059
Hsin-lo	2737-4099
Hsiu-to	2794-6416
Hsüan-tsang	2881-6700
hui-shih	2345-5824
jen-hsü	3100-2861
Jen-wang-ching-shu	3099-7037-1123-5861
jih	3124
Kan-chou	3223-1289
kuang ju *Shen-mi-chi*	3590-3157-5719-4464-431
K'uei-chi	3648-399
Manji Dai-nippon zoku-zō-kyō	7032-5943-3124-5025-2865-6718-1123

pa-wan-szu-ch'ien fa-men	4845-7030-5598-906-1762-4418
ping-yin	5284-7426
P'u-t'i-liu-chih	5387-6233-4083-937
Sheng-lun	5754-4253
So-ch'üan-tsung	5465-1672-6896
Ta-fan-kuo ta-te san-ts'ang fa-shih	5943-1798-3738-3124-6162-5415-6718-1762-5760
T'an-k'uang	6068-3606
Tun-huang	6571-2290
Tz'u-en	6965-1743
wei	7079
Wei-shih-san-shih-sung	7064-5825-5415-5807-5559
wu-chieh-che	7189-626-236
yen	7334
Yen pa-wan szu-ch'ien che	7334-4845-7030-5598-906-263
Yü-ch'ieh-lun	7636-581-4253
Yü-ch'ieh-shih-ti-lun	7636-581-5760-6198-4253
Yüan-ts'e	7722-6759
yün	7745

Realism of the Sarvāstivāda School

Yuichi Kajiyama

'REALISM' AND THE THEORY OF CATEGORIES form the two fundamental characteristics of the philosophy of the Sarvāstivāda School. It does not recognize the existence of substance and defines the ultimate reality (*dharma*) as an elementary force-factor with a particular own-being and operation. This does not prevent us from calling the Sarvāstivādin a realist. Sarvāstivāda philosophy is realism in the sense that it admits the existence of external realities separate from and independent of our cognition and ideas.

However, the realism of the Sarvāstivāda philosophy is closely connected with its theory of categories and *dharmas*; in other words, the former is a corollary of the latter. The Buddhist refutation of the existence of *ātman* is made by analyzing the personality in five groups of component elements (*pañca-skandha*), *viz.* body (*rūpa*), sensations (*vedanā*), representations (*saṃjñā*), volitions (*saṃskāra*), and consciousness or understanding (*vijñāna*), and by declaring that only these components are real and that *ātman* or 'self' is merely a name for a conceptual whole which does not exist as a separate reality. This breakdown of the whole into its constituent elements forms the spirit of the Sarvāstivāda theory of categories.

The theories of twelve departments (*dvādaśa-āyatana*), eighteen domains (*aṣṭādaśa-dhātu*), and five classes with seventy-five *dharmas* can be interpreted as analyses of human cognition. Let us consider the theory of eighteen domains as a typical example. Cognition is classified into six kinds: visual, auditory, olfactory, gustatory, tactile, and mental. Each cognition is analyzed again in terms of its three component elements: the instrument, the object, and consciousness. Thus the number of the component elements of cognition amounts to eighteen altogether. These eighteen elements are real, but cognition as a whole is not.

When we are perceiving an external object, say a book, or when we are thinking of an idea, we are usually not conscious of the division of that cognition into the three elements. The world of cognition appears at first as an inseparable whole, and it is only through our logical reflection that it is divided into the three. This is the view of the Sautrāntikas. The Sarvāstivāda philosopher, however, does not believe in the reality of the whole. What is real to him is only the three component parts, i.e., the instrument of cognition, the object, and consciousness. In the case of visual perception, for example, the eyes, the color, and consciousness or understanding of what is seen are realities but visual perception as a whole is not. In the case of cognition of an idea the mind as instrument, the idea as object, and consciousness as subject are admitted as real, but not the cognition as a whole. In this case we have to note that the mind as an organ is actually the mind at the preceding moment (*manas*) and that consciousness is the mind at the present moment (*vijñāna*).

What is the fundamental principle underlying the theory that component elements are real while a whole is not? Evidently the denial of a whole has the same purpose as the denial of *ātman*. But this is merely a teleological explanation. What is the epistemological and ontological principle? In order to understand this, we will examine a particular theory of the Sarvāstivāda School, the theory that color-form is perceived by the eyes and not by consciousness.

The Sarvāstivādins as well as the Naiyāyikas think that an external object is perceived by sense-organs. The Sautrāntika philosophers, beginning with Dharmakīrti, vehemently criticize this theory, saying that cognition is a determining operation belonging to knowledge and therefore cannot be ascribed to a sense-organ which is by nature physical and does not have the attribute of consciousness.[1]

The same problem as to whether it is the eye or consciousness which perceives an object has been discussed by philosophers after Dharmakīrti, but this had already been questioned at the time of Vasubandhu. Over the years the Sarvāstivādins have adhered to their opinion in spite of criticism by other schools.

In the *Abhidharmakośa* scholars such as Dharmatrāta appear asserting that consciousness perceives, while others maintain it is the eye. The authoritative theory of the Sarvāstivāda School supports the latter view, the chief advocate of which is Vasumitra. The Sautrāntika is introduced in this work as maintaining that color-form is perceived by consciousness in association with some of the mental *dharmas*. The essentials of the controversy between Dharmatrāta and Vasumitra can be briefly condensed in dialogue form, as follows.[2]

Vasumitra: The eye is called the perceiver not because it judges but because it has the function of seeing color-form.

Dharmatrāta: If the organ of an eye cognizes by itself, visual perception may occur even at the time when another kind of perception, say an auditory one, is taking place. But it contradicts the established theory of the Sarvāstivāda School itself that two cognitions cannot arise at one and the same time.

Vasumitra: We do not say that all eyes perceive at all times but that only eyes which are in operation because of their coexistence with consciousness see. Consciousness, however, does not cooperate with two or more sense-organs at a time.

Dharmatrāta: If so, why don't you call consciousness the perceiver, because it is the very cause of visual perception?

Vasumitra: If consciousness were the perceiver it could see even an object concealed behind a wall, since consciousness is not a resisting entity. This, nevertheless, is not experienced. Therefore, we have to conclude that it is the eyes which see and not consciousness.

Dharmatrāta: If you mean that the eyes come into direct contact with an object to see it and that, therefore, the eyes cannot see what is concealed by another resisting thing, how then do you explain the fact that the eyes can see an object placed behind glass, crystal, water, etc.?

Thus we have to say that visual consciousness sees the object with the cooperation of the sense-organ of an eye. The words of the *Sūtras* that the eyes see color-form are merely a metaphorical expression.

Vasumitra: If, as you say, it is visual consciousness which sees, what is it that understands the perception? One and the same consciousness cannot have two different functions, seeing and understanding.[3]

Dharmatrāta: Seeing and understanding are not separate functions.[4]

Interrupting their discussion, the Sautrāntika enters the arena and ridicules both parties. In his opinion visual perception is not the simultaneous operation of color-form, the sense-organ, and consciousness. On the contrary, according to him, when visual consciousness arises from the causes of the eyes and color-form, it should be understood as a causal effect. The three exist at different moments. The Sarvāstivādins say that the eyes see and that consciousness understands; but this is merely verbal convention and not a truth.[5]

Saṃghabhadra in his *Abhidharmanyāyānusāriśāstra* strongly opposes the Sautrāntika theory introduced above. His argument may be summarized as follows. All conditioned things are alike insofar as they are produced out of their causes and conditions. Nonetheless, everything has its own-being and operation. Earth is produced from its cause, but it has the particular own-being of hardness and the particular operation of supporting other things. In the same way the eyes, color-form, and consciousness are all produced by their causes, but each of them has a separate and distinct own-being and function which is not common to other things. The eyes are different from color-form and consciousness, and the same thing can be said about the other two. Therefore we should admit that each element has its own reality, although a whole composed of all these elements is not real. The eyes are what see, color-form is what is seen, and consciousness is what understands. The Sautrāntika is wrong in saying, in effect, that differences among these three elements do not exist and that one should not be attached to verbal convention. Ordinary people are mistaken in being attached to the whole. We must deny the reality of the whole, but not that of the component elements.

The Sarvāstivādins deny the reality of *ātman* or *pudgala* and its function, but not that of the elements.[6]

Vasumitra as well as Saṃghabhadra repeatedly argues that a reality means a *dharma* having a separate own-being (*svabhāva*) and function (*kriyā, kāritra*) and that a real element cannot have two or more natures and functions. This is the fundamental concept of Sarvāstivāda realism which is reflected clearly in the discussion of whether it is the sense-organ or consciousness which perceives. Moreover, we realize that this is also the fundamental concept of the theory of categories. In this theory a phenomenon as a whole is divided into as many elements as the number of its component natures. If a *dharma* has two or more natures and functions the division of a phenomenon is useless. The essential nature of consciousness is illumination and its function understanding. If it perceives as well as understands, what is the use of establishing the eye and consciousness as different *dharmas*? To assign only one own-being and function to a *dharma* is to regard the *dharma* as real. If this principle is ignored the whole system of categories collapses.

This principle led the Sarvāstivādins to another important theory, *i.e.*, the theory that consciouness has no content. The content of consciouness or the form of cognition belongs to its object, since consciousness, of which the own-being is illumination, cannot have as its own the image of the object, which is another own-being. The image or form belongs to the object, which is external to consciousness. What necessarily follows from this theory is that when we are conscious of a thing—physical, mental or logical—it exists as external to consciousness. This is nothing but the theory of knowledge without images (*nirākāra-jñāna-vāda*), a point which we will come back to at the end of this article.

A firm belief common to the Vaiśeṣika, Naiyāyika, and Sarvāstivāda philosophers affirms that the objects of our cognition and speech really exist. That is to say, correct knowledge and words have their corresponding objects in the external world. Praśastapāda says, in effect, that to be existent (*astitva*), to be an object of cognition (*jñeyatva*), and to be expressed in a word or in words (*abhidheyatva*) mean the same thing. Vasubandhu, introducing the Sarvāstivāda theory, states that cognition cannot occur without an object external to it.[7]

This belief leads these three schools to a substantiation of ideas. A human idea must have its counterpart in the external world, without which the former cannot arise. If an idea or word exists, the object of that idea or word is also exists externally. It becomes clearer when we examine the theory of the three schools regarding the contents of ideas. To take the example of the unconditioned *dharmas*, *i.e.* space (*ākāśa*) and the two kinds of cessation (*nirodha*) or non-existence, these are considered to be eternal and external realities by the Sarvāstivādin, whereas they are not real in the view of the Sautrāntika and other schools. The later Nyāya-Vaiśeṣika School also includes absence (*abhāva*) in its list of the categories of realities. The fourth of the five classes with seventy-five *dharmas*, the mind-dissociated (*cittaviprayukta-saṃskāra*) subsumes fourteen *dharmas*, many of which are merely concepts to us. The Sarvāstivada School, however, considers them externally existent.

The Sautrāntika philosophers, whose way of thinking is radically opposed to that of the Sarvāstivādins, say that the object of cognition is not external to cognition but an essential part of it. Furthermore, they say that there is no actual difference between the object, the subject, and cognition because they are one and the same entity and because the division into three parts is merely a logical construction.[8] The Sarvāstivādins, however, declare that cognition as a whole is unreal, and that only the elements of it are real. To accord reality to the component elements means to externalize the elements which are contained in the whole. We propose to call this way of thinking of the Sarvāstivāda philosophers the 'spatial externalization of elements'.

This externalization of the component elements of cognition is also carried out by the Sarvāstivādins in the realm of time. The Sautrāntikas, on the one hand, are known to have proclaimed that only a thing at the present moment is real, and that the same thing in the past is not, nor is it in the future.[9] The Sarvāstivādins, on the other hand, say that in its own-being a thing remains the same throughout all three times. The very designation 'Sarvāstivāda' is derived from the fact that the philosophers of this school assert the reality of every *dharma* in all three times.[10]

According to the theory of momentary flux (*kṣaṇikavāda*) as understood by the Sautrāntika, everything is a stream of momentary events. A thing disappears at the very moment in which it is produced and a different event succeeds that which has disappeared, just as a sprout arises from its seed. The steady light of a lamp is really a continual flow of instantaneous flames, to cite yet another example. Our recognition identifying the present moment of a thing with the past moment of it is mere imagination.[11] Therefore only the present moment of a thing is real. The Sarvāstivādins, being Buddhists, maintain that everything disappears at every moment. But this momentary flux is admitted only in the phenomenal world. They recognize existence of the own-being of a thing (*svabhāva, dravya*), which, subsisting in a changing thing, never undergoes change itself. They call a thing present when its constant own-being comes into the situation in which it operates. Presence means the same as the operation of a thing. But it does not mean that the thing is existent only at the present moment, since, though deprived of its operation, it exists as a constant own-being in all three times.[12]

The Sautrāntikas as well as modern minds may contend: You, Sarvāstivādins, assert that a thing exists not only in the present but also in the past and future. A rock in the Himalayas in your opinion exists in all three times even though it is not cognized by anyone; or a book you lost last year is not cognized by your sense-organ but just thought of by your mind. It means that the rock or the book is none other than an idea, a content of your consciousness, and not a physical object. Therefore you cannot say that the rock or the book remains with the same own-being.

The Sarvāstivādins, however, do not agree. They do not admit that a book consisting of matter loses its own-being and becomes an immaterial idea. Just as neither mental nor logical *dharmas* become matter, so matter does not change into an idea. If a *dharma* changed its nature in accordance with a different time and situation, the system of categories and elements would be easily broken.

Now let us examine the most important theory after which the Sarvāstivāda School is named, *i.e.*, the theory that every *dharma* having a constant own-being is real throughout the three times. This theory cannot be understood without presupposing what has been introduced above. In the *Abhidharmakośa*, as proof that a thing is real in the three times the Sarvāstivādins assert the following facts:

1) every cognition has its object; 2) past *karma* produces its effect in present and future time; 3) the testimony of the *Sūtras*.[13] We will discuss only the first because it is the most directly related to the epistemology of the school.

The proof is as follows: If the own-being of a past or future thing is not real, our consciousness of a past or future thing would have no object. But there cannot be a cognition without an object; otherwise it would follow that we would not be able to think of a past or future thing. It is a fact, however, that we can think of a past or future thing. Yaśomitra, commenting on this passage of the *Abhidharmakośa*, formulates the argument in a syllogism which goes:

> As in the case of visual perception (cognition always has a real object);
> Consciousness is by nature cognition;
> Therefore, consciousness has a real object.[14]

To the Sautrāntika philosophers and most of us, consciousness of an object which we saw in the past or will see in the future is memory or imagination. And the existence of the memory of an object or its imagination does not prove the existence or reality of the object. The Sautrāntikas do not qualify memory and imagination as valid means of cognition (*pramāṇa*), and approve inference as related to reality only indirectly. The major premise of Yaśomitra's syllogism refers only to the fact that sense-perception is not possible without a real object. But from this we cannot deduce the conclusion that memory or imagination also has a real object.

The Sarvāstivādins, however, do not regard a representation in our mind as an idea. Consciousness or cognition itself is the illuminating faculty, without any content or image. Therefore, if consciousness apprehends an image, an object which has that image must exist outside consciousness. If a past object is known, it means that the past object is now existing. Perception is one thing and consciousness another. But both are not different insofar as they are cognitions, and cognition means for consciousness to understand an object which is external to it.

Four theories about the difference between past, present, and future times are introduced and criticized in the *Abhidharmakośa-bhāṣya*. The most important and authentic theory among them is the one proposed by Vasumitra. It maintains that difference among the three times is no more than difference in situation (*avasthā*). Although everything remains the same in its own-being throughout the three times, the own-being is combined with a function (*kāritra*) at the present and not at the past and future times.[15]

The Sautrāntika criticizes this theory of situation vehemently. When Vasumitra talks of the combination of own-being and function, it is presupposed that function is different from own-being. In order that function be distinguished in the three times it must have another sub-function, which however will lead to an infinite regression (*anavasthā*). Thus, function must be a permanent entity like own-being. The permanence of function, however, makes a difference among the three times impossible. Therefore, it is necessarily derived that function is not different from own-being but part and parcel of it. But this alternative does not solve the problem in question either. If an own-being having function A as part and parcel of its self comes to have function B at the next moment, this is tantamount to saying that the own-being has become a different own-being. And what does change cannot be called an own-being.[16]

Against the Sarvāstivādins maintaining that a jar in past and future times exists because it becomes an object of cognition, the Sautrāntika argues that in that case no difference can exist between the present jar and the one in the past and the future. The Sarvāstivādins, attempting to establish a difference, say that a jar in the present is a conglomeration of atoms while a jar in the past and the future had and has its atoms, in dispersal, and that this is the difference among the three times.

Answering in this way, however, the Sarvāstivādins reveal an inconsistency in their own theory. When one thinks of, or in the Sarvāstivādins' word 'cognizes', a past or a future jar one does not think of atoms but of the jar as a conglomeration of atoms. Otherwise one cannot actually be said to think of a jar. Besides, the above theory contradicts one of the Sarvāstivādins' main doctrines: that atoms do not exist separately but always in conjunction with one another. Therefore, it is false that a jar in the past and future is broken into separate constituent atoms. Even if we admit that atoms of a jar in the past and future are dispersed but exist, the concept of permanence of atoms destroys the Sarvāstivādins' doctrine that all conditioned *dharmas* are impermanent.[17]

At the end of this controversy the Sarvāstivādins almost confess inability to explain their theory of permanent own-being having the present function. As Buddhists, they are also exponents of the theory that every conditioned thing is a flux of momentary events which disappear as soon as they arise. However, they can hardly coordinate their theory of permanent own-being with that of the universal flux of phenomena.

The Sarvāstivādins seem to distinguish between two kinds of times: the time of perception and the time of thought. Own-being, as it is defined by them, is the object of thought and speech, and thus exists not in the phenomenal world but in the permanent world. It exists not in the time in which our perception takes place, but in the time of thought in which we speculate and remember. To the Sarvāstivādins, human cognition is a synthesis of momentary functions as objects of perception and of permanent own-being as objects of thought.

In the above discussion we repeatedly came across the Sarvāstivādins' theory that the object of consciousness, be it material or non-material, is an entity separate from consciousness. We also mentioned that this is what is usually called 'the theory of knowledge without an image' (*nirākāra-* or *anākāra-jñāna-vāda*). The details of this theory must be understood in comparison with 'the theory of knowledge with an image (*sākārajñānavāda*), which we cannot deal with at length in this article. For the time being, we will refer to a simple example.

Suppose that you are perceiving a book in front of you. Does the form (*ākāra*) of the book belong to the book outside your knowledge or is it your own representation? If it is your representation, it is not external to your knowledge, and you are cognizing your own knowledge. The image of the book is part and parcel of your consciousness, and the external world is not perceived by you. If so, you cannot be sure of the existence of the external world and you have either to deny it with the Vijñānavādins or to just infer or postulate with the Sautrāntikas that something must be present external to our mind though not seen. This is the principal idea of the *sākārajñānavāda*.

According to this theory, the fact that a book is cognized means that knowledge is cognizing its own self. That is to say, the necessary corollary of the *sākārajñānavāda* is that cognition is none other than self-cognition (*svasaṃvedana*). Self-cognition does not mean that a cognition perceives another cognition but that a cognition is conscious of itself.

The *nirākārajñānavādin*s think that knowledge cannot be conscious of itself. What is known by knowledge is different than knowledge. The image or form belongs to the object, and knowledge illuminates it. This is true, they say, not only of the object of sense-perception but also of the cognition of non-material objects. Mental or logical *dharma*s are, insofar as they are known by knowledge, existent outside knowledge or in the external world. The Naiyāyika, a *nirākārajñānavādin*, asserts that he perceives, by means of the sense-organs, all six kinds of realities: substance, qualities, actions, universals, particulars, and the relation of inherence.[18] The Sarvāstivādin includes mental and logical *dharma*s among the external realities which become the objects of the cognitive organs.[19]

The *sākārajñānavāda* is maintained by the Sāṃkhya Vedānta as well as the Sautrāntikabauddha. The theory, in Satkari Mookerjee's words,[20] "holds that knowledge of external reality is made possible by virtue of the objective reality leaving an impress of its likeness on the mirror of consciousness." The *nirākārajñānavāda* is maintained by the Nyāyavaiśeṣika, Mīmāṃsaka, Jaina, and the Vaibhāśikabauddha, and "the theory maintains that our consciousness is clear like a clean slate and does not depart an inch from its intrinsic purity even when it apprehends the external reality. Consciousness is an amorphous substance and remains so in all its activities. It is like light and reveals the object with its form and qualities without undergoing any morphological articulation in its constitution."

Śāntirakṣita as well as Kamalaśīla enumerates for criticism's sake three kinds of epistemological attitudes regarding the relation of knowledge and object. The *nirākārajñānavāda* or *anirbhāsajñanavāda* maintains that an object is cognized by knowledge not endowed with its image; *sākārajñānavāda* or *sanirbhāsajñānavāda* that an object is cognized by knowledge having its image; and *anyanirbhāsajñānavāda* that an object is cognized by knowledge endowed with an image different from that of the object.[21] The last, however, may be included in the second (*sākāranirbhāsajñānavāda*) as a special case. In his *Madhyamakālaṃkāra*, Śāntirakṣita calls the Sarvāstivādin *anākārajñānavādin* and the Sautrāntika *sākārajñānavādin*. Kamalaśīla explains that the *anākāravādins* are of the opinion that external reality has form (*ākāra*) while knowledge is without form.[22]

Eventually all four schools of Buddhism come to be classified from the perspective of *ākāravāda*. According to Guṇaratna, the Vaibhāṣikas or Sarvāstivādins say that knowledge has no image but becomes a means to cognize an object when it coexists with the latter and all other conditions; the Sautrāntikas and the Yogācārins say that knowledge endowed with an image is the means of cognition; and the Mādhyamikas maintain that the difference between the means and object of cognition is [false] as in a dream, and emancipation is arrived at through the understanding of *śūnyatā* (emptiness).[23]

Mādhava describes in the *Sarvadarśanasaṃgraha* the same kind of classification: The Vaibhāśikas uphold [the theory] that [cognition occurs when] an object is accompanied by knowledge; the Sautrāntikas think that the external object cannot be grasped by perception [but that it can be postulated by inference; hence, knowledge cognizes only its own image]; the Yogācārins all agree that knowledge is in possession of an image, and the Mādhyamikas hold that pure illumination independent [of an image] is the highest truth.[24]

Mādhava and Guṇaratna wrote their passages in the fourteenth and fifteenth centuries respectively, and we are not certain of the Buddhist texts from which the two non-Buddhist scholars derived their knowledge of the Buddhist theories. But we have enough reason to suppose that the two scholars gathered some of their materials from Bodhibhadra's *Jñanasārasamuccayaṭīkā* and Mokṣākaragupta's *Tarkabhāṣā*, both of which were written in the eleventh or twelfth century. According to these two Buddhist scholars, the Sarvāstivādins in regard to the image of cognition are of the opinion that although knowledge produced by sense-organs has no images [of atoms], atoms, when assembled together, appear as an existent.[25]

Not much material is available regarding the doctrines of the Sarvāstivāda School in its later stage. Much of what we have seen above in connection with the *nirākārajñānavāda* of this school is a reconstruction from fragmentary sources compiled from the texts of other schools. The *nirākāravāda* as a distinct form in opposition to the *sākāravāda* must have developed after Dharmakīrti and Śāntirakṣita.

It was these two philosophers who first described the *sākārajñānavāda*'s peculiarity and criticized the epistemological viewpoint of the Sarvāstivādins, and in doing so gave the name *nirākārajñānavāda* to their theory.[26] This does not mean, however, that this theory of consciousness having no image and of sensation occuring when consciousness, an object, and a sense-organ coexist simultaneously was created only after the seventh or eighth century. The Sarvāstivāda School maintained it since olden times, even before its designation as '*nirākārajñānavāda*'.

T. Stcherbatsky, summarizing the theory of cognition of the Sarvāstivādins as it appears in the *Abhidharmakośa*, states: "Their explanation of the origin of knowledge was in perfect agreement with their ontology, *i.e.*, with the theory of a plurality of separate, though interdependent, elements (*dharma*). The phenomenon of knowledge was a compound phenomenon, resolvable into a number of elements simultaneously flashing into existence. Being conceived as momentary flashes, the elements could not move toward one another, could not come into contact, could not influence one another; there could be no 'seizing' or 'grasping' of the object by the intellect. But, according to the laws of interconnexion (*pratītya-samutpāda*) prevailing between them, some elements are invariably appearing accompanied by others arising in close continguity with them. A moment of color (*rūpa*), a moment of the sense-of-vision-matter (*cakṣuḥ*), and a moment of pure consciousness (*citta*), arising simultaneously in close contiguity, constitute what is called a sensation (*sparśa*) of color. The element of consciousness according to the same laws never appears alone, but always supported by an object (*viṣaya*) and a receptive faculty (*indriya*)."[27]

As mentioned previously, the essential nature of the *nirākārajñānavāda* consists in the negation of the self-cognition of consciousness. In the seventh chapter of the *Abhidharmakośa*, knowledge is classified into ten kinds. And in the course of discussion, a question is raised as to whether there is any kind of knowledge having everything as its object. The Sarvāstivādins reply negatively. The questioner continues to contend that knowledge that everything is devoid of *ātman* must have everything as its object. In reply to this, a verse by Vasubandhu states, in effect:

> The knowledge of ordinary people (*saṃvṛtijñāna*) understands all things excepting its own complex to be devoid of *ātman*.

Saṃvṛtijñāna, one of the ten kinds of knowledge dealt with here, means ordinary knowledge, different from a saint's knowledge intuiting religious truth, a yogin's knowledge perceiving the mind of another person, and other special kinds of knowledge. This part of the *Kośa* is concerned mainly with the objects of the ten kinds of knowledge. Hence, the object of ordinary knowledge is now in question. There is, however, no knowledge which is other than *saṃvṛtijñāna* and which has everything as its object. Thus, the verse comes to mean that knowledge in general does not cognize its own complex. Its own complex consists of one moment of the cognition itself; the ten mental *dharmas* that are always associated with it; the four *dharmas* of origination, subsistence, decay, and extinction; and the *dharma* of attainment (*prāpti*). These occur simultaneously in close relation. According to Vasubandhu's own commentary on the above verse, the cognizant is one thing and the cognized another; therefore, knowledge cannot know itself. The ten mental *dharmas* associated with knowledge, being concerned with the same objects as those of knowledge, cannot be known by knowledge. *Prāpti* as well as the four *dharmas* of phenomenal aspects are too close to knowledge and for this reason they are not known by knowledge, as an eye-drop solution dropped on an eye cannot be seen by it.[28]

The same problem is also treated in the *Mahāvibhāṣāśāstra*, compiled in the second or third century. In the ninth volume of this work, the Mahāsāṃghikas assert that just as a lamp illuminates other things as well as itself, knowledge illuminates itself as well as other things. The Dharmaguptakas maintain that knowledge apprehends itself and the mental *dharma*s associated with it; the Mahīśāsakas hold that knowledge apprehends the four phenomenal aspects; and the Vātsīputrīyas say that *pudgala* knows everything. Against these different theories the Sarvāstivādins maintain the same theory evident in the *Kośa*. Even the knowledge of ordinary people, which has the greatest range of objects, cannot know itself. Therefore, all knowledge is not self-cognizant. This is the established opinion of the Sarvāstivāda school.[29]

In the *Mahāvibhāṣāśāstra* various reasons are enumerated to disprove the self-cognition of knowledge. Let us consider a few of them here. If knowledge knows itself, the Sarvāstivādins say, there would be no distinction between the subject and the object in all phenomena. And the world itself would fall if the relations of cause and effect, of the maker and the thing made, the establisher and the established, the knower and the known, etc., were not recognized. Moreover, the Sarvāstivādins say, a finger cannot touch itself, a sword cannot cut itself, an eye cannot see itself, and a wrestler cannot defeat himself. In the same way, knowledge does not know itself. If knowledge knows itself, the *Mahāvibhāṣāśāstra* continues, the Buddha should not have taught that consciousness arises depending on an object and a sense-organ, and that these three elements are separate and distinct.

From the foregoing we conclude that Sarvāstivāda realism is based on the idea of *dharma* which is possessed of a particular own-being and function and on the theory of knowledge without image.

I express my heartfelt gratitude to Professor Luis O. Gómez who, having read this paper, gave me useful suggestions, and to Miss T. Sugimoto for her correction of the English text.

This article is part of an unpublished work entitled *Basic Structure of the Sarvāstivāda Philosophy*. Due to limitation of space I have omitted the first section, which deals with the theory of categories of the school.

Abbreviations Used in Notes References

AK & AKBh: *Abhidharmakoṣabhāṣya of Vasubandhu*, ed. P. Pradhan, K.P. Jayaswal Research Institute, Patna, 1967.

ANA: *Abhidharmanyāyānusāriśāstra*, by Saṃghabhadra, Taishō, No. 1562, Vol. 29, p. 329ff.

Kando: *Kandō Abidatsuma Kusharon*, ed. Kyokuga Saheki, Hozokan, Kyoto.

MA & MAV: *Madhyamakālaṃkāra and its Vṛtti*, by Śāntirakṣita, Peking Reprint Edition, Nos. 5284 & 5285, Vol. 101.
NBT: *Nyāyabindu of Dharmakīrti with Nyāyabinduṭīkā of Dharmottara*, ed. T. Stcherbatsky, *Bibliotheca Buddhica*, Vol. 7, 1918.
SDS: *Sarvadarśanasaṃgraha of Sāyanamādhava*, ed. V.S. Abhyankar, *Government Oriental Series*, Class A, No. 4, Poona.
TBh: "Tarkabhāṣā of Mokṣākaragupta," in *Tarkabhāṣā and Vādasthāna*, ed. H.R. Rangaswami Iyengar, Mysore, 1952.
TBh-tr: *An Introduction to Buddhist Philosophy—An Annotated Translation of the Tarkabhāṣā of Mokṣākaragupta*, Yuichi Kajiyama, *Memoirs of the Faculty of Letters*, No. 10, Kyoto University, 1966.
TRD: (*Shaddarśanasamuchchaya by Haribhadra with*) *Guṇaratna's Commentary Tarkarahasyadīpikā*, ed. L. Suali, Bibliotheca Indica, Vol. 167.

NOTES

1. Śāntirakṣita, for example, says in TS, vv. 2000-2001: "Knowledge is by nature opposed to insentient matter; this immateriality is nothing but the self-cognition of knowledge. The self-cognition of knowledge is not to be analysed into action and its agent, since knowledge, being a single unity without compartments, cannot be divided into the three parts" [*viz.*, the knower, the known, and the knowing]. Cf. also NBT 15, 18-21; TBh 16 (TBh-tr. 48, with notes).
2. AKBh 30-31; Kando 2, 14b-15a, b.
3. The theory that two or more cognitions cannot occur at once is common to the Sarvāstivāda, Vaiśeṣika, and Naiyāyika. The theory is a corollary of the Nyāya-Vaiśeṣika admission of *manas* as a single substance of the size of an atom. *Manas* links *ātman* and the sense-organ when cognition takes place; but, because *manas* is a single entity, it cannot connect two sense-organs with *ātman* at one time. Hence, two sense-cognitions do not arise at one time. Cf. *Nyāyasūtra*, 1.1.16: *yugapajjñānānutpattir manaso liṅgam*. The Sarvāstivādins subscribe to this theory despite their denial of *ātman*.
4. The same kind of discussion is found in "Tarkasopāna of Vidyākaraśānti" in G. Tucci, ed., *Minor Buddhist Texts*, Part I, (SOR 9), 281, 6-9. Mokṣākaragupta, following Dharmakīrti, argues that the means of valid knowledge is not the sense-organ but consciousness. TBh-tr. § 2.6 with n. 21.
5. An external object which stimulates the sense-organ precedes the latter by one moment. The consciousness of the object takes place one moment after the sense-organ functions. Hence, three moments are necessary for a perception to be completed. Cf. NB 1, s.9; TBh 14 (TBh-tr. § 6.1).

6. Cf. ANA 367 c.

7. Cf. *Praśastapādabhāṣya ed. with Nyāyakandalī*, Vizianagaram Sanskrit Series, p. 16: "*ṣaṇṇām api padārthānām astitvābhidheyatvajñeyatvāni.*" Śrīdhara comments: "*astitvaṃ svarūpavattvam . . . yasya vastuno yat svarūpaṃ tad eva tasyāstitvam;*" AKBh 295: "*sati viṣaye vijñānaṃ pravartate nāsati . . .*;" Kando 20, 2b. See also the proof of the existence of own-being throughout the three times further on in this article.

8. The external object itself is not perceived, but is inferred. The object of cognition is an image which is caused to arise in knowledge by the external reality. The object, subject, and resulting cognition are in reality one and the same entity, which is divided into three parts only by logical analysis. See No. 1 above.

9. AKBh and AK Chap. 5, v. 27 (Kando 20, 4b-9a) contains the controversy between both schools on the reality of past and future *dharmas*.

10. Cf. AK Chap. 5, v. 25: *tadasti (= sarvakālāstitā)–vādāt sarvāstivādā iṣṭāḥ*; Kando 20, 2a.

11. Cf. TBh-tr. 28.2.

12. Cf. AK Chap. 5, v. 26 with AKBh; Kando 20, 3a ff.

13. Cf. AK Chap. 5, v. 2 with AKBh.

14. *Yaśomitra, Abhidharmakośavyākhyā*, ed. U. Wogihara, 469, 15-16: "*sādhanaṃ cātra, sadālambanam eva manovijñānam, upalabdhisvabhāvatvāt, cakṣurvijñānavad iti.*"

15. Cf. AK Chap. 5, v. 26 with AKBh; Kando 20, 3a-b.

16. AKBh 297, 19 ff.; Kando 20, 3a-b..

17. Cf. AKBh 299, 24-300, 2; Kando 20, 7a-8.

18. Cf. *Nyāyavārttika* of Uddyotakara & *Nyāyavārttikatātparyaṭīkā* of Vācaspatimiśra, included in *Nyāyadarśanam*, ed. A.M. Tarkatirtha, *Calcutta Sanskrit Series*, No. 18, pp. 94-95. To the Naiyāyika, perception is essentially perceptual judgment rather than sensation. Not only substance, quality, and motion, but concepts, as well as logical relations, are cognized by perception. Uddyotakara classifies perception into six kinds according to the variety of its objects. This theory, shared by the Sarvāstivādin, is opposite to the Sautrāntika theory of perception (*pratyakṣa*) which is never associated with concepts.

19. The Sarvāstivādins define the internal as what causes ego-consciousness and the external as what does not. In their classification of 18 *dhātu*s, the six kinds of cognitive organs and the six kinds of consciousnesses are internal and the six kinds of objects including *dharmas* as the eighteenth *dhātu* are external. Here *dharmas* include the mental, the mind-dissociated, and the unconditioned.

20. S. Mookerjee, *The Buddhist Philosophy of Universal Flux*, University of Calcutta, India, 1935, p. 77.

21. TS v. 1999 with TSP.

22. MA, MAV vv. 116-17 = TS vv. 1999-2000.
23. Cf. TRD 46-47; TBh-tr n. 148.
24. Cf. SDS 46, 368-371; TBh-tr. n. 148.
25. TBh-tr. § 30 with n. 381. TBh is closely related to *Jñānasārasamuccaya*, falsely ascribed to Aryadeva. Bodhibhadra's commentary on the latter is available in Peking Reprint Edition No. 5252; Guṇaratna, the author of TRD, names TBh as one of the ten most distinguished works of Buddhist philosophy. See TBh-tr. Introduction.
26. See for example the discussion between the Sarvāstivādin and the Sautrāntika in Dharmakīrti's *Pramāṇavārttika*, "Pratyakṣa," vv. 371-387, with Manorathanandin's commentary.
27. Th. Stcherbatsky, *The Central Conception of Buddhism*, Susil Gupta (India) Ltd., Calcutta, 1961 (First edition, London, 1923), p. 46.
28. Cf. AK Chap. 7, v. 18 with AKBh; Kando 26, 14a.
29. Cf. Taishō 27, 42c.

Haribhadra's Quotations from Jñānagarbha's *Anantamukhanirhāradhāraṇīṭīkā*

Hisao Inagaki

I

Haribhadra was an eighth-century *Svātantrika* of the Mādhyamika School, who, according to Mkhas-grub-rje, held views similar to those of Ārya-vimuktisena and Bhadanta-vimuktisena.[1] In the opening verses of his commentaries on the *Abhisamayālaṃkāra* he mentions these two Vimuktisenas[2] and in the 'great' commentary quotes from their works as well as from Nāgārjuna, Asaṅga, Āryadeva, Vasubandhu, Dignāga, and others. This indicates a close relationship between Haribhadra and the two Vimuktisenas regarding fundamental points of doctrine, but for the practical method of pursuing the way to enlightenment he turned to the Yogācāra system, in particular the *Mahāyānasūtrālaṃkāra*.[3] As for the method of presentation of themes and the exposition of terms and concepts, he seems to have availed himself of the works of other *ācāryas*. According to H. Amano, Haribhadra followed Vinītadeva's system of explaining the objective of the treatise (*ārambhaprayojana*) in terms of *sambandha, prayojana, abhidheya,* and *prayojanaprayojana*, and used relevant passages from Kamalaśīla's *Tattvasaṃgrahapañjikā* to explain them, often reproducing them with little change in wording.[4]

This paper is presented as a further demonstration of Haribhadra's indebtedness to his predecessors. The reader will find that Haribhadra owed a great deal to Jñānagarbha in explaining important terms in the *Abhisamayālaṃkārāloka*.

The texts examined in this paper are:

1. *Abhisamayālaṃkārāloka Prajñāpāramitāvyākhyā*, edited by U. Wogihara, Tokyo, 1932–35; abbreviated as *Āloka*.
2. *'phags pa sgo mtha' yas pa sgrub pa'i gzung rgya cher 'grel pa* (*Ārya-anantamukhanirhāra-dhāraṇī-ṭīkā*), Tibetan Tripiṭaka, Vol. 79; abbreviated as *Ṭīkā*.

II

Etymological and doctrinal explanations of Buddha's common epithets are found in the *Āloka* and the *Ṭīkā*. The comparisons below indicate that Haribhadra not only borrowed Jñānagarbha's views but used his words with little alteration. I have followed the passages with English paraphrasing to aid in demonstrating this.

(1) *Āloka:* (*tathāgato 'rhan samyaksambuddha* ity ebhis tribhiḥ padaiḥ śāstṛtva-sampadaṃ darśayati.) sā ca śāstṛtva-sampad dvidhā. vaktṛtva-lakṣaṇā pratipattṛtva-lakṣaṇā ca. tatra yatraiva te dharmā vyavasthitās tathaiva gadanāt tathāgata ity anenāviparīta-dharma-daiśikatvād vaktṛtva-sampad uktā. pratipattṛtva-lakṣaṇā ca jñāna-prahāṇa-sampad-bhedena dvividhā. tatra arīn hatavān *arhann* ity anena prahāṇa-sampad uktā. arayaś ca rāgādayaḥ kleśāḥ sarva-kuśala-dharmopaghātārthena. iyaṃ ca prahāṇa-sampat pūrvam uktā. tat-pūrvakatvāj jñāna-sampadaḥ. *samyag* aviparītaṃ[5] *sam*antād dharmāvabodhāt *samyaksambuddha* ity anena jñāna-sampad uktā. aviparītasarvajñājñānādhigama-yogāt. (p. 183, lines 8–17.)

Ṭīkā: de la ston pa nyid phun sum tshogs pa rnam pa gnyis ni gsung ba nyid kyi mtshan nyid dang/ sgrub pa nyid kyi mtshan nyid do// de la gsung ba nyid kyi mtshan nyid ni *de bzhin gshegas pa* zhes gsungs pa yin te/ chos rnams ji ltar gnas pa de kho na bzhin du gsungs pas na de bzhin gsung ba zhes bya ba'i phyir ro// 'dis ni phyin ci ma log par chos ston pa po nyid yin par bstan to// sgrub pa nyid kyi mtshan nyid ni spangs pa dang/ ye shes phun sum tshogs pa'i ngo bo byid rnam pa gnyis te/ go rim bzhin du *dgra bcom pa yang dag par rdzogs pa'i sangs rgyas* zhes gsungs pa yin no// (p. 70 c.)

In the above [verse], the two aspects of the attainment of the state of the [true] teacher (*śāstṛtva-sampad*) are the aspect of being an expounder (*vaktṛtva*) and that of being a practitioner (*pratipattṛtva*).

The former is shown by *tathāgata*; for, because he expounds *dharmas* as they really are, he is called "one who thus expounds." This explains the state of one who expounds *dharmas* without perverting them. The aspect of being a practitioner is of two kinds, attainment of avoidance (*prahāṇa-sampad*) and of wisdom (*jñāna-sampad*). They refer to *Arhat* and Samyaksambuddha respectively.

dgra rnams bcom pas na *dgra bcom pa* ste/ 'dis ni spangs pa phun sum tshogs pa bstan to// dgra dag ni 'dod chags la sogs pa nyon mongs pa rnams te dge ba'i chos thams cad la gnod pa byed pa'i phyir ro// spangs pa phun sum tshogs pa 'di sngar smos pa ni/ de ye shes phun sum tshogs pa'i sngon du 'gro ba'i phyir ro// yang dag pa phyin ci ma log par kun nas sangs rgyas pas na *yang dag par rdzogs pa'i sangs rgyas* shes bya'o// 'des ni ye shes phun sum tshogs pa bstan te/ thams cad mkhyen pa'i ye shes phyin ci ma log pa bstan pa'i phyir ro// (p. 69 c–d.)

Arhat is so called because he has destroyed (*hata*) the enemy (*ari*); this shows the attainment of avoidance. The enemy refers to evil passions (*kleśa*) such as greed because they harm all good *dharmas*. The attainment of avoidance is presented first because it precedes the attainment of wisdom. *Samyaksambuddha* is so called because he is enlightened truly (*samyak-*), that is, unpervertedly (*aviparītam*), and completely (*samantāt*). This shows the attainment of wisdom, for this explains the Omniscient's unperverted wisdom.

(2) *Āloka*: tad evam aviparīta-dharma-daiśikatvena sarva-kleśa-prahāṇena sarvākāra-dharmāvabodhena ca śāstṛtva-sampad asādhā-raṇā paripūrṇā ca Bhagavataḥ kathitā. tathā hi na bāhyānām aviparīta-dharma-daiśikatvam asti sarva-kleśāprahāṇāt. tasmād ete na bhūta-śāstāraḥ. śrāvaka-pratyekabuddhās tu yady api bhūta-śāstāraḥ sarva-kleśa-prahāṇāt. na tu sarvākāra-sarva-dharma-śāstāraḥ sarvākāra-sarva dharmānavabodhāt. Bhagavān punar yathokta-nyāyena bhūta-śāstā sarvākāra-śāstā ceti pratipāditam. (p. 183, lines 18–24.)

Ṭīkā; de'i phyir de ltar phyin ci ma log par chos ston pa po nyid dang/ nyong mongs pa thams cad spangs pa dang/ rnam pa thams cad du chos[6] thams cad thugs su chud pas[7] bcom ldan 'das kyi ston[8] pa nyid phun sum tshogs pa thun mong ma yin pa dang yongs su rdzogs par[9] bstan te/ 'di ltar phyi rol pa rnams la ni phyin ci ma log par chos ston pa po nyid med de/ nyon mongs pa thams cad ma spangs pa'i phyir ro// de nyid kyi phyir de dag yang dag p'i ston pa ma yin no// nyan thos dang rang sangs rgyas rnams ni nyon mongs pa thams cad spangs pa yin pa'i phyir/ yang dag pa'i ston pa yin mod kyi/ rnam pa thams cad du chos thams cad khong du chud pa ma yin pas na rnam pa thams cad kyis ston pa ma yin no// bcom ldan 'das ni yang dag pa'i ston pa dang rnam pa thams cad kyis ston pa yin no// (p. 70 c–d.)

For this reason, the *Bhagavat*'s uncommon (*asādhāraṇa*) and perfect (*paripūrṇa*) attainment of the state of the [true] teacher is shown by the fact that he expounds *dharmas* without perverting them, that he has cast off all evil passions, and that he has realized all aspects of all *dharmas*. Non-Buddhists lack the quality of one who expounds *dharmas* without perverting them because they have not removed all evil passions; and for this very reason they are not true teachers (*bhūtaśāstṛ*). Because *śrāvakas* and *pratyekabuddhas* have removed all evil passions they are indeed true teachers, but since they have not realized all aspects of all *dharmas* they are not teachers of all aspects of all *dharmas* (*sarvākārasarvadharmaśāstṛ*). The *Bhagavat*, indeed, is the true teacher and the teacher of all aspects [of *dharmas*].

(3) *Āloka*: yena sā śāstṛtva-sampal labhyate tad darśayati. *vidyā-caraṇasampanna* iti anena śāstṛtva-sampadaḥ prāpti-hetuṃ darśayati. tatra vidyā samyag-dṛṣṭiḥ. samyak-saṃkalpādīni śeṣāṇy aṅgāni cara-ṇaṃ. yataḥ samyag-dṛṣṭyā tattvaṃ dṛṣṭvā samyaksaṃkalpādibhiś caraṇa-bhūtair gacchati. (anyathā 'paśyann acaraṇo gantum asamartha iti bhāvaḥ. tābhyāṃ sampanno yuktaḥ.) adhiprajñaṃ vā śikṣā vidyā. adhicittam adhiśīlaṃ ca śikṣā caraṇaṃ. prajñāyāḥ pūrva-parikarma-bhūtatvena puraś-caraṇaṃ caraṇam iti kṛtvā. vidyāyās tu pūrva-gra-haṇaṃ tatpariśuddhyā śīla-samādhyoḥ pariśuddhitaḥ. (tayā hi pra-jñayā cakṣuṣeva paśyaṃs tābhyāṃ ca śīla-samādhibhyāṃ caraṇā-bhyām iva gacchan gantavyam anuprāpnotīti vidyā-caraṇa-śabdena tisraḥ śikṣā nirdiśyante.) (p. 183, line 24; p. 184, line 4.)

Ṭīkā: ston pa nyid phun sum tshogs pa de gang gis 'thob pa de ni *rig pa dang zhabs su ldan pa* zhes bya bas bstan to// (p. 70 d.)

By virtue of what he attains, the state of a [true] teacher is rendered by 'possessed of knowledge and practice' (*vidyācaraṇasampanna*).

rig pa ni yang dag pa'i lta ba'o// yang dag pa'i rtog pa la sogs pa yan lag bdun ni zhabs te/ yang dag pa'i lta bas de kho na gzigs nas yang dag pa'i rtogs pa la sogs pa zhabs su gyur pa rnams kyis[10] gshegs pa'i phyir ro// yang na bslab pa gsum ni rig pa dang zhabs te/ lhag pa'i shes rab kyi bslab pa ni rig pa'o// lhag pa'i sems dang lhag pa'i tshul khrims kyi bslab pa ni zhabs te/ shes rab kyi sngon du yongs su sbyong bar gyur pa ni zhabs te sngar spyod pa yin pa'i phyir ro// rig pa sngar smos pa ni de yongs su dag pas tshul khrims dang ting nge 'dzin youngs su dag par 'gyur ba'i phyir ro// (p. 69 d.)

Knowledge (*vidyā*) refers to the right view (*samyag-dṛṣṭi*), and the [other] seven elements (of the Eightfold Noble Path) such as right thought (*samyaksaṃkalpa*) are practice (*caraṇa*). After having seen reality with the right view, he walks with right thoughts, which have become his 'feet'. Or the three disciplines (*trīṇi śikṣāṇi*) can be regarded as knowledge and practice. The training of superior wisdom (*adhiprajñā*) is knowledge, and that of superior thought (*adhicitta*) and superior *śīla* (*adhiśīla*) is practice. Practice (*caraṇa*) constitutes the acts preliminary to [developing] wisdom, and so here it means 'preceding' (*puraścaraṇa*). The reason knowledge is mentioned first is that one must develop it before one can develop *śīla* and *samādhi*.

(4) *Āloka*: sā ca tādṛṣā dvividhā 'pi śastṛtva-sampat. tāṃ *sugata* ity anenācaṣṭe. tathā hi lokottareṇa mārgeṇa śobhanāṃ jñāna-prahāṇa-sampadaṃ gataḥ su-gataḥ surūpavat. a-punar-āvṛttyā vā suṣṭhu gataḥ su-gataḥ sunaṣṭa-jvaravat. niṇśeṣaṃ vā gataḥ su-gataḥ suparipūrṇa-ghaṭavat. artha-trayaṃ caitad bāhya-vīta-rāga-śaikṣāśaikṣebhyo viśe-ṣaṇārthaṃ. (p. 184, lines 4–9.)

Ṭīkā: ston pa nyid phun sum tshogs pa rnam pa gnyis pa de ci 'dra ba de yang *bde bar gshegs pa* zhes bya bas bstan to// de yang legs par zhes bya ba la sogs pa don gsum smos pas ci rigs par bshad par bya'o// (p. 70 d.)

The two aspects of attaining the state of the true teacher are shown by *sugata*, which has three meanings. (See below.)

di ltar 'jig rten las 'das pa'i lam nas ye shes dang spangs pa phun sum tshogs par legs par gshegs pas na *bde bar bshega pa* ste gzugs legs pa bzhin no// yang na phyir mi ldog par gshegs pas na *bde bar gshegs pa* ste rims nad legs par sos pa bzhin no// ma lus par gshegs pa'i phyir yang *bde bar gshegs pa* ste bum pa shin tu gang ba bzhin no// don 'di gsum yang phyi rol pa'i[11] 'dod chags dang bral ba dang/ slob pa dang/ mi slob pa rnams las rang gi don phun sum tshogs pa bye brag tu bya ba'i phyir ro// (p. 69 e; p. 70 a.)

He is called *sugata* because he has "attained the distinguished" perfection of wisdom and avoidance by the supraworldly path, just as [one may have attained] a beautiful form. Or he is called *sugata* because one has "reached non-retrogression," just as fever may be completely gone. Also, he is called *sugata* because he has "gone to the utmost," just as a bottle may be completely filled. These three meanings [of *sugata*] are also meant to distinguish the [*Bhagavat*'s] attainment of self-benefit from that of non-Buddhists who have rid themselves of greed, those who are still in training, and those who no longer need training.

(5) *Āloka*: asyāś ca śāstṛtva-sampado dvividhaṃ karmeti prathanaṃ bhavyābhavya lokāvalokanaṃ karma darśayati. *lokavid* iti bhabyābhavya-loka-parijñānād asau loka-vid ity ucyate. (p. 184, lines 11–14.)

Ṭīkā: ston pa nyid phun sum tshogs pa de'i phrin las rnam pa gnyis la/ sems can skal ba dang ldan pa dang skal ba dang ldan pa ma yin pa la gzigs pa'i phrin las gang yin pa de ni *'jig rten mkhyen pa* zhes bya bas bstan to// (p. 70 d.)

Of the two kinds of acts accompanying the attainment of the state of the [true] teacher, the act of observing whether sentient beings are possessed of stored goodness (*bhavya*) or not is indicated by the term 'knower of the world.'

'jig rten mkhyen pa ni skal ba dang ldan pa dang skal ba dang ldan pa ma yin pa mkhyen pa'i phyir ro// (p. 70 a.)

He is called 'knower of the world' because he knows [whether people of the world] are possessed of stored goodness or not.

(6) *Āloka*: dvitīyaṃ bhavya-vinayanaṃ karma darśayati. *anuttaraḥ puruṣadamyasārathir* iti bhavyābhavyāl lokān vyavalokya Bhagavān ye puruṣā eva damyā damanārhā damayituṃ vā śakyā bhavyās tān vinayati. teṣāṃ sārathi-bhāva-gamanāt. vinayaṃ hi sārathi-bhāvaḥ asan-mārgād apanīya san-mārge pratiṣṭhāpakatvāt. guṇa-viśeṣādhāyakatvāc cāśvādi-sārathivat. anuttara-grahaṇaṃ sārathi-bhāva-viśeṣanārthaṃ. dur-damānām api keṣāṃcit puruṣa-damyānāṃ tīvra-rāga-dveṣa-moha-mānānām ārya-Sundaranandāṅgurīmālorubilvākāś-

yapa-mahārājakapiṇa-prabhṛtīnām damaka iti pradarśanārthaṃ. (p. 184, lines 16–23.)

Ṭīkā: skal ba dang ldan pa 'dul ba gang yin pa de ni *skyes bu 'dul ba'i kha lo bsgyur ba bla na med pa* zhes bya bas bstan to// (p. 70 d.)

The act of training those who are possessed of stored goodness is indicated by the term 'supreme charioteer of men to be tamed'.

skal ba dang ldan pa dang skal ba dang ldan pa ma yin pa thugs su chud nas skal ba dang ldan pa rnams 'dul bar mdzad pas na/ *skyes bu gdul ba'i kha lo bsgyur ba bla na med pa* zhes gsungs te/ 'dis ni gzhan gyi don phun sum tshogs pa bstan to// gdul bar 'os pa dang/ gdul bar nus pa yin pa'i phyir *'dul ba* ste/ skyes bu nyid 'dul ba yin pa'i phyir *skyes bu 'dul ba'o*// de dag gi *kha lo bsgyur ba* ni lam ngan pa nas bzlog ste/ lam bzang por 'dzud pa'i phyir dang/ yon tan gyi khyad par skyed pa'i phyir te rta la sogs pa'i kha lo bsgyur ba bzhin no// *bla na med pa* smos pa ni gdul dka' ba 'dod chags dang/ zhe sdang dang/ gti mug dang/ nga rgyal gyi shas che ba/ 'phags pa mdzes dga' dang/ sor phred dang/ lteng rgyas 'od srung dang/ rgyal po chen po ka pi na la sogs pa 'dul ba yang yin no zhes bstan pa'i don to// (p. 70 a.)

Having examined whether they are possessed of stored goodness or not, he edifies those possessed of it; hence he is called 'supreme charioteer of men to be tamed'. This shows his accomplishment of others' benefit. The phrase 'to be tamed' (*damya*) is used because they are fit or capable of being tamed, and the phrase 'men to be tamed' (*puruṣadamya*) is used because men must indeed be tamed. He is their 'charioteer' (*sārathi*) because he leads them away from the path of misery to the right path; also because he helps them develop excellent qualities as does a charioteer his horses. 'Supreme' (*anuttara*) is meant to indicate that [the *Bhagavat*] is the [only] one who [can] tame [even] those who are [most] difficult to tame, who have intense greed, anger, stupidity, and arrogance, such as Ārya Sundarananda, Aṅgulimāla, Uruvilvākāśyapa, and Mahārāja Kaphiṇa.

(7) *Āloka*: tac ca bhavya-vinayana-karma yatra sthitaṃ tad darśayati. *śāstā devānāṃ ca manuṣyāṇāṃ ce*ti. . . (p. 184, lines 23–24.)

Ṭīkā: skal ba dang ldan pa'i 'dul ba'i phrin las gang dag la gnas pa de ni *lha dang mi rnams kyi ston pa* zhes bya bas bstan to// (p. 70 d.)

Here the acts of training of those who are possessed of stored goodness are demonstrated by the 'teacher of heavenly and human beings'.

(8) *Āloka*: . . . prakṛṣṭā buddhir asyeti buddhaḥ. . . . prakṛṣṭā ca buddhir navabhir ākāraiḥ. sarvajña-jñānena ayatna-jñānena anupadiṣṭa-jñānena savāsana-saṃkleśāvaraṇa-prahāṇa-jñānena nikhila-jñeyāva raṇa-prahāṇa-jñānena sarvākāra-sarva-sattvārtha-karaṇa-śaktyā karuṇā-sampattyā 'kṣayatā-sampattyā 'tulatā-sampattyā ca samagraiḥ. (p. 184, line 30; p. 185, line 5.)

Ṭīkā: blo khyad par du 'phags pa 'di la yod pas na *sangs rgyas* zhes bya'o// blo khyad par du 'phags pa yang rnam pa dgu ste/ thams cad mkhyen pa dang/ rnam pa thams cad mkhyen pa dang/ bsgrim mi dgos par mkhyen pa dang/ lung phog pa med par mkhyen pa dang/ nyon mongs pa dang shes bya'i sgrib pa bag chags dang bcas pa spangs pa dang/ rnam pa thams cad du sems can thams cad kyi don mdzad par spyod pa dang/ thugs rje phun sum tshogs pa dang/ zad mi shes pa phun sum tshogs pa dang/ mtshungs pa med pa phun sum tshogs pas so// (p. 70 b.)

He is called *Buddha* because he has distinguished intellect. The distinguished intellect is of nine kinds: 1) all-knowing (*sarvajña*), 2) knowing all aspects (*sarvākārajña*), 3) knowing effortlessly (*ayatna-jñāna*), 4) knowing things untaught (*anupadiṣṭajñāna*), 5) rejecting hindrances of evil passions and hindrances regarding things to be known together with their lingering tendencies (*savāsanasaṃkle-śajñeyāvaraṇaprahāṇa*), 6) performing beneficial acts for all sentient beings in every way (*sarvākārasarvasattvārthakaraṇaśakti*), 7) attaining compassion (*karuṇāsampatti*), 8) attaining inexhaustibility (*akṣayatāsampatti*), and 9) attaining unsurpassed status (*atulatā-sampatti*).

III

There are several further passages in the *Āloka* which Haribhadra is believed to have reproduced from Jñānagarbha's *Ṭīkā*. In one, Haribhadra explains how Maitreya acquired his name in much the same way as Jñānagarbha explains how Amoghadarśin acquired his.

In the following quotations from the *Āloka*, the punctuation of Wogihara's edition has been altered to match that in the corresponding parts of the *Ṭīkā*.

Āloka: 1. maitreyo nāma samādhiḥ tal-lābhāt. 2. kasyacit samādher maitreyatvaṃ phalaṃ tad-adhigamāt. 3. pūrva-praṇihita-maitrī-phalābhisamayād. 4. īdṛśo vā guṇās tena maitrī-vimokṣa-mukha-prabhā-vitatvād arjitā yenāsau maitreyo jāta iti *Maitreya*. (p. 325, lines 19–22.)

Ṭīkā: 1. ting nge 'dzin thob pa ni/ mthong ba don yod ces bya ba'i ting nge 'dzin te/ de thob pa'i phyir/ byang chub sems dpa' yang mthong ba don yod ces gsungs pa dang/ 2. ting nge 'dzin de'i 'bras bu thob pa ni/ ting nge 'dzin 'ga' zhig gi 'bras bu mthong be don yod pa nyid de/ de thob pa'i phyir/ mthong ba don yod ces gsungs pa dang/ 3. smon lam gyi 'bras bu thob pa ni/ sngon gyi smon lam gyi 'bras bu thob pa'i phyir/ mthong ba don yod ces gsungs pa dang/ 4. yon tan bsgrubs pa'i 'bras bu thob pa ni/[12] des gang gis mthong ba don yod par hyur pa de lta bu'i yon tan bsgrubs pas na de'i phyir mthong ba don yod ces gsungs pa'o// (p. 53 c–d.)

1. Attainment of a *samādhi*: there is a *samādhi* named *amogha-darśin*; because he has attained it, Bodhisattva Amoghadarśin is so called. 2. Attainment of the fruit of a *samādhi*: the fruit of a specific *samādhi* is the state of *Amoghadarśin*; because he has attained it, he is called *Amoghadarśin*. 3. Attainment of the fruit of the vow: because he has attained the purpose of his former vow [to become 'one with the unfailing sight'], he is called *Amoghadarśin*. 4. Attainment of the fruit of producing merits: because such merits (as his, *i.e.*, the unfailing sight) are produced by the manner in which he became one with the unfailing sight, he is called *Amoghadarśin*.

In another passage, referring to Buddha's refusal to enter *parinirvāṇa* as long as there remains even one being to be saved, Haribhadra says in the *Āloka*:

> syān matis tathāgata-vineya-sattvāsambhavāt parinirvāṇam iti. tad atra cintyam. kiṃ buddha-rūpa-vineyā eva sattvā na vidyante. kiṃ vā rūpāntara-vineyā apīti. yadi pūrvaḥ pakṣaḥ tadā Śakrādi-rūpa-saṃdarśana-vineya-jana-sambhavāt tādrūpyeṇa kiṃ nāvatiṣṭhate. (p. 146, lines 15–19.)

We find a similar explanation in the *Ṭīkā*:

> de bas na ji srid du gzung par bya ba'i sems can gcig tsam yod pa de srid du de dag mya ngan las 'da' ba ni mi rigs pa dang/ sangs rgyas kyis gdul ba'i sems can med du zin kyang// brgya byin la sogs pa'i gzugs kyis gdul ba yod pa'i phyir ro// (p. 52 c-d.)

Therefore, as long as there is even one sentient being to be taken in, he (*i.e.*, Buddha) is not supposed to enter *nirvāṇa*. Even if there is no sentient being to be taught by Buddha, there are beings to be taught [by him] in the form of Indra and so forth.

Jñānagarbha maintains that the *nirmāṇakāya* enters *nirvāṇa* but not the *saṃbhogakāya*. He quotes the following verse of the *Suvarṇaprabhāsa* as Scriptural evidence:

> sangs rgyas mya ngan yod mi 'da'//
> chos kyang nub par mi 'gyur te//
> sems can yongs su smin mdzad phyir//
> yongs su mya ngan 'da' ba ston// (p. 52 d.)
> (na buddhaḥ parinirvāti na dharmaḥ parihīyate/
> sattvānāṃ paripākāya parinirvāṇa deśayet//)[13]

The fact that Haribhadra quotes the same verse[14] following the above explanation suggests a strong possibility that he has availed himself of Jñānagarbha's views on this point also.

In another passage from the *Āloka* we find the following explanation of the numerical terms describing the number of Buddhas who have passed into *nirvāṇa*:

> *aprameyāprameyāṇām* ityādi laukika-vīta-rāgāṇāṃ śaikṣāṇām aśaikṣaṇāṃ pratye-buddhānāṃ bodhisattvānāṃ ca yathākramam *aprameyāsaṃkhyeyāparimāṇācintyāparyantānāṃ* jñāna-pathātītatvenāprameyādayo veditavyāḥ. (p. 329, lines 13–16.)

It is very likely that Haribhadra borrowed Jñānagarbha's views on the significance of the similar terms describing the number of kalpas which have elapsed, for it is said in the *Ṭīkā*:

> *grangs med pa* ni 'jig rten pa'i 'dod chags dang bral ba rnams kyi shes pa'i lam las 'das pa'o// *ches grangs med pa* ni slob pa 'dod chags dang bral ba rnams kyi[15] shes pa'i lam las 'das pa'o// *yangs pa* ni mi slob pa

rnams kyi shes pa'i lam las 'das pa'o// *rgya cher gyur pa* ni bse ru la sogs pa'i shes pa'i lam las 'das pa ste// sogs pa smos pas ni rang sangs rgyas tshogs dang spyod pa rnams bsdu'o// *tshad med pa* ni bde bar gshegs pa'i sras rnams kyi shes pa'i lam las 'das pa'o// (p. 69b.)

'Innumerable' (*asaṃkhyeya*) signifies 'beyond the knowledge of common men who have rid themselves of greed'. 'More than innumerable' (*asaṃkhyeyatara*) signifies 'beyond the knowledge of those still in training' (*śaikṣa*). 'Numerous' (*vipula*) means 'beyond the knowledge of those who no longer need training' (*aśaikṣa*). 'Extensive' (*vistara*) means 'beyond the knowledge of solitary sages and others'. 'Others' includes pratyekabuddhas who live in groups (*vargacārin*). 'Immeasurable' (*aprameya*) means 'beyond the knowledge of the *sugata*'s sons' (*i.e., bodhisattvas*).

IV

The above examples will be sufficient to illustrate Haribhadra's indebtedness to Jñānagarbha. Jñānagarbha, who lived in the eighth century,[16] was Śāntirakṣita's predecessor, and is considered to be the originator of the Yogācāra-Mādhyamika School[17] to which Śāntirakṣita, Kamalaśīla, and Haribhadra belonged.[18] The facts that Haribhadra was Śāntirakṣita's disciple[19] and that he quotes from Kamalaśīla's *Tattvasaṃgrahapañjikā* indicate further that he was well acquainted with Jñānagarbha's thought. Even though it is difficult, at present, to find any significant link between them in fundamental doctrinal points, the evidence which has been presented above of Haribhadra's heavy reliance on Jñānagarbha's views on the meanings of important terms like Buddha's epithets brings to light the hitherto hidden relationship between the two scholars and helps clarify the lineage of the Yogācāra-Mādhyamika School.

NOTES

1. Mkhas Grub Rje's *Fundamentals of the Buddhist Tantras*, translated by F. D. Lessing and A. Wayman, The Hague and Paris: 1968, p. 97: "Ārya Vimuktasena, Bhadanta Vimuktasena, Haribhadra, Buddhajñānapāda,

Abhaya, and so forth, explained it (*abhisamayālaṇkāra*) as Svātantrika." Haribhadra's life is generally dated in the eighth century. E. Conze gives the probable year of his death as 770 (*The Prajñāpāramitā Literature*, The Hague: 1960, p. 120), and recently R. Kano gave his life span as 730-795 (*Genkanshōgonron no kenkyū*, Tokyo: 1972, p. 17). Earlier, P. L. Vaidya postulated that the *Āloka* was composed during 776-808 or 800-808 (Buddhist Sanskrit Texts, No. 4, xiv).

2. *Āloka*, ed. Wogihara, p. 1; *Sphuṭārtha, Tibetan Tripiṭaka*, Vol. 90, p. 273d.

3. *Gaekwad's Oriental Series*, No. 62, *Abhisamayālaṃkārāloka*, ed. G. Tucci, Baroda: 1932, pp. 27-31; R. Mano, *loc. cit.*, p. 18.

4. H. Amano, "Genganshōgonron no chosakumokuteki ni tsuite," *Journal of Indian and Buddhist Studies*, Vol. 17, No. 2, pp. 895-905.

5. The text reads ". . . -sampadaḥ *samyag* aviparītaṃ."

6. The Peking version omits *thams cad du chos.*

7. *pa* in the Peking version.

8. *stod* in the Peking version.

9. *pa* in the Peking version.

10. *kyi* in the Peking version.

11. *pa* in the Peking version.

12. Derge, Narthang, and Peking omit *ni*/.

13. *Suvarṇaprabhāsa*, 2. 30.

14. The verse quoted by Haribhadra (p. 147, lines 5-6) reads:

> "na buddaḥ parinirvāti dharmo 'ntardhīyate na ca/
> sattvānāṃ paripākāya nirvāṇaṃ tūpadarśayet//"

15. *kyis* in the Peking version.

16. Jñānagarbha's life span is given by J. Nagasawa as c.700-760 (*Daijōbukkyō yugagyō shisō no hattenkeitai*, Tokyo: 1969, pp. 4-16.

17. *History of Buddhism by Bu-ston*, translator E. Obermiller, Heidelberg: 1932, Vol. 2, p. 135. Tsong-kha-pa's pupil Mkhas-grub-rje considered Jñānagarbha to be an adherent of the Sautrāntika-Mādhyamika theories held by Bhāvaviveka and attributes the foundation of the Yogācāra-Mādhyamika School to Śāntirakṣita (*Mkhas Grub Rje's Fundamentals of the Buddhist Tantras*, p. 93; also, *History of Buddhism by Bu-ston*, pp. 135-6, footnote). In the *Saṃdhinirmocanabhāṣya*, however, Jñānagarbha declared the relative and provisional existence of empirical things which was based on *ālayavijñāna* while maintaining in the *Anantamukhanirhāradhāraṇīṭīkā* that all things are void and originally unproduced. Being a versatile scholar well-versed in the doctrines of Yogācāra, Mādhyamika, and Esotericism, Jñānagarbha should not be dismissed simply as a Yogācāra-Mādhyamika; but his theory along this line of thought certainly led to a fuller development of the Yogācāra-Mādhyamika doctrine of Śāntirakṣita. Cf. J. Nagasawa, *op. cit.*, p. 275.

18. *History of Buddhism by Bu-ston*, Vol. 2, p. 135.

19. Haribhadra learned the Mādhyamika doctrine from Śāntirakṣita (*Geschichte des Buddhismus*, translator A. Schiefner, St. Petersburg: 1869, p. 219). Haribhadra and Vimuktisena are also mentioned as Śāntirakṣita's disciples in *Mkhas Grub Rje's Fundamentals of Buddhist Tantras*, p. 91.

The Editing of Buddhist Texts

Lewis R. Lancaster

When Erasmus compiled his edition of the Greek New Testament from half a dozen manuscripts and rushed it into print, the work came to be called the *Textus Receptus* and for nearly four centuries undeservedly dominated the field of New Testament study.[1] In Buddhist studies related to Mahāyāna there is also a *Textus Receptus*, or perhaps we should say *Textus Recepti*, since the Buddhist texts are so numerous. These texts are the Sanskrit editions that have been published over the last century. From these editions have come the translations and studies on which Western scholarship has been based and from which we derive most of our descriptions of the doctrines of Mahāyāna. Thus, in an often unspoken but nevertheless practiced idea, the Sanskrit extant manuscript tradition and the edited versions of it are taken as the 'original' or the closest we can ever hope to come in the effort to determine the autograph.

The source of these 'Received Texts' of Mahāyāna is for the greater part in India, in Pala-Dynasty palm leaves and scattered copies from later centuries or in Nepalese manuscripts which are often late copies of the eighteenth or nineteenth century and show all the signs of erosion which can occur because of scribal errors. Thus most of our printed texts are based on material that at its oldest dates to the ninth century.[2] While such texts, a few as old as a thousand years, are ancient in terms of extant writings, they date from a relatively late period for Indian Buddhism, a time when the tradition was in the waning years of its development.

Naturally, scholars are very excited when new manuscripts become available. Romantic journeys to Central Asia with remarkable finds of old material have become legendary.[3] In more recent times the discovery of the cache of birchbark manuscripts in Gilgit[4] made available new material for editing and evaluating existing Sanskrit editions. But for all of the excitement generated by these new finds, it should be pointed out that the fragments brought from the sands of Central Asia or the crumbling ruins of the *stūpa* at Gilgit contain material which was in part already at hand. On the shelves of our libraries, at the time when the Gilgit fragments were being deposited in their present locations, scholars had in printed edited form some of the same information to be found in these manuscripts. That is to say, the Chinese Buddhist canon was already available.

From the second century onward, Buddhist missionaries were hard at work translating their sacred texts from Sanskrit or some form of Prakrit into Chinese. The efforts required to accomplish this task, and the difficulties that had to be overcome, have often been described. However, scholars have wondered and remarked about the seemingly impossible task of translating complex doctrinal statements full of technical vocabulary by missionaries who probably could not read or write Chinese or perhaps even speak it. There has arisen some suspicion about these translation efforts. How accurate can they be? Is there not room for doubt about their success when one thinks of them being put together by a group, with a missionary reading or reciting the original, a helper or the missionary putting them into colloquial language from which the Chinese could be taken, another setting down the characters, and perhaps yet another polishing it for style? And when this was all completed, who was there to check the outcome against the original? Without dictionaries for terminology, with no previous translations to serve as guides, one can marvel that the work of the early missionaries in China was ever accomplished and at the same time question the accuracy of the work.[5]

The Chinese has always been of limited value for the editor who wishes to reconstruct the exact Sanskrit word and form. In the translation task, these early missionaries were faced with the Indic nouns in three numbers; with three genders; with the verb in three persons and three numbers; with present, imperfect, imperative, optative, perfect, aorist, future, and conditional modes and tenses; with active, middle, and passive voice; and with intensive, desiderative, and causative conjugations. There were also numerous particles and compounds, which were comprised of several members. The target language, on the other hand, had no inflections for case, number, tense, mood, or voice. The relationship between the component characters was established by position, stress, or particles. In isolation a one-character word was neither singular nor plural, nominal, verbal, adjectival, past, present, future or agent.

Thus, few editors have given much attention to the Chinese when working with the Sanskrit manuscripts. It has been the Tibetan translations which have received the most attention. It is the Tibetan which can often provide answers about vocabulary, since the equivalents are more standardized than among the Chinese translators, and it is the Tibetan particles which can often settle issues regarding Sanskrit syntax.

What then are the values of the Chinese translations for the editor? While they will perhaps never determine whether the active or middle voice was used in the original Indic texts, they can play an important role in deciding on the content. It is the content of a text which can indicate how it has changed over the centuries and how the focus and use of technical terms have undergone transmutation. Further, one of the great advantages of the Chinese translations is that we know the date of their completion and know they came from one of the best scribal traditions in the world. In South Asia the scribe was and still is often illiterate, a copyist working by quantity, possibly unable to read or understand any of the material being copied. For anyone who works with Nepalese manuscripts, the truth of scribal error becomes a terrible reality. It is fairly safe to say that the later the manuscript copy the more distorted it becomes. But in China, writing is the skill of a learned man, and the expertness of one's writing is a sign of culture and training. Therefore, only the best and most learned were chosen to do the writing. When we compare a T'ang-dynasty manuscript with a thirteenth-century woodblock and a modern printing of the same text, we find a few different characters or an occasional alternate way of writing the character, but the text is found to have been transmitted with remarkable fidelity over these centuries. It is for this reason that the editing of a Chinese Buddhist text from existing sources is normally a dull task, and the discoveries of little significance.[6] With this in mind, we can make use of the extant copies with some assurance that they are not too different from the autograph of earlier centuries.

The questioning of the value of the early Chinese translations is by no means limited to the modern textual editor. Complaints were constantly being made by the Chinese themselves. Hsüan-tsang, faced with the 100,000-line *Prajñāpāramitā* text,[7] thought to follow the example of his illustrious predecessor Kumārajīva—that is, to make an 'abbreviation' of the text. That night, after making this decision, Hsüan-tsang in a horrible nightmare saw the visions of hell open up before him, and on awakening he made a solemn vow not to perish but to publish in complete form.[8] Thus even in the T'ang dynasty the earlier Chinese versions were under suspicion. When the first *Prajñāpāramitā* text, in 8000 lines, had been made available by the translation bureau of An Shih-kao and the efforts of Lokakṣema,[9] the Chinese were distressed to learn that their prized version was a shortened one and that there was a complete, longer version ready and waiting in Central Asia and India. They were never content until this version, in 25,000 lines, was put safely into their hands.[10] From this came their maxim, "The longest version equals earliest version." All shorter versions were thereafter considered incomplete or abbreviated by translators such as Kumārajīva. This idea is still found on the shelves of our libraries.[11]

Modern scholars have in some ways followed the same principle with regard to the Chinese translations. The Sanskrit text, the 'received text', is the standard; and when Kumārajīva's version is compared with the Sanskrit the differences that occur are often said to be merely Kumārajīva's style. If, for example, one compares Kumārajīva's version of the *Vajracchedikāprajñāpāramitāsūtra* with the Sanskrit edition of Max Müller,[12] it appears to be a shortened version with words left out or whole phrases omitted.

However, a new day is beginning for the Chinese translations.

With the discovery of the Gilgit fragments as well as those from Central Asia, we now have a more complete picture of the Sanskrit for this well-known Mahāyāna text.[13] The Chinese translations are numerous and date from 400 A.D. to 703 A.D. They were done by some of the greatest names in Chinese Buddhist history: Kumārajīva, Bodhiruci, Paramārtha, Hsüan-tsang, and I Ching.

In the text passage reproduced below, the oldest Chinese version of Kumārajīva is compared with the printed edition of the extant Sanskrit manuscripts used by Max Müller. Contrasted with these is a third, the Gilgit manuscript, representing the oldest Sanskrit version yet discovered. All of the words belong to the Müller edition; those that are italicized are found in the Gilgit version; and those with equivalents in Kumārajīva's translation are marked with asterisks.

> *Bhagavān āha*[14]
>
> *tat kiṃ manyase subhūte dvātriṃśan mahāpuruṣalakṣaṇais tathagato* 'rhan samyaksambuddho *draṣṭavyaḥ/*
>
> Subhūtir *āha*
>
> *no* hīdaṃ *bhagavan* na dvātriṃśan mahāpuruṣalakṣanais tathagato 'rhan saṃyaksambuddho draṣṭavyaḥ/ *tat kasya hetoḥ/ yāni* hi *tāni* bhagavan *dvātriṃśan mahāpuruṣalakṣaṇāni tathagatena bhāṣitāny/ alakṣaṇāni* tāni bhagavaṃs tathagatena bhāṣitāni/ *teno-cyante dvātriṃśan mahāpuruṣalakṣaṇānīti/*
>
> *bhagavan āha*
>
> *yaś ca khalu punaḥ subhūte strī vā puruṣo vā* dine dine *gaṅgāna-dīvāluka*samān *ātmabhāvān parityajet/* evaṃ partiyajan gaṅgāna-dīvālukāsamān kalpāṃs tān ātmabhāvān parityajet/ *yaś ceto* (MM 30) *dharmaparyāyād antaśaś catuṣpādikām api gāthām udgṛhya pare-bhyo deśayet* samprakāśayed/ *ayam eva tato nidānaṃ bahu*taraṃ *puṇya*skandhaṃ prasunuyād *aprameyam asamkhyeyam/*

When Kumārajīva is compared with the Müller edition his work does appear to be abbreviated, but this is not the case when it is placed alongside the earlier Gilgit text. It would appear from this type of comparison that Kumārajīva's version represents a Sanskrit tradition quite similar to that preserved in the Gilgit ruins. Hsüan-tsang need not have had his nightmare of being like Kumārajīva; he had only to accept the fact that Buddhist *sūtra*s were documents undergoing constant and at times radical changes through the centuries. For many believers such as Hsüan-tsang it was impossible to imagine that anyone could have altered the words of the Buddha, so they explained differences by blaming the translators, accusing some of them of altering texts deliberately. For the modern scholar who relies on the comparison of the late Sanskrit manuscripts with the early Chinese versions, the time has come when it is necessary to justify assertions about the differences to be found in the Chinese. On what basis can one assume that the Chinese is in error or a deliberate abbreviation of the translator? The time is past when Kumārajīva can be ridiculed and used as a bogey to frighten the translator in his dreams. The proof is becoming more formidable every year that in the Chinese we have an invaluable source of evidence for making new editions with some assurance that these translators knew their craft and practiced it with vigor and accuracy.

[This paper was presented at the International Congress of the History of Religions at the University of Lancaster, England, in the summer of 1975].

NOTES

1. Bruce Metzger, *The Text of the New Testament: Its Transmission, Corruption, and Restoration*, Oxford University Press: 1968, p. 95 ff.
2. C. Bendall, *Catalogue of Buddhist Sanskrit Manuscripts in the University Library of Cambridge*, Cambridge University Press: 1883.
   R. Mitra, *The Sanskrit Buddhist Literature of Nepal*, Calcutta, Sanskrit Pustak Bhandar (reprint), 1971.
These along with other similar catalogues give an indication of the dating of extant manuscripts.
3. A. Stein, *On Central Asian Tracks*, London: Macmillan and Co., 1933.
4. N. Dutt, *Gilgit Manuscripts*, Vol. 1, Srinagar, Kashmir: 1939.
5. K. Ch'en, *Buddhism in China*, Princeton University Press, 1964, p. 365 ff.
6. A glance at the footnotes listing alternate readings in the *Taishō Shinshū Daizōkyō*, Tokyo: 1924–29, is sufficient to establish the nature of those variations.
7. E. Conze, *The Prajñāpāramitā Literature*, 's Gravenhage: Mouton & Co., 1960, pp. 37–40.
8. See T. 2154-557b ff.
9. Conze, pp. 51–52.
10. Conze, pp. 40–45.

11. See R. Shih, *Biographies des Moines Éminents* (*Kao seng tchouan*) *de Houei-Kiao* (tr. and annotated), *Bibliotheque du Muséon*, Vol. 54, Louvain: Institut Orientaliste, 1968. p. 13, note 51 describes Lokakṣema's translation as an excerpt of the larger 25,000-line text.

12. F. M. Müller, *Buddhist Texts From Japan* (*Anecdota Oxoniensia Arya Ser.*), Vol. 1, Oxford: Clarendon Press, 1881.

13. G. Tucci, *Minor Buddhist Texts, Serie Orientale Roma*, Vol. 9, Rome Instituto Italiano per il Medio ed Estremo Oriente, 1956.

14. See E. Conze, *Vajracchedikāprajñāpāramitāsūtra, Serie Orientale, Roma*, Vol. 13, Rome: Instituto Italiano per il Medio ed Estremo Oriente, 1974, pp. 38-39.

Kumārajīva's version is T. 235-750a:20 ff.

Piracy in South China in the Nineteenth Century

Man-kam Leung

THE APPEARANCE OF PIRATES in South China in the early nineteenth century was a phenomenon which symbolized the decline of Ch'ing power. Pirates became active during the last years of the Ch'ien-lung period (1736–1795). Their activities coincided with the White Lotus rebellion in the northwest during this period. This paper is a preliminary study of sea piracy during the Chia-ch'ing period (1796–1820) with particular emphasis on the career of the pirate chief Ts'ai Ch'ien (d. 1809).

THE ORIGINS OF THE CHINESE PIRATES IN THE EARLY NINETEENTH CENTURY

The activities of the pirates in South China in the nineteenth century were closely linked with the internal political situation in Annam during this period. The struggle between Nguyên Quang-Toán and Nguyên Phúc-Ánh for the throne of Annam after 1792 created chances for many Chinese adventurers in South China. Nguyên Quang-Toán was hard pressed for funds for his war efforts. In order to increase his revenue he sent half of his fleet, manned mainly by Chinese desperados and renegades, to venture into Chinese waters for loot. They left in the summer and returned to Annam in the autumn, and were known to the Chinese as the 'barbarian fleet' (*i-t'ing*). As time went on the Annamese pirates were joined by Chinese pirate groups—the *Feng-mei* gang the the *Shui-ao* gang. After 1795, with the Chinese pirates as their guides, the Annamese ships went as far as Fukien and Chekiang waters. Annamese ships were larger and better equipped with armaments than the Chinese navy. Outnumbering and outgunning Chinese coastal defenses, the pirates were roaming at will the South China Sea. In 1796 the term *t'ing-fei* ('boat bandits') first appeared in Chinese government documents to designate the Chinese and Annamese pirates in these areas.[1] By this time the pirate situation in Fukien and in Chekiang had become so bad that the court repeatedly pressed local authorities for positive action against the pirates. The counteraction taken by the local officials was to keep on sending reports to the court that many pirates had been captured or had voluntarily surrendered to the authorities. One retired grand counselor from Fukien complained in family letters to Peking of the widespread piratical activities in his home province. When the Chia-ch'ing emperor heard of this complaint and asked the Fukien authorities for an explanation,[2] the acting governor-general of Chekiang and Fukien, Kuei-lun (d. 1800), answered the imperial query by saying that flooding around the Chang-chou and Ch'üan-chou areas had driven many poor people into unemployment, and that these unemployed may have gone to sea as pirates. However, the governor-general assured the emperor that these pirates were only small-timers, and would be disbanded and dispersed by the authorities in no time. But when the emperor received the news in July that 47 officers and soldiers were killed in action against the pirates, the court demanded an explanation. The Tartar general Ha-tang-a of Fu-chou memorialized, "The pirates speak Cantonese, and some of them are dressed in foreign [Annamese] costumes."[3] Ha-tang-a apparently tried to blame the authorities in Kwangtung for the pirate activities in the Fukien area. The court rebuked Ha-tang-a by asking him, "Can we allow foreign bandits to have their way to rob us in our waters?"[4] However, the governor of Kwangtung, Chu Kuei (1731-1807), still got the blame for the pirate activities in the Fukien and Chekiang areas. Chu was dismissed from his post, much to the displeasure of the Chia-ch'ing emperor, because Chu was his former teacher and one of his trusted counselors.

The situation in the Fukien and the Chekiang areas continued to deteriorate until 1800, when the Chia-ch'ing emperor assumed personal control of the government, and Juan Yuan (1764–1849) was appointed governor of Chekiang. By this time the Annamese pirates were gradually fading from the scene, and the Chinese pirates took over. The leaders among them were Ts'ai Ch'ien in Fukien and Chekiang, and Chu Fen (d. 1809) in the Kwangtung area.

Juan Yuan arrived in Chekiang in the fall of 1799. Juan was a young bureaucrat eager to prove himself to the Chia-ch'ing emperor. In fact, his appointment to this post was secured by Chu Kuei, his own former teacher and a trusted minister of the Chia-ch'ing emperor. As Chu Kuei had earlier been blamed for his failure to curb the pirate activities in Kwangtung, Juan Yuan's appointment to Chekiang might have been an attempt on Chu's part to restore his defamed honor by sending one of his capable lieutenants to the troubled areas. If that were the case, Juan Yuan disappointed neither his former teacher nor the Chia-ch'ing emperor.

Juan Yuan was not new to the pirate activities in Chekiang. When he had been a director of education in this province in 1795 he had already had a bitter experience with the way in which the pirates operated. One of the candidates for the civil service examination complained to him in tears that his mother and his wife were both kidnapped by the pirates for ransom. He raised enough money to pay for the life of his mother, but not enough to ransom his wife. Consequently, his wife was killed by the pirates. Juan Yuan felt very strongly about this tragedy, but was not able to do anything about it.[5] Suppression of pirates was outside the jurisdiction of the director of education.

THE OPERATIONAL TECHNIQUES OF THE PIRATES

Financial Sources: Ransom, Booty, and Protection Fees

Ransom was one form of income for the pirates. If the money was paid, the victims were usually returned unharmed, as in the case of the candidate's mother mentioned above. However, if the ransom was not paid, the kidnapped victim was often killed as an exemplary action against any resistance to cooperation. The other form of income for the pirates was booty from raids. When the Annamese were still active, booty was often shipped back to Annam for disposal. Targets of the raids were not so much the coastal villages as the seaborne Chinese junks trading between China and Southeast Asia at that time. Taking such booty was often lucrative. In order to avoid being attacked at sea, the Chinese junk merchants often donated handsome protection fees to the pirates. In return, the pirates issued certificates of impunity. To a lesser degree, the levy of protection fees was also imposed on the coastal fishermen. In 1803, the court instructed the governor-general of Chekiang and Fukien, Yü-te (d. 1809), to investigate the protection-fees racket. The emperor told Yü-te:

> I was informed recently that in Fukien the pirates and the secret society members are joint partners in crime. In coastal ports, every merchant ship which goes overseas has to pay $400 in barbarian currency [Spanish dollars]. Any ship returning from abroad has to double this amount. The fee is handed to Ts'ai Ch'ien. If this fee is paid, nothing will happen. Otherwise any unwilling merchant will lose his fortune as well as his life. Furthermore, on land the membership of the secret societies is enormous. Even some of the clerks and policemen in the government services are joining these societies. The local authorities helplessly watch this growing trend, but do not dare to do anything about it. If this trend does not stop in time, it will result in great disaster. I therefore instruct you to investigate secretly. You should send capable men in your office to infiltrate into these societies by disguising themselves as merchants willing to cooperate, in order to discover the true identities of the ringleaders and their whereabouts. In this way, the ringleaders of these societies may be captured in one sweep of action. Once they are captured, they should be executed immediately. The lives of lower-ranking members, or members who were forced to join these societies, should be spared. If you can tackle several such cases in this way, people will be greatly impressed and may divert their minds towards better things. If we execute scores of criminals to save the lives of millions, how great will be the number of merit points in our karma! As for Ts'ai Ch'ien, he is the big evil pirate. As long as he is not removed, there will be no peace in our waters. I guess that those who share the booty with Ts'ai are mostly members in the secret society. The best way to conduct a secret investigation is to look around in the monasteries, flower boats [floating bordelloes?], and opium dens. Then you can find clues and information. If you proclaim

> openly and send out troops to make arrests, this will simply drive the guilty ones into open revolt. Any open action against them not only will bring you no result, but will also cause great damage to your investigation. Be careful and be secretive.[6]

The emperor's advice might have worked if the vested interests in local areas had not outweighed those of the central government.

Organized Corruption: Political Bribes and 'Kickbacks' to the Ch'ing Officials

The pirates, in order to have their booty effectively disposed of or their supply guaranteed, needed some connections on land to serve as partners in crime. Members in the secret societies performed this function as co-partners with the pirates. However, in order to avoid being harassed by the authorities, the pirates also needed information concerning troop movements or any news of dangers to their operation. It was in this respect that bribes and 'kickbacks' to the Ch'ing officials came into the picture. In 1800, the Chia-ch'ing emperor charged that there were financial kickbacks known as *hai-feng* ('salary from the sea') to local officials serving in the coastal areas.[7] In return, the local authorities supplied the pirates with information about any plans unfavorable to their operations. The usual practice was that the pirates divided their booty into three shares. The clerks and policemen in the local *yamen* were entitled to one share, the local army and navy unit to another share, and the pirates themselves kept the third share. Thus, as the Chia-ch'ing emperor pointed out, crimes committed by the pirates were seldom solved because local authorities were actually business partners of the pirates.

This intricate web of organized corruption was one of the major factors contributing to the perpetuation of the pirate problem. More than once a particular pirate group was able to save itself through connections with the local authorities. The biggest kickback known to have been transmitted was to Yü-te, the governor-general whom the Chia-ch'ing emperor had entrusted with the investigation of the connections between the pirates and the members of the secret society. In 1803, when Ts'ai Ch'ien was pursued by Li Ch'ang-keng (1750–1808) into the Fukien area, the relentless attack of Li made

Ts'ai lose many of his ships. He therefore informed Yü-te that he was willing to surrender to him. His message was accompanied by a gift of 100,000 taels of silver, with a note that the governor-general should order Li Ch'ang-keng's fleet to move from the upwind position by returning to port. Yü-te complied and Ts'ai escaped.

Raiding Techniques

The Annamese ships were larger and better equipped in weaponry. Their masts measured up to eighty Chinese feet. Their cannon weighed as much as 4,000 catties. All ship surfaces were protected by ox-skins and nets to ward off enemy fire. When a raid took place, the Annamese ships acted as naval cover for their Chinese collaborators. Their cannon fire often neutralized the barrage from the coastal defense. Their bigger ships kept the smaller Chinese vessels at bay. In this way, the Chinese pirates were able to charge ashore with relative ease under the protection of the firing umbrella of the Annamese ships. Before a raid was planned, spies were sent ashore to gather information about a particular area. This technique was to continue even when the Annamese pirates left the scene.

THE DESTRUCTION OF THE ANNAMESE PIRATES AND THE RISE OF TS'AI CH'IEN

When Juan Yuan arrived in Chekiang in the fall of 1799, the situation there was really pathetic. According to his estimate, the combined strength of both Annamese and Chinese pirates was about 200 ships with 20,000 men. The Chinese navy in Chekiang was only about three to four thousand men with one hundred ships, none of which equalled the technical mastery of the Annamese ships.[8] This sad situation might well be illustrated by the expressed confidence of one of the pirate chiefs. When a civil servant on his payroll informed him of the arrival of a new governor, adding that things might become different or even difficult, the pirate feasted his informant, and then pointed to his big ship, saying boastfully, "I sailed this big ship with a food supply to last me ten months. My cannons weigh several thousand catties. I just come here to collect my share of the revenue. That governor, he had better be careful (because he is the one who has troubles). He is no match for me."[9]

At this time, the Annamese fleet was commanded by a Chinese renegade known as Lun Kuei-li, a Cantonese by origin. His real Chinese name was Wang Kuei-li. He joined the Annamese army of Nguyên Quang-Toán in 1794; and because of valor in battle he rose rapidly in rank. Eventually he was entrusted with naval operations in Chinese waters. He divided his navy into three task forces: front, middle, and rear. He himself commanded the rear task force which had about 28 ships. Early in 1800, more than thirty Annamese ships gathered in Chekiang and anchored among the offshore islands near the Lin-hai and Wen-chou areas. At this time the Chinese pirate groups, the *Shui-ao* and the *Feng-mei* gangs, each having about sixty to seventy ships, were also gathering there. Ts'ai Ch'ien's group of about seventy ships were also roaming in this area.[10] A general alarm was sounded through Chekiang province. Juan Yuan succeeded in stirring up differences between the two Chinese pirate groups of the *Shui-ao* and the *Feng-mei*, and occasional skirmishes were fought among them. The reason for this massive convergence of pirate ships in this area was probably that they were waiting for the fishing season in the Chou-shan archipelago area, which was in April and May of each year.[11] In June, the Annamese ships and their Chinese ally, the Feng-mei group, were pushing towards Sung-shan County; and a landing was also in preparation. This change in anchorage area may have been due to the signal of a coming hurricane. Around 7 P.M. on June 21, 1800, the hurricane came; and most of the pirate ships were destroyed. About eight hundred pirates were captured alive, including Lun Kuei-li himself. About four to five thousand pirates were drowned. After this, the Annamese ships disappeared from Chinese waters. But the destruction of the Annamese fleet only made way for the rise of Ts'ai Ch'ien.

Ts'ai Ch'ien was a native of T'ung-an County, Fukien Province. Not much is known of his family background except that he was a commoner and went to sea around 1795 to become a pirate. His name first appeared in government documents in 1798, when the authorities reported that his ships had left Taiwan for the mainland.[12] By this time he was already referred to as a pirate chief. In 1800, when the Annamese ships and other pirates were destroyed by the hurricane in the Chekiang area, his ships were left intact. By force, intrigue, or persuasion, he was able to incorporate the remnants of the Annamese ships and other pirate groups under his leadership. With these new elements joining his force, his power exploded. On land, he concluded an alliance with the secret societies to guarantee his supplies. He centered his activities around the Chekiang and Fukien areas with occasional excursions into Taiwan. The Ch'ing government could do very little to curb his activities, because its ships were inferior to those of Ts'ai; and the whole naval force was plagued with the problem of organized corruption. Juan Yuan realized this; and in 1800 he made several suggestions to the emperor to improve the situation. Juan's proposed changes were:[13]

1. On land, the government should vigorously enforce the *pao-chia* system to track down any subversive elements in the society. Fishermen and merchant ships going to sea must have authorization from the government concerning cargo and the nature of their voyage, thus cutting off supplies to the pirates. In the coastal areas, every one had to carry a certificate of identity.
2. At sea, the existing battleships in the navy should be abandoned. Better and larger ships, modelled after the Annamese pattern, should be built to improve the fighting abilities of the naval vessels. These new battleships should also be equipped with cannon captured from the Annamese pirates or new cannon cast after the Annamese models.
3. Officials should organize local defense units in their areas.
4. The naval forces in Chekiang should be unified under one commander. Juan Yuan recommended Li Ch'ang-keng for this position. At that time, Li Ch'ang-keng was probably the best naval officer in the whole Ch'ing navy.

The Chia-ch'ing emperor agreed to all these proposals. But implementing the changes took time. Ts'ai Ch'ien was therefore left free to roam the South China Sea at will.

In May, 1802, his ships were destroyed by a hurricane around the Fukien area; but the government navy at Fukien was reluctant to wipe him out. In January, 1803, he went to Chekiang to pay tribute to the Buddha at the P'u-t'o Monastery in Ting-hai County. It was there that he was ambushed by Li Ch'ang-keng. By this time, Juan Yuan had already equipped his Chekiang navy with the new battleships known as *t'ing-t'ing*. Because of this, Li was able to inflict heavy losses on Ts'ai's fleet. Ts'ai escaped towards Fukien with Li hot on his trail. Realizing that his end might be near if something were not done immediately, Ts'ai informed Yü-te, the governor-general of Fukien and Chekiang, that he was willing to surrender to him. Yü-te accepted his offer of surrender and ordered the Chekiang navy to return to port. Once the pressure from the Chekiang navy was relieved, Ts'ai refused to honor his pledge to surrender and escaped to sea again. However, after his traumatic encounter with Li Ch'ang-keng's formidable armada of *t'ing-t'ing* battleships, Ts'ai realized that he needed better ships than those of his opponents from Chekiang. He therefore bribed the ship builders and merchant seamen in Fukien to construct bigger and better ships than those of the *t'ing-t'ing* class. After these ships were completed, the merchants were to sail them into the open sea and hand them over to Ts'ai Ch'ien. Then they were to come back and report to the authorities that they had been robbed by the pirates of their cargo and their ships. By this method, within a period of less than a year, Ts'ai was able to rebuild his fleet with better ships and better equipment.

The ship builders in Fukien were able to accomplish this because some legal loopholes existed in the Ch'ing maritime statutes. For battleships, the construction was subject to rigorous prescriptions regulating their layout and equipment. But a merchant ship did not have to subscribe to this kind of regulation, and could be built according to any blueprint one wished. However, a merchant ship could easily be converted into a formidable battleship if the original design permitted it.

In the autumn of 1804, with these new battleships in hand, Ts'ai Ch'ien was able to intercept rice shipments from Taiwan on their way to Fukien. The booty was so handsome that he was able to share it with Chu Fen in Kwangtung. Chu Fen was very grateful for his generosity, as his food was in short supply at that time. Because of this favor from Ts'ai, Chu was willing to join him in his raids in Fukien. The Fukienese navy was afraid or unwilling to stop the activities of Chu and Ts'ai. It happened that Hu Chen-sheng, a commander in the Chekiang navy, was passing through Chekiang with 24 ships transporting building materials for the new ships in the Chekiang navy. Yü-te ordered Hu to attack the pirates; but because of lack of support from the Fukien navy, Hu's whole fleet was annihilated, and Hu himself was killed in action. The Chia-ch'ing emperor was angry and ordered court-martials for those who failed to render support to Hu in his time of need. The emperor also ordered that a unified command of the Chekiang and Fukien navies should be created; and he appointed Li Ch'ang-keng to this new post. The sole duty of this new commander was to suppress Ts'ai Ch'ien.

In August, 1804, Chu Fen and Ts'ai Ch'ien appeared in Ting-hai, Chekiang with a fleet of about one hundred ships. When Li Ch'ang-keng saw the formation of the pirate ships stretching out in one horizontal line, he sailed his ships up and smashed right into the middle of the enemy line. In this way, he broke the enemy formation into two sections. He went for Ts'ai himself and succeeded in destroying Ts'ai's sails; but a hurricane suddenly came up, and Ts'ai was able to flee again. Afterward, Ts'ai blamed Chu for his defeat. Chu was angry and broke his partnership with Ts'ai, returning to Kwangtung.

In the autumn of 1805, Ts'ai Ch'ien sailed toward Taiwan with an armada of more than 100 ships. He blockaded the Lu-erh-men with sunken ships. Lu-erh-men was the key harbor in the southern part of western Taiwan and the center of communications between this island and the mainland. With the support of bandits on land, he declared himself *Chen-hai-wang*, 'the king who stabilized the sea'. The combined land and sea invasion forces boasted a strength of twenty thousand men. They pushed southward as far as the present-day Kaohsiung area.

The Chia-ch'ing emperor severely reprimanded Yü-te and appointed a new imperial commissioner to deal with the rebels. But before the imperial commissioner could assume his duty the invasion force had been stopped on land by the local defense units and at sea by Li Ch'ang-keng's navy.

When Ts'ai was busy attacking cities, Li Ch'ang-keng and his Chekiang navy attacked Ts'ai's fleet from the sea. Li succeeded in trapping Ts'ai's main fleet at Lu-erh-men. But once again Ts'ai was able to buy his way out through his good relationship with the Fukien navy. When the tide turned, the Fukien navy guarding the harbor let Ts'ai escape to sea with his fleet.

Li Ch'ang-keng complained to the emperor bitterly afterwards, "When Ts'ai broke out from Lu-erh-men, he had with him about 30 ships. Their sails were rotten and his supply of ammunition was insufficient. However, when he got back to Fukien, all the sails were changed into new ones and all his ships were repaired and cleansed—a completely new fleet, with new supplies of ammunition. In this kind of situation, how can this pirate be destroyed?"[14]

The Chia-ch'ing emperor dismissed Yü-te from his post. By this time, those in the Fukien navy were worried for fear of being impeached by Li for their shady dealings with Ts'ai Ch'ien. When the new governor-general, A-lin-pao (d. 1809), a Manchu, arrived, what he heard of Li was hostile criticism from officials in the Fukien administration. Within a period of two months A-lin-pao sent off three secret memorials to the emperor, charging Li with cowardice and incompetence as a naval commander.[15] This aroused the suspicions of the emperor. It happened at this time that Juan Yuan had to resign from his office because his father had passed away. The emperor therefore instructed Ch'ing-an-t'ai, the successor to Juan Yuan as governor of Chekiang, to report to him in secret whether A-lin-pao's charges against Li were true. Fortunately for Li, Ch'ing-an-ta'i was an upright official and reported back to His Majesty in the negative on all charges against Li. The Chia-ch'ing emperor was furious, rebuking A-lin-pao by asking him how he was able to pass judgment on Li after being in office for only two months, and warning him of the consequences of any further unfounded criticism of Li.

In January, 1808, Li pursued Ts'ai into Kwangtung waters. With only three ships left in Ts'ai's fleet, the capture of Ts'ai was almost certain. Unfortunately, Li, when he closed in, was hit by a bullet in the throat, and died the following day. When Li was hit his second-in-command, Chang chien-sheng, a naval officer in the Fukien navy, panicked and ordered the whole task force to retreat. Ts'ai Ch'ien once again escaped into Annamese waters. When the Chia-ch'ing emperor received the news of Li's death, his hands trembled as he held the memorial, and he wept. On the recommendation of Juan Yuan, His Majesty then ordered Wang Te-lu (1771–1842) and Ch'iu

Liang-kung (1771-1817), two of the most capable lieutenants in Li's navy, to take over the task of suppressing Ts'ai Ch'ien.

Juan Yuan was reappointed to his former post as governor of Chekiang. When he arrived in Hangchou in April, 1808, he designed a new battle technique for use against Ts'ai. He suggested to the navy that in the next battle encounter with the enemy, it should concentrate on attacking Ts'ai's own flagship by separating him from the rest of his fleet. This technique worked. Ts'ai was annihilated in September, 1809, by the combined naval forces of Chekiang and Fukien, headed by Ch'iu Liang-kung and Wang Te-lu.

FACTORS CONTRIBUTING TO THE DEFEAT OF TS'AI

Failure to Establish a Permanent Base of Operation

The crucial factor responsible for Ts'ai's defeat, in my opinion, was the fact that he was never able to establish a permanent operational base. More than once, he tried to invade Taiwan, probably out of a desire to use this island as his base. This plan failed to materialize. The failure to establish a permanent base out of the reach of the Ch'ing naval power put him in a very precarious position with respect to problems of supply and maintenance of his ships.

Minimal Technological Differences Between the Two Sides

In this naval war between the pirates and the Ch'ing navy, each side fought with the same type of vessels and weaponry. There was no major technological breakthrough with regard to weapons and shipbuilding. The ultimate outcome of this war would naturally be determined by which side had control over most of the material sources and manpower. The Ch'ing government had such control; and their victory was therefore inevitable.

Change in Provincial Leadership

In his fourteen years of activities as a pirate Ts'ai Ch'ien was more than once able to buy his way out of trouble by bribing the provincial leadership, especially in his home province, the Fukien area. Since

1799 the post of governor-general of Chekiang and Fukien had been occupied by two Manchu administrators: Yü-te from 1799 to 1806, and A-lin-pao from 1806 to 1809. It was only when Fang Wei-tien (1756–1815), a Chinese, was appointed to this post in 1809 that talented officers in the Chekiang and Fukien navy were valued. With the help of the administrative abilities of Juan Yuan, another Chinese at Chekiang, the pirates in these two provinces were finally wiped out.[16] This showed that Manchu talents in the Ch'ing administrative hierarchy had greatly declined. It was the Chinese élite that effectively ran the country.

CONCLUSION: WHO WERE THESE PIRATES?

From the trial and interrogation records of the captured pirates, we find that most of them were natives of two provinces: Fukien and Kwangtung. Most of them were former fishermen living in the coastal areas. They became pirates because of famine or unemployment, for lucrative benefits, many leaving families and relatives on land. The life of the pirate was hard. Also, loneliness and the constant fear of being captured by the authorities placed many pirates under emotional strain. Many practiced sodomy because of the lack of orthodox sexual outlets aboard ship.[17]

As for the financial aspects, piracy was extremely attractive. The main sources of pirate income were not booty but rather profits from trade and the levy of protection fees on Chinese junks travelling between China and Southeast Asia. The pirates were designated as such by the Ch'ing authorities because in the eyes of the government they practiced a lifestyle verging on a marginal and extra-legal existence in the accepted order of Chinese society. They were actually merchant seamen and traders, who tried to make a living out of the sea trade. Piracy was only an occasional exercise of their skill. The fact that Ts'ai Ch'ien was able to buy the services of the Fukien sea merchants and ship builders was a proof of his credibility as a good businessman who always honored his commitments and paid his bills. To paraphrase a modern economic term, his credit rating was high among those in the seafaring community of the Chia-Ch'ing period.

NOTES

1. *Ch'ing-Jen-tsung shih-lu hsüan-chi*, Taiwan wen-hsien ts'ung-k'an edition, Taipei: 1963, p. 6.
2. *Ibid.*, p. 3.
3. *Ibid.*, p. 7.
4. *Ibid.*, p. 7.
5. *Ch'ing-ch'i-hsien lei-cheng hsüan-pien*, Taiwan wen-hsien ts'ung-k'an edition, Taipei: 1967, Vol. 8, pp. 1353-4.
6. *Ch'ing-Jen-tsung shih-lu hsüan-chi*, p. 43.
7. *Ibid.*, p. 28.
8. *Lei-t'ang-an-chu ti-tzu-chi*, ed. Lo Shih-lin, Chapter 1, p. 36a.
9. *Ch'ing-ch'i-hsien lei-cheng hsüan-pien*, Vol. 8, p. 1354.
10. *Ibid.*, p. 1358.
11. The pirates went there to levy protection money from the fishermen and to share the haul of fish.
12. *Ch'ing-Jen-tsung shih-lu hsüan-chi*, p. 12.
13. *Lei-t'ang-an-chu ti-tzu-chi*, Chapter 1, pp. 32b–33a.
14. *Ch'ing-Jen-tsung shih-lu hsüan-chi*, p. 82.
15. Wei Yuan, *Sheng-wu chi*, Ssu-pu pei-yao edition, Vol. 4, p. 29a.
16. *Ibid.*, Vol. 4, p. 32b.
17. See the trial records of the captured pirates in *T'ai-an hui-lu hsin-chi*, Taiwan Edition wen-hsien ts'ung-k'an, Taipei: 1967.

CHINESE CHARACTERS IN TEXT AND NOTES (MATHEWS' DICTIONARY NUMBERS)

A-lin-pao	1-4022-4946
Chang Chien-sheng	195-860-5747
Chang-chou	188-1289
Chen-hai-wang	298-2014-7037
Ch'ing-an-t'ai	1171-26-6023
Ch'ing-ch'i hsien lei-cheng hsüan-pien	1171-512-2699-4244-358-2898-5231
Ch'ing-Jen-tsung shih-lu hsüan-chi	1171-3099-6896-5821-4200-2898-503
Ch'iu Liang-kung	1215-3941-3698
Chu Fen	1346-*

*Not listed in Mathews' Dictionary; as Mathews' #1868, but with radical #85 instead of #32.

Chu Kuei	1346-3609
Ch'üan-chou	1674-1289
Fang Wei-tien	1802-7067-6350
Feng-mei	1894-7109
Fu-chou	1978-1289
Ha-tang-a	2003-6087-1
hai-feng	2014-1885
Hu Chen-sheng	2167-313-5748
i-t'ing	2982-6410
Juan Yuan	7710-7707
K'uei-lun	3655-4247
Lei-t'ang-an-chu ti-tzu-chi	4236-6117-33-1336-6201-6939-431
Li Ch'ang-keng	3852-213-3339
Lin-hai	4027-2014
Lo Shih-lin	4099-5776-4022
Lu-erh-men	4203-1744-4418
Lun Kuei-li	4247-3636-3869
Nguyên Phúc-Ánh	7710-1978-7488
Nguyên Quang-Toán	7710-3583-6846
Sheng-wu chi	5753-7195-431
Shui-ao	5922-48
T'ai-an hui-lu hsin-chi	6008-28-2349-4200-2739-508
t'ing-fei	6410-1820
t'ing-t'ing	6414-6410
Ts'ai Ch'ien	6673-881
T'ung-an	6615-26
Wang Kuei-li	7037-3636-3867
Wang Te-lu	7037-6161-4196
Wei Yüan	7104-7728
Yü-te	7666-6162

A History of Tantric Buddhism in India
with Reference to Chinese Translations

Yukei Matsunaga

INTRODUCTION

THE ORIGIN AND DEVELOPMENT of Tantric Buddhism in India has not yet been adequately reported. Dr. B. Bhattacharyya has stated that, according to Tibetan tradition, the Tantras were introduced by Asaṅga from Tuṣita heaven to earth, and immediately after their introduction they were transmitted secretly, in an uninterrupted manner, from preceptor to disciple for nearly 300 years before they received publicity through the mystic teachings of the Siddhas and Vajrācāryas.[1]

The origin of Tantrism is related in Indian and Tibetan legends in the form of myths, as is only natural in the history of a mystical religion. Today it is necessary to search for the origin of Tantrism through historical documents and material that is detached from such mythological traditions. However, it is difficult to trace the origin and development of Tantrism in India through such material as only a little survives. Indeed, so few specimens of the Tantric literature and related works which flourished after the eighth century remain in existence that this early material cannot serve as an adequate source for historical research.

Material on Tantrism can be found in the remains of the non-Āryan Indus civilizations as well as in the Vedas, which are the oldest surviving historical documents of the Indo-Āryans. For example, gods appear in the *Ṛg-veda* and the *Atharva-veda*, and numerous magic rituals from the latter text were handed down within the later Buddhist Tantras. There are also many non-Āryan goddesses who appear again in the Tantras. It is said that Mahāyāna Buddhism, especially Tantric Buddhism, expanded under the influence of this Hindu culture. Even so, there is little source material which directly relates the history of Tantric Buddhism. However, just as we can trace the development of Mahāyāna Buddhism by following the history of Chinese translations, so, through a similar process, it is possible to understand the history of Tantric Buddhism. Since we can identify with considerable credibility the periods in which the Chinese translated certain texts, the latest possible dates for the writing of certain *sūtras* have been agreed upon in reference to these periods. For example, there are several Chinese translations of such Mahāyāna *sūtra*s as the *Saddharmapuṇḍarīka-sūtra* and the *Prajñāpāramitā-sūtra*. Just as Buddhist scholars can identify the important historical changes in the contents of these *sūtras* by comparing the translations of each one, so can the lines of development of the Buddhist Tantras be postulated through variations in the Chinese translations. There are six Chinese translations of the *Mahāmāyūrī*. These extend from the fifth-century translation by Kumārajīva to the eighth-century translation of Amoghavajra. By comparing these it is possible to know the processes by which the *vidyā* were gradually changed into *dhāraṇī* which were suitable for Buddhism. These *vidyā* were used to avert calamities, and had been widely believed in by the masses. Similarly, if we compare the numerous Chinese translations of such *sūtras* as the *Mātaṅga-sūtra* or the *Anantamukha-sūtra*, which have their origins in the second century, we can observe the processes which changed a Mahāyāna text, by the gradual addition of *dhāraṇī*, into an esoteric text.

We cannot determine the earliest period of the composition of *sūtra*s which had their origin in India merely by looking at the period of the Chinese translations. However, those *sūtra*s which were translated in China from around the first century to the eighth century, when viewed in terms of the rate of cultural interchange between China and India, show obvious differences over a period of a few years or several centuries of a kind that makes it possible for us to surmise the period of their composition. Even in the Tibetan translations made after the eighth century the situation remains the same. However, the period from the middle of the ninth century until around the end of the tenth century was a dark age for Buddhism in both China and Tibet. Since there were hardly any translations of *sūtras* made during this period, it is difficult to know and follow the history of the translations or the development of Buddhism in India at that time.

In this paper I will try to trace the development of Tantric or Esoteric Buddhism in India up to the middle of the eighth century, referring principally to Chinese translations but at times to Tibetan translations. The origin of Tantrism has been argued from various viewpoints by Indian and Western scholars; but research based on Chinese translations has rarely been introduced into the arguments. On the other hand, results achieved by Japanese scholars in this area of investigation have been published.[2] In addition, I will try to trace the development which resulted in the emergence of Buddhist Tantrism by referring to magic spells, rituals, the pantheon, and the goal of prayer.

MAGIC SPELLS

Magic spells used to avert calamities were an essential element in the everyday life of the ancient Indian people. They were used from antiquity even in the Buddhist *saṅgha*. The *paritta* used in the schools of Southern Buddhism is one such spell. In Northern Buddhism, among the Dhammaguttas who had separated from the Theravādin School of the Mahīṃsāsakas around 300 years after the death of Buddha, the *Vidyādhara-piṭaka* was compiled separately from the Tripiṭaka.[3] In the *Sheng ching* (*Jātakanidāna*), which was translated by Dharmarakṣa in 285 A.D., magic spells for averting the influence of thieves, evil spirits and demons are explained by the Buddha.[4] By the first part of the fifth century, even in Dharmakṣema's translation of the *Ta-pan-nieh-p'an-ching*[5] and in Fa-hsien's translation of the *Ta-pan-ni-*

yuan-ching,[6] magic spells used to escape calamities begin to appear. These came to be frequently described in later *Mahāyāna-sūtras*.

While the *Mo-teng nü-ching*[7] translated in the middle of the second century is a common *Mahāyāna-sūtra*, when it was retranslated as the *Mo-teng-ch'ieh-ching* (T.21.1300) at the beginning of the third century it became a *dhāraṇī* text with numerous kinds of *dhāraṇī*. In the case of the *K'ung-ch'üeh-wang-chou-ching*,[8] which had its origin in the *Moraparitta* and which was translated by Kumārajīva at the beginning of the fifth century, when it became a work of the same name in Saṃghavarman's translation (T.19.984) at the beginning of the sixth century it had nearly expanded to the present form of the Sanskrit *Mahāmāyūrī*. Similarly, in the progression from I-ching's early eighth century translation of the same text under the title *Ta-k'ung-ch'üeh-chou-wang-ching* (T.19.985) to Amoghavajra's translation of about the middle of the eighth century with the title *Fo-mu-ta-k'ung-ch'üeh-ming-wang-ching* (T.19.982), the names of *nāgas*, *yakṣas*, rivers, mountains, and so forth became extremely detailed. The numbers of *dhāraṇī* increased and became lengthy, and all had come to be arranged in the form of a *dhāraṇī* text. The gradual expansion of the *dhāraṇī*s can also be witnessed in the *Anantamukha dhāraṇī*,[9] which had nine different Chinese translations ranging from the middle of the third century to the eighth century, and in the *Puṣpakūṭa-dhāraṇī*[10] and the *Ch'ih-chü-shen-chou-ching*,[11] both translated several times from the third century to the beginning of the eleventh century.

Furthermore, the *dhāraṇī*, which were originally used as a means of unifying the mind and of entering into *samādhi*, were now recited for the purpose of increasing the power of memory. In the *Hua-chi-t'o-lo-ni-shen-chou-ching*,[12] which was translated at the beginning of the third century, *dhāraṇī* are explained which have as their goal the memorization of the contents of the *sūtra* and of the teachings of the Buddha. Also, since the *dhāraṇī* were considered a condensed form of the *sūtra*, the hope of averting misfortune through the recitation of an entire *Mahāyāna-sūtra* came to be fulfilled in the recitation of a single *dhāraṇī*. Thus the *paritta* and the *dhāraṇī*, came to have equivalent religious functions. As a result of this mixing, the *dhāraṇī*, which had been used as a means of unifying the mind, came to be recited for the purpose of removing misfortune; and in the *tantra* such *dhāraṇī* became numerous. Also, the *mantra*s, which were praises of the gods—and the *vidyā*, which represented the wisdom of the Buddha—were indiscriminately confused with the *dhāraṇī*. Consequently the special features which they originally had were lost, and all three idioms came to have identical functions.

RITUALS

After the beginning of the Christian era there flourished, as a concomitant of the influential expansion of the Kuṣana dynasty, a cultural exchange among Greece, Rome, and India. The art of Gandhāra prospered under the influence of Greek sculpture. At approximately the same time in the region of Mathurā, Buddhist images in purely Indian forms began to be created. This tendency is reflected in the description of the construction of Buddha images to be found in Lokarakṣa's translation of the *Pan-chou-san-mei-ching* (179 A.D.).[13] Again, in Chih-ch'ien's translation of the first half of the third century,[14] offerings of flowers and candles before the Buddha and rituals wherein *dhāraṇī* are recited were first explained.

In 320 A.D., when Candragupta founded the Gupta dynasty, there was an effort to revive Brahmanism. During this period the theoretical system of Mahāyāna Buddhism was completed by such Buddhist scholars as Maitreya, Asaṅga, and Vasubandhu. Simultaneously Buddhism absorbed on a large scale the rituals of Brahmanism, the deities of Hinduism, and numerous additional Buddhas, Bodhisattvas, and deities into its pantheon. After this period the rituals and pantheons of Buddhism changed from simplified and unsystematic matters into complicated and systematic ones. This was a gradual development, clearly indicated by each of the Chinese translations of the period.

The ritual of the *abhiṣeka* which was performed at the coronation of the king in ancient India also entered into Buddhism. This ceremony appears in a *sūtra* translated at the beginning of the fifth century, when it was performed as a ritual leading to Buddhahood. The *abhiṣeka* appears to have become established as a Buddhist ritual at the latest by the end of the fourth century.[15] Similarly, in the translations of the *Mātaṇgī-sūtra* of the second and third centuries *homa* is depicted as the usual fire-ceremony of Brahmanism. However, in the *Mahāmāyūrī*,[16] which was translated by Śrīmitra around 320 A.D., the *homa* ceremony, together with three other rituals (the ritual of drawing a boundary-line for protection against evil, the ritual of sprinkling the earth with cows' urine, and the ritual of burning poppy seeds in fire), appears to be described as a Buddhist ceremony.

In the *sūtra*s that were translated from around the beginning of the fifth century, separate *dhāraṇī* and ritual systems are dedicated to some Bodhisattvas.[17] Thus a method of meditation before the Buddha practised after entering a pagoda, offering flowers to the Buddhas, and purifying the ground with mud has been briefly described.[18] There is also a description of *hsün-kuan* wherein one visualizes some Buddha in a particular meditation hall and expands that visualization, and of *ni-kuan* wherein one gathers all the Buddhas into oneself through a visualization process. Both of these were handed down in later Buddhist *yoga* and came to occupy an important place in *Yogatantra* and *Anuttarayogatantra*. During this period (the fourth and fifth centuries) meditation was directed toward unspecified Buddhist images, but subsequently descriptions began to appear in which particular meditative techniques were focussed upon such Bodhisattvas as Avalokiteśvara, Maitreya, Samantabhadra, and Ākāśagarbha, and even upon such Buddhas as Amitābha and Bhaiṣajyaguru.

The *Ta-chi-i-shen-chou-ching*, which was translated by T'an-yao at the end of the fifth century, is important as a *sūtra* which indicates the development of Buddhist ritual during the time of the Gupta dynasty. In it the ritual of drawing a boundary-line for protection against evil and the *homa* ritual are explained in even greater detail. Previously there had been texts which differentiated the *dhāraṇī* according to the goal of the prayer, and it is interesting that in this *sūtra* the Buddhas, Bodhisattvas, and deities that have come to be worshipped are distinguished in a similar manner.[19] Thus, if we compare the worship of certain unspecified Buddhas who have as their function the removal of misfortune with the earlier rituals that were performed with the same goal in view, we can see a remarkable development.

The *Ta-fang-teng-wu-hsiang-ching*, translated by Dharmakṣema at the beginning of the fifth century, is the earliest Buddhist text which describes *dhāraṇī*s and rituals for the inducement or cessation of rain.[20] Later on, in the *Ta-fang-teng-ta-yün-ching-ch'ing-yü-p'in* (*Mahāmegha-sūtra*) translated by Jñānayaśas (Jinayaśas) in the latter part of the sixth century,[21] detailed rituals for the inducement or cessation of rain are established. The farming rituals of the non-Āryans also entered into Buddhism at this time and became orthodox Buddhist rituals.

There also appeared in the Gupta period certain medical *sūtra*s which advocated the use of *dhāraṇī* to alleviate the pain of toothaches and headaches. Rituals directed toward various Bodhisattvas and deities derived from Hinduism were also established.

Moreover, in the *Mou-li-man-t'o-lo-chou-ching*, which was translated at the beginning of the sixth century, depictions of Buddhist statues with many faces and hands appear, and these are found in later Tantric Buddhism. In addition *mudrā*s are explained for the first time,[22] and these together with *mantra*s have come to be related.[23] Accordingly, in fifth-century India, rituals of meditation bound to *mudrā*s and *mantra*s are known to have been gradually established.

In the *Shih-i-mien-kuan-shih-yin-shen-chou-ching*, which was translated by Yaśagupta in the latter part of the sixth century, the ritual of *Avalokiteśvaraikadaśamukha* ('Avalokiteśvara with eleven faces') appears for the first time. One century later various forms of Avalokiteśvara observances are introduced such as Nīlakaṇṭha, Hayagrīva, Cundī, and Amoghapāśa; and rituals connected with each of these Avalokiteśvaras are established. By the beginning of the seventh century the numerous varieties of venerated Buddhas, *mudrā*s, and *mantra*s are explained and systematized as belonging to certain groups according to the goal of the prayer. In addition, because the special characteristics of various Buddhas and Bodhisattvas were thought to be expressed by short letters (*bīja*) and particular concrete objects (*samaya*) such as a bell or a *vajra*, techniques for meditation on these rather than on Buddhist statues were explained.[24] All of these developments gave rise to the three kinds of meditation on *bīja*, *samaya*, and Buddhist statues which are described in the *Mahāvairocana-sūtra*.

Such texts as the *Susiddhikara-sūtra*, *Subāhuparipṛcchā-sūtra*, and *Guhya-sūtra* incorporate the rituals of *Śānta*, *Pauṣṭika*, and *Abhicārika*, all of whom have their source in the *Atharvaveda*. They further establish three types of *homa* ritual which are distinguished according to the goal of the prayer. These three types of *homa* ritual were handed down intact in the *Mahāvairocana-sūtra*. The Tantras which drew upon the system of the *Tattvasaṃgraha-sūtra* added the *Vaśīkaraṇa* and *Ākarṣaṇa* to the three mentioned above, and thus there developed five kinds of *homa* ritual.

THE PANTHEON

In short, we know that the magic spells and rituals in the *sūtra*s which were translated from the first century to the beginning of the seventh century gradually became arranged and systematized. The Buddhist pantheon was organized, and moreover there was rapid development in the construction of the *maṇḍala*, resulting in its appearance in those *sūtra*s which were translated after the seventh century.

Among the five Buddhas that appear in the center of the *maṇḍala*, the four that surround the central image—*i.e.*, Akṣobhya, Ratnaketu, Amitāyus, and Dundubhisvara—were introduced into China at the beginning of the fifth century. They appear in Dharmakṣema's translation of the *Suvarṇaprabhāsa-sūtra*[25] and in Buddhabhadra's translation of the *Kuan-fo-san-mei-hai-ching*.[26] The names of three of these four Buddhas are similar to those of the Buddhas in the *Garbhodbhava-maṇḍala*. Thus, for a period of two hundred years, the composition and names of these four Buddhas do not appear to have changed at all.[27]

In the *T'o-lo-ni-chi-ching*, translated in the middle of the seventh century, the number of Buddhas, Bodhisattvas, and deities increased rapidly; and various *mudrā*s, *mantra*s and methods of worship were established. The majority of the Buddhas, Bodhisattvas, and deities of the *Garbhodbhava-maṇḍala* had already appeared, but had not yet been included in the design of the *maṇḍala*. However, since the need to arrange the various forms of the Buddhas, Bodhisattvas, and deities (which had increased to an unusual extent) had already arisen, the twelve volumes of this *sūtra* were divided into five categories: Buddhas (Vols. 1-2), Bodhisattvas (Vols. 3-6), *vajra*s (Vols. 7-9), deities (Vols. 10-11), and miscellaneous information (Vol. 12).

Of the five Tathāgatas who formed the basis of the *maṇḍala*, the names and locations of the four mentioned above were settled by the fifth century. However, sudden changes occur in the translations of Bodhiruci at the beginning of the eighth century. In the ninth volume of Bodhiruci's translation of the *Amoghapāśa-sūtra*, Śākyamuni has been added as the central Tathāgata, Lokanātha replaces Dundubhisvara in the northern quarter, and Ratnasambhava replaces Ratnaketu in the southern quarter.[28] These changes are thought to indicate the processes which gradually gave rise to the *Vajradhātu-maṇḍala*. At the same time, the four Bodhisattvas Kṣitigarbha, Maitreya, Samantabhadra, and Mañjuśrī–are placed in the four corners; and when Kṣitigarbha is replaced by Avalokiteśvara, these become the four Bodhisattvas of the *Garbhodbhava-maṇḍala*. The Bodhisattvas and deities that are explained in other parts of this *Amoghapāśa-sūtra* greatly resemble those included in this *Garbhodbhava-maṇḍala*. Finally, in Volume 22 of this *sūtra*, the five Tathāgatas–Vairocana (center), Akṣobhya (east), Ratnasambhava (south), Lokeśvararāja (west) and Amoghasiddhi (north)–are explained;[29] and so the five Tathāgatas of the *Vajradhātumaṇḍala* are known to have been established.

In Bodhiruci's translation of the *I-tzu-fo-ting-lun-wang-ching*, the five Tathāgatas–Śākyamuni (center), Ratnaketu (east), Samkusumitarāja (south), Amitābha (west), and Akṣobhya (north)–are described.[30] Accordingly, though the placement of the Tathāgatas in the *maṇḍala* is different here with the exception of Amitābha, the names of the five Tathāgatas in both the *Garbhodbhava-* and the *Vajradhātu-maṇḍala*s are found.

The construction of the *maṇḍala*s mentioned above was first indicated in Bodhiruci's translations at the beginning of the eighth century; and this was handed down in both the *Garbhodbhava-maṇḍala*, which underwent no further variations in later ages, and in the

Vajradhātu-maṇḍala, which was the source for many of the *maṇḍalas* in *Anuttarayoga-tantra*. The *Garbhodbhava-maṇḍala* became the authoritative drawing for the *Mahāvairocana-sūtra*, while the *Vajradhātu-maṇḍala* became the authoritative drawing for the *Tattvasaṃgraha-sūtra*. The Bodhisattvas and deities which had previously been arranged without order now came to be systematically drawn with fixed standards in these two *maṇḍalas*. The above two *sūtras* appeared in the period extending from the middle to the end of the seventh century A.D.

THE GOAL OF PRAYER

The goal of writing, reading, and preserving the *dhāraṇīs* and *Mahāyāna-sūtras* focussed on such worldly benefits as recovery from illness or the removal of misfortunes. The goals of the rituals, which were described in texts translated from the third to the beginning of the seventh century, were directed for the most part toward such ends. In contrast, in those *sūtras* translated by Chih-t'ung, Atikūṭa, Punyodaya, and Hsüan-tsang, all of whom were active around the middle of the seventh century, rituals were performed for the attainment of *Anuttarasamyaksambodhi*. This situation is representative of changes in the goals of rituals performed in India in the first half of the seventh century at the latest. Such a tendency, moreover, has become quite evident in the *Mahāvairocana-sūtra* and the *Tattvasaṃgraha-sūtra*.

Mudrās appear in Buddhist texts around the fifth century and are used in various rituals in conjunction with *mantras* and *dhāraṇīs*. When we come to the *Mahāvairocana-sūtra* we find that meditations have been combined with *mudrās* and *mantras*. Moreover, the possibility of attaining Buddhahood through the practice of a yoga which unites the three mysteries of body (*mudrā*), speech (*mantra*), and mind (*samādhi*) is now explained for the first time. Spiritual elements in the ritual which place emphasis on an external *kriyā* have also been added. All of these are established as the practice of Buddhist yoga in the *Tattvasaṃgraha-sūtra* and, of course, in *Anuttarayoga-tantra*.

Mahāvairocana-sūtra

Śubhakarasiṃha translated the *Mahāvairocana-sūtra* into Chinese in 724 A.D., while Śīlendrabodhi and dPal-brtsegs translated it into Tibetan approximately a century later. If we compare these two translations we find that the chapter order is different and that certain sections differ somewhat in content. When we examine these two *sūtras* in their entirety we can see that the Tibetan translation is more systematically arranged. At any rate, we know that the contents of this *sūtra* changed even in the eighth century. In the ninth century, furthermore, due to the prosperity of the Vajrayāna which drew upon the tradition of the *Tattvasaṃgraha-sūtra*, little research was done in India or Tibet on the *Mahāvairocana-sūtra*.

The *Mahāvairocana-sūtra* must finally have been completed at the latest by 724 A.D., when it was translated by Śubhakarasiṃha. It is also possible that the original text was completed by 685 A.D., since Wu-hsing, who sojourned in India at this time, obtained this *sūtra*. The travelog of Wu-hsing reports that "recently many people in India have vouchsafed the teachings of Esoteric Buddhism."[31] On the basis of this account we know that Esoteric Buddhism was prospering by the end of the seventh century. If, moreover, one takes into account such works as Atikūṭa's translation of the *T'o-lo-ni-chi-ching*, which is considered one of the sources for the formation of the *Mahāvairocana-sūtra*, and Bodhiruci's translation of the *I-tzu-fo-ting-lun-wang-ching*, it seems probable that the *Mahāvairocana-sūtra* was composed during the period extending from the early to the middle part of the seventh century.

Tattvasaṃgraha-sūtra

There are various translations of the *Tattvasaṃgraha-sūtra*. These are Vajrabodhi's translation of the *Chin-kang-ting-yü-chung-lüeh-ch'u-nien-sung-ching*[32] in 723 (four volumes), Amoghavajra's translation of the *Chin-kang-ting-i-ch'ieh-ju-lai-chen-shih-she-ta-ch'eng-hsien-teng-ta-chiao-wang-ching*[33] in 753 (three volumes), and Shih-huo's translation of the *I-ch'ieh-ju-lai-chen-shih-she-ta-ch'eng-*

hsien-teng-san-mei-ta-chiao-wang-ching[34] in 1002 (thirty volumes). The Tibetan translation at the beginning of the eleventh century by Śraddhākaravarma and Rin-chen bzang-po[35] is almost consistent with Shih-huo's translation, which is similar to the Sanskrit text presently in existence. The Tibetan translation indicates the latest developed stage of the *Tattvasaṃgraha-sūtra*. Thus, through each of these translations the *Tattvasaṃgraha-sūtra* developed into the Sanskrit text presently in existence.[36]

Vajrabodhi, according to his biography, travelled to southern India at the age of 31 and began a seven-year period of study under Nāgabodhi, a disciple of Nāgārjuna. At this time, it is recorded, he studied the *Vajraśekhara-yoga-sūtra*,[37] this being another name for the *Tattvasaṃgraha-sūtra*. According to a Chinese source Vajrabodhi's birthdate is conjectured as 671 A.D., and so his thirty-first year would correspond to the year 701 A.D. Based on this account we know that the *Tattvasaṃgraha-sūtra* existed in southern India around 700 A.D. Accordingly, the date for the composition of the shortest text of the *Tattvasaṃgraha-sūtra* can be set at around the end of the seventh century. Also, because of the existence of the *Kosalālaṃkāra* of Śākyamitra[38] and of the *Tantratattvālokakarī* of Ānandagarbha,[39] both of which are commentaries on the largest text of the *Tattvasaṃgraha-sūtra*, and because of the fact that both commentators were active in the latter half of the eighth century, we know that the largest text of the *Tattvasaṃgraha-sūtra* had been completed by the end of the eighth century.

KRIYĀ- AND ANUTTARAYOGA-TANTRA

In a commentary on the *Mahāvairocana-sūtra* by Buddhaguhya, who is known for his exchanges with the Tibetan king Khri-srong-lde'u-btsan who flourished in the middle and latter part of the eighth century, the three kinds of Tantra—*Kriyā*, *Caryā*, and *Yoga*—are presented. However, there is no mention of *Anuttarayoga-tantra*.[40] From this it may be concluded that at that time the *Anuttarayoga-tantra* had no influence. The majority of the translations of *Anuttarayoga-tantra* texts, including the Tibetan ones, came into being after the eleventh century. The original source for the *Guhyasamāja-*

tantra can be detected in the *Shih-pa-hui-chih-kuei*,[41] which was translated by Amoghavajra who returned to China from India in 746 A.D. carrying numerous Sanskrit texts. However, the *Guhyasamāja-tantra* presently in existence could certainly not have been completed at this time. Aside from its mythological origins, the *Anuttara-yoga-tantra* must have prospered only after the middle of the eighth century, as witnessed in historical documents.

In India and Tibet there is a fourfold classification of Tantra into *Kriyā*, *Caryā*, *Yoga*, and *Anuttarayoga*. This is a classification based upon the contents of the Tantra; and when the periods in which the texts were translated are considered, it also indicates the actual historical development of the Tantric system. The *Mahāvairocana-sūtra*, which is a *Caryā-tantra* text, and the *Tattvasaṃgraha-tantra*, which is a *Yoga-tantra* text, were both formed in the seventh century. The former had no further conspicuous development. Surprisingly, apparently only a very short time-span was involved before the latter developed into *Anuttarayoga-tantra* by the end of the eighth century, for both *Caryā*- and *Yoga-tantra*s were still flourishing at the end of the previous century. We do know that by the first half of the seventh century many texts of the *Kriyā-tantra* class had been developed, and that the *Anuttarayoga-tantra*s were established after the second half of the eighth century.

Within *Kriyā-tantra* texts such as the *Mañjuśrīmūlakalpa*[42] we find newer and older sections. The ninth chapter of the text resembles a *sūtra* translated by Maṇicinta in A.D. 702[43] as well as a *sūtra* translated by I-ching around the same period.[44] There is another old chapter recognized as having been completed by the seventh century. On the other hand, since the fifty-third chapter was referred to by King Gopāla of the Pāla dynasty,[45] we know that this section had been completed by the middle of the eighth century. Accordingly, this is an example of a *Kriyā-tantra* text which overlapped the period of *Anuttarayoga-tantra* through a process of continuous compilation.

By ordering the periods of the translation of the Buddhist Tantras as above, it is possible to see a process of change from unsystematic texts to systematic ones, from simple to complicates ones, and from external rituals to serious internal meditation. On the basis of this examination of the particular periods in which the *sūtra*s or Tantras were translated, we know that Tantrism had not yet arisen by the second or third century. Rather, it had its roots in this period; and through a gradual process of development it attained its greatest popularity after the seventh century A.D.

NOTES

1. Gaekwad's Oriental Series, No. 53, Introduction, pp. xxxiv–xxxv.
2. Seigai Omura, *Mikkyo Hattatsu Shi* (A History of Esoteric Buddhism), 5 Volumes, Tokyo: 1918; Yukei Matsunaga, *Mikkyo no Rekishi* (A History of Tantric and Esoteric Buddhism), Kyoto, 1969.
3. *I-pu-tsung-lun-lun-shu-chi*, *Manjizokyo* 1-83-3-220.
4. T. (=Taishō *Tripiṭaka*), Vol. 3, pp. 84–5.
5. T., Vol. 12, p. 370.
6. T., Vol. 12, p. 856.
7. T., Vol. 14, No. 551.
8. T., Vol. 19, No. 988.
9. T., Nos. 1009–1018.
10. T., Nos. 1356–1359.
11. T., Nos. 1351–1355.
12. T., No. 1356.
13. T., Vol. 13, p. 899c.
14. T., Vol. 21, p. 875a.
15. This is observable in the *Ta-fang-kuang-fo-hua-yen-ching* (*Avataṃsaka-sūtra*, T., Vol. 9, p. 572b) translated by Buddhabhadra in 420 A.D., and in the *Ta-ch'eng-pei-fen-t'o-li-ching* (T., Vol. 3, p. 238c) translated by an unknown hand in 431 A.D.
16. This *Mahāmāyūrī* is no longer extant, but we know of its existence through a quotation in the *Mahāmāyūrī* which was translated by Saṅghabhadra (T., Vol. 19, pp. 458c–459a).
17. *Ch'i-fo-pa-p'u-sa-so-shuo-ta-t'o-lo-ni-shen-chou-ching* (T., Vol. 21, pp. 536–561).
18. *Kuan-fo-san-mei-hai-ching* (T., Vol. 15, pp. 696–697).
19. T., Vol. 21, pp. 579b–580c.
20. T., Vol. 12, p. 1084c.
21. T., Vol. 19, pp. 500–506.
22. T., Vol. 19, p. 661.
23. T., Vol. 20, pp. 149a–152a.
24. *Kuan-tzu-tsai-p'u-sa-sui-hsin-chou-ching* (T., Vol. 20, pp. 457–470).
25. T., Vol. 16, pp. 335–6, 345.
26. T., Vol. 15, p. 688.

27. They have no distinguishing features in any of the following *sūtras* which were translated up to the end of the seventh century: T., Vol. 21, p. 226; T., Vol. 18, p. 876a; T., Vol. 14, p. 699a–b; T., Vol. 16, p. 404a–b, etc.
28. T., Vol. 20, p. 270.
29. T., Vol. 20, p. 346b.
30. T., Vol. 19, p. 247a–b.
31. T., Vol. 75, p. 431a.
32. T., Vol. 18, No. 866.
33. T., Vol. 18, No. 865.
34. T., Vol. 18, No. 882.
35. Tohoku, No. 479.
36. Sanskrit text of the *Tattvasaṃgraha-sūtra*, edited by K. Horiuchi, Koyasan: 1968–70.
37. T., Vol. 55, p. 875b.
38. Tohoku, No. 2503.
39. Tohoku, No. 2510.
40. Tohoku, No. 2663, fol. 261.
41. T., Vol. 18, pp. 287a–b.
42. T. G. Śāstrī, *The Āryamañjuśrīmūlakalpa*, Trivandrum Sanskrit Series, No. 70, 1920; No. 76, 1922; No. 84, 1925; Tohoku, No. 543; T., No. 1191.
43. T., Vol. 19, No. 956.
44. T., Vol. 20, No. 1182.
45. R. Sānkrityāyana and K. P. Jayaswal, *An Imperial History of India* (Sanskrit text), Lahore, 1934, p. 66 (text).

Transcendent Perception in Jaina Logic with Special Reference to Buddhist Logic

Hojun Nagasaki

I

IN ORDER TO DISCUSS the concept of transcendent perception in Jaina logic, we have to begin with the system of logic found in the *Pramāṇamīmāṃsā* by Hemacandra (1088–1171 A.D.), one of the most important works on Jaina logic. In this work, valid knowledge (*pramāṇa*) is represented by both *pratyakṣa* (perceptual cognition) and *parokṣa* (non-perceptual cognition). Perceptual cognition or *pratyakṣa* is comprised of two categories, transcendent perception (*mukhya*) and empirical perception (*sāṁvyavahārika*). Etymologically, the term *mukhya* means 'belonging to the face' or 'foremost'; thus, it designates what is the supreme facet of all cognitions, just as the face can be said to be the supreme part of the body. Three forms of cognition are included under the category of *mukhya* or transcendent perception: *avadhi* (visual intuition), *manaḥparyāya* (intuition of the modes of the minds of others), and *kevala* (pureness). *Kevala* is the full manifestation of the luminous nature of the self obtained when all obstructing karmas are completely removed through the practice of meditation. The cognitions of *avadhi* and *manaḥparyāya*, likewise, depend on the degree to which obstructions have been removed, the latter cognition being obtained only in the *guṇasthāna* of the sixth to twelfth stages.[1]

The following chart depicts the complete system of logic found in the *Pramāṇamīmāṃsā*.

CHART I

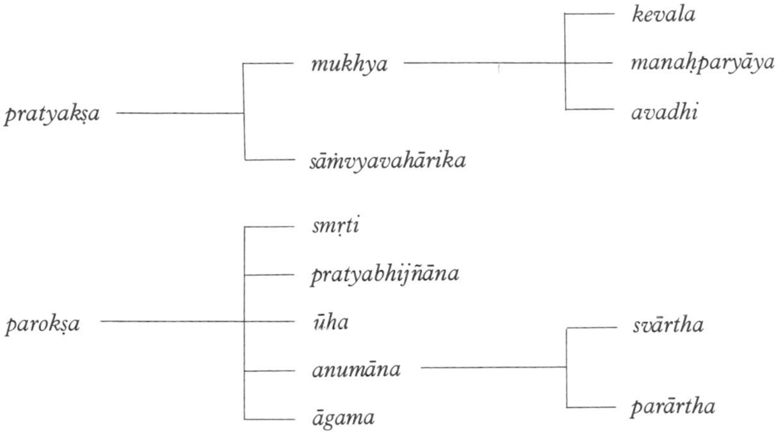

However, according to earlier epistemological sources in Jaina tradition, the original connotation of *pratyakṣa* was 'transcendent perception' (comprised of the triad of *avadhi*, *manaḥparyāya*, and *kevala*) and was exclusive of empirical perception. *Parokṣa* was conceived of as consisting of *mati* (sensuous knowledge) and *śruta* (scriptural knowledge). Chart II, adapted from the *Tattvārthādhigama-sūtra* of Umāsvāti (*circa* 400–500 A.D.), should depict this clearly.

CHART II

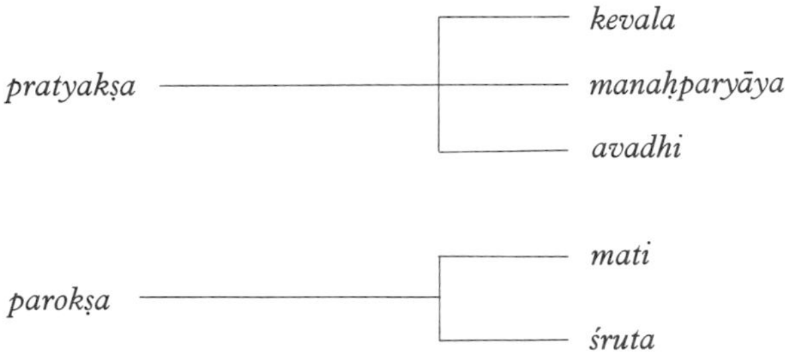

This chart represents the epistemological system traditionally found in the Jaina *Āgama*. It is significant to note that *pratyakṣa* is seen as being generated without the help of any sense channel. It is *mati* which is referred to as the cognition obtained through the *indriya* (sense channel) as well as *anindriya* (non-sense channel). This is included under the category of *parokṣa*, along with *śruta* (cognition brought about through the agency of scriptural authorities).

In comparing Charts I and II, we find that *pratyakṣa* in Chart I consists of transcendent perception as well as empirical perception, the latter being obtained through the sense channels. In other words, the triad of *avadhi*, *manaḥparyāya*, and *kevala*, enumerated under *pratyakṣa* in Chart II, is entitled 'transcendent perception' (*mukhya*) in Chart I. The one segment of *mati* which deals with sense intuition in Chart II has been separated and moved into the category of *pratyakṣa* in Chart I under the heading of 'empirical perception' (*sāṁvyavahārika*).

Now we must determine who, why, and when these innovations were introduced, inasmuch as they depart from the traditional pattern of Jaina epistemology. It has already been reported by other scholars[2] that indications of the rise of a new system can be detected in the *Āgama* around the sixth century. Jinabhadra (*circa* 550 A.D.) refers to intuition obtained by means of the senses with the term *sāṁvyavahārika-pratyakṣa* (empirical perception), while the triad of *avadhi*, *manaḥparyāya*, and *kevala* was included under the heading *pāramārthika-pratyakṣa* (transcendent perception). Siddhasena Divākara (*circa* 650–750 A.D.), the author of the first systematic work on Jaina logic, also divides *pratyakṣa* into two categories, *alaukika* (transcendent) and *laukika* (empirical), while *anumāna* (inference) and *śabda* (the words of the scriptural authority) are enumerated under *parokṣa*. In the *Laghīyastraya* of Akalaṅka (*circa* 750 A.D.), *pratyakṣa* includes *mukhya* and *sāṁvyavahārika* (see Chart III), a system which was subsequently adopted by Māṇikya Nandi, Hemacandra, and other logicians.

As for the use of the terms *pratyakṣa* and *parokṣa*, there seem to be shades of difference between traditional Jaina epistemology and Jaina logic. What was originally intended when the term *pratyakṣa* was used to denote the triad of *avadhi*, *manaḥparyāya*, and *kevala*? A

CHART III

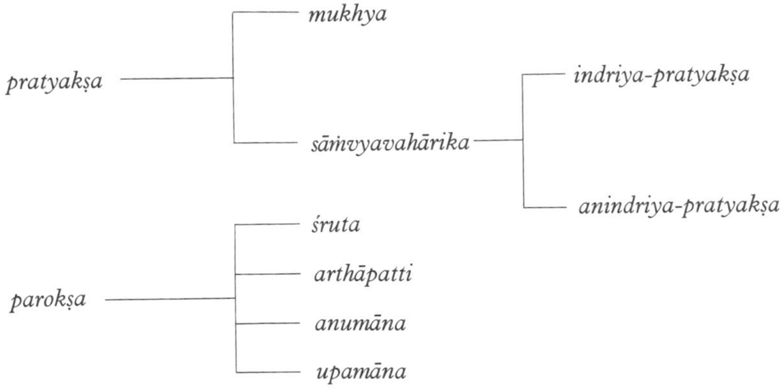

key to this problem is the fact that the term *pratyakṣa* was not generally understood to mean 'super-sensuous transcendent intuition', but was usually regarded to mean 'empirical intuition obtained by means of the senses'.

Hemacandra gives the following etymological definition of the word *pratyakṣa.*[3] The prefix *prati* implies 'to be resident' or 'to be dependent'. The term *akṣa* has two connotations: It means *jīva* (self) in that it derives from the root √*aś* or √*akṣa*, meaning 'to pervade' or 'to embrace'. *Akṣa* (*i.e.*, *jīva*) is that which pervades all substance, space, time, and modes. What is therefore resident (*prati*) in *jīva* (self) is called *pratyakṣa*. *Akṣa* also denotes *indriya* (sense-organ) in that it embraces an object; thus, what is dependent upon the sense-organs is also called *pratyakṣa*.

Parokṣa has two connotations: cognition which is placed beyond the realm of *akṣa* (*i.e.*, *jīva*), and cognition which is left untouched by the sense-organs.

Now, according to traditional Jaina epistemology (Chart II), *pratyakṣa* denoted cognition which is resident in *jīva*, while *parokṣa* denoted cognition which is not resident in *jīva*. *Parokṣa* was therein considered to be empirical perception as well as all other valid cognitions generated apart from *jīva*. In contrast to that, *pratyakṣa*, according to the system of Jaina logic (Charts I, III), has been expanded to include both transcendent perception which is resident in *jīva* and empirical perception which is dependent upon the sense-organs.

Of the two definitions of *pratyakṣa*, the first one (*i.e.*, cognition which is resident in *jīva*) derives from the original interpretation of the Jaina.[4] The second definition (*i.e.*, cognition which is dependent upon the sense-organs) came to be included under *pratyakṣa* during the course of the philosophical development of the Jaina school.

Why was the second definition added by Jaina logicians? From about the sixth century, it had become common practice to hold discussions with the masters of different schools over philosophical issues. In general, every school of philosophy, with the exception of the Jaina, was using *pratyakṣa* in the sense of 'empirical intuition'. The Jaina school could not simply maintain its own traditional meaning of *pratyakṣa* against the general consensus. In order to bring its system into line with the logic of other schools, its logicians sought to supplement traditional Jaina structure by introducing some innovations in its system of philosophy. This gradual development, which began from about the sixth century, is evident in the writings of logicians from Siddhasena onward.

Under traditional epistemology, *pratyakṣa* consisted of the triad of *avadhi*, *manaḥparyāya*, and *kevala*, while all other forms of cognition were included under *parokṣa*. What was the original intention of traditional epistemology? Clearly, it was a comprehensive religious system with *kevala* (pureness) at its apex. *Kevala* was the absolute perception which could reside in *jīva* and which was attained when obstructing karmas were completely removed through the practice of meditation. *Manaḥparyāya* and *avadhi* corresponded to different stages prior to the ultimate attainment of *kevala*.

How was it possible for Jaina epistemology to draw closer to the logic systems of other schools and yet preserve its traditional religious structure? In this regard, the influence of Buddhist logic upon the formation of the new Jaina system is undeniable. The concept of the *yogin*'s intuition (*yogi-pratyakṣa*), which was regarded as a type of perceptual cognition by the Buddhist masters from Dignāga onward, begins to play an important role.

II

Dignāga (*circa* 480–540 A.D.), an eminent Buddhist master in India, presents this definition of the term *yogi-pratyakṣa* (yogin's intuition) in his *Pramāṇasamuccaya*:

> The *yogin*'s intuition of a thing in itself unassociated (*avyatibhinna*) with the teacher's intuition [is also a type of perception].

> The *yogin*'s intuition which is not associated (*avyavakīrṇa*) with any conceptual construction of the *āgama* (the authoritative words of the teachers) and which apprehends only a thing in itself is also perception.[5]

Dignāga makes it clear that *pratyakṣa* is defined as being devoid of conceptual construction (*kalpanā*) and as taking the particular (*svalakṣaṇa*) for its object. Inasmuch as the yogin's intuition is freed from conceptual construction, it is qualified as a kind of perception. But as far as Dignāga's definition of the yogin's intuition is concerned, it is far from clear whether it is a perception brought forth in meditation or whether it is the wisdom of Enlightenment. Nor does it make it clear what it is that the yogin is actually supposed to perceive.

Dharmakīrti (period of known activity 634–673 A.D.) gives the following definition of the yogin's intuition in his *Nyāyabindu*, which will help to clarify matters. He states:

> The yogin's intuition is the cognition produced upon the final consummation of intensive meditation upon reality (*bhūta-artha-bhāvanā-prakarṣa-paryanta-jaṃ yogi-jñānaṃ ceti*).[6]

Dharmottara elaborates further upon this in his commentary in the *Nyāyabinduṭīkā*:

> 'Reality' (*bhūta*) is the true object. Reality of this order, such as the Four Noble Truths, is perceived by means of valid knowledge. 'Meditation (*bhāvanā*) on reality' implies keeping [the true object] continuously in mind. 'Intensity (*prakarṣa*) of meditation' means that the cognition containing the image of the object of meditation is approaching clarity. 'The final consummation (*paryanta*) of intensive meditation' is the stage in which the clarity is still not quite perfected.

> When the clarity [of the yogin's intuition] is still to be attained, there is progress [toward its consummation]. On the other hand, when it is completed, there is no further progress possible. Therefore, the condition prior to complete clarity is called 'the final consummation of intensive meditation'. The cognition which is generated from that final consummation contains the complete and vivid image of the object of meditation as though it were actually present before [the yogin]. This is 'the yogin's intuition' (*yoginaḥ-pratjakṣa*).[7]

We must note that Dharmottara's interpretation infers that the yogin's intuition represents the transcendent perception generated by the final consummation of contemplation upon the Four Noble Truths. The commentary continues as follows:

> On this matter [the process is divided into three stages. The first] stage in which the vision begins to become clear is that of 'intensive meditation' (*bhāvanā-prakarṣa*). When the object of meditation is perceived as though it were veiled by mica, that is 'the stage of final consummation of intensive meditation' (*prakarṣa-paryanta-avasthā*). When the yogin perceives the object of meditation as clearly as though it were a small grain in the palm of his hand, this is 'the yogin's intuition' (*yoginaḥ pratyakṣa*).[8]

It is of importance that Dharmottara divides the process into three stages, *i.e.*, *bhāvanā-prakarṣa*, *prakarṣa-paryanta-avasthā*, and *yoginaḥ pratyakṣa*.[9] An advanced interpretation employing a similar format is given by Vinītadeva in his commentary on the *Nyāyabindu*. In this work, reality (*bhūta*) stands for the Four Noble Truths. Intensive meditation upon reality (*bhūta-artha-bhāvanā-prakarṣa*) is comprised of four stages, (*viz.*) *smṛty-upasthāna*, *uṣmagata*, *mūrdhan*, and *kṣānti*. The final consummation of intensive meditation upon reality (*bhūta-artha-bhāvanā-prakarṣa-paryanta*) corresponds to *agradharma* (*laukika-agradharma*).[10]

Uṣmagata, *mūrdhan*, *kṣānti*, and *agradharma* are the preparatory stages to Enlightenment and are referred to as 'the four stages of *kuśala-mūla*' (roots of merit). According to Vinītadeva, after one completes the practice of *smṛty-upasthāna*, one gradually proceeds through these four stages before reaching the final attainment of the *yogin*'s intuition.

The mention of *smṛty-upasthāna*, *uṣmagata*, etc., should bring to mind the reference to the 'three orders of sages' and the 'four stages of *kuśala-mūla*' in the *Abhidharmakośabhāṣya*.[11] These were regarded as the stages of practice prior to reaching *dṛṣṭi-mārga*, the stage wherein one enters the ranks of sainthood. The 'three orders of sages' consist of the five contemplations to subdue the false mind' and two *smṛty-upasthānas*. The first *smṛty-upasthāna* is to contemplate separately upon the body (*kāya*) as offensive, sensation (*vedanā*) as misery, the mind (*citta*) as impermanent, and phenomena (*dharma*) as insubstantial. The second *smṛty-upasthāna* is to contemplate on all four collectively as offensive, miserable, impermanent, and insubstantial. After finishing the contemplations on the 'three orders of sages', one then proceeds to the 'four stages of *kuśala-mūla*' (*viz.*, *uṣmagata*, *mūrdhan*, *kṣanti*, and *agradharma*) wherein one contemplates on the Four Noble Truths.

Agradharma is the last stage in which man remains attached to *saṃsāra*, for beyond this point, man, possessed of genuine insight into the Four Noble Truths, enters the ranks of sainthood in *dṛṣṭi-mārga*. *Smṛty-upasthāna* and the others, which Vinītadeva describes as stages in which one attains the *yogin*'s intuition, correspond to the above-mentioned stages preparatory to the attainment of sainthood in the Sarvāstivādin School.

Concerning the term *bhūta-artha* (the true object of reality) found in Dharmakīrti's definition of the yogin's intuition, all commentators on the *Nyāyabindu* regard the object to be the Four Noble Truths. In each of the five stages prior to the attainment of the yogin's intuition which Vinītadeva maintains, the Four Noble Truths must be regarded as the object of meditation for the yogin. In the *Abhidharmakośabhāṣya*, however, the four *smṛty-upasthānas* of the preparatory stages are not associated with the contemplation of the Four Noble Truths. This difference can be attributed to the variations in practices between the yogins of the Mahāyāna and the Sarvāstivādin concerning *smṛty-upasthāna*.

In the *Madhyāntavibhāga-bhāṣya*, *smṛty-upasthāna* is discussed in relation to the Four Noble Truths. There it states:

> Through the body (*kāya*), gross wickedness (*dauṣṭhulya*) is manifested. By contemplating upon this, one arrives at the 'Noble Truth of Suffering' (*duḥkha-satya*), since the body is characterized by the prop-

> erty of possessing wickedness. Gross wickedness [which is manifested by the body is derived from the fact that it] is the state of suffering due to conditioning (*saṁskāra-duḥkhatā*) [because existence is so impermanent and undependable that it is thus a cause of suffering]. By reason of the fact [of suffering due to conditioning], the sages perceive all existence with depravities (*āsrava*) as being [the state of] suffering.
>
> Sensation (*vedanā*) is a cause for craving (*tṛṣṇā*). By contemplating upon this, one reaches the 'Noble Truth of the Arising of Suffering' (*samudaya-satya*).
>
> The mind (*citta*) is the seat which adheres to a self (*ātman*). By contemplating upon this [as impermanent, etc.], one arrives at the 'Noble Truth of the Cessation of Suffering' (*nirodha-satya*), because one subdues the fear of destroying a [non-existent] self.
>
> By contemplating upon phenomena (*dharma*), one does not become bewildered by the qualities of defilement and purity, and thus attains the 'Noble Truth of the Way which leads to the Cessation of Suffering' (*mārga-satya*). Therefore, in the initiation [of conditions favorable to Enlightenment], *smṛty-upasthāna* is declared [as the means] for the realization of the 'Four Noble Truths' (*catuḥ-satya*).[12]

The above quotation supports the argument that *smṛty-upasthāna* is also employed in practices for the realization of the Four Noble Truths. This provides us with an understanding of the role *smṛty-upasthāna* plays in the preparatory stages of the yogin's intuition in Mahāyāna Buddhism. An arragement of *smṛty-upasthāna* coupled with the four stages of *kuśala-mūla* can now be presumed to have comprised the preparatory stages which were actually practiced by both the Sarvāstivādins and the Mahāyānists. In the *Madhyāntavibhāga-bhāṣya*, the thirty seven conditions favorable for Enlightenment (*bodhi-pakṣa*) are presented in the following sequence: the four *smṛty-upasthāna*, the four *samyak-prahāna*, the four *ṛddhi-pāda*, the five *indriya*, the five *bala*, the seven *bodhy-aṅga*, and the Eightfold Noble Path. These represent the states to be actualized in intensive practices structured in accordance with the degree of development one has attained in the process of bringing to maturation one's religious awareness. It is most significant that the five *indriya* and the five *bala* are discussed in connection with the four stages of *kuśala-mūla* in the *Bhāṣya*. The sentence in question reads, "The [five] *indriya* correspond to *uṣmagata* and *mūrdhan*, and the

[five] *bala* correspond to *kṣānti* and *laukika-agradharma*."[13] Sthiramati[14] elaborates on these elements and differentiates them into the following ranks and grades:

CHART IV

the *indriya*	the lowest rank		*uṣmagata*
	the middle rank		*mūrdhan*
	the highest rank		
the *bala*	the lowest rank		*kṣānti*
	the middle rank		*kṣānti*
	the highest rank	inferior grade	*kṣānti*
		mediocre grade	*kṣānti*
		superior grade	*agradharma*

The superior grade of the highest rank of *bala* is regarded as equivalent to the stage of *agradharma*. The seven *bodhy-aṅga*, a step above the five *bala*, would consequently correspond to *dṛṣṭi-mārga*, the rank of sainthood.[15]

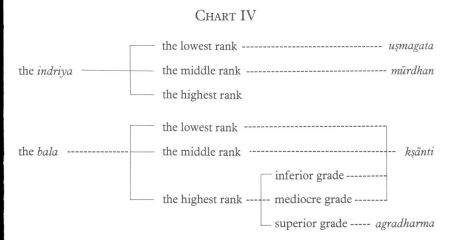

Now let us recapitulate what we have surveyed thus far. First, from the presentation above, it should be clear that the successive stages of practice (*smṛty-upasthāna*, four *kuśala-mūla*, *dṛṣṭi-mārga*) are in fact completely integrated with the thirty-seven conditions favorable to Enlightenment (*bodhi-pakṣa*), as was evident in the *Madhyāntavibhāga-bhāṣya*. Second, as has been mentioned previously (in connection with Vinītadeva's expanded definition of Dharmakīrti's concept of the yogin's intuition), the same stages (*viz.*, *smṛty-upasthāna*, *uṣmagata*, *mūrdhan*, *kṣānti*, and *agradharma*) were found to correspond to the attainment of the yogin's intuition. Through these two avenues, we can now see that the stages corresponding to the *bodhi-pakṣa* are at the same time those which correspond to the attainment of the yogin's intuition. It is thus possible for us to synthesize a more comprehensive understanding of the actual nature of practices employed in Mahāyāna toward the attainment of the yogin's intuition. This is a salient point that has hitherto been neglected. We can now safely suppose that the yogin's intuition corresponds to the absolute perception of the Buddhist Truth attained in the stage of *dṛṣṭi-mārga*.

After passing through these stages, one comes to a realization of the Four Noble Truths which is identical to the attainment of the yogin's intuition. It is clear that the yogin's intuition is attained by going through these stages of meditation; however, the yogin's intuition itself is beyond meditation, as it is attained only after going beyond the final mundane stage of *agradharma*. Thus, it represents a form of transcendent perception generated in the ranks of sainthood and which fully corresponds to the absolute knowledge obtained in *dṛṣṭi-mārga*.

III

The yogin's intuition is one of the four types of *pratyakṣa* (perception) in Buddhist logic, since it is freed from conceptual construction. The commentators on the *Nyāyabindu* properly segregated it from the other types of *pratyakṣa*, regarding it as a form of transcendent perception. The yogin's intuition is not a perception wrought in meditation, but represents the absolute perception of Buddhist Truth itself. It has been reported that Buddhist logicians beginning with Dharmakīrti exerted a profound influence on Jaina logicians. When the Jaina masters were confronted with the problem of introducing a new system of logic into the existing Jaina structure, the yogin's intuition claimed by the Buddhists may have provided a good model to follow. Under this influence, the Jaina tradition could still keep *kevala* (as well as *avadhi* and *manaḥparyāya*) as one of the *pratyakṣa* under the heading of *pāramārthika-pratyakṣa* or *mukhya* (transcendent perception), while *sāṃvyavahārika-pratyakṣa* (empirical perception) was added to bring the Jaina system into line with the logic of the other schools. Thus, *pāramārthika* or *mukhya* corresponds to the yogin's intuition, and *saṁvyavahārika* does not disagree with other types of *pratyakṣa* found in Buddhist logic. Buddhist influence is also apparent from the fact that the terms *pāramārthika* and *sāṁvyavahārika*, both specific to Buddhist philosophy, were adopted by Jaina logicians to denote transcendent perception and empirical perception.

NOTES

1. Spiritual development (*guṇasthāna*) is divided into fourteen stages. *Kevala* constitutes the thirteenth and fourteenth stages within which the soul receives final emancipation.

2. Atsushi Uno, "A Study of Jaina Epistemology, with Special Reference to '*Jñāna*' and '*Pramāṇa*'," *Journal of Indian and Buddhist Studies*, Tokyo: Vol. 16, No. 2, March, 1968. Nathmal Tatia, *Studies in Jaina Philosophy*, Benares: 1951, pp. 28-29.

3. *Pramāṇamīmāṁṣa* 1.1.31, ed. by S. Saṅghavi, M. K. Śastri, D. M. N. Tīrtha, *The Sancalaka-siṅghi Jaina Granthamālā*, Amedabad-Calcutta: 1939.

4. *Sarvārthasiddhi* 1.12.

5. Masaaki Hattori, *Dignāga, On Perception*, Harvard University Press, Cambridge: Mass., 1968, pp. 27, 94.

6. *Nyāyabindu* 1.S.11, *Bibliotheca Buddhica*, Vol. 7, Petrograd: 1918, pp. 11-12.

7. *Nyāyabinduṭīkā*, *Bibliotheca Buddhica*, Vol. 7, p. 11; *Dharmottarapradīpa*, Tibetan Sanskrit Works Series, Vol. 2, Patna, India, 1955, pp. 67-68.

8. *Ibid.*, *Bibliotheca Buddhica*, Vol. 7, p. 12; Tibetan Sanskrit Works Series, Vol. 2, pp. 68-69.

9. Yuichi Kajiyama, *An Introduction to Buddhist Philosophy*, Memoirs of the Faculty of Letters, Kyoto University, No. 10, Kyoto: 1966, p. 53n.

10. *Nyāyabinduṭīkā* (*rigs pa'i thigs-pa'i rgya-cher 'grel-pa*), The Tibetan Tripiṭaka, Peking Edition, Tokyo-Kyoto, 1957, Vol. 137, No. 5729, *Mdo-'grel* CXI *zhe*, 7b-8a); Vinītadeva's *Nyāyabinduṭīkā* translated into Japanese by Shoko Watanabe, *Acta Indologia*, Vol. 1, Naritasan Shinshoji, Japan: 1970, p. 254; T. Stcherbatsky, *Buddhist Logic*, Vol. 2, Leningrad: 1930, pp. 31-32n.

11. *Abhidharmakoshabhāṣya of Vasubandhu*, ed. by P. Pradhan, Tibetan Sanskrit Works Series, Vol. 8, Patna, India: 1967, p. 343f.; Chinese version of the *Abhidharmakośabhāṣya*, Chapter 23, *Taishō Shinshū Daizōkyō*, Vol. 29, p. 118cf.

12. *Madhyāntavibhāga-bhāṣya*, ed. by Gadjin M. Nagao, Tokyo, Japan: 1964, p. 50.

13. *Ibid.*, p. 53.

14. *Madhyāntavibhāgaṭīkā de Sthiramati*, par S. Yamaguchi, Nagoya, Japan: 1934, p. 179.

15. *Ibid.*, p. 180.

The *Kuan-wu-liang-shou Fo-ching*: Its Origin and Literary Criticism

Julian F. Pas

THE *Kuan-wu-liang-shou-Fo-ching* (hereinafter abbreviated as *Kuan-Fo-ching* or KFC) is one of the most cherished Sūtras of the Pure Land Schools. This text is very well known in the West through the English translation by J. Takakusu in the *Sacred Books of the East* (*SBE*) series,[1] in which he adopts as the supposed Sanskrit title *Amitāyur-dhyāna-sūtra*. This is a shortening of the title reconstructed by B. Nanjio, *Buddha-bhāshitāmitāyur-buddha-dhyāna*(?)-*sūtra*.[2] Most Western authors have accepted this assumption, and use the shortened title *Amitāyur-dhyāna-sūtra* whenever they refer to this text. Sometimes Western and Japanese authors just call it the *Meditation Sūtra*, presuming the correctness of *dhyāna* in the title. However, other scholars have adopted an alternative version, *Amitāyur-buddhānusmṛti-sūtra*, which has led to a different English title, the "Visualization Sūtra."

In fact, the whole discussion has lost most of its relevance since recent studies have discovered that the original was not written in Sanskrit at all (see below). For this reason I prefer to use the Chinese title only, even more so because the term *kuan* may open up completely new perspectives as to the basic intention of the book and may enable us to situate the Sūtra correctly within the development of Buddhist meditation.

ORIGIN

A unanimous tradition holds that the *Kuan-Fo-ching* was translated into Chinese by a monk from the Western Regions, Kālayaśas, between 424 and 442 A.D.[3] At that time, Kālayaśas lived in the capital of the Southern court of the Liu Sung dynasty in Chien-yeh (present-day Nanking).

His biographer[4] writes that although he was well acquainted with the Abhidharma and the Vinaya, and had a clear understanding of the Sūtras, he specialized in meditation: "When he 'started out on a trip of inspective meditation' (*yu kuan*) it sometimes happened that for seven days he did not rise, but was continuously raptured in *samādhi*."[5] He propagated Buddhism in various countries. When he arrived at the Sung capital, he first lived in the Tao-lin monastery at Chung-shan.[6] "A monk, Pao-chih, admired his method of meditation, and the monk Seng-han asked him to translate two Sūtras: *Sūtra of 'Inspection' of Yao-wang and Yao-shang* and *Sūtra of 'Inspection' of the Buddha of Infinite Life*, and he (monk Seng-han) took the text in dictation."[7] These two Sūtras were instrumental in disseminating the mysteries of the Pure Land throughout the land of the Sung. Next Kālayaśas went to Chiang-ling. In the nineteenth year of *Yü-chia* (442 A.D.) he traveled to Szu-ch'uan, where he spread everywhere the teaching of meditation (*ch'an*). He returned to Chiang-ling, where he died at the age of sixty.[8]

The *KFC* has allegedly been translated three times: besides the Kālayaśas version there was one whose translator is unknown and another attributed to Dharmamitra (356–442 A.D.);[9] but this seems rather unlikely, since it is very probable that both translators must have known each other and would not likely translate the same text. Presently only one translation is extant (T. 365) and its transmission is beyond any doubt quite reliable.[10] The major historical problem concerning the *KFC* is that of the place and date (and language) of its original composition. It was traditionally thought that the Sūtra was written in Sanskrit. However, at the present time, opinions are divided between two views: some regard the Sūtra as a Chinese work, even a forgery;[11] others consider a Central Asian origin more likely.[12]

The criteria used to solve the problem are of different natures: there are external and internal criteria, which, together, may help us to formulate a reasonably solid theory. The external evidence in this case proves to be rather weak, while the internal criteria are rather convincing. Among them are two kinds which are of practical importance: first, a comparison between the *KFC* and related texts, the so-called *Kuan* Sūtras, second, the critical examination of the *KFC* text itself.

With regard to external criteria, there is the total lack of any Sanskrit manuscript and the absence of a Tibetan version. This is of course a weak argument if it stands alone. But further there is the fact that the translators of this Sūtra and of the other *Kuan* Sūtras are all Central Asian monks, apparently belonging to a particular school of meditation, promulgated in these texts. Also, as external evidence, there is a Uighur fragment of the *KFC* discovered by the Otani expedition in the neighborhood of Turfan; but the fragment is late and appears to be based on the Chinese version.[13]

To return to a possible Sanskrit original, it must be taken into account that if the Chinese text of Kālayaśas was based on a Sanskrit original, this must have existed and have been written around (or before) the beginning of the fifth century. The *KFC* and the related Sūtras are all written later. However, there is no indication that such Sūtras were written in India proper around that time. Kasugai suggested the end of the fourth century in Gandhāra. Nakamura suggests Central Asia.[14] Fujita's view is that the close relationship of the translators to Central Asia can best be explained if the origin of the Sūtra(s) is located there: both Kālayaśas and Dharmamitra are Central Asians; and the *Maitreya Sūtra* was written around Turfan.

Furthermore, Fujita says, Buddhist art specialists have made a study of the relation between Buddhist art and the *KFC*: the Sūtra is a gold mine from an iconographic viewpoint, and surviving Buddhist art also enables us to put a *terminus post quem* for the composition of the Sūtra. *E.g.*, in Meditation Nine, 'Meditation on the Images', it is said that Amita measures "six hundred thousand *niyuta*s of *koṭi*s of *yojana*s innumerable as are the sands of the River Gaṅgā."[15] It seems that such a description of the Buddha reflects the actual existence of massive Buddha statues, and, to speak more concretely, may refer to the colossal stone-carvings of Bāmiyān (in Afghanistan), of which the approximate date is given as "the relatively late period between 300 and 600."[16] Central Asian statues, carved from stone and of large dimensions, were already made as early as around 400 A.D.,[17] which gives a more accurate *terminus post quem* for the date of the *KFC*.

There is no decisive evidence to prove that the *KFC* was actually written in Central Asia; but if India is ruled out, the arguments in favor of Central Asia are stronger than for Chinese origin. Among the arguments put forward to claim Chinese origin there are two main categories. First of all there are the similarities between the *KFC* and the other *Kuan* Sūtras. The literary dependence of the *KFC* on these other Sūtras cannot be denied, but the influencing process could have taken place as well in Central Asia as in China. Therefore this argument is not convincing. The second kind of reasoning is based on the presence in the text of Chinese ways of thinking and distinctively Chinese style-elements: but as will be shown shortly, this proves that exactly these parts of the Sūtra may have been composed by a Chinese author and can thus be considered interpolations. The basic Sūtra text is not affected by this argument. Finally, there seems to be another argument against Chinese origination: the long and unanimous tradition that holds Kālayaśas responsible for the translation. Even if this attribution proved uncertain, the fact that the text was translated shows that it was not originally written in Chinese.

Some internal criteria have already been mentioned but need further elaboration, especially the inner relationship between the *KFC* and the other *Kuan* Sūtras. Several texts belonging to this group have been preserved in Chinese, but there is no Sanskrit original for any of them. This group may be considered to represent the final stage in the development of 'Buddha-vision' or 'Buddha-inspection', already introduced in the *Sukhāvatī-vyūha-sūtra* and further elaborated in the famous text *Pan-chou san-mei ching*.

A. Soper[18] distinguishes three stages in the development of this method of Buddha-meditation or 'visualization', including an elementary stage attested to in a work ascribed to Nāgārjuna (but according to E. Zürcher certainly not composed by him).[19] In the *Mahā-prajñā-pāramitā-śāstra*, translated by Kumārajīva as *Ta Chih-tu lun* (T. 1509), it is said that "one of the powers achieved through becoming a Bodhisattva" is the ability to see all the Buddhas of the Ten Quarters, realized in the ecstasy called *pratyutpanna-samādhi*.[20] An intermediate stage is described in the *Pan-chou san-mei ching* (see below), and a third much more advanced stage is represented by the *KFC*.

This distinction of three stages, aside from its focus on the Amita cult only, has the weakness of over-simplifying the matter. The first and second stages are not so clearly distinguishable, at least not when the distinction is based on the above-mentioned texts. It is very likely that the *Pan-chou san-mei ching* is older than the *Ta Chih-tu Lun*, which even perhaps quotes from it; for it mentions a Sūtra called *Pan-chou sūtra* which seems to be an abbreviation of *Pan-chou san-mei ching*.

It seems preferable to tentatively distinguish two main stages in the development of Buddha-visualization in meditation. A more detailed analytic comparison of the texts might eventually lead to the establishment of more stages.

EARLY STAGE

The early stage is characterized by its emphasis on visualizing the Buddhas of the Ten Quarters rather than individual Buddhas or Bodhisattvas. The *terminus a quo* for this development corresponds with the period in which the worship of the Ten Buddhas and the belief in their respective *Buddhakṣetra*s was already well established (*i.e.*, probably later than the *Smaller Sukhāvatī-vyūha-sūtra*, which shows a less developed Buddhology in that it still moves in a stage of belief in the Buddhas of the Six Directions).

Furthermore, there seems to have been another important factor which influenced the development of the whole movement of Buddha-visualization. Although early Buddhists took over many elements of Hindu cosmology, among which is included the Hindu belief in various heavens, Buddhists could not be attracted any longer by the ideal of rebirth in one of these heavens, even the highest one, since their ultimate goal was attainment of *nirvāṇa*. Instead these heavens were in some way sublimated, inasmuch as they were identified with the various stages of *dhyāna*[21] and could thus be reached in this life. With the elaboration of the theory of *Buddha-kṣetra*s, it may have been a logical consequence that, in a parallel way, these pure Buddha-lands were thought to be reachable through meditation; so that a vision of these *kṣetra*s and even of the respective Buddhas reigning over them became a highly desirable result of mental concentration.

Initially perhaps none of the Buddhas of the Ten Directions was pre-eminent. Several texts show that visualization was directed toward the Ten Buddhas without distinction. In another text ascribed to Nāgārjuna, the *Daśabhūmi-vibhāṣā-śāstra,*[22] often quoted to prove that Nāgārjuna was a devotee of Amitābha, there is indeed one reference to the visualization of the Buddhas. It is given in Chapter Nine, "On the Easy Practice": "I only wish that the Tathāgatas increasingly bestow on me their compassion, and grant me, in the present life, a vision of themselves before my eyes."[23]

However, the most famous Sūtra treating this early aspect of Buddha-visualization is the *Pan-chou san-mei ching*, of which the reconstructed Sanskrit title is given as *Pratyutpanna-buddha-saṃmukhāvasthita-samādhi-sūtra,*[24] and which E. Zürcher translates as the *samādhi* "during which the Buddhas are made to appear before one's eyes."[25] Elsewhere he more or less explains this as a "form of mental concentration which enables the devotee to behold all Buddhas 'as if they were standing before his eyes'."[26]

This was one of the earliest texts translated into Chinese. Two of the four extant translations (of a total of seven) were made by Lokakṣema between 168 and 188 A.D.[27] These two versions "pose problems of textual criticism which have not yet been solved."[28] E. Zürcher further reports that Japanese scholars have reached widely divergent conclusions: one view holds that T. 418, the version in sixteen chapters, is the original from which T. 417, the version in eight chapters, was abridged.[29]

The date of the original composition is said to be quite early: Mochizuki suggests the first century B.C., since this is the earliest text in which the visualization of the Buddhas is explained.[30] A special place is given to the vision of Amita, which means either that the author himself was a worshipper of Amita or that he wrote the Sūtra in a place where the Amita cult was already practiced. It seems likely that the *PCS* is in fact the earliest document in which the Amita cult is attested.[31]

On close investigation of the text (especially T. 418), however, it does not seem impossible that the references to Amita have been interpolated. The reason is that the mentioning of Amita Buddha only, in a context which purports to teach a *samādhi* to visualize all the Buddhas of the Ten Quarters, seems artificial and out of place.[32] It seems more probable that the *PCS* was composed during the first century A.D.

LATER STAGE

Whereas the *Pan-chou san-mei ching* was translated into Chinese at a very early date (*ca*. 179 A.D.), the other *Kuan* Sūtras, among which the *KFC* is one of the most influential, were translated much later, from about the end of the fourth till the middle of the fifth century A.D. It is not easy to give any conclusive results as to the place and date of origin of these Sūtras.

The extant Sūtras belonging to the *kuan* group are six in number.[33] They are arranged below, with explanations, according to their hypothetical dates. T. 409 and T. 643 seem comparatively early; T. 365 and T. 1161 are almost certainly among the latest ones; T. 452 and T. 277 are difficult to locate, so it is not unreasonable to relate them to a middle period.

(1) *Kuan Hsü-k'ung-tsang P'u-sa ching* (*KHP*),[34] T. 409, Vol. 13 (Nj. 70); *Sūtra on Visualizing the Bodhisattva Akāṣagarbha*,[35] translated by Dharmamitra between 424 and 442 A.D. (Liu Sung dynasty).

It appears that the Sūtra is not homogeneous but is a compilation of various fragments, some with a Hīnayāna tendency and others of a more Mahāyāna character. The interlocutor is Upāli, traditionally considered a compiler of the Vinaya. There is no stress on visualization, more importance being given to a ritual of confession and to *dhāraṇīs* for healing and forgiveness of 'sins'. The Buddhology of the text is confusing: there are lists of thirty-five Buddhas[36] and of thirty-five Buddhas of the past;[37] of fifty-three Buddhas of the past,[38] of the seven Buddhas and of the six Buddhas of the Six Directions; later also of the Buddhas of the Ten Directions. Calling the names of the Buddhas is considered important. Although Bodhisattva Avalokiteśvara is named, the Buddha of the West is not Amitābha, but either *Tsao-wang Shen-t'ung Yen-hua Fo* (in the list of six)[39] or *Ta-pei Kuang-ming Wang Fo* (in the list of ten).[40]

One receives the impression that the Sūtra is not concerned with meditation but moves rather in the atmosphere of magical Buddhism and ritual confession.

(2) *Fo-shuo Kuan Fo San-mei Hai Ching* (*KFSH*),[41] T. 643, Vol. 15 (Nj. 430), *Sūtra on the Sea of Mystic Ecstasy Attained by Visualizing the Buddha*,[42] translated by Buddhabhadra sometime between 398 and 421 at the Southern Court of the Eastern Chin.

There are reasons to believe that this was one of the earliest *Kuan* Sūtras translated into Chinese and adhering to the Hīnayāna rather than the Mahāyāna school. The object of meditation here is Śākyamuni. A great deal of the text is devoted to stories about his life, and "the general effect is not very different from that reached in the latest Hīnayāna narratives."[43] Soper suggests the area around Nagarahāra as the place of composition. The episode about the Buddha subjugating the evil Nāga king and leaving his own 'shadow' in the Nāga cavern betrays the author's special interest in the famous place of Buddhist pilgrimage and suggests a resemblance to an Iranian tradition about the struggle between good and evil, light and darkness.[44]

(3) *Fo-shuo Kuan Mi-lo P'u-sa Shang-sheng Tu-shi-t'ien Ching* (*KMST*),[45] T. 452, Vol. 14 (Nj. 204); *Sūtra of Meditation on Maitreya Bodhisattva's Rebirth on High in the Tuṣita Heaven*,[46] translated in Southern China in 455 by the exiled Northern Liang Prince of An-yang.

The text was brought from the Central Asian city of Turfan.[47] Although Soper thinks that this Sūtra is rather late and intimates a variety of sources, it can as well be argued that it is one of the earlier Sūtras of the group. However, the title *Kuan* is hardly appropriate since "no technique of visualization is offered."[48] Some similarities with the *KFC* are striking—the water of eight qualities in the Tuṣita lakes; the distinction between correct meditation and heterodox meditation; the promise of rebirth in Tuṣita Heaven if one performs *buddhānusmṛti* and calls the name of Maitreya; and the promise of extinction of sins. Although these similarities, strictly speaking, could have been copied from other *Kuan* Sūtras, it is more likely that the Sūtra was written before the *KFC*.

(4) *Fo shuo Kuan P'u-hsien P'u-sa Hsing-fa Ching* (*KPP*),[49] T. 277, Vol. 9 (Nj. 394), *Sūtra on the Practice of Visualizing the Bodhisattva Samantabhadra*,[50] translated by Dharmamitra between 424 and 442 A.D. (Liu Sung dynasty).

The introduction of the Sūtra already gives away its Mahāyāna origin. Ānanda asks the Buddha, "How will sentient beings after Buddha's *nirvāṇa* produce the *bodhi*-mind, cultivate the Mahāyāna Sūtras, [and] practice the right-mindfulness and concentration on the true realms . . .?"[51] Moreover, several times the text mentions the *Lotus Sūtra*.

The title *Kuan* is again not wholly justified. Although the Sūtra starts off by describing a method of *kuan* practiced in order to visualize Bodhisattva Samantabhadra, the major part is devoted to confession of sins in order to obtain a vision of the Buddhas of the Ten Directions. Purification of the six sense-organs comprises the basic message.

There are no proofs of the origin of the text, and not much is known about the origin of the cult of Samantabhadra; but Soper suggests Nagarahāra because of its links with the *KFSH*.[52]

(5) *Fo shuo Kuan Yao-wang Yao-shang Erh P'u-sa Ching* (*KYWS*),[53] T. 1161, Vol. 20 (Nj. 305); *Sūtra Spoken by the Buddha on Visualizing the Two Bodhisattvas Bhaiṣajyarāja and Bhaiṣajyasamudgata*,[54] translated by Kālayaśas between 424 and 442 at the southern capital (Liu Sung Dynasty).

Nanjio says that this was the second translation; the earlier one was reported lost in the *K'ai-yüan Lu*.[55] The relative lateness of this Sūtra appears evident from its borrowing of ideas from the *Lotus Sūtra* and the *Sukhāvatī* literature. It also mentions the *KFSH* and demonstrates close links with the *KFC*.

The conclusions to be drawn from this general review are not too exciting. However, some facts seem to be well established.

First, the general period in which these Sūtras were composed seems to have been between 300 A.D. (or perhaps somewhat earlier) and 400 A.D. They were all translated into Chinese around the first half of the fifth century. With varied degrees of success, all of these texts purported to teach particular methods of meditation which predicated particular centers of origin and development. However, the *kuan* method did not arise all of a sudden. Several conditions predetermined its origin, *e.g.* the cult of the Buddhas (of the Ten Directions) and Bodhisattvas and a developed iconography. It also seems that the use of *dhāraṇīs* and the invocation of Buddhas and Bodhisattvas through mantras was universally practiced.

Furthermore, one of the aims of meditation had become to achieve a mystical vision of the Buddhas: first the Buddhas of the Ten Directions in general, later particular individual Buddhas. For all of these reasons, it would appear that the origin of the *Kuan* Sūtras can be situated *ca.* 300 A.D.

Second, there are several useful indicators of the place(s) of origin of the *Sūtras*. The area in and around Kashmir seems the most probable choice: it is not pure accident that almost *all* the translators of the *Kuan* Sūtras are connected with Kashmir. Buddhabhadra[56] studied there; Dharmamitra[57] was born there; the Prince (or Marquis) of An-yang, while staying in Khotan,[58] studied meditation under *dhyāna*-master Buddhasena, who came from Kashmir and was considered one of the most famous *dhyāna* teachers.[59] About Kālayaśas, we only know that he was from the Western Regions; but his specialty being meditation, it is not presumptuous to believe that he was in some way related to Kashmir.

When analyzing the contents of the various Sūtras, it is beyond doubt that some of them are closer to Hīnayāna (*KFSH*, T. 643), others unmistakably Mahāyāna (*KPP*, T. 277; *KFC*, T. 365), and some are a mixture (*KHP*, T. 409; *KMST*, T. 452; *KYWS*, T. 1161). This seems to add weight to the hypothesis about the area of origin: Kashmir was a stronghold of the Sarvāstivādins,[60] and in many other places of Central Asia Hīnayāna and Mahāyāna communities lived side by side, *e.g.* Kucha.[61] It would not seem surprising that both Hīnayāna and Mahāyāna groups developed this kind of meditation, even in a competitive way, and that various centers chose their own Buddha or Bodhisattva as the particular object of visualization. This method, in fact, has nothing distinctively Mahāyānistic: *e.g.*, the Sūtra which teaches the vision of Śākyamuni could be a further development of *Buddhānusmṛti*, which was a popular Hīnayāna method of meditation. Similarly, the worship of the Ten Buddhas was not exclusively practiced by Mahāyāna followers. What makes the method more radically Mahāyānistic is the general context in which it moves. That some of the *Kuan* Sūtras are a mixture of both schools of Buddhism could be explained either through the fact of actual coexistence of both *yāna*s in the same areas, resulting in mutual influence and perhaps even in a mixed form of Buddhism; or through resorting to the hypothesis that some of the Sūtras, originally Hīnayāna in character, were taken over and manipulated by Mahāyāna followers. Both possibilities are acceptable; a more thorough analysis of the texts may bring to light which of the two is the correct one.

Coming back to the *KFC*, a comparison with the other Sūtras of the group shows better its distinctive merits: it is the most organized and methodical of them all, even if some interpolations must be recognized. The Sūtra as a whole suggests that it was built on some preceding texts and that the method of visualization and examination was brought to perfection. Even superficial comparison of the vocabulary demonstrates its literary dependence on the other *Kuan* Sūtras as well as on the *Pan-chou san-mei ching*. If the latter served as a base for Hui-yüan's Amita-worship, the great success of the *KFC* in China caused the *PCS* to gradually lose its place of eminence.

The study of all the texts related to Buddha-visualization is very interesting. On the one hand it may become a source of more information about the development of Central Asian Buddhism; on the other hand it seems an important link in the development of *dhyāna* (*ch'an*) in China, not only of Pure Land *Buddhānusmṛti* but probably also of the later Chinese school that took the name of *Ch'an* (*Zen* in Japan).

THE QUESTION OF INTERPOLATIONS

In the above examination of the probable date and place of origin of the *KFC* it was mentioned that the Sūtra has been augmented by interpolations. A detailed study of this problem is very exciting, and will shed new light on the development of the Amita cult.

As far as is apparent from various studies of the *KFC*, this question has never been raised by scholars, and resolving it, *a fortiori*, has never been attempted. This is not surprising in the case of the Buddhist monks who wrote commentaries on the Sūtra. They accepted the Buddhist scriptures as they were, with deep respect and great faith. They were apparently not aware of the question or not interested in it, since each part of the sacred text was beyond suspicion or doubt. It is more surprising in the case of scholars who study the text analytically. The solution to this question is very important, though, since it can illuminate the reasons why various commentators disagreed in some of their interpretations or even explain why a particular commentator contradicted himself in various parts of his exegesis.

In the present study there is no pretense of completeness, and only the major points of importance will be touched upon. We will try to arrive at some conclusions through a process of gradual exclusion.

First Step: The (Sixteen) Topics of Meditation

A careful and critical study of the present text of the *KFC* leads to the impression that not all of the sixteen topics are authentic, *i.e.*, they do not apparently go back to the first redaction. Reading some passages in the Chinese commentaries strengthens this impression. From the text itself emerges the following fundamental reason: it is evident that the author[62] divided the meditation topics into two separate but parallel sets.[63] The first set is introduced by the appearance of Śākyamuni (4) who enables Vaidehī to see the *Sukhāvatī* of the West (8). Here the Queen says, "O World-Honored One, people such as I can now see that land by the power of Buddha, but how shall all those beings who are to come after Buddha's Nirvāṇa . . . see the World of Highest Happiness of the Buddha Amitāyus?"[64]

Thereupon Śākyamuni starts the discourse and explains how to meditate on the various aspects of *Sukhāvatī*. This is the first set of topics (Meditations 1-6). After the sixth exercise there is a clear interruption in the discourse, introduced by "Listen carefully, listen carefully. Think over what you have heard"—the same sentence which introduced the first part of the speech.[65] Then there is the climax of the whole Sūtra, when "Buddha Amitāyus stood in the midst of the sky with Bodhisattvas Mahāsthāma and Avalokiteśvara attending on his right and left respectively."[66] After this 'Buddhophany', Vaidehī addressed herself again to Śākyamuni: "O Exalted One! I am now able by the power of Buddha to see Buddha Amitāyus together with the two Bodhisattvas. But how shall all the beings of the future meditate on Buddha Amitāyus and the two Bodhisattvas?"[67] Thus far the text offers a perfectly symmetrical parallelism which cannot be explained as accidental and was consciously intended. Whatever in the text destroys this original symmetry must be considered a manipulation by a later interpolator. Therefore, since the former set of meditations contained six topics, we can rightly expect six new topics for the latter part of the discourse. However, there are seven, followed by another three—the three grades of rebirth.

If we apply this first (negative)[68] internal criterion to the number of meditations, we have to conclude that the three so-called meditations on the three grades of rebirth are secondary or interpolated. That this first exclusion is valid is supported by several subsidiary considerations. First is the nature of these meditations. From a logical viewpoint, these descriptions can hardly be called visualizations or examinations. They actually list the various moral conditions for being reborn, which is essentially different from the former topics. Second, the Sūtra text states that the Buddha discourses in answer to Vaidehī's questions. (This is the usual procedure in Buddhist Sūtras.) The information given in Meditations 14–16 is not really part of his answer. Shan-tao has felt this difficulty. He says that Meditations 1–13 are the answers of the Buddha to the Queen's questions but that Meditations 14–16 are a spontaneous (*i.e.*, *motu proprio*) explanation.[69] Third, an argument observed in the (Chinese) text itself is that the vocabulary and use of certain expressions indicate a different authorship.

SECOND STEP: THE REMAINING (THIRTEEN) TOPICS

After this first exclusion there are thirteen meditations left, which is a rather odd number in Buddhist numerology. It is, however, not impossible that the semi-final redactor of the *KFC* adopted the scheme of thirteen degrees of *kṣānti* as a model for thirteen meditations, since *kṣānti* is an important subject throughout the Sūtra. Still, this similarity does not prove that the original version consisted of thirteen meditations. There are better reasons to presume that ten were the original number. 'Ten' is a holy number in Buddhism, and at one time (comparatively late) it became prevalent in various lists of Buddhist terminology, *e.g.*:

a) ten *bhūmi*s: originally seven, three added later;[70]
b) ten *pāramitā*s: originally six, four added later, and supplementary;[71]
c) ten powers (*daśabāla*);
d) ten (objects of) mindfulness: developed from six to eight, finally ten;
e) ten directions, or The Buddhas of the Ten Directions: developed from four to six, finally ten;
f) ten objects of meditation: ten *kasina*s, ten kinds of foulness, ten recollections (see 'mindfulness' above).

The last group may have inspired the author of the *KFC* to adopt the number 'ten' for his own scheme of meditation topics, since the text in fact deals with *anusmṛti* (as the corrected title suggests).

This is all based on assumptions, since no real proof is available. Other alternatives are possible, such as an original number of eight or twelve meditations. As mentioned above, the first set of topics in the *KFC* consists of six; if this number is doubled we arrive at a total of twelve. The other choice, sixteen, also has some arguments in its favor. Since the *KFC* is doctrinally closely related to the *Pan-chou San-mei Ching* of which two versions exist, one in eight chapters and another in sixteen, it would not seem impossible that it inspired the secondary redactor to double the original number of eight meditations. In this case, however, the presumption is uncertain as the eight-chapter version might be an abridgement of the sixteen-chapter original work.

When the thirteen remaining meditation topics are considered individually there are further indications that some are not authentic. First of all, Meditation Thirteen is suspect. As already mentioned, it breaks the symmetry, although this argument in itself is not strong enough. But in the terminology there appears something unusual. The other meditations are concluded with stereotyped formulas like

"Such is the perception of the sun, which is the First Meditation,"[72] and "Such is the perception of the trees, and it is the Fourth Meditation."[73] However, the conclusion of Meditation Thirteen is, "Such is the meditation that forms a joint perception of the Buddha and Bodhisattvas, and it is the Thirteenth Meditation."[74]

Moreover, the topic presented here is not really a new one but a repetition of former topics. It would only be acceptable if it were a recapitulation of them. Finally, some of the ideas expressed are not in harmony with the rest of the Sūtra. For example, the reference to "the ancient prayer" of Amita is the only allusion to Dharmākara's original vows.

Next, when analyzing the contents of Meditation Three, which is called "Perception of the Land," it is hard to avoid the impression that it is patchwork: it appears that some textual disruption has taken place solely to achieve the number of meditations needed. Indeed, no new object of meditation is offered here.

Further, meditations Ten and Eleven, with the two Bodhisattvas as respective objects, when carefully compared with the meditation on Buddha Amita, lead to the conclusion that originally there was only one meditation instead of two. The present descriptions of the two Bodhisattvas are so extensive and detailed, and extoll the greatness of these Bodhisattvas so much, that their glory exceeds that of Amita himself. The chapter on Amita is rather short (probably augmented with some interpolations, because there are duplicates), whereas the chapters on his two attendants are comparatively long. It therefore seems very probable that the original meditation was divided into two at one time when the cult of Avalokiteśvara reached its zenith. Supreme worship of him is already discernible here and hardly agrees with the intention of the original author.

If all of the above assumptions are integrated, the following scheme appears to be the authentic outline of the Sūtra:[75]

The External Splendors	*The Internal Splendors*
1) The Setting Sun	6) The Throne
2) The Land of Amita	7) The Images of Amita and Bodhisattvas
3) The Trees	8) The True Body
4) The Lakes	9) The Two Bodhisattvas
5) General View	10) General View

This new division of the Sūtra topics has the advantage of showing in a more striking manner both the symmetric parallelism of the two groups and the particular method used in this kind of meditation.

The parallelism manifests itself as follows. Meditations One and Six are both introductory: the setting sun directs the mind's attention toward the location of the Land; the throne toward the place where Amita is. Meditations Two and Seven are parallel inasmuch as both present a first glimpse of the respective realities of the Land and of the Buddha. Subsequent Meditations Three and Four vs. Eight and Nine concern the true realities of the Land and the Buddha-Bodhisattvas respectively. Finally, Meditations Five and Ten are both recapitulations, or complete reviews of what was seen in the previous exercises.

The particular method used in this kind of meditation consists of seeing, *i.e.*, visualizing and examining, the features of the Land and its inhabitants, either through the help of visual aids such as iconographic representations or through mental projection–imagination. Further, the practitioner begins by visualizing the various details of a topic and gradually arrives at inspection of its essentials even to the point of absorption into a state of trance (*sāmādhi*).

Returning to the dispute about the title of the Sutra and reviewing the whole argument in the light of the critique just completed, one may conclude with the great probability that the original Sūtra consisted of ten forms of *anusmṛti*, adapted to the needs of the followers of the Amita cult. Later glossarists perhaps first added the three chapters on the grades of rebirth, which then made a further addition of three more meditations necessary just to obtain another meaningful numerical series. However, this later process could have taken place the other way around as well.

The question of interpolations is not yet exhaustively covered through the elimination of the above passages. There seem to be several more pericopes that may be of later origin. Without detailing the reasons (except to say in general that these passages do not agree with the basic message of the Sūtra or that they betray its secondary character for reasons of vocabulary, among others), the following passages are likely interpolated: the three 'pure actions' necessary for rebirth;[76] the passage after the Seventh Meditation;[77] the text about the *Dharmadhātu-kāya*;[78] and the passage on the Buddha's mind.[79]

It appears that some of the major interpolations are due to a Chinese intervention. Foremost in this respect is the interpolation of the Three Grades or Nine Modes of Rebirth. The Chinese term used for 'modes' is *p'in*, which in ordinary contexts has a variety of meanings: '*Rang, Würde; Grad, Klasse, Sort, Reihe; Gegenstand, Ware; Ordnung, Regel; Haltung, Benehmen, Wesen, Character, Persönlichkeit; Eigenschaft, Qualität*'.[80] In Chinese history *p'in* has a special meaning in the expression *chiu-p'in*—the nine official grades for both civil and military ranks of eminence, of which the names and insignia are listed by H. Giles.[81] This system of Nine Categories (*chiu-p'in chih-tu*) was instituted during the period of the Three Kingdoms by the Wei dynasty (220–264 A.D.) either by Ts'ao Ts'ao or by his son Ts'ao P'ei.[82] It was a system of selection of government officials based on the personal abilities of candidates. According to their qualities they were assigned to one of nine classes.

It seems quite likely that this system of ranking the qualities of individuals, first used for political purposes, was adopted by the Buddhists and applied in the spiritual sphere: the Nine Modes of Rebirth are equally based on personal qualities of the believer.[83] This is in substantiation of the view expressed earlier—that this part of the Sūtra is an interpolation. If the original text was written in Central Asia, this section was inserted by a Chinese.

Another conclusion arrived at through the application of critique is that the *KFC* reflects a much more developed Pure Land ideology than the two *Sukhāvatī-sūtra*s in the following areas, briefly indicated here. The *KFC* was predetermined by the *SVS* since it builds on a previous knowledge of the description of *Sukhāvatī* and divides the various features into separate units as topics for meditation. The place of the two great Bodhisattvas has become more prominent, and the resulting 'triad' perhaps points to Iranian influence,[84] although it seems perfectly possible that Avalokiteśvara already had an earlier and separate cult. The fundamental approach toward Amita and his Buddha-land is different from the approach in the *SVS*. The *KFC* is not a devotional book but a manual of *buddhānusmṛti*. Instead of presenting the explicit goal of rebirth in *Sukhāvatī* as the main message of the discourse, it encourages the practitioner to strive for a more immediate object, the vision of Amita *in* *this life*: "Those who practice the *samādhi* . . . in accordance with this Sūtra will be able to see, in the present life, Buddha Amitāyus and the two great Bodhisattvas."[85]

CONCLUSION

The study of the *Kuan-Fo-ching* is extremely interesting because it is a document that, under an appearance of simplicity, opens up perspectives of spiritual and mystical experiences. It once occupied a place of eminence among Central Asian and Chinese meditators and still attracts Japanese and Western Buddhists today, although its interpretation in modern times is not always based on the real meaning of the text. Summarizing, it is no exaggeration to say that the *KFC* is a most interesting document in Buddhist religious literature for the following reasons.

1. It testifies to the practice of a remarkable method of Buddhist meditation which is unique to Buddhist mysticism and perhaps to mysticism in general. As the method probably presupposes the development of visual aids such as Buddha-images (statues, paintings, mandalas), it has certain similarities to Tantric practices of meditation, and a comparison between the two would be very revealing. More than thirty years ago, Carl Jung, much impressed with this Buddhist meditation text, wrote of his impressions about its psychological value.[86] He found striking similarities between this method of *dhyāna* and the methods of psychoanalysis.

2. The *KFC* offers a rich field of study with regard to Sūtra development. On the one hand it is doctrinally related to several other texts, some of them more general in scope (aiming at a vision of all the Buddhas of the Ten Quarters), others emphasizing the vision of a particular Buddha or Bodhisattva. On the other hand the present text of the *KFC* betrays several layers of composition, and in this respect again a critical study of the Sūtra is quite revealing.

3. This text is a representative sample of the study of the history of Buddhist exegesis, since numerous commentaries on it have been written in both China and Japan.

For these reasons, it is rather surprising that Müller hesitated to include the *KFC* in his collection of the *Sacred Books of the East*. "I was so much disappointed at the contents of the Sūtra, that I hesitated for some time whether I ought to publish it in this volume."[87] However, acquiescing to the wishes of his Japanese Pure Land friends, for whom the Sūtra is one of the most cherished Scriptures, he decided to publish the English translation (by J. Takakusu) with the result that nowadays the Sūtra is one of the best-known Mahāyāna texts in both the East and the West.

CHINESE CHARACTERS (MATHEWS' DICTIONARY NUMBERS)

ch'an	5650
cheng-kuan	351–3575
Chiang-ling	638–4067
Chiu-p'in (*chih-tu*)	1198–5281 (986–6504)
Chung-shan	1503–5630
hsieh-kuan	2625–3575
Hsien-tsai Fo hsi-tsai-ch'ien-li San-mei	2684–6657–1982–2506–6657–919–3921–5415–4411
Hsi-yü chih Fo-chiao	2406–7676–935–1982–719
Kao-seng chuan	3290–5453–1446
kuan	3575
Kuan Fo San-mei Hai Ching (T. 643)	3575–1982–5415–4411–2014–1123
Kuan Hsü-k'ung-tsang P'u-sa Ching (T. 409)	3575–2821–3722–6718–5387–5410–1123
Kuan P'u-hsien P'u-sa Hsing-fa Ching (T. 277)	3575–5384–2671–5387–5410–2754–1762–1123
Kuan-shih-yin Kuan-ching	3575–5790–7418–3575–1123
Kuan(-wu-liang-shou)-Fo-ching (*shu*) (T. 365)	3575(–7180–3943–5846)–1982–1123(–5861)
Kuan Yao-wang Yao-sheng Erh P'u-sa Ching (T. 1161)	3575–7501–7037–7501–5669–1751–5387–5410–1123
Pan-chou San-mei Ching (T. 416–419)	4881–1291–5415–4411–1123
Pao-chih	4956–973

p'in	5281
Seng-han	5453-2017
Shih-chu P'i-p'o-sha Lun (T. 1521)	5807-1337-5158-5347-5606-4253
Shih-fang hsien-tsai Fo hsi-tsai-ch'ien-li Ting	5807-1802-2684-6657-1982-2506-6657-919-3921-6393
Ta Chih-tu Lun	5943-933-6504-4253
T'ang Ch'ang-ju	6116-213-3145
Tao-lin	6136-4022
Ta-pei Kuang-ming Wang Fo	5943-4992-3583-2460-5415-1982
Tsao-wang Shen-t'ung Yen-hua Fo	6730-7037-5719-6638-7335-2217-1982
Wei-chin Nan-pei-ch'ao Shih-lun-ts'ung	7104-1088-4620-4974-233-5769-4253-6921
yu-kuan	7524-3575

ABBREVIATIONS

BEFEO *Bulletin de l'Ecole Française de l'Extrême-Orient*

BKD Ono's *Bussho Kaisetsu Daijiten* (Encyclopedia of Buddhist Works)

EB *The Eastern Buddhist*

IBK *Indogaku Bukkyōgaku Kenkyū* (Journal of Indian and Buddhist Studies)

KFC(S) *Kuan-Fo ching* or *Kuan-wu-liang-shou-Fo ching* (*Shu*) (T. 365) (T. 1753)

KFSH *Kuan Fo san-mei Hai ching* (T. 643)

KHP *Kuan Hsü-k'ung-tsang P'u-sa Ching* (T. 409)

KMST *Kuan Mi-lo P'u-sa Shang-sheng Tu-shi-t'ien Ching* (T. 452)

KPP *Kuan P'u-hsien P'u-sa Hsing-fa Ching* (T. 277)

KSC *Kao-seng Chuan*

KYWS *Kuan Yao-wang Yao-shang Erh P'u-sa Ching* (T. 1161)

MEB Mochizuki's *Bukkyō Daijiten* [Encyclopedia of Buddhism]

Nj. Nanjio, *Catalogue of the Chinese Translations of the Buddhist Tripiṭaka*

PCS *Pan-chou San-mei Ching*

RBS *Revue Bibliographique de Sinologie*

SBE *Sacred Books of the East*

T. Taishō edition of the Chinese Tripitaka

NOTES

1. M. Müller, ed., *Sacred Books of the East*, Vol. 49, *Buddhist Mahāyāna Texts*, First Edition. Oxford: Clarendon Press, 1894. Reprinted Delhi: Motilal Banarsidass, 1968. J. Takakusu's translation is in Part 2 of the book, pp. 161-204. The following translations have also been made of the *KFC*.

a) Bhikku Assaji, trans., *The Sūtra of Visualizing the Buddha of Immeasurable Length of Life, Bilingual Buddhist Series I: Sūtras and Scriptures* (Taipei: Buddhist Culture Service, 1962), pp. 155-192.

b) Yoshitaka Kawagishi, trans., *Buddha-Bhaṣita Amitāyur Dhyāna Sūtra* (*Meditation on Buddha Amitāyus*). New York: American Buddhist Academy Press, 1949.

c) Lu K'uan Yü (Charles Luk), *The Secrets of Chinese Meditation*. (London: Rider and Co., 1964), pp. 85-106 ("The Sūtra of the Contemplation of Amitāyus").

d) A partial translation is included in J. Eracle, *La Doctrine Bouddhique de la Terre Pur, Introduction à Trois Sūtras Bouddhiques* (Paris: Dervy-Livres, 1973), pp. 78-88 ("Le *Sūtra* de la Contemplation du *Buddha* de la Vie Infinie").

2. B. Nanjio, *A Catalogue of the Chinese Translations of the Buddhist Tripiṭaka* (Oxford: Clarendon Press, 1883), p. 58, No. 198.

3. See P. C. Bagchi, *Le Canon Bouddhique en Chine*, vol. 1 (Paris: 1927), pp. 391 ff. See also R. Shih, trans. and annot., *Biographies des Moines Eminents* (Louvain: 1968), I. 147 ff.

4. *KSC*, T. 2059, 50. 343, C. 11-23.

5. *Ibid.*, p. 343, C. 13-14; R. Shih, *op. cit.*, p. 147: "Quand il entrait en contemplation, il y restait parfois sept jours sans en sortir."

6. Now a suburb of Nanking.

7. *KSC*, *loc. cit.*, p. 343, C. 16-18.

8. *Ibid.*, p. 343, C. 21-23.

9. G. Ono, ed., *BKD*, [Encyclopedia of Buddhist Works], Tokyo, 1968-69 reprint, p. 198c.

10. *Ibid.*, Ono also lists 16 earlier Buddhist canons in which the Sūtra text appears.

11. For instance L. Hurvitz, *RBS*, 1959, No. 634, says that the *KFC* is a "well-known 'spurious sūtra' of Chinese provenance."

12. A recent study of the various opinions on this question was written by K. Fujita, *IBK* 17 (1969), pp. 465-472. ("The Problem of Compilation of the *Kuan-wu-liang-shou-ching*"). According to this article some Japanese scholars such as Nakamura and Kasugai favor a Central Asian origin. Others, like Tsukinowa and Suzuki, are of the opinion that a Chinese origin is more probable.

13. *Ibid.*, p. 465. See also R. Fujimoto, *An Outline of the Triple Sūtra of Shin Buddhism* 2:3 Kyoto, 1960.

14. K. Fujita, *op. cit.*, p. 466.
15. *SBE* 49, Part 2: 180.
16. D. Seckel, "The Art of Buddhism" in *Art of the World*, (New York: 1964), p. 62. See also S. E. Lee, *A History of Far Eastern Art*, (New York, 1964), p. 132. This dates the Bāmiyān statues around the fourth and fifth centuries A.D. Fa-hsien, who traveled to India from 399 A.D. until his return to China in 414, does not mention the Bāmiyān statues in his travel account. He would probably have heard of them or seen them if they had existed at that time since he was in the neighborhood of Bāmiyān (Gandhāra, Peshawar, Nagarahāra, and maybe even Kabul). See also J. Legge, *A Record of Buddhistic Kingdoms*, pp. 21–40.
17. K. Fujita, *op. cit.*, p. 469.
18. A. Soper, *Literary Evidence for Early Buddhist Art in China* (Ascona, Switzerland: Artibus Asiae Publishers, 1959), p. 143.
19. E. Zürcher, *The Buddhist Conquest of China* (Leiden: Brill, 1959), p. 212.
20. A. Soper, *op. cit.*, p. 143. The author does not give an exact reference, but the idea is found in T. 1509, 33. 50: 306 A. 12–13 and in 34.51: 308, C. 10–14. The latter states, "The Bodhisattvas possess a *samādhi*, called '*samādhi* of inspecting (*kuan*) all the Buddhas of the Three Worlds'. When a Bodhisattva enters into this *samādhi*, he can distinctly see all the Buddhas of the Three Worlds and hear their discourses on the *dharma*."
21. See L. Renou, J. Filliozat, *et al.*, *L'Inde Classique* 2.2271: 532ff. (Hanoi, 1953).
22. Kumārajīva, trans. *Shih-chu P'i-p'o-sha Lun*, T. 1521, Vol. 26.
23. *Ibid.*, p. 44, B. 19–20.
24. *MEB*, p. 4252b; *Hōbōgirin*, *Ann.*, p. 25; Nj., p. 73. The translations of this presumed title are various. A. Andrews, "Nembutsu in the Chinese Pure Land Tradition," *EB* 3:21 1970, renders it as "Seeing All Buddhas Samādhi Sūtra." A. Soper, *op. cit.*, p. 143, renders it as "Sūtra on the Meditation [that Brings before One] Everything that Exists through the Ten Quarters." These translations do not seem accurate. In addition to the short Chinese title, *Pan-chou San-mei Ching*, there is a longer one given as a sub-title which appears to be a translation of the Sanskrit: *Hsien-tsai Fo hsi-tsai-ch'ien-li San-mei*, or *Shih-fang hsien-tsai Fo hsi-tsai-ch'ien-li Ting*.
25. E. Zürcher, *op. cit.*, p. 333, Note 95.
26. *Ibid.*, p. 220. Another translation similar to Zürcher's is given by P. Demiéville, "La *Yogācārabhūmi* de Saṅgharakṣa," *BEFEO* 54:353 Note 2 (1954). "*Sūtra* de la concentration durant laquelle apparai [ssen]t face à face le[s] Buddha[s] en présence immédiate."
27. T. 417 and 418. The former is missing in Nj.; the latter is Nj. 73. The other translations are T. 416 (Nj. 75) and T. 419 (Nj. 76). S. Mochizuki, *Bukkyō Keiden Seiritsu Shiron* (Kyoto: 1946), p. 190, suggests 179 A.D. as the date of translation.

28. E. Zürcher, *op. cit.*, p. 35.

29. *Ibid.*, pp. 332 ff., Note 95. According to S. Mochizuki, *op. cit.*, p. 192, T. 416 is certainly the latest translation; among the three remaining ones, T. 419 is the oldest (four chapters), followed by T. 417 (eight chapters) and T. 418 (sixteen chapters).

30. *Ibid.*, p. 195.

31. *Ibid.*, p. 196. If this is correct, it would follow that the formula "from one day to seven days, keep his name in mind with thoughts undisturbed" (*SBE*, *loc. cit.*, p. 99) appearing in *SSVS*, and other formulas found in the *LSVS* and the *KFC*, are all based on the *PCS* (*ibid.*, p. 196).

32. The references to Amita are in T. 417, p. 898a–b and in T. 418, p. 905a–b.

33. Originally there must have been more than six: at least one *Kuan-*Sūtra is reported in ancient catalogs, The *Kuan-shih-yin Kuan-Ching*. It is mentioned in the *Ch'u san-tsang chi-chi* and the *Chung-ching Mu-lu*, which states that it was translated by the Marquis of An-yang (T. 2146, 55: 116c).

34. The reconstructed Sanskrit title (Nj., p. 30) is *Ākāṣagarbha-bodhisattva-dhyāna-sūtra* (?).

35. A. Soper, *op. cit.*, p. 206, Note 17.

36. T. 409, Vol. 13. 678, A. 14–8.5.

37. *Ibid.*, p. 678, B. 6–16.

38. *Ibid.*, p. 678, C. 7–29.

39. *Ibid.*, p. 679, A. 10–11.

40. *Ibid.*, p. 679, A. 27.

41. The reconstructed Sanskrit title (Nj., p. 104) is *Buddhadhyāna-samādhisāgara-sūtra.*

42. A. Soper, *op. cit.*, p. 184. For a discussion of the Sūtra, see *ibid.*, pp. 184–192.

43. *Ibid.*, p. 184.

44. *Ibid.*, p. 185.

45. No Sanskrit title given by Nj.

46. A. Soper, *op. cit.*, p. 215. For a description of the contents, see *ibid.*, pp. 215 ff.

47. P. C. Bagchi, *op. cit.*, p. 222. A. Soper, *op. cit.*, p. 216 thinks that for this reason the *KMST* may have been composed at Turfan "so that it represents a provincial imitation."

48. *Ibid.*, p. 216.

49. No Sankrit title given by Nj.

50. A. Soper, *op. cit.*, p. 222.

51. T. 277, Vol. 9: 389, C. 5–6.

52. A. Soper, *op. cit.*, pp. 223, ff.

53. The Sanskrit title reconstructed by Nj., p. 79, is *Bhaishajyarāja-*

bhaishajyasamudgati (or *-gata*) *-sūtra*. Nj. leaves out *dhyāna*, although his translation of the title includes 'meditation'.

54. A. Soper, *op. cit.*, p. 203. For a general discussion of the Sūtra, and of the underlying cult see *ibid.*, pp. 203–210.

55. Nj., *op. cit.*, p. 79.

56. See P. C. Bagchi, *op. cit.*, pp. 341–346. A. Soper, *op. cit.*, p. 218, adds the following: "In this geographical connection, it may be noted that the Chinese monks' biographies in several instances name Kashmir as the country in which Maitreya was particularly accessible to human worshippers by the route of mystic ecstasy. The famous missionary and translator Buddhabhadra is said to have visited Tuṣita in a trance while he was studying in Kashmir, some time around A.D. 400."

57. P. C. Bagchi, *op. cit.*, pp. 388–391.

58. *Ibid.*, pp. 221–223.

59. *Hsi-yü chih Fo-chiao*, p. 341.

60. See *l'Inde Classique*, 2.2321.562:30. See also R. Gard, *Buddhism*, (New York: G. Braziller, 1962), p. 30.

61. See Liu Mau-tsai, *Kutscha und seine Beziehungen zu China vom Zweiten Jahrhundert* V.C. *bis zum Sechsten Jahrhundert* N.C., 1.28 Wiesbaden, 1969.

62. 'Author' in the present context always refers to the original composer of the Sūtra in distinction from later interpolators.

63. In the following discussion the numbers between parentheses refer to the chapters of the Sūtra as given in Takakusu's English translation.

64. *SBE*, 49, Part 2; 169 (8). The Chinese text: T. 365, Vol. 12: 341, C. 25–27.

65. *SBE*, *loc. cit.*, p. 175 (15). Chinese: T. 365, *loc. cit.*, p. 342, C. 14–15. The Chinese text of the first passage, T. 365, *loc. cit.*, p. 341, C. 15 is identical with the second.

66. *SBE*, *loc. cit.*, pp. 175 ff.

67. *SBE*, *loc. cit.*, p. 176 (15). The Chinese text, T. 365, *loc. cit.*, p. 342, C. 20–22 almost perfectly parallels the citation in Note 64.

68. Negative since it shows discrepancy with the internal unity of the Sūtra.

69. Commentary on *KFC*, T. 1753, Vol. 37:347, C. 11–14.

70. H. Dayal, *The Bodhisattva Doctrine in Buddhist Sanskrit Literature* (London: Kegan Paul, 1932), p. 271.

71. *Ibid.*, p. 167.

72. *SBE*, *loc. cit.*, p. 170 (9); Chinese text: T. 365, *loc. cit.*, p. 342, A. 4.

73. *SBE*, *loc. cit.*, p. 173 (12); Chinese text: T. 365, *loc. cit.*, p. 342, B. 21.

74. *SBE*, *loc. cit.*, p. 187 (21); Chinese text: T. 365, *loc. cit.*, p. 344, C. 6–7.

75. Compare with the scheme in Takakusu's translation:

The External Splendors	*The Internal Splendors*
1) The Setting Sun (9)	7) The Throne (16)
2) The water and Icy Ground (10)	8) The Images of Buddha and Bodhisattvas (17)
3) The Land (11)	9) The True Body (18)
4) The Trees (12)	10) Avalokiteśvara (19a)
5) The Lakes (13)	11) Mahāsthāmaprāpta (19b)
6) General View (14)	12) Universal View (20)
	13) Joint View (21)
	14) 15) 16) } Three Grades of Rebirth (22-30)

76. *SBE, loc. cit.*, p. 167 (7).
77. *Ibid.*, p. 177 (16).
78. *Ibid.*, p. 178 (17).
79. *Ibid.*, p. 187 (18).
80. Rüdenberg, *Chinesisch Deutsches Wörterbuch*, No. 4773, p. 351. Cf. Mathews, *Chinese-English Dictionary*, No. 5281, p. 724.
81. Giles, *Chinese-English Dictionary*, Table I, p. [1].
82. See T'ang Ch'ang-ju, *Wei-chin Nan-Pei Ch'ao Shih-lun-ts'ung*, Second Edition, Peking: 1957. pp. 85-126. See also D. Holzman, "Les Sept Sages de la Forêt des Bambous et la Sociéte de leur Temps," *T'oung-pao*, 44:317-46, 324 (1956). See also E. Zürcher, *Buddhist Conquest*, p. 44.
83. Although this system of ranking officials into nine groups may have been the direct source of inspiration for the introduction of nine modes of rebirth, it is not impossible that the ultimate source was the cosmology of Chinese philosophers like Huai-nan-tzu (second century B.C.) who thought that Heaven consisted of 'nine divisions'. See Y. L. Fung, *History of Chinese Philosophy*, 1:399.

The division into nine ranks also had quite different applications in Chinese history, *e.g.*, the nine groups of 'great imperial concubines' during the T'ang dynasty. See N. Toan and L. Ricaud, *Une Traduction juxta-linéaire commentée de la Biographie officielle de l'Impératrice Wou Tsö-t'ien, d'apres le Texte du Hsin T'ang-shu* (Saigon, 1959), pp. 83 ff.; "La Hiérarchie féminine à la Cour des T'ang."
84. A. Soper, *op. cit.*, pp. 141-155.
85. *SBE, loc. cit.*, p. 200 (32). Chinese text: T. 365, *loc. cit.*, p. 346, B. 9-10. For a more detailed study of the meditation aspect of the *KFC* and Shan-tao's view on it, see my article "Shan-tao's Interpretation of the Meditative Vision of Buddha Amitāyus," *History of Religions*, 14: 99-116 (1974).
86. C. G. Jung, "Zur Psychologie östlicher Meditation," in *Bulletin de la Société Suisse des Amis de l'Extrême-Orient* (*Mitteilungen der Schweizerischen Gesellschaft der Freunde Ostasiatischer Kultur*) 5:33-53 (1943).
87. *SBE, loc. cit.*, p. xxi.

"The Dharma that Came Down from Heaven": a Tun-huang Fragment

Hugh E. Richardson

An eighth-century document relating to Tibetan Buddhism that seems to have gone unremarked is No. 370 (5) in the *Catalogue of Tibetan MSS from Tun-huang in the India Office Library*,[1] which is reproduced here with the permission of the Librarian. It is the last part of a scroll 366c. × 27c. in size on which there are four other miscellaneous Tibetan religious works written on the back of a Chinese manuscript. It is obviously incomplete, amounting only to some twenty-six *śloka*s whereas a *bam-po*, as it is described, should contain 300 *śloka*s of two to four lines each. The handwriting is clumsy and there is much dubious orthography and many mistakes some of which have been corrected while others have not. The impression it leaves is that it was a copying exercise abandoned unrevised when it had been spoiled by so many errors. The fragment therefore bears out the description "sacred waste" given by Sir Aurel Stein to the cache of MSS in Chinese, Tibetan, and other Central Asian languages which he discovered in 1906 in a cave-temple at Ch'ien-fo-tung some 12 miles south of the oasis and town of Tun-huang.[2] Recently Professor Fujieda Akira has suggested convincingly how the documents probably came to be walled up during improvements to the cave-temple in the eleventh century to get them out of the way rather than to conceal them from predatory hands.[3]

Although the majority of the MSS are copies of religious works, there are also many lay documents which, in the Tibetan collection, include letters, petitions, contracts, veterinary works, divination manuals, hunting laws, translations of extracts from the Rāmāyana, stories about Confucius, and—best known and most valued—the historical annals and chronicle which have been edited and translated by Professors Bacot, Thomas, and Toussaint.[4] All these must have owed their survival, in company with the religious works, to the sanctity attached to the written word in any form.

It is not clear how the Chinese MSS, some of which date from as early as the fifth century and come from remote places, found their way to the cave; but those in Tibetan seem to be the debris of a clerical center[5] which employed local scribes and was probably modelled or superimposed on a pre-existing Chinese copying office. As many of the MSS are fragmentary or even mere scribbling on the back or between the lines of Chinese documents, it seems probable that they originated near the place where they were found; for it is unlikely that anyone would trouble to carry such waste the 12 miles from the city simply to store it.

The provenance of the original documents will be considered later. First a translation is presented of the fragment. Allowances are made for the errors, of which a list is given in the appendix together with a transcription of the text.

A VOLUME ON THE *DHARMA* THAT CAME DOWN FROM HEAVEN

The lords of men, sons of the gods, the excellent ruler Srong-brtsan the king divinely manifested, and the *btsan-po* Khri Srong-lde-brtsan, these two who brought benefit to all beings in the world of men in this land of Tibet, learned the doctrine of Gautama Śakya that most excellent medicine like the flower of the Udambara, the *dharma* of the Perfection of Wisdom that became the Mother of those who have attained final bliss in the Three Ages, famed as the unsurpassed Great Vehicle the very essence of suchness which destroys the extremes of being and not-being. They received that doctrine and devoted themselves to it and caused it to spread among all creatures. For its enduring maintenance an inscription was written on a stone pillar as a compact between ruler and subjects.

Such wise teachings are the Ocean in which the deeds of ruler and subjects are as Mount Sumeru. The tradition of such actions being long established, the bounds of the dominion increased and the land of Tibet was happy. Harvests were good, diseases of men and cattle rare. The sound qualities and right behavior of the people increased; and, far from shunning the rites of gods and men, they revered them and, clinging even more strongly to those principles, they did not fail in proper respect and affection towards teachers and parents, brothers, sisters, and kinsmen, and to those who through age are in a position of honor. And since there was a feeling of love towards all, no one committed theft or robbery against anyone else; shameful acts such as lying and fornication were shunned; honesty and good qualities increased. Although they (the kings) had the bodies of men, their ways were those of the gods. In other kingdoms and among other men that has not happened before, and it is not likely in the future. Even among the gods such a thing is rare.

When the king the father died, because the son was young the good religion and old learning were, indeed, eclipsed. How then is it that the excellent way of truth, the virtuous religion, adherence to the ten rules of religious discipline, the royal laws of the king the lord of men, and obedience to the instructions of wise parents continue according to the customs of Tibet?

Because of the nature of the world from its beginning, from the *nirvāṇa* of Śakya until the coming of Byams-pa Mu-tri (Maitreya), many self-originating Buddhas come into being suddenly and unannounced by prophesy. Religious texts,[6] the Dharma and the Vajrayāna, the seven successive Buddhas and their Scriptures: the three groups do not coincide; each has its separate tradition, and the *dharmas* are, as it were, a seed. . . .

This text contains several points of historical interest. It adds to the evidence of the Tun-huang Chronicle[7] and the *sKar-cung*[8] inscription that Tibetans in the eighth and ninth centuries regarded Srong-brtsan sgam-po, who lived some 200 years earlier, as the first patron of Buddhism in their country.

The "vow of king and people inscribed on a *rdo-rings*" refers to the pillar at bSam-yas.[9] It can be dated between 779 A.D. when the monastery was completed, and 782 A.D., the last year in office of Zhang rGyal-gzigs shu-theng,[10] who was Chief Minister when a *bka'-tshigs* (edict) embodying such a vow was promulgated by Khri Srong-lde-brtsan.[11]

The allusion to the eclipse of religion when the king was young echoes what is said in a second edict of Khri Srong-lde-brtsan about the suppression of Buddhism when he was young and its restoration by him when he came of age. That is repeated in an edict by his son Khri Lde-srong-brtsan which, together with the two edicts of his father, is recorded in the *Chos-'byung* of dPa'-bo gtsug-lag phreng-ba (1565).[12] The brief comment in our fragment is, as far as I know, the only original evidence actually from the time of the kings about those events which later historians embellished with much pious and picturesque detail. Together with the passage about the vow of the king and people it adds further confirmation of the authenticity of the three edicts which dPa'-bo gtsug-lag appears to have copied from originals in the archives at bSam-yas.

It should be noted that the edict of Khri Lde-srong-brtsan shows that there was also some resistance to Buddhism when he came to the throne, and that he too reasserted royal support of the faith, joining his ministers and people in a vow to that effect as his father had done.[13] That seems to have escaped later historians who, for the most part, are confused about the identity of Khri Lde-srong-brtsan. But it is improbable that the eclipse of religion "when the king died, because the son was young" could refer to his reign. He was not the immediate successor of Khri Srong-lde-brtsan who died ca. 797–800 A.D. but was established on the throne after the death of his elder brother Mu-ne bTsan-po and a period of disputed succession around 805 A.D. He cannot have been young when his father died, for at his own death in 815 A.D. he was succeeded by a grown son. If he had been on the throne when the document was written, his name might have been expected to appear at the beginning. It must have been written after the capture of Tun-huang by the Tibetans, which Professor Demiéville dates in 787 A.D.[14] and Professor Fujieda in 782 A.D.[15]

Even before that event, whenever it was, the narrow valley where the caves of Ch'ien-fo-tung are situated had probably been in the hands of the Tibetans for some time. They had taken Su Chou and Kan Chou as early as 766 A.D.; and in 767 they captured the strategic city of Kua Chou dominating the junction of the northern and southern routes across Central Asia. Sha Chou (Tun-huang), some 75 miles to the southeast—the only surviving stronghold on the fortified *limes*—had been bypassed and surrounded by the Tibetans for several years before its fall;[16] but it is unlikely that there would have been any literary activity until the establishment at Sha Chou itself of a Tibetan administration as one of the five *mthong-khyab khri-sde* under the overall jurisdiction of the bDe-blon[17] whose headquarters were to the northeast of Lan Chou. So a date for the document after 782 A.D. and before 805 may be accepted.

Whether the text was composed locally or is a copy of an original brought from Central Tibet is largely speculation. Some of the MSS from the cave have a connection with Central Tibet, for example, many of the religious texts translated from Sanskrit, and the historical chronicles and annals of which echoes are found in histories such as that of dPa'-bo gtsug-lag (who of course could not have seen the Tun-huang MSS).[18] Others such as administrative documents, petitions, and the prayers at the foundation of the De-ga gyu-tshal Chapel are clearly of local origin. The language of those prayers, which F. W. Thomas describes as magniloquent,[19] suggests that the similarly enthusiastic language and spirit of our fragment may be the product of a colonial frontier régime. By comparison, eulogies of Khri Srong-lde-brtsan in the commemorative inscription at the burial ground at 'Phyong-rgyas[20] and in the Tun-huang Chronicle[21] are spare and formal.

Assuming a local origin for the document, it may be inquired whether any influence specifically from the China border is traceable in its religious content. For it was at Sha Chou and other cities of the frontier captured by the Tibetans that their previously rather tentative practice of Buddhism, which had just received an injection of new life through the visits of Padmasambhava and Śantarakshita, came into contact with a society in which the faith had flourished for over four centuries and where, under the T'ang dynasty, Chinese teachers had recently developed a school of *dhyāna* philosophy tinged with Taoism.[22] And it was from Sha Chou, probably soon after its capture by the Tibetans, that the leading figure in that school—the Master Mahāyāna—was invited to the Tibetan court. There his doctrine of immediate enlightenment through complete quietism—known to the Tibetans as *ston-min*—quickly won a following that threatened the supremacy of the Indian teachers of Śantarakshita's school, who expounded the way of gradual enlightenment through the accumulation of knowledge and merit, and of Padmasambhava's, whose followers sought special powers through strenuous forms of mystical training.[23]

The Master Mahāyāna was supported by the 'Bro clan, originally from the Yang-tung people, whose territory appears to have been to the southeast of Tun-huang. They may have become vassels in Tibet under Srong-brtsan sgam-po,[24] and for over a century had been allied by marriage to the Tibetan royal family. There are signs that, at least from the early eighth century, they had leanings toward the culture of China. The influential Queen Khri-ma-lod, Khri Srong-lde-brtsan's grandmother, was of 'Bro; and one of his own queens, a devout Buddhist and patroness of the Chinese master, was also from that clan.

By the time of Mahāyāna's visit the Buddhist revival in Central Tibet had rapidly secured a footing in affairs of state. The Tibetan nobility soon saw the political potential of high rank in the Buddhist church. Before the end of the eighth century a monk of the noble family of Myang acted as guardian to the young Khri Lde-srong-brtsan;[25] and the first successor of the Indian Master Śantarakshita as principal abbot in Tibet was a member of the Central Tibetan family of dBa's[26] which had a long record of political rivalry with the 'Bro.

There were therefore other controversial elements associated with doctrinal differences, one in the field of Tibetan domestic politics and another in the wider sphere of international relations. At that time India was no threat to Tibetan power, while with China there was a long-standing and active hostility.

The religious controversy became so bitter that the king arranged a public debate. There are many signs of the effectiveness of the arguments of the Chinese teacher and of their lasting influence; but internal and foreign considerations were, perhaps, responsible for the official rejection of his doctrines.[27] The Master Mahāyāna returned to Sha Chou, where he continued to be an important figure both in religion and politics.[28]

We should hardly expect to find evidence of that doctrinal debate in a popular eulogy of the sort with which we are dealing; but the emphasis, in the fragment that survives, on the active pursuit of good works, and the appreciative mention of the Vajrayāna, appear to follow the official line.

In the brief account it gives of the origins of Buddhism there are several peculiarities to which Dr. D. L. Snellgrove has kindly drawn my attention. The separation of *chos* (*dharma*) and Vajrayāna is unusual. It is not clear how the Seven Buddhas are intended to fit into the pattern or precisely what the three categories are which do not coincide. They appear to be (1) Śākyamuni's *Dharma*, (2) texts relating to the Seven Buddhas, and (3) the Vajrayāna. That classification agrees with no known arrangement of Buddhism. The three are usually Śrāvakayāna (the early disciples' way), Pratyekabuddhayāna, and Bodhisattvayāna; or, alternatively, Early Buddhism, Perfection of Wisdom, and Mind-Only (Vijñānavādin). The fragment perhaps represents an early stage of Tibetan religious thinking when they had not yet clarified their views on the various stages in the development of Buddhism.

NOTES

1. L. de la Vallée Poussin, *Catalogue of the Tibetan Manuscripts from Tun-huang in the India Office Library*, Oxford: 1962, p. 122.
2. M. A. Stein, *Serindia*, Oxford: 1921, Vol. 2, p. 820; and Map 78.
3. Akira Fujieda, *The Tunhuang Manuscripts*, I. Zinbun, Kyoto: 1966, pp. 15-16.

4. F. W. Thomas, *Tibetan Literary Texts and Documents Concerning Chinese Turkestan*, Vol. 2 (*TLTD*), London: 1951; M. Lalou, *Inventaire des Manuscrits Tibétains de Touen-houang*, Vols. 1–3, Paris: 1939–1961; J. Bacot, F. W. Thomas, and C. Toussaint, *Documents de Touen-houang relatifs à l'histoire du Tibet* (*DTH*), Paris: 1940.

5. Akira Fujieda, *The Tunhuang Manuscripts*, Vol. 2, Zinbun: 1969, p. 36.

6. The reading *zhu* appears to be faulty. It might possibly refer to the work of revising translations of religious texts, but that seems out of context. The copyist wrote but deleted the letter '*g*'. I have arbitrarily guessed that *gzhung* was intended.

7. *DTH*, p. 118.

8. H. E. Richardson, "The sKar-cung Inscription," *Journal of the Royal Asiatic Society* (*JRAS*), 1973, pp. 13, 15.

9. G. Tucci, *The Tombs of the Tibetan Kings* (*TTK*), Rome: 1950, p. 43.

10. P. Pelliot, *Histoire Ancienne du Tibet*, Paris: 1961, pp. 110–113; and *DTH*, p. 153.

11. Tucci, *TTK*, p. 46.

12. *mKhas-pa'i dga'ston*, Vol. *ja* (*PT*), ff. 110a and 128b; and Tucci, *TTK*, p. 47.

13. *PT*, f. 129a; Tucci, *TTK*, p. 52; and Richardson, "The sKar-cung Inscription."

14. P. Demiéville, *Le concile de Lhasa*, Paris: 1952, p. 177.

15. Fujieda, Vol. 2, p. 22.

16. Demiéville, *op. cit.*, pp. 172, 173.

17. *DTH*, p. 115.

18. R. A. Stein, "*Deux Notules d'histoire ancienne du Tibet*," *Journal Asiatique* (*JA*), 1963; G. Uray, *Traces of a Narrative of the Old Tibetan Chronicle in the mkhas-pa'i dga-ston*, Monumenta Serica, Vol. 26.

19. Thomas, *TLTD*, pp. 92–108.

20. H. E. Richardson, "A New Inscription of Khri Srong Lde Brtsan," *JRAS*, 1964.

21. *DTH*, pp. 118 and 160–161.

22. Demiéville, *op. cit.*, pp. 47, 58.

23. Tucci, *Minor Buddhist Texts* (*MBT*), Vol. 2, Rome: 1958; and Demiéville, *op. cit.*

24. Pelliot, *op. cit.*, p. 89.

25. Richardson, "Tibetan Inscriptions at Zhva'i Lha Khang," *JRAS*, 1953, p. 2.

26. Thomas, *TLTD*, pp. 85, 86; *PT*, ff 113a–114b.

27. Tucci, *MBT*, pp. 64, 65, 151, and 154.

28. Demiéville, *op. cit.*, pp. 262, 271, 272, and 278.

APPENDIX A

A Reproduction of the Fragment

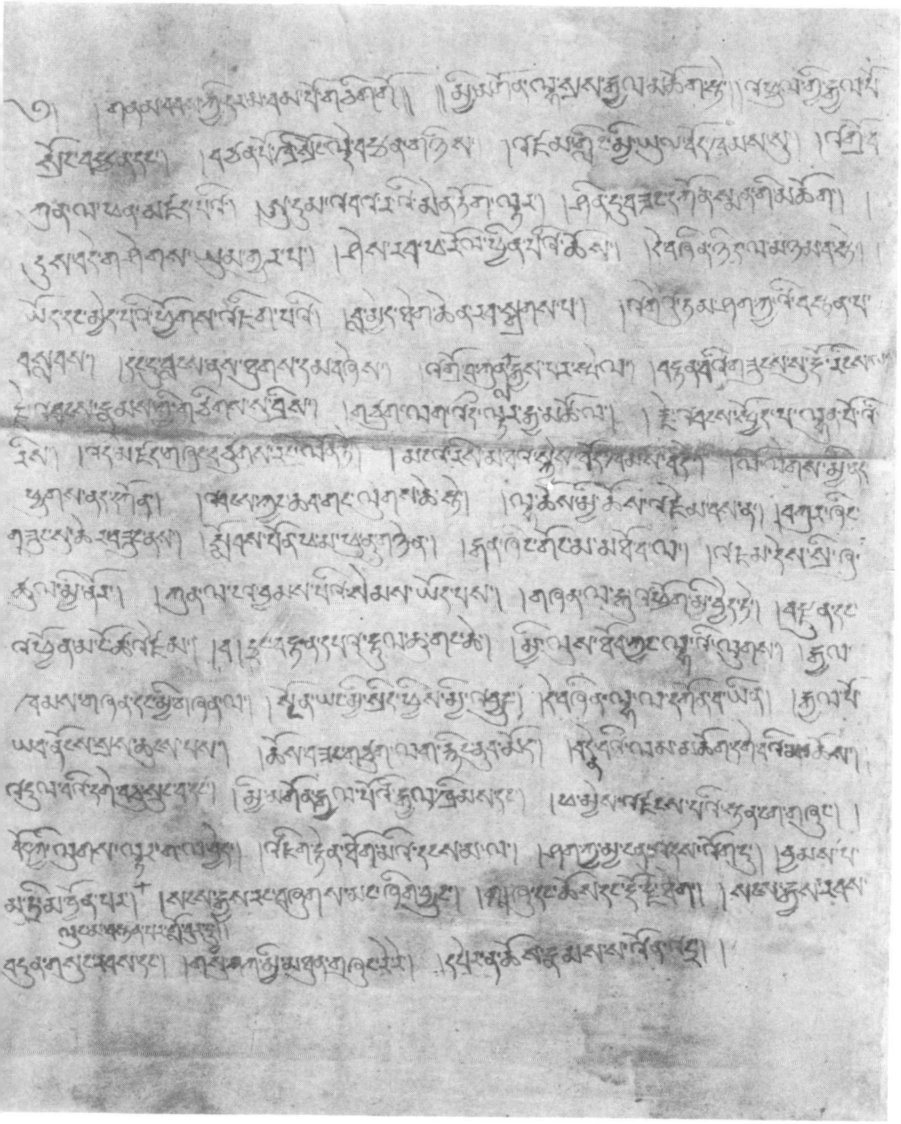

APPENDIX B

Transcription of the Tibetan Text*

(1) gnam babs kyi dar ma bam po gcig go / / / / myi mgon lha sras rgyal mchog ste / / 'phrul gyi rgyal po (2) srong brtsan dang / / btsan po khri srong lde brtsan gnyis / / 'dzam gling myi yul bod khams su / / 'gro ba (3) kun la phan mdzad pa'i / / u dum 'ba' ra'i men tog ltar / / shin du bzang dkon sman gi mchog / / (4) dus bde gshegs yum gyur pa / / shes rab pha rol phyin pa'i chos / / de bzhin nyid la mnyam ba ste / / (5) yod dang myed pa'i phyogs 'jig pa'i / / bla myed theg chen rab sgrags pa / / 'ge'u tam shag kya'i bstan pa (6) bslabs / / dang du blangs nas thugs dam bzhes / / 'gro ba kun la rgyas par spel / / brtan ba'i gzungs su rdo rings la / / (7) rje 'bangs rnams kyi gtsigs su bris / / gtsug lag 'di ltar rgya mtsho la / / rje 'bangs spyod pa lhun bo'i (8) ris / / 'di mdzad gzhung btsugs ring lon te / / mnga' ris mtha' skyes bod khams bde / / lo legs myi nad (9) phyugs nad dkon / / 'bangs kyang chab gang lugs che ste / / lha chos myi chos 'dzem bas na / / bkur zhing (10) gzung su cher bzung nas / / slobs pon pha ma phu nu gnyen / / rgan zhing gong ma mtho ba la / / 'jam des sri zhu (11) tshul myi nor / / kun la nga' byams pa'i sems yod pas / / gzhan la rku 'phrog myi byed te / / brdzun dang (12) 'phyon ma ngo tsha 'dzem / / ba / drang brtan dpa' rtul chu gang che / / myi lus thob kyang lha 'i lugs / / rgyal (13) khams gzhan dang myi gzhan la / / sngon yang myi srid phyis myi 'byung / / de bzhin lha la dkon ba yin / / rgyal po (14) yab nongs sras chungs pas / / chos bzang gtsug lag rnying nub mod / / bden ba'i lam mchog dge ba'i chos / / (15) 'dul ba'i dge bcu srung ba dang / / myi mgon rgyal po'i rgyal khrims dang / / pha myes 'dzangs pa'i stan ngag gzhung / / (16) bod kyi lugs ltar ga la byed / / 'jig rten thog ma'i dangs ma la / / shag kya mya ngan 'das 'og du / / byams pa (17) mu tri ma byon par / / lung ma bstan par glo bur tu / / sangs rgyas rang bzhugs mang zhig byung / / zhu dang chos dang rdo rje theg / / sangs rgyas rabs (18) bdun gsung rabs dang / / gsum ka myi mthun gzung re re / / dper na chos rnams sa 'on 'dra / /

*The beginning of each of the 18 lines, which measure about 27 × 27 c., is numbered in the transcription.

APPENDIX C

SCRIBAL ERRORS

Some of the errors that make the document look like a rather inexpert writing exercise are noted below:

At the beginning of L. 4. the metre requires another syllable which should, presumably have been *gsum*. In L. 6 *la* has had to be inserted below the line. L. 7 the *ba* of *'bangs* is badly botched. L. 12. an irrelevant letter *ba* has been isolated by an extra *shad* but has not been deleted. L. 14 the *na* of *bden* has been added below the line; and an unwanted letter *ma* has been partly deleted. L. 17. a sentence has been inserted below the line; and further on, an unwanted *ga* has been isolated by an extra *shad* and deleted. L. 18. the *ka* of *gsum ka* has had to be rewritten; and, after the next sentence, the writer seems to have given up.

The text cannot have been revised or some corrections might have been made and obscurities cleared up, e.g.: Ls. 5. and 16. *shag kya* read *sha' kya*. L. 10. *slobs pon* read *slob dpon*. L. 11. where there is one more syllable than the metre requires, the copyist may have transformed *kun la 'ang* into *kun la nga*. The doubtful reading *zhu* in L. 17. might have been clarified (see note 6.); and perhaps *ris* at the beginning of L. 8. ought to be *ri*. Revision might have imposed consistency on such forms as *pa'i* and *po'i* where in some instances the *'a-chung* bearing the vowel sign has been separated by a *tsheg*. The use of *ba* and *pa* and *tu* and *du* might also have been made consistent; but in early *mss* liberty in such forms is not uncommon.

On Non-Symbolic Motifs in Indian Art

R. Morton Smith

SOME MAY THINK this a rather irrelevant article, but to this writer the philologist's and philosopher's customary indifference to art is only a regrettable part of the dehumanization of humanist studies. If Tibetan art is inseparable from Tibetan Buddhism, the reverse is also true if we want to study the latter, and not ourselves. Indian art is probably the most important source of Tibetan art, and the difference between Hindu and Buddhist, orthodox and heretical art are of little significance. Most of the symbolism is shared, and the attitude toward art is the same; though as the heretics may have used art first, orthodoxy may follow rather than lead.

Art begins as artifacts rather than art—frequently as the magical artifact. The Indo-European world was permeated by magic, and this continued through Vedic times in India into the Formative period. While the magical may be ignored by the developing philosophy, it is never absent from the religion or even the language; the sacred language of Sanskrit retains the power of the *brahma* word. Since religion dominates the art, we may expect to find an important magical factor in the art too. There it takes the form of symbolism; and while some symbolism teaches, some (*e.g.* the form of the temple or *stūpa*) makes the magical assertion, the non-verbal symbol, like the sacred word helping the truth to be substantiated. Hence the rule that we suggest in this article: that generally the non-symbolic decoration does not prosper in the prestigious art of Indian tradition, Hindu or heretical.

'Prestigious art' is what we call the major arts: ambitious sculpture, painting, and architecture dominated by the ideology—that is, by the *brahman*. Pottery and textiles might long retain the unsymbolic but the prestigious always decends in art; and motifs from it such as the lotus petal and the creeper vine had pervaded pots already on the Barhut medallions. They also pervade textiles; but the evidence we have is paradoxically unfavorable. One would expect textile patterns to be shown sooner in painting than on sculpture, but I have not in fact identified flowers on clothing at Ajanta or Bagh. Stripes are common, maybe because of weaving on a narrow hand loom; and one can find simple geometric patterns, *e.g.* contiguous white crosses on a black ground, one cross wide. If we look at the *yakṣa/ī*s on the Barhut gates there are certainly flower and leaf patterns on textile headdresses; but on other clothing such patterns do not seem to be shown much before the middle of Stern's Period I at Ellora (Badami I and III, 570+ A.D.). The floral pattern on Śīva at Mahakuteśvara and the chevron and half-flower at Hutsappaya and Aihole are still done in narrow strips. This is no longer so on Indian textiles found at Fostat of the twelfth century on, perhaps because the patterns are dyed, not woven. The patterns—lotus petal, flower in square, pearl festoon with intervening tassel and filled with lion—can easily be paralleled in the sculpture of the same period or earlier.

We should emphasize that that which is non-symbolic is often not prominent and frequently has to be hunted for when it does occur. The exception is the railing in the Western Caves, but quite a lot of that is, with the *kuḍus*, representational—balconies and *caitya*s (cells which magically accommodate the divine, and thus increase merit for the donors). When the motif becomes symbolic—*e.g.* when the bead-and-reel becomes floral, or the dentil becomes greatly elongated into a lotus-petal (as shown by the intervening tips)—it may become prevalent and flourish.

It can be presumed that foreign motifs were originally non-symbolic to the Indian. The foreigners to be expected in India were

Greek, and some of the favorite Greek motifs do not even appear in India. The egg-and-dart motif, exceedingly popular in the fourth century B.C. and in Hellenistic times, does not even appear in Gandhara. The Hellenistic/Roman Cupids bearing garlands only survive when the Cupid becomes an Indian *gaṇa*, as at Amaravati. It is still found on the north pillar at Kailasa; also at Mallikarjuna and Pattadkal in the same form and also at Pattadkal in the Pāpanātha and Virūpākṣa Temples. When Cupid became a *gaṇa*, the wreath also changed. It was apt to change its foliage after every full or half curve. At Amaravati it was carrying several different stripes of decoration. In one place at Mallikarjuna and Kailasa (the north pillar) it seems to have become a plain creeper; but elsewhere, both there and at Virūpākṣa and Pāpanātha at Pattadkal, it has become a pearled garland. The symbolism is Indian; the Greek laurel of conquest is meaningless in India.

The Greek key motif I have found twice: once on a panel of two keys at Mirpurkhas *ca.* 500 A.D., and once on a small dividing panel on the ceiling of Ajanta I of much the same date. There is also at Ajanta XVII a small dividing panel on the ceiling with a meander that encloses a T, alternately upright and upside down. I have not found this elsewhere; but there is near it a small panel of the same pattern in continuous curve (making Y rather than T), which I think is paralleled elsewhere. There is a quite complicated derivative of the Greek key at Harwan (*ca.* 300 A.D.), the border of a floor tile (beneath a lotus petal), which could be compared with plaques on a garland bordering a half-lotus of *ca.* 200 A.D. at Amaravati.

The bead-and-reel motif is a most popular decoration in Greece; it undergoes developments as early as Sanchi II, and with these we are not concerned here. The original form appears on the Aśokan pillar capitals in different places at Basarh, Lauriya-Nandangarh, Sankasya, and Kumrahar. In Sanchi II and Barhut it appears around lotus medallions but not later. However, it continues at points on the capital complex through Barhut and Mathura at Amaravati and Jaggayyapeta. At Sanchi II and Mathura we find bead-and-reel as the frame of a design (scene or creeper). This is paralleled in early Amaravati, and even in a late example from the Amaravati School at Anuradhapura in Ceylon. In the east, at Bodhgaya and Amaravati, it appears on pot-bases of pillars in conjunction with other decorations, usually immediately above or below the belly of the pot. It is not there at Sanchi I or Mathura.

In the west, bead-and-reel is decidedly rare outside the early site at Pitalkhora, where it is used as at Mathura: once round three sides of a panel of lotus; once over a frieze of *kinnara*s; under Gajalakṣmī elephants over a door; and possibly at the bottom of a bell capital. Otherwise I have found it only at Manmodi round a lotus center, and also, roughly executed, round a panel of auspicious signs at Junagarh; both were over doors.

Since the bead-and-reel motif is Greek, one would expect to find it very common in Gandhara; but examination does not produce the expected. There are two forms, the ordinary rounded and the flat. The flat form may originally represent beam-ends as it is not found vertically, but it is found round a gable-end inside. However, it is the flat form that appears first in Gandhara, if one follows Marshall or Ingolt. This form is commonly used under one band or scene which is over another. The ordinary rounded form does not seem to be used horizontally except on the short sides of panels filled with a *yakṣī* or *yakṣa*, on columns; otherwise we find it as the vertical border of a jamb. We do not find bead-and-reel on pots or pillars; nor do we find developments of it other than the flat one in Gandhara. Usage is Indian rather than Greek, and this is confirmed by the appearance of bead-and-reel at Butkara (Swat) round a gable roof, which can be paralleled at Mathura and Amaravati *ca.* 200 A.D. Although bead-and-reel may continue in Gandhara, this had no impact on India proper; though the flat form does appear with other Gandhara motifs at Devni Mori in the fourth century A.D.

Another motif that seems to run independent courses in India and Gandhara is the dentil, which points downward in Gandhara but upward in India. It is a very popular motif in Gandhara, though surprisingly hard to find in the contemporary Mediterranean. It occurs immediately under a roof or molding above scenes horizontally or vertically adjacent. It is exported from Gandhara to China only through transformation into lotus petals, as shown by the intervening tips or rim. At Sanchi II the dentil forms three sides of a railing pillar, but at I and III it is above scenes on the crossbars of the *toraṇa*. It is absent thereafter, or virtually so. All I can find is teeth and counter-teeth with an intervening line round two lotus medallions, and its decorating or representing foliage on some other medallions at Barhut. It is also round a lotus medallion at Sanchi III. It is otherwise absent from Barhut, Bodhgaya, and Mathura, but can be found edging a series of petals on the pillar-lotuses at Amaravati and also at Alluru. The dentil also appears at Bhaj under the right-hand *kuḍu* only, and at Kondane under *kuḍu* under ziggurat under bigger *kuḍu*. Ziggurat is substituted for dentil at Sanchi I, though not consistently, and this may explain the dentil in the West, where ziggurat is so common. In late Gupta and post-Gupta times one can easily find very sharp dentils; but they are, as in Buddhist China, lotus petals, as is indicated by the intervening tips. At Somnathpur there is a band of such lotus petals under divine figures, which becomes a plain upward dentil for a short strip. Otherwise the decoration is long dead.

Along with the dentil we should consider the ziggurat, a stepped pyramid usually of four steps. The motif takes two forms, plain and with an intervening opening lotus-bud which fills the free space at the top. This latter is the form on the Barhut coping and pillars and is also at Ananta Gumphā at Khandagiri in Orissa as well as on the west gate at Sanchi over the caryatid *gaṇa*s. Elsewhere it is plain: at Sanchi I on the north and east gates, at Sanchi III over caryatid *gaṇa*s, at Bodhgaya, and at Rānī Gumphā at Khandagiri. In all these places it is used above scenes, horizontal on the coping and vertical on pillars. At Mathura, on the pillar, the *kuḍu* has usually expelled the ziggurat; but the ziggurat holds out on at least one pillar, which has two ziggurats with a frond/'tree of life' in between. We have the ziggurat over a frieze at Bhaj *vihāra* and at Pitalkhora, both early in the west, where it is always plain. We have mentioned its occurrence at Bhaj and Kondane; but it forms a frieze in the *vihāra* hall at Nadsur, and on the right of the main entrance to Ajanta XII, over a *kuḍu*.

The ziggurat is also common on *harmikā*s either on the top or on the top plinth. At Junnar one is found on the top two plinths and at Ajanta XXVI one covers all the plinths. At Sanchi I and Nasik III it is on top, as also on a small *stūpa* in Swat, Gandhara, and on a model from Jaulian, Taxila. At Bhaj, Bodhgaya, and Barhut it is on the side of the plinth; at Karle and the other caves, as well as at Amaravati, it is absent from the *harmikā*. The only other ziggurats I can find are in a Mauryan fragment from Sarnath with a civic crown within the outline and above a *stūpa* railing in Gandhara. There is also in Gandhara, especially at Butkara and at the Dharmarajika *stūpa* at Taxila, a pattern of inverted ziggurats which forms the base for one *mithuna* scene over another. Though the *mithuna* is Mathuresque I cannot find this motif at Mathura, except possibly on a late fragment illustrated by Mme. Hallade, where a *kuḍu* is below and between the ziggurats.

Parallel with the dentil, one might look for the chevron. I cannot find it alone, though it is common enough when filled with a half-flower.

The rope pattern is another early motif. It is a member of the bell-capital complex usually seen immediately above the bell lotus-petals. However, in three places on the Aśoka columns it is immediately underneath, as it is once at Mathura. It is found above at Rampurva, Lauriya Nandangarh, Besnagar, Barhut, Mathura, and on representations of pillars at Sanchi II, Barhut, and early Amaravati. Like the bead and reel, it appears on the base of pots functioning as the base of pillars, as at Bodhgaya, Ananta Gumphā at Khandagiri, Amaravati, and Jaggayyapeta. On pot-bases of pillars it does not seem to appear at Sanchi or in the western caves. The rope is found round lotus medallions, at Barhut, once at Mathura, and at Nasik III, where Mathura influence is apparent in the railing uprights. On copings a rope that looks very much like bead-and-reel supports bells at Barhut and Mathura, and a realistic rope does so on a *toraṇa* at Mathura; but on one coping the bells have disappeared and only the rope is left. At Amaravati on a coping we have a rope above bells; but the bells have become concave, and the intervening spaces have turned into lotus petals which are much more obvious than the bells. We also find a rope above and below a creeper motif under a half-lotus at the foot of a railing pillar. The rope is another motif like the preceding, obsolete in the unity of Indian art of Gupta times since it could not compete with the pearled garland. It is never Gandharan.

Next we may consider 'leaning triangles'. 'Weaving' might be a better name, but the width is only a half-weave, the perpendicular of one of the triangles. The triangles tend to be scalene, and are shaded at right angles to contiguous triangles. The use of this motif resembles that of the rope: at Barhut it is a torus above the bell capital; it also surrounds a lotus medallion and decorations round a *kuḍu* and a doorpost. It does not appear at Bodhgaya, Sanchi, or Mathura, nor in the western caves, except at Karle where it forms one of the rings on the underside of the umbrella. But this motif has a modest life in the southeast: at Jaggayyapeta it is round the rim of a bell capital, and at Amaravati and Nagarjunikonda it is on a plinth at the top or bottom of pillars. It also appears on *harmikā* plinths and making one of the patterns on composite garlands on a pot at Nagarjunikonda, on *gaṇa*s at Amaravati, on the edge of a seat at Nagarjunikonda and Alluru, as the border of a scene at Nagarjunikonda and Amaravati, and once at Amaravati where it forms the basis of a half-lotus on a railing pillar.

The leaning triangles motif has a mild vogue in the northwest; it is not on pillars or pots any more than the rope is, nor on *harmikā*s; but it is to be found on a plinth above an acanthus column at Surkh Kotal. At Harwan in Kashmir it is twice used as a border on floor tiles. It borders an ivory plaque in Taxila, and is the base for a scene at Rhode, Gandhara, and at Butkara on a jamb. It makes a late appearance at Mirpurkhas as the border of a slab with the Buddha-image and, strangely, shows up under a Buddha in China.

The criss-cross motif is common as a representation of surfaces such as leather and textile, but as a decoration it occurs only on capitals at Barhut and Mathura. It is a smaller mesh at Mathura, where it is often used for the forepart of animals' wings. In painting it can be found, usually badly drawn, in small panels on the Ajanta ceilings. It is not used in Gandhara but might be seen in degenerated form as the Gandharan lenticulated garland. At Barhut, on the capitals, it takes the form of diagonal in square. At one place in Gandhara, on a 'miracle at Śrāvastī' decorative panel beside the Buddha-image, there are two small panels of criss-cross and one of checkers. This is enough to emphasize the general absence.

The railing is used as the base for the portrayal of scenes. It begins plain, at Sanchi and Barhut. The earliest railings tend to have little or no space between the horizontals—a form still found even in Barrett's middle period at Amaravati. The real railing had bigger spaces at Bodhgaya, as had the ornamental one at Khandagiri. It is still plain in the upper floor at Rānī Gumphā, Khandagiri, and early Mathura, down to about 50 A.D. (or not quite so late). It is plain on the Amohini plaque of 15 A.D. But already on the north gate at Sanchi I and on the lower floor at Rānī Gumphā there is a half-moon top and bottom, and the post is probably meant to be octagonal as there is a rim at each edge. It is also sometimes divided into three equal grooves, as happens at Gaṇeśa Gumphā Khandagiri. This kind of pillar can in fact be found at Mathura with lotus medallions on it (and on representations with the medallions in Middle Amaravati); but when used as ornamentation in Mathura, the central groove is reduced to a thick line forked at each end.

In the western caves, the railing is plain down to Karle. Over the donors at Kanheri, as well as under, we find it with three grooves and lotus medallions or half-medallions. It appears in the same manner on the top plinth of a capital under elephants. The veranda railing is of the same type, to be found also in Middle Amaravati. On Nasik III, the railing medallions are much more protuberant on the veranda; and this variety with protuberant lotus appears in late Amaravati.

The other place where railing appears is on the *harmikā* of *stūpa*s on the *gala* or the plinth. On the *gala* it is originally representational, as can be seen at Barhut; but it seems to be ornamental on all the *stūpa*s on the gates at Sanchi I. At Bhaj and Karle it is ornamental on the *gala* and on the plinth, where it appears at Junnar also. Nasik III displays a combination, with plain railing under *mithuna*s up the door and on the *gala* but with a protuberant form on the *vedikā*. At the *caitya*, Nasik XIII, there is a mid-Amaravati form of railing on the side stair but it is plain elsewhere. On Amaravati *harmikā*s, railings seem to be as often representational as ornamental, but up through Barrett's Middle Period they are plain. Protuberant medallions appear only in the late period; the railing is on the *gala*, not the plinth, which is plain till the late period and then receives motifs like the pearled garland. Gandhara *harmikā*s do not show the railing but use other motifs like flowers.

The motifs so far considered were all extinct, or virtually so, by Gupta times. I have found one unsymbolic (I imagine) motif which is quite successful in India—checkers. Not visible in the first native tradition—Sanchi, Barhut, early Mathura, Amaravati, or the early western caves—it seems to begin in Gandhara (Ingholt's second and third period; Marshall's third and later maturity) as a substitute for a railing, *e.g.* for the *vedikā* around *stūpa*s, or a balcony. We then find checkers up jambs and the sides of frontons, across the top as the basis of a scene of Buddha on a throne. They are also used to fill space between gables on a frieze. Triangular checkers are also tried but do not find favor.

At Mathura (Kaṇkālī Tīlā), probably Kushan, checkers decorate two *kuḍu* arches and form their bases. At Devni Mori they occur on and fill *kuḍu*s. At Ajanta I and XIX there is a band of checkers round a doorway. This is paralleled beside the *kuḍu*s at Burdwar Sagar, at Bhuvaneśvara up pilasters, on both sides of the creepers at Mukteśvara and Yameśvara, and on a small panel beside a *kirin* at Rajarani temple. On pillars we can find checkers round the top of a Gupta pillar at Mathura, at Gyraspur (Gwalior, ninth century), and at the Vaitāl Deul, Bhuvaneśvara, above and below the torus of a gate pillar. In western India the Moslems take over checkers, using them at the base of pillars at Champanir and Mahmudabad. At Mahmunabad they occur both over a window and under it beneath a Moslem version of the *kuḍu*. Back east, checkers form the ubiquitous background of the Konarak sculptures.

Checkers are also used for windows, horizontally and diagonally. They occur at Bhuvaneśvara in the Mukteśvara and Parasurāmeśvara Temples, at Khajuraho in the Pārśvanātha, in the eleventh century Udayaśvara at Udaipur, and in small panels at Ahmedabad in the Jami Masjid. I have not found them elsewhere in Southeast Asia, but they do occur at Pagan on the Nanpaya *ca.* 1060 A.D., where the solid squares have been ornamented with florets. Such a checkered window may be the origin of checkers in fifteenth- and sixteenth-century Bengal at Baranagar and Murshidabad, where the raised squares have become florets.

Some late patterns may appear unsymbolic, such as the lozengein-rectangle, popular as a frieze on mosques in western India and visible in the Neminātha Temple at Mount Abu. But examination may well show this motif to be a degenerated floret; and both forms, plain and floret, are found doing the same duty at the Ṛṣabhanātha Temple of Abu. The plain pattern cannot be found before 1000 A.D.

The motifs discussed here are, I suspect, virtually absent from Tibet as far as Indian influence is concerned. Meanders and frets can easily be found on metalwork under Chinese influence. One can find a lotus petal transformed back into a dentil along a beam under a roof. But architecture is again under Chinese influence. On the Indian side, however, one suspects the rule that it is the symbolic that survives.

SPECIFIC REFERENCES

D. E. Barrett, *Sculptures from Amaravati in the British Museum*, London, British Museum, 1954.

Nirmal Kumar Bose, *Canons of Orissan Architecture*, Calcutta: R. Chatterjee, 1932.

Ananda K. Coomaraswamy, *La sculpture de Bodhgaya*, Paris, *Les éditions d'art et d'histoire*, 1935 (= *Ars Asiatica*, Vol. 18).

Henry Cousens, *The Antiquities of Sind*, Calcutta: Government of India Central Publication Branch, 1929 (= *Archaeological Survey of India, New Imperial Series*, Vol. 20).

Henry Cousens, *The Chālukyan Architecture of the Kanarese Districts*, Calcutta: Government of India Central Publication Branch, 1926 (= *Archaeological Survey of India, New Imperial Series*, Vol. 42).

Sir Alexander Cunningham, *The Stūpa of Bharhut*, London: India Office, 1879.

J. Fergusson and J. Burgess, *The Cave Temples of India*, London: W. H. Allen and Co., 1880.

A. Goswami, *Designs from Orissan Temples*, Calcutta: Thakkur's Press and Directory, 1950.

Harald Ingholt, *Gandharan Art in Pakistan*, New York: Pantheon Books, 1957.

Ram Chandra Kak, *Ancient Monuments of Kashmir*, London: India Society, 1933.

V. A. Smith, *The Jain Stūpa and Other Antiquities of Mathurā*, Allahabad: Archaeological Survey of India, 1901.

GENERAL REFERENCES

Ludwig Bachhofer, *Early Indian Sculpture*, 2 vols., New York: Pegasus Press, 1929 (reprinted: New York, Hacker Art Books Inc., 1972).

Klaus Fischer, *Schöpfungen Indischer Kunst*, Köln: M. DuMont Schauberg, 1959.

Louis Frédéric, *Art of India* (*Temples and Sculptures*), New York: Harry Abrams, n.d.

Stella Kramrisch, *Art of India*, London: Phaidon Press, 1965.

H. Zimmer and J. Campbell, *The Art of Indian Asia*, 2 vols., New York: Pantheon Books, 1955.

Non-Cognitive Language in Mādhyamika Buddhism

Mervyn Sprung

INTRODUCTION

THIS PAPER WANTS TO LOCK HORNS with a central question in the philosophy of Mādhyamika Buddhism: how can natural language serve the purposes of enlightenment. It is perhaps foolish to attempt this as no one has yet locked horns with Mādhyamika who has not been thrown—and lost his horns in the struggle. The question deals with a philosophy of language but concerns the human predicament, the concern of all classical philosophies. How to extricate the human from his natural predicament without mutilating his greatest gifts? Courageous bondage may be more enlightened than passive liberation. To discuss any question in Mādhyamika apart from this central concern would be, I believe, to distort it; and the question of language is no exception. Nāgārjuna, Āryadeva, Candrakīrti, and the others do not develop an explicit philosophy of language; but we should be able to learn a great deal if we study what they say about it. If we do not isolate this from the central concern of their thought, it should light up some approaches to Mādhyamika understanding of the human predicament and its transcendence.

THE NATURAL PREDICAMENT

The Buddhist of whatever school has so much in common with what might be called a naturalist, and what is most often called a nihilist, that he is at pains to defend himself against the charge of being one. He turns naturally to the phenomena, inner and outer (mostly the former), of everyday existence, and tests their behavior by his own experience. He is without obtrusive presuppositions and cool in his analysis. He is quite fearless in drawing his conclusions about the meaningless of the natural order and the virtually hopeless predicament of all beings, including the human, who are seemingly inextricably interwoven with it.

The Mādhyamika understanding of the human being begins with a spontaneous conscious event (*ayoni ṣo manaskāraḥ*, *Prasannapadā*, p. 452). This is not a 'state', nor an 'act'; it is an unaccountable psychic spontaneity below the level of all other acts and faculties. It is dynamic, volative, action-bent, generating and carrying all differentiated human activities. This underived beginning is understood as a thirst or hunger (*taṇhā*) for not less than everything, but, in that sense, for inexhaustible existence itself. This is perhaps an attempt to describe the nature of the psyche itself, an attempt recalling Freud, Neitzsche, and Schopenhauer.

The most primary set of acts resting on *taṇhā* consists of the judgements 'good' and 'not-good' and fixing a world of putative things based on these (*śubhāśubhaviparyāsa*). In a world with this skeleton-structure it is possible for the *kleśa*s to arise. These are the basic afflictions of beings, the express finitude of natural existence, the limitations within which beings must decide and act. They may be many—any form of helplessness due to pre-formed value judgements—but the Mādhyamika texts speak, classically, of three: *rāga*, *dveṣa*, and *moha*. These are: (1) being attracted to what is considered 'good', (2) being averse to what is considered 'not-good', and (3) being deluded by the putative substantiality of the good and not-good things. The *kleśa*s dictate the basic forms of involvement in the world. Specific actions of responsible individuals arise within these limitations and of course from action consequences must arise as 'fruition', to use the Buddhist term. Fruition may require many birth-death episodes because of inexorable *karma*.

In this way beings are driven, by the nature of existence itself, to perpetuate their hopeless strivings and ambitions meaninglessly. No aspect of natural human existence escapes this condemnation. There is no value sense nor faculty of reason which is of another origin and not an integral part of 'kleshic' finitude. Reason especially, or more strictly speaking intellect, is as much in the service of the pervasive hunger for existence as are passions and ambitions. The intellect is an expression of this hunger. In the natural man, strictly as such, there is no divine spark either in the form of a universal reason (Aristotle) or of a transcendent love of the good (Plato) or of immanent *brahman* (Vedānta).

LANGUAGE IN ITS NATURAL SETTING

This view of the natural predicament of humans obviously severely restricts the possible views of the nature of human language. There is nothing in man's nature which could infuse meaning, other than empirically generated meaning, into human language. There is here no Upanishadic immanent *brahman*, no platonic memory of the forms of Being or any Christian God-created soul. Language must be as afflicted, as diseased as all other elements on the natural scene. It can hardly be used to uncover truth. It has no revelatory power. *Vāc* is not the most precious gift of the Vedic Gods, nor Heidegger's *Sprache* as the 'house of being'; *vāc* means mere words or verbal utterances. Language is integrally meshed with the blind drives which turn the wheel of meaningless existence.

Under a few rubrics I would like to suggest how Mādhyamika understands language in its natural setting. There is an initial complication: Mādhyamika uses no one Sanskrit word with a range of meaning comparable to 'language'. *Vāc* is used, of course, but most often I think in the plural, to refer to verbal utterances. Again the conferring of a name (*abhidhāna*) is frequently set off against what receives the name (*abhidheya*). The Sanskrit term *prapañca* is perhaps the favorite term but, as I shall suggest, it covers both the name and the thing named; so it is not a word for language. Another term, *prajñapti* is often used; but it betrays rather a Mādhyamika theory of language and is in no sense a general term for language. To speak thematically of language therefore is to impart a contemporary concept and problem to Mādhyamika Buddhism—but I am going to assume that this is legitimate.

The most obvious function of words, the Mādhyamika philosophers think, is to confer names on things. Candrakīrti, in his *Prasannapadā* draws the boundaries around *duḥkha* (p. 493) or, as he normally calls it, *saṃvṛti*, by saying it is the totality of the transactions of naming and receiving names and of knowing and being known. And he says (p. 364) that only if an object of thought has a specific character can speech (*vācas*) function in relation to it. Naming, however, is not a cool affair of the intellect, a pasting of labels on wine bottles to designate their contents. Far from it. Naming is an integral part of the fear-ridden 'kleshic' existence in which it appears, serves its purpose, and persists. When he is pushed to explain how the notion of self-existence of particular things arises, and after he has shown how untenable the notion is, Candrakīrti explains (p. 264) that it is in order to dispel their apprehensions and fears that men say "things are self-existent" and project the notion of self-existence, so constituting the world of the everyday. 'Names covering over the abyss of fear', Nietzsche would have said. In any case it appears that speaking must serve the purposes of a being caught up in the basic afflictions.

Much becomes clear from the use of the term *prapañca*. It is sometimes taken to mean 'language', as it includes the name as well as what is named; it is sometimes translated as 'phenomena', as it includes the object-correlate of a name. Certainly both aspects should be kept together, and so I translate the term as 'named-thing'. As it is most often used as a collective noun, like 'forest' or 'army', I think of it as 'the manifold of named-things': the entire world that can be captured in language and which must be coped with by means of language. Its reference is usually outward; it is the external pole corresponding to the *loka*, the ordinary man; *prapañca* is *saṃvṛti* when this is understood as made up of named-things. It is this inseparability of the names of speech and what is named through speech that is characteristic of Mādhyamika. I think we can say that there is no thing without a name: naming and coming into existence within a *loka*, a personal world, are one and the same event with two aspects. Nor can there be names without something named. There are of course empty words like 'the horns of a rabbit' but, according to Mādhyamika, no empty names.

At the risk of appearing to retract this very point it must be remembered that no Buddhist has ever thought that the things of the everyday—the commonest recipients of names—exist *realiter*. They are held to be temporary aggregates of component elements, owing their apparent existence to the ignorance and fears of men. King Milinda's chariot stands as the paradigm of this doctrine. The components of the chariot—wheels, axles, tongue, etc.—are held to correspond to their respective names; but nothing which can be directly perceived over and above these components corresponds to the word 'chariot'. The word 'chariot' refers to the assemblage of lesser things, which would be 'parts' if there were anything for them to be parts of. At this level it is clear that the word 'chariot' functions differently than the words 'wheel', 'axle', 'tongue', etc. For one thing it *presupposes* them. Only if something is named by such words can the word 'chariot' function, whereas these words can function without the term 'chariot'. Again, whereas on this level the lesser names function by one-to-one reference, the wheel in question being the sole referent of the name 'wheel', the word 'chariot', having no such referent, functions rather by suggesting, virtually prescribing, certain appropriate ways of dealing with wheels, axles, tongues, etc. When invited to mount into a chariot one does not straddle the tongue nor cling to the wheel. 'Chariot' is not a name of something; it is a *prajñapti*, a way of conveying a message.

Now the lesser parts in their turn are obviously as much dependent on their own still lesser parts as the chariot was on them. The Buddhist pushes the reduction, as everyone knows, to the level of a small list of irreducible elements, the *dharma*s. These are directly given in either outer or inner perception, mostly the latter. As they have no parts and so depend on nothing other than themselves, each may properly be named, so most schools supposed, without the use of *prajñapti*. The

Mādhyamika refuses to concede this uniqueness, however; in his view *dharmas* too are composite, surreptitiously resting on the notions of a self-existent substance (*svabhāva*) and its attributes. It must follow that *dharmas*, elsewhere ontologically sacrosanct, are as irrevocably *prajñaptis*—elements of speech—as are all other putative realities.

The bewildering conclusion is inescapable—though no Mādhyamika, as far as I know, ever formulated it this way—that at no level and at no point does language in fact name anything. It does not 'refer', as we say. Its function is rather to bind together a world which is by nature disjointed and meaningless, and to be the means of moving about with practical effectiveness in it. Language, in short, has no cognitive function; its role is instrumental; it suggests what to expect from things and what to do with them: it conducts. Words are guides; they preserve proven ways of coping with things. They are, to risk a neologism, ductal or ducational. A name suggests a way. This is perhaps most strikingly so in the case of the notion of person. 'Person' is a signal instance of *prajñapti*; the names 'person' (*pudgala*) or 'I' (*ahaṃkāra*) serve very well to bring order into situations, to arouse expectations, to focus memory, to guide reactions, to lend unity to existence. They are cognitively worthless, but this does not hinder their usefulness.

That language in Mādhyamika thought can have no cognitive function becomes even clearer when we consider two further thrusts of Nāgārjuna's analysis: one, that all *dharmas* (putative attributions) are false; and two, that the very terms 'attribute' and 'subject of attribution' are unintelligible and hence illusory. Nāgārjuna recalls a statement imputed to Buddha when he formulates (13.1) "Whatever is not what it pretends to be is unreal." (*tan mṛṣā moṣadharma yad*) In this picturesque and, I find, devastating phrase Nāgārjuna thrusts language outside the bounds of truth. Every attribute is by definition purloined, borrowed under false pretense and, as it were, put on display at its false owner's home. Nor is the point merely that attributes are interchanged, mixed up. The falseness lies in anything pretending to own, in full title, attributes which are merely borrowed: pretending to be what it is not. To elude the obvious liar's paradox here Nāgārjuna says the notion of *śūnyatā* must be introduced; but more of that later.

This cardinal point receives a special investigation under the heading 'Subject and Attribute' (*lakṣyalakṣaṇam* 5). Nāgārjuna attempts to convince us that both of these notions are unintelligible. If you wish to speak of a subject of attribution apart from any attributes, you are speaking of nothing; and if the subject is nothing, how can any qualities be attributed to it? End of subject. If you wish to speak of attributes apart from any subject, you are attempting to attribute a quality without having anything to attribute it to, to offer a characteristic of what has no character. An attribute must be an attribute *of*, or it is not an attribute, whatever else it may be. Now Mādhyamika believes that the cognitive function of language rests on attribution, *i.e.*, makes sense only on the model of an epistemic object and what may be predicated of it. It follows that verbal assertions, whatever else they may do for humans, do not serve to know anything in the way in which we ordinarily presume we know something, *i.e.*, being able to say what something is.

The final point in the critique (emasculation) of natural language concerns the notion of 'is'. The most elementary presumption of an assertive use of language is the notion 'is'. If there is no 'isness' ('areness') in things, *i.e.*, if things 'are' not thus or thus, then assertions about them are adrift in a meaningless ocean of words. Now if there is any one essential view in Mādhyamika, it is that the 'isness' of things is illusory, or, lest 'thing' mean only tangible entity, the 'isness' of any putative ontological existent, including, of course, the phenomenon of consciousness. Required indeed to constitute an everyday world, an arena for 'kleshic' struggles, 'isness' misleads us into an illusory sense of the reality of things. 'Isness', in the form of *svabhāva* (self-existence), makes sense only the way things truly are (*tattvam*), not of the way they ordinarily are. This thought lies so deep in Mādhyamika thinking that it is the unspoken background of all its arguments. It is explicit in the investigation into self-existence when (15.6,7) it is said that those who think in terms of 'is' and 'not is' do not grasp the Buddha's teaching. Buddha is said to be enlightened precisely because he comprehends existence and non-existence in the true way. No doubt is then left that this true way is to avoid using these notions of anything in the everyday world.

THE PROBLEM OUTLINED

Thus the Mādhyamika understanding of ordinary language. Language is born of and serves the timeless need of men to comfort and deceive themselves with a world of 'pretend' reality. It serves an intellectual faculty which is subject to 'kleshic' demands; all reasoning, based on the everyday understanding of language, must fail to be knowledge, must fail to be anything more than sophisticated screams from the seminars and classrooms of *duḥkha*. Śāntideva says quite simply, quite devastatingly, "The intellect and the delusive everyday are one." (*Buddhiḥsaṃvṛtir ucyate* 9.2): Is this the end? If the intellect has condemned itself to be severed from truth is it not trapped in its own flybottle? Are its pronouncements pretending to truth not the babblings of a great infant who draws attention to his wants but is without the faculty to express himself clearly? Is human talk not mere bedlam? And, if it is, should the Mādhyamika, the one who has drawn our attention to this state, not be the first to button up his lips and to withdraw into the horrors of unfulfilled silence?

This places us squarely in front of the central problem of Buddhist philosophy, a problem which can be only sketched in at this time. The Buddhist does not restrict himself to a description of 'kleshic' existence (*duḥkha*); his one concern is to put an end to it. So he speaks about the possibility and the nature of a way which would go beyond the natural order; he speaks as if we were already beyond it; yet he does this using natural language. How does he understand his own ability to make language serve the purpose of getting beyond *duḥkha*, to make statements which concern the true way of things? Is he not doomed to absurdity? Must he not demand more of language than his own conception of it will permit? Most especially, how can the Mādhyamika, the severest of skeptics, the Buddhist who tells us that verbal utterance is inoperative in ultimate truth (493), extricate himself from his own self-stultifying naturalist views?

One might well, on a first reading of the texts, find an abundance of evidence that Mādhyamika does abandon language to *saṃvṛti* and condemn himself to silence. Candrakīrti refers to the Buddha's night of enlightenment when he uttered not one syllable, being freed from everything with name (539). Nāgārjuna states that the true way of things (*tattvam*) is not expressible through the names for things (*prapancair aprapañcitam* 18.9); and he argues that it is unintelligible to assign any attribute, drawn from the realm of the *skandha*s (the nameable), to the *tathāgata*, a synonym for the way things really are.

But by itself this emphasis would only deepen the absurdity (language drawing a boundary around itself!) and give an unbalanced result. We must, it seems to me, understand Mādhyamika in such a way as to justify its talking about the matters which concern it most. This is, of course, a problem in its own right and demands persistent study of the word and spirit of the texts. At this time I shall merely sketch some of the ways open to us to complete the Mādhyamika philosophy of language, without attempting to be definitive and certainly not exhaustive.

The terms around which a study of this intriguing question must, it seems to me, center are: (1) *prajñapti* (the non-cognitive nature of words), (2) *śūnyatā* (the absence of being in particulars), (3) *satya-dvayam* (the dual context of language), and (4) *bodhisattva* (embodied enlightenment).

All names are *prajñapti*s, suggestions of the way thought and behavior should go; language cannot describe states of affairs, yet serves to convey intentions. In a specific Mādhyamika sense, *prajñapti*s are terms conducive to entering and proceeding on the Buddhist way. Nāgārjuna says this of his own most favored idea—*śūnyatā*. "The true way of things we hold to be the devoidness of self-existence in them; this devoidness is a conducive (or 'conductive') notion (*prajñapti*) presupposing the everyday world; it alone is the middle way (24.18)." When this is placed alongside Candrakīrti's chain of synonyms (p. 264)—*dharmatā*, *śūnyatā*, *svabhāva*, *tathatā* and *tattvam*—it seems we may fairly conclude that the entire treasury of preferred Buddhist terms, not excluding *buddha* and *nirvāṇa*, are not meant to have cognitive value but function in a conducive way within the Buddhist enterprise. Nāgārjuna pronounces, with his usual audacity, "No truth has been taught by a Buddha for anyone, anywhere, at any time." Can it be that everyday language, freed from the misconception that it refers to self-existent things, becomes available, in the mouths of the wise, to guide beings in the direction of Buddhist freedom?

Śūnyatā, the term which more than any other lures us into the intricacies of Nāgārjuna's thought, is an invitation to proceed through the everyday without treating anything in it as either in being or illusory. This holds not only for entities but for the short list of irreducible realities—the *dharmas*. *Śūnyatā* has the superficial appearance of nihilism, but is intended to open the world to the presence of what is not entity but rather the truth of entities. Words themselves are not real as particulars, but are as open to the presence of what is not particular as is any other putative constituent of the everyday world. By nature, then, language is capable of functioning effectively in the dimension of what 'transcends' the everyday: that, whatever it is, has been the true character of both the everyday world and of language from the beginning. It is Nāgārjuna's genius to use the one term *śūnyatā* to evoke the nature of both bondage and freedom, of both the everyday and what resolves it.

We are at this point very close to the notion of the two truths, *satyadvayam*—a notion Mādhyamika makes distinctive use of. The *locus classicus* is Chapter 24 of Nāgārjuna's *Kārikās*. "The teaching of the Buddhas is wholly based on there being two truths: that of a personal, delusive world and truth in the highest sense." "Those who do not clearly comprehend the due distinction between the two truths cannot clearly know the hidden sense of the Buddha's doctrine." "Except as based on the language of everyday transactions, the ultimate truth cannot be pointed out; if the ultimate truth is not grasped, *nirvāṇa* cannot be attained (24.8,9,10)."

The apparent clear cleavage between the two truths might be expected to discourage any attempt to draw on the language of the everyday for purposes of making statements about truth in the highest sense. But the last *Kārikā* (24.10) opens another possibility: "Except as based on the language of everyday transactions, the ultimate truth cannot be pointed out." It is clear that there is only one language available, that of the everyday; and yet by using it the truth which is beyond the everyday may be pointed out or 'taught'. Any word suggesting knowing or description is conspicuously absent from this formulation. 'Pointing' is a word describing behavior.

Candrakīrti deals with this problem in a way which contributes something to a discussion of the possibility of metaphysics. Commenting on Nāgārjuna's characterization of the ultimate truth, "not dependent on anything other than itself, at peace, not manifested as named-things, beyond thought construction, not of varying form—this is the true way of things (18.9)," he says, "nonetheless even what lies beyond naming must be characterized drawing on conventional usage by a transfer of terms accepting the conventional assumptions 'this is real', 'this is not real', and so on (372)." This passage and many others raise questions of the use of metaphor, analogy, and implicit models at the point where thought struggles to reach into a dimension which appears to be other than the empirical, questions which remain unresolved in spite of millenia of concern.

Another Mādhyamika, Āryadeva, pre-dating Candrakīrti by three or four hundred years and the immediate successor to Nāgārjuna, has taken up the notion of the two truths in what seems to me to be a more promising way. He says that the two truths are *reciprocally* interdependent as the great and the small (p. 88). Buddha taught the *dharma* basing it on both the everyday and the superior truth. Both are true and not false if understood in reciprocal dependence. Buddha can say to Ānanda, "Go to the town of Śrāvastī and beg your food" without speaking falsely because: (1) his words are in accord with everyday usage, (2) he knew there was in truth no town, no food, no Ānanda, and (3) he used the everyday concepts and words in the interests of Ānanda's enlightenment.

It is false, Āryadeva says, to state that a date fruit is small or that a cucumber is large. But it is not false to claim that a date is smaller than a cucumber nor that this is larger than a date. If this notion is applied to the two truths we may reach some interesting interpretations. Truth in the highest sense, if affirmed in its own terms and without reference to the everyday, is no more true than is everyday truth apart from the clarifying light of the higher truth. A metaphysics of *śūnyatā* (the higher truth) held to be abstractly 'true' is the purest *saṃvṛti*; it is, by definition, false. All theories are 'samvritic'; there is no second privileged realm to which philosophical theories refer. Either of the two 'truths', taken separately from the other, is false. Only when the lower truth is spoken in the understanding of *śūnyatā* (the higher truth) or when the *śūnyatā* understanding is turned onto the everyday, is what is said *not* false.

Even at this point the puzzle remains: outside of a cognitive context, what can it mean to speak of truth and falsehood? The most difficult problems of Mādhyamika thought become discernible here and demand separate and extensive study. My own attempt at penetration would take up the notion of the middle way as a possibility of satisfying the demands of ontology and epistemology, or as a possibility of carrying on after both ontology and epistemology have been left behind. Nāgārjuna does say that *śūnyatā* is itself the middle way (24.18). This allows us to think that the middle way is not a path that leads to some goal outside itself but is itself the goal, integrating and transmuting, somehow, the theoretical and practical into what is both and yet neither. The middle way seems to join the two truths and provide the depths of understanding out of which it is possible to speak truly, that is, to use words which are conducive to enlightenment.

The *bodhisattva* stands as evidence of the Buddhist faith that this is possible. He embodies *śūnyatā*; he does not need the distinction of the two truths; his way is the middle way. Language, which ran head-on into the *aporia* of the natural predicament, may recover its evocative power in the mouth of one who has discovered that, despite all the evidence to the contrary, man carries his potency to freedom in himself as a natural being and never was, in truth, caught in a natural predicament.

REFERENCES

Mūlamadhyamakakārikās de Nāgārjuna avec La Prasannapadā Commentaire de Candrakīrti. Publié par Louis de la Vallée Poussin, St. Petersburg, 1913. Nāgārjuna's *Kārikās* are indicated by chapter and number. Thus (1.1) indicates Chapter 1, *Kārikā* 1.

Prasannapadā. Candrakīrti's commentary on Nāgārjuna's Kārikās. All references connected with Candrakīrti are to the text published by de la Vallée Poussin. This (1) indicates page 1 of the *Prasannapadā*.

Bodhicaryāvatāra of Śāntideva, with the commentary or *Pañjikā* of Prajñākaramati, edited by P. L. Vaidya. Mithila Institute, Darbhanga, 1960.

Śataśāstra by Āryadeva. *Pre-Dignāga Texts in Buddhist Logic*. G. Tucci.

Phenomena and Reality in Vijñaptimātra Thought (I)

On the Usages of the Suffix 'tā' *in Maitreya's Treatises*

Shōkō Takeuchi

INTRODUCTION

VIJÑAPTIMĀTRA DOCTRINE was theorized by Vasubandhu in the light of Sūtras such as the *Sandhinirmocana-sūtra*, the *Mahāyāna-abhidharma-sūtra*, the Śāstras of Maitreya, and the treatises of Asaṅga. This doctrine, which alludes to *śūnyatā* (the philosophy attributed to Nāgārjuna who was active around the second or third century A.D.), re-accepted the doctrinal structure of the Abhidharma, which had been thoroughly refuted by Nāgārjuna and had become philosophically systematized as the teaching of Asaṅga and Vasubandhu. We should keep in mind that both Asaṅga and Vasubandhu were not only great philosophers but also great Yoga-ācārya. Due to their religious experiences, their philosophy became fathomlessly profound. It can be said that they established not only the doctrine of Mahāyāna Buddhism in India which developed after them but also that they were very influential in the development of Mahāyāna doctrines in China. The Vijñaptimātra doctrine systematized by Vasubandhu was not limited to the thoughts of one school but became the basic theory underlying the entire Mahāyāna movement in India.

In China, the main current of the Vijñaptimātra doctrine was systematized by K'uei-chi, a disciple of Hsüan-tsang, into the doctrine of the Fa-hsiang School. K'uei-chi referred to the Sūtras and Śāstras translated into Chinese by Hsüan-tsang as the fundamental texts. Since then, the tenets of the Fa-hsiang School have been studied as a basic teaching of Buddhism by all schools in China and Japan. But in China and Japan this doctrine has been considered 'pseudo-Mahāyāna' and has been placed a step lower among Mahāyāna doctrines. Why has it been considered lower? It is due to the fact that the Chinese way of thinking is different from that of India; moreover, the Vijñaptimātra doctrine itself underwent changes.

When Indian Buddhism was first introduced and acccpted in China, the Buddhist way of thinking was naturally assimilated into or became acclimatized to the Chinese culture. For example, according to the Vijñaptimātra doctrine, the defiled *ālaya-vijñāna* is taken to be the 'bedrock' of the existence of sentient beings. In Vijñaptimātra doctrine, the structure of the illusive world is explained on the basis of thc *ālaya-vijñāna*. In contrast to that, there is the doctrine of the Tathāgata-garbha, according to which the potentiality of attaining Buddhahood is contained within senticnt beings. Looking at the illusive world from an Enlightened view, the Tathāgata-garbha theory holds that the basis of world structure is the pure *Buddhatva*. At first glance these two doctrines may seem to contradict each other, but in India they never did. Although it can be said that the former seeks spiritual awakening and is always introspective and that the latter is more affective in practice background, and that therefore the two differ in the manner in which they expound the Buddha's teachings, they are not inconsistent or contradictory. Many of Vasubandhu's works belong to Vijñaptimātra thought; but there are also works such as the *Buddhagotraśāstra* which are typical of the latter. In China, however, because these two schools of thought are put on the same plane, they assumed a critical attitude toward each other, as was the case with the ancient Chincse view of human nature, which according to some schools was considered originally good while others considered it negative. Chinese scholars of the Vijñaptimātra School claimed that the Tathāgatha-garbha School's doctrine was not authentic, while the scholars of the Tathāgata-garbha School criticized the other.

It can be said that this resulted from the difference in the Indian and Chinese way of thinking. The former preferred a religious approach, whereas the latter preferred a logical one. In view of that fact, it is inappropriate to claim that the Chinese interpretation is wrong from the Indian standpoint, or to view Indian Buddhism from a Chinese perspective; because although Indian Buddhist thought and Chinese Buddhist thought have had frequent contact, they have developed independently of each other.

It is worth noting that the translation of Buddhist Scriptures caused the Chinese refraction. They were translated into Chinese whenever they were introduced into China. They were not, however, literal, as were the Tibetan translations. The Chinese, because their cultural environment was different, put a great deal of effort into gaining a correct understanding. It is therefore difficult to reproduce the original text by reading Chinese translations. Out of kindness the Chinese translators, in order to render the translated words more euphonically, translated a single original word into two or sometimes even three words. In annotating the translated words, the Chinese commentators added new meanings to each of them. Thus, in spite of their kind intentions, the translators and commentators contributed to changes in doctrine. Buddhist Scriptures which were translated in that manner became the basis for Chinese speculation and developed into what is called 'Chinese Buddhism'. Therefore, it is most natural that Chinese Buddhism has its own idiosyncratic color and tone in contrast to Indian Buddhism.

Generally speaking, these facts can be considered the reasons for the differences between Vasubandhu's theories and the theories of the Fa-hsiang School. But this is not all. A change took place in the Vijñaptimātra School itself. This change was not entirely of Chinese origin; it was due, in part, to Dharmapāla's interpretation. We cannot claim that the Fa-hsiang School resulted from a transfer of Dharmapāla's thoughts alone. It is conceivable that in addition there was the above mentioned Chinese interpretation of Indian Buddhism.

Concerning *hetu-pariṇāma* and *phala-pariṇāma*, I have compared and contrasted Sthiramati's Sanskrit text of the *Triṃśika-vijñapti-bhāṣya* with the *Ch'eng Wei Shih Lun*, attributed to Dharmapāla, and have shown that both are consistent.[1] Nevertheless, the Fa-hsiang School has a different interpretation. This can be attributed to the refractions in translation, not to Dharmapāla's interpretation. But because we can neither find Dharmapāla's original commentary on the *Triṃśika-vijñapti-kārikā* nor refer to his other works concerning the Vijñaptimātra doctrine, we have no basis for deciding what is really Dharmapāla's interpretation and what are modifications added by the translator, Hsüan-tsang. There is, however, a fundamental difference between the Vijñaptimātra doctrine of Vasubandhu and the doctrine of the Fa-hsiang School. This difference can be found in their respective views of the *tri-svabhāva* theory, regarding the interpretation of the relation between 'phenomena' and 'reality', as is suggested in the title of this paper.

THE *TRI-SVABHĀVA* THEORY

According to the treatises of Maitreya, Asaṅga, and Vasubandhu, the *tri-svabhāva* (threefold-aspect) theory is based on *paratantra-svabhāva*. All things exist as *paratantra* and *pratītya-samutpāda*. Those who are unable to fully understand this truth just as it is remain in *samāropa-apavāda-darśanaṃ* which is *parikalpita-svabhāva*. To be enlightened to this truth is the realization of *pariniṣpanna-svabhāva*. The *tri-svabhāva* theory is a world view ranging from delusion to Enlightenment.

The mutual relations of the threefold aspects (*tri-svabhāva*) is tersely shown in the *Triṃśika-vijñapti-kārikā*,[2] which reads:

> *niṣpannas tasya pūrveṇa sadā rahitatā tu yā.*[3]

Here, *tasya* means *paratantra-svabhāva* and *pūrveṇa* means *parikalpita-svabhāva*. The above statement can be rendered into English as follows:

> In *Paratantra-svabhāva*, the getting rid of *parikalpita-svabhāva* is the realization of *pariniṣpanna-svabhāva*.

However, the statement as it stands cannot be applied to the inter-pretation of this verse in the *Ch'eng Wei Shi Lun*.[4] According to the Fa-hsiang School, the interpretation of the verse is as follows:

> *Pariniṣpanna-svabhāva* is that which is attained by getting rid of *parikalpita-svabhāva*. And it is the absolute reality (*tathatā*) as *āśraya* on which *paratantra-svabhāva* depends.

According to this interpretation the word *rahitatā* is broken into two components, *rahita* and the suffix *tā*. Absolute reality (*tathatā*) is indicated by tā. Ordinarily the suffix *tā* is used in Sanskrit when an ab-stract noun is formed; it does not possess an independent meaning. However, according to the Fa-hsiang interpretation, *pariniṣpanna-svabhāva* is *tā*, *i.e.*, *tathatā*, but *paratantra-svabhāva* itself is not *tathatā*. In the *Ch'eng Wei Shi Lun*, it is said that

> twofold non-substantiality (*dvaya-śūnya*) is not *pariniṣpanna-svabhāva*.

This is likened to the wind driving away the clouds and fog, and revealing the moon clearly—the wind is the 'wisdom of the twofold non-substantiality' and the moon is *tathatā*. Consequently, in the *Ch'eng Wei Shi Lun Shu Chi*,[5] we find the following explanation:

> *Tathatā* is the nature of non-substantiality (*śūnyatā*) and is not non-substantiality (*śūnya*) itself. By *śūnya*, *tathatā śunyata* is revealed.

This thought is a source of a rigid distinction between 'phenomena' and 'reality', the salient feature of Fa-hsiang doctrine, which can be diagrammed:

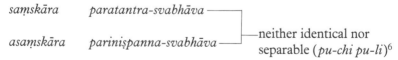

The relationship shown above between *paratantra* and *pariniṣpanna* deviates from the *tri-svabhāva* theory which Vasubandhu advocated. For Vasubandu the relationship is expressed by *anekatva-ananyatva* (neither identical nor different) and *nānya-nanānya* (neither different nor not different). According to the Fa-hsiang School, the relation between 'phenomena' and 'reality' differs from Vasubandhu's view. The *Ch'eng Wei Shi Lun Shu Chi*[7] states that the relation between *paratantrasvabhāva* and *parinispanna-svabhāva* is the relationship which holds between *āśrita* (that which depends on something else) and *āśraya* (that on which something depends); but the relationship between *āśrita* and *āśraya* is not one of *anekatva-anayatva* (neither identical nor different). However, in the Fa-hsiang School, it is said that it is 'neither identical nor different' because it is 'neither identical nor separable'. But strictly speaking, 'neither identical nor separable' is not 'neither identical nor different'.

The relation between 'phenomena' (*sarva-dharma*) and 'reality' (*tathatā*) is explained at length by the following metaphor. When a house is built of wood, it is said that the house stands for 'phenomena' and the wood stands for 'reality'. In this case, it is clear that the relationship which holds between the house and wood is one of 'neither identical nor different'. In contrast to this, there is another view which states that the wood is not 'reality'; a piece of land on which the house is to be built is needed first, and it is this land which is 'reality'.

The former view is held by a school called Ekayāna, while the latter view is the one upheld by the Fa-hsiang School. The relationship between 'phenomena' and 'reality' according to the latter view is one of 'neither identical nor separable'. As the metaphor shows, the house and the land are mutually related; however, the land can never be the house. Therefore, the relationship between the land and the house cannot be said to be one of 'neither identical nor different'.

The way in which 'phenomena' and 'reality' are conceived, as demonstrated by the relationship between the house (*āśrita*) and the land (*āśraya*), is unique to the thought of the Fa-hsiang School. Originally the relationship between 'phenomena' and 'reality' was explained as 'neither identical nor different' simply by adding the suffix *tā* to a word, *e.g.*, *dharma* and *dharmatā*, *tathā* and *tathatā*, and so on. But the unique way in which the Fa-hsiang School explained this relationship originated in its interpretation that the suffix *tā* has an independent meaning of its own. We have already seen examples of this use of the suffix in the word *rahitatā* (T.V.K.) and *śūnyatā* (*Ch'eng Wei Shi Lun Shu Chi*).

At this point I would like to present a few cases of the suffix *tā* as used in Śāstras by Nāgārjuna, Maitreya, and Vasubandhu.

SOME USAGES OF THE SUFFIX '*tā*'

The term *śūnyatā* was used by Nāgārjuna for the purpose of expressing a principle of Mahāyāna Buddhism. Together with *pratītya-samutpāda* and *madhyamā-pratipad*, Nāgārjuna used *śūnyatā* as one of the key terms of the doctrine.

Nāgārjuna's use of the suffix *tā* can be found in his *Madhyamaka-kārikā*,[8] from which a few examples will be given.

> *yaḥ pratītyasamutpādaḥ śūnyatāṃ tāṃ pracakṣmahe /*
> *sā prajñaptirupādāya pratipat saiva madhyamā* (24.18)
> *apratītyasamutpanno dharmaḥ kaścinna vidyate*
> *yasmāt tasmād aśūnyo 'hi dharmaḥ kaścinna vidyate* (24.19)

In 24.18 *pratītyasamutpāda* = *śūnyatā*, and in 24.19 *pratītyasamutpāda* = *śūnya*. Thus we can see that *śūnyatā* and *śūnya* are used without distinction.

However, in Maitreya's *Dharma-dharmatā-vibhaṇga*[9] we find a special use of the suffix *tā*, *viz.*, in the distinction between *dharma* and *dharmatā*. According to Maitreya's text, *dharma* is 'that which is to be extinguished' (*parihatavyaṃ*), and it has the nature of delusion—a phenomenon of *saṃsāra*. In comparison to that, *dharmatā* is 'that which is to be realized (*sākṣātkartavyaṃ*), *i.e.*, *nirvāṇa*. This can be verified by the following Śāstras:

(a) *anutpannāniruddhā hi nirvāṇamiva dharmatā* // M.K. 18.7
(*dharmatā* is truly the unproduced and non-extinguished *nirvāṇa*)

(b) *dharmatāṃ pratividhyēha*[10]
(*dharmatā* is 'that which is to be realized')

(c) *dharmadhātu vinirmukto yasmād dharmo na vidyate*[11]
(because a *dharma* which is freed from the *dharmadhātu* does not exist . . .)

From those passages the meaning of the word *dharmatā*, as used in the *Dh. V.*, can be easily understood.

The distinctive feature of the *Dh. V.* is to demonstrate the polarity of the terms *dharma* and *dharmatā* by showing that *dharma* is contextually related to the phenomenon of *saṃsāra*, which is to be extinguished. The relationship between the terms *dharma* and *dharmatā* is stated in the *Dh. V.* as follows:

chos nyid ni chos med pa tsam gyis rab tu phye ba yin pa
(*dharmatā* is clearly distinguished by merely negating *dharma*)

Moreover, by merely adding the suffix *tā* to the word *dharma*, the polarity of the terms *dharma* and *dharmatā* is shown as *saṃsāra* and *nirvāṇa*, which are to be strictly distinguished. Although the above analysis demonstrates that *saṃsāra* and *nirvāṇa* are distinguished in the sense that the former is to be extinguished and the latter is to be realized, the two are after all identical.

To recapitulate, the function of the suffix *tā* is to indicate the state to be realized. This is similar to the function of the terms *tathatā* and *tatha*: *tathatā* is distinguished from *tatha* by its meaning 'that which is to be realized'. This understanding corresponds to the tenet of the Fa-hsiang School, which takes the suffix *tā* in the term *rahitatā* (*T.V.K.* 21) as a state to be realized, discussed in the previous section.

'*SAT*' - '*ASAT*' - '*SAT*'

Now, let us look into the use of the terms *śūnya* and *śunyatā* in Maitreya's work, the *M.A.V.* It opens with the following *kārikā*:

abhūta-parikalpo 'sti dvayam tatra na vidyate /
śūnyatā vidyate tv atra tasyāṃ api sa vidyate (1.1)[12]

and is followed with

na śūnyaṃ nāpi cāśūnyam tasmāt sarvam vidhtyate /
satvād asatvāt satvāc ca madhyamā pratipac ca sā (1.2)[13]

A comparison of those two *Kārikās* shows at a glance the difference between the meaning of *śūnyatā* (1.1) and *śūnya* (1.2). But according to Vasubandhu's commentary on the *M.A.V.*, the first half of 1.2 is a quotation from the *Prajñāpāramitāsūtra* and is therefore not original to the *M.A.V.* itself.

In the *M.A.V.*, however, we find the following *kārikā*:

dvayābhāvo hy abhāvasya bhāvaḥ śūnyasya lakṣaṇaṃ /
na bhāvo nāpi cābhāvaḥ na pṛithaktvāika lakṣaṇaṃ // (1.13)[14]

In Vasubandhu's commentary on 1.13, the terms *śūnyasya lakṣaṇaṃ* are commented upon by *śūnyatāyā lakṣaṇaṃ*; therefore, in accordance with that commentary, the first half of *M.A.V.* 1.13 can be understood as follows:

śūnyatāyā lakṣaṇaṃ —— *dvaya-abhāva* (A)
—— *abhāvasya bhāva* (B)

From the above, we can see that (A) corresponds to '*dvayam na vidyate*' (*M.A.V.* 1.b) and that (B) corresponds to '*śūnyatā vidyate tv atra tasyāṃ api sa vidyate*' (*M.A.V.* 1.1cd). Now, the question is, is it suitable to consider *M.A.V.* 1.1 similar to *M.A.V.* 1.13?

M.A.V. 1.1 expounds the existence of *abhūta-parikalpa*, the non-existence of *dvaya* (*i.e.*, *grāhya* and *grāhaka*), and the existence of *śūnyatā*. In *M.A.V.* 1.2 *madhyamā-pratipad* is elucidated by the formula 'existence (*satva*) - non-existence (*asatva*) - existence (*satva*)'. This corresponds to the formula cited in *M.K.* 24.18. There *madhyamā-pratipad* was elucidated '*pratītya-samutpāda* (*sat* = exist) - *śūnyatā* (*asat* = not exist) - *upādāya-prajñapti* (*sat* = exist)'. Thus, although the two texts are similar in their formulation, they are not in complete accord with each other.

It is clear that in the *M.A.V.* *abhūta-parikalpa* is both *paratantra-svabhāva* and *pratītyasamutpāda*. But in the *M.K.* '*pratītyasamutpada*' is explained as *prapañcopaśamam*,[15] while in the *M.A.V.*, as just pointed out, it is *abhūta-parikalpa*, and according to Vasubandhu's commentary it is also *vijñāna-parināma*.

The above discussion indicates a dissimilarity in doctrinal characteristics. In the *M.K.* *asat* is *śūnyatā* and *sat* is *upādāya-prajñapti*. In the *M.A.V.* *asat* is *dvayasya abhāva* and *sat* is *śūnyatā*. The term *upādāya-prajñapti* can be analyzed into the following components: *upa* (on) + *ādāya* (to take) + *prajñapti* (to make known). *Śūnyata* is a realm of silence where words are unattainable. For this reason, it is said that *śūnyatā* is *asat*. But *śunyatā* must appear in the realm of *sat* where words are attainable and can explain it. If it remained in the realm of silence it would remain meaningless to us. Therefore, when *śūnyatā* presents itself in the realm of *saṃvṛiti* (delusive world), this process is called *upādāya-prajñapti*. Hence, in the *M.K.*, *upādāya-*

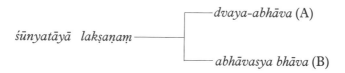

prajñapti refers to the retrospective working of *śūnyatā*. In comparison, in the *M.A.V.* *śūnyatā* is *sat* realized through *dvayasya abhāva*. Although the second item in the formula of *madhyamā-pratipad* expressed in the *M.K.* (*i.e.*, *śūnyatā* = *asat*) and the third item in the *M.A.V.* (*sat* = *śūnyatā*) are both *śūnyatā*, in the former text it is *asad* and in the latter it is *sat*. In either case, *śūnyatā* is placed at the summit of the path toward Enlightenment. The phrase *tasyām api sa vidyate* in the *M.A.V.* corresponds to *upādāya-prajñapti*, explained in *M.K.*

In the *M.A.V.*, *śūnyatā* and *abhūta-parikalpa* are identified as *satva*. This indicates that the retrospective working of *śūnyatā* explained in the *M.K.* is expressed in the *M.A.V.* by the term *śūnyatā*. Accordingly, the formula '*sat* - *asat* - *sat*' in the *M.K.* involves both a path toward Enlightenment and its retrospective working, but in the *M.A.V.* only the former comes to surface. This indicates the essential difference between the two doctrines.

Now we must consider the terms *dvayasya abhāva* in the *M.A.V.* As we have already seen (*M.A.V.* 1.13), *dvayasya abhāva* together with *abhāvasya bhāva* are regarded as *śunyatā-lakṣaṇaṃ*. In that sense, *dvayasya abhāva* is not other than *śūnyatā*. In *M.S.A.* 9.78 it is said that "the non-existence is the highest existence."[16] Vasubandhu comments on this as follows:

> Non-existence is the negation of *parikalpita-svabhāva*,
> and the highest existence is *pariniṣpanna-svabhāva*.

The *Dh.V.*[17] explains that the non-existence of *dharma* is *dharmatā*. Thus, aside from *dvayasya abhāva* there is no true *bhāva*: *abhāvasya bhāva*.

However, *M.A.V.* 1.1 cannot be understood in that manner. The verse in question states that *abhūta-parikalpa* exists, but (he himself) does not contain any duality such as *grāhya* and *grāhaka*. Now, the *tri-svabhāva* as explained by Maitreya means that "in *paratantra-svabhāva* the getting rid of *parikalpita-svabhāva* is the realization of *pariniṣpanna-svabhāva*." The expression "in *paratantra-svabhāva*" corresponds to the word *tatra* in the statement *dvayan tatra na vidyate* (*M.A.V.* 1.1) in *M.A.V.* 1.1, *tatra* does not mean that *abhūta-parikalpa* is left as an existence behind the "non-existence of *grāhya* and *grāhaka.*" According to Vasubandhu's commentary, *tatra* is explained as *abhūta-parikalpo grāhya-grāhaka vikalpaḥ.*[18] Therefore *dvayasya abhāva* is nothing but *abhūta-pariklapasya abhāva*. But *M.A.V.* 1.1 says "*śūnyatā vidyate tv atra tasyāṃ api sa vidyate.*" This implies that *abhūta-parikalpa* still exists after *dvayasya abhāva* has been realized. In Vasubandhu's commentary, *abhūta-parikalpa* is explained as '*yat . . . avaśiṣtam*' (that which is left over).[19] In this case, '*yat . . . avaśiṣtam*' and the aforesaid '*tatra*' do not express an arithmetic remainder. *Dvayasya abhāva* is a thorough negation of *abhūta-parikalpa*. *Yat . . . avaśiṣtam* and *tatra* express that *abhūta-parikalpa* negated as *dvayasya abhava*, revives on *śunyatā* again. Strictly speaking, *dvayasya abhāva* (*M.A.V.* 1.1) and *śūnyatā* are not synonymous.

An innovated term which expresses the fact that the characteristic of the Vijñaptimātra doctrine is a path toward Enlightenment is the term *asal-lakṣaṇānupraveśopāya-lakṣaṇa* which means the characteristic of the *anupraveśa* to penetrate into the non-existence of *abhūta-parikalpa.*[20] This is usually expressed as follows:

> *vijñapti* exists; *artha* does not exist;
> *vijñapti* does not exist also.

Here, *vijñapti* is *abhūta* (not true). This can be known only retrospectively. The Vijñaptimātra doctrine explains the structure of an illusive world from the standpoint of *abhūta-parikalpa*. It explains that the first insight develops as to the fact that all things are *vijñaptimātra*; then gradually even *vijñapti* is seen to be non-existent. This process is implicit in the statement *asal-lakṣaṇānupraveśopāya lakṣaṇa*. By means of such a process the existence of *paramārtha* is realized. In Nāgārjuna's doctrine such a process toward Enlightenment is not explained fully. The salient feature of the Vijñaptimātra School is to elucidate that process.

In the section dealing with *āśraya-paravṛitti-praveśa* in the *Dh. V.*,[21] four steps of *prayoga* are explained:

1. *upalambha-prayoga*, which is the *prayoga* to become aware of *vijñaptimātra*;
2. *anupalambha-prayoga*, which points to the awareness that *artha* does not exist;

3. *upalambhānupalambha-prayoga*, which points to the awareness that if *artha* does not exist then *vijñapti* also does not exist; and
4. *nopalambhopalambha-prayoga*, which points to the awareness that both *vijñapti* and *artha* do not exist and the two are identical.

Of these four *prayoga*s, the third one corresponds to *dvayasya abhāva*, and the fourth one corresponds to *śūnyatā* and *abhūta-pari kalpa*. In Vasubandhu's *Trisvabhāva-kārikā*, the first three *prayoga*s are expounded in *Kārikā* 36 and the fourth one in *Kārikā* 37.[22]

Therefore, what is expounded as *asal-lakṣaṇānupraveśopāya-lakṣaṇa* is totally the path toward Enlightenment; but the retrospective side as exemplified by the term *upādāya-prajñapti*, found in the *M.K.*, does not come to the surface. From *dvayasya abhāva abhāvasya bhāva* (*śūnyatā*) are the process toward Enlightenment, therefore they are not identical. Accordingly, in *M.A.V.* 1.1 the statements *dvayam tatra na vidyate* and *śūnyatā vidyate* are not identical.

THE PROBLEM STATED

In this respect, the relation between *dvayasya abhāva* and *śunyatā* as expounded in the *M.A.V.* (especially in 1.1) closely resembles the relationship between *śūnya* and *śūnyatā* expounded by the Fa-hsiang School. But in *M.A.V.* 1.13 there is a statement that *dvayasya abhāva* is also *śūnyatā-lakṣaṇa*. This does not pertain to the aforementioned process of *asal-lakṣaṇānupraveśa* but is a statement made from the standpoint of *śūnyatā*.

In the doctrine of the Fa-hsiang School, the path toward Enlightenment is expounded schematically, so that only *asal-lakṣaṇānupraveśa* comes to the surface. Thus, the Fa-hsiang School would distinguish *śūnyatā* from *śūnya* as the state to be realized. This caused a change in the way that the Fa-hsiang School understood the *tri-svabhāva*, especially in terms of the relationship between *paratantra-svabhāva* and *pariniṣpanna-svabhāva*. As a result, in the

Fa-hsiang School the relationship between Phenomena and Reality cannot be expressed without consideration of the relationship of 'neither identical nor separable', as was diagrammed in the second section.

However, as mentioned above, textual sources indicate a singularity of relationship between 'phenomena' and 'reality', *i.e.*, between *paratantra-svabhāva* and *pariniṣpanna-svabhāva*, as was evident in the relationship between *dharma* and *dharmatā* in the *Dh.V.* and between *śunya* and *śunyatā* in the *M.A.V.* In both the *Dh.V.* and the *M.A.V.*, the process of *asal-lakṣaṇānupraveśa* is expounded, and these śāstras emphatically state that 'phenomena' and 'reality' are identical. In the Fa-hsiang School, this is ignored.

It is with this interpretation that we encounter a new problem. Was it due to Dharmapāla's personal views that the separation between 'phenomena' and 'reality' took place, or was that a result of Hsüan-tsang's interpretation, given in his translations of Dharmapāla's works? The answer will be discussed in a future article.

NOTES

1. Shoko Takeuchi, "Hetupariṇāma and Phalapariṇāma" in *Journal of Indian and Buddhist Studies*, Vol. 3, No. 2, Tokyo, pp. 303-305.
2. Hereafter abbreviated T.V.K.
3. S. Lévi, *Vijñapti-mātratā Siddhi*, Paris, 1925, p. 39.
4. The *Ch'eng Wei Shi Lun* is a commentary on the T.V.K. attributed to ten great commentators such as Dharmapāla, Sthiramati, and so on. It is said to have been translated into Chinese by Hsüan-tsang. See Wei Tat, *Ch'eng Wei Shih Lun, Doctrine of Mere-Consciousness*, Dai Nippon Printing Co. (H.K.) Ltd., Hong Kong: 1973, p. 53.
5. J. Takakutsu, *Taishō Shinshu Daizōkyo*, The Taisho Shinshu Daizokyo Kanko Kai, Tokyo: First Edition, 1927, Vol. 43.
6. The compound *pu-chi pu'li* (neither identical nor separable) is probably of Chinese origin, as I cannot find its corresponding equivalent in Sanskrit texts. Therefore, to make the distinction between it and *anekatva-ananyatva*, I have translated *pu-chi pu-li* into English as 'neither identical nor separable'.
7. *Taishō Shinshu Daizōkyo*, Vol. 43, p. 564a.
8. Hereafter abbreviated M.K. The references given are from Louis de la Vallée Poussin, *Mūlamadhyamakakārikās* (*Madhyamikasūtras*) *de Nāgārjuna*, St. Pétersburg: 1903-1913.

9. Hereafter abbreviated *Dh.V.*; see Josho Nozawa, "The *Dharmadharmatāvibhaṅga* and the *Dharmadharmatāvibhaṅga-vṛtti*" In *Studies in Indology and Buddhology, presented in Honor of Prof. Susumu Yamaguchi*, Hozokan, Kyoto, 1955, p. 19.

10. S. Levi, ed., *Asaṅga, Mahāyāna-sūtralaṃkara* (hereafter abbreviated *M.S.A.*), Paris, 1907. See 20-21.17 and .22, pp. 178, 79.

11. G. M. Nagao, ed., *Madhyāntavibhāgabhāṣya* (hereafter abbreviated M.A.V.), Suzuki Research Foundation, Tokyo, 1964, p. 67. See also, *M.S.A.* 13.11 and .12, *op. cit.*, p. 67.

12. G. M. Nagao, *op. cit.*, p. 17. The verse can be rendered into English as follows: "The universal constructor of phenomena (*abhūta-parikalpa*) exists. (But he himself) does not contain any duality (such as *grāhya* and *grāhaka*). Non-substantiality), he (universal constructor) is included too."

13. *Ibid.*, p. 18. English rendition: "[It is said that] all things are neither void nor non-void. According to [the formula] 'existence non-existence existence' the Middle Path is explained."

14. *Ibid.*, pp. 22-23.

15. Poussin, *op. cit.*, p. 11 (*M.K.* 1.1).

16. S. Levi, *op. cit.*, p. 48: *yā 'vidyamānatā saiva paramā vidyamānatā* (1.13).

17. J. Nozawa edition, *op. cit.*, p. 25, 11.2-3.

18. G. Nagao edition, *op. cit.*, p. 18, 1.1.

19. *Ibid.*, p. 18, 1.5.

20. *Ibid.*, p. 19, 1.22. See also D. L. Friedman, *Sthiramati*, "*Madhyānta-Vibhāgaṭīkā*," *Analysis of the Middle Path and the Extremes*, Utrecht: 1937, p. 29.

21. Nozawa, *op. cit.*, pp. 34-35.

22. See *Yamaguchi Susumu Bukkyogaku Bonshu*, Vol. 1, Shunju-sha, Tokyo: 1972, p. 129.

A New Vision of Reality

Tarthang Tulku Rinpoche

MANY DIFFERENT WAYS OF VIEWING the world are now available to us. Very precise and specialized views, theories, or models of reality are being defined in conformity to different perspectives. But I feel that none of these available models can provide a sufficient basis for fully confronting reality, and that they often merely serve to give theoretical confirmation to a common feeling of helplessness in the face of situations over which we 'have no control'. A more total and profound confrontation with 'what is' may, aside from affording us a greater measure of theoretical accuracy, also facilitate the discovery of personal freedom and peace. Both the physical and social sciences are also seeking models with the intent of promoting an increase in intrapersonal and interpersonal harmony and in control of the natural order. But I feel that the available approaches have little likelihood of success because *both* the theories and the problems they are concerned with are expressions of 'hidden' forces or dynamic principles.

An understanding of these principles which are unaccounted for contributes to our picture of why things are a certain way, and also to our ability to change or improve our lives. Moreover, an unusual feature in this case is that a complete understanding of these principles may enable us to transcend our 'control and improvement' orientation altogether. The accuracy of our view of reality and the corresponding implementation of human values may merge, becoming the one fact of a vigorously lived-out vision or insight.

One facet of this latter view of 'reality' involves 'time'. In this view, 'time' is not seen in quite the usual way. But it stands in such an important relationship to current conceptions of time that both ordinary time (henceforth written '$time_1$') and my new notion '$time_2$' should be first discussed briefly. Time involves various senses of 'time', but the two of concern here are (1) time as a variable in the physical sciences generally, and in physics in particular and (2) felt or lived time.

For centuries the physical sciences have sought to know 'why' and by what agency things are as they are. Early theories centered around the power of things—objects—to behave in certain ways, and to bring about certain effects. Objects were thought to 'do' things, and to do so by virtue of a power which was theirs by their very nature or essence. This 'power and object orientation' has largely been replaced by an attention to frequencies of event patterns, typical sequences. 'Power' is now considered an archaic term and has been redefined in terms of sequences of events that are so regular as to be 'law-like'. (Later in our discussion we will see that just as power can be replaced by 'law-like regularity', so these regularities can in turn be viewed as a function of what I will call '$time_2$'.)

Ordinary objects themselves can be redefined in terms of patterns of motion on the part of atomic and sub-atomic particles. At a certain micro-level of analysis, objects are entirely constituted by a characteristic movement—they *are* such and such a movement, rather than *doing* it in a 'subject as agent of the verb' sense. It is interesting to consider that although science now deals in terms of sequences of events—typical temporal series—science is not capable of investigating this flow of time itself. One can investigate any particular state, occurrence, or series by studying the way it relates to certain base-level law-like trends. But one cannot meaningfully ask *why anything should happen at all.* No empirical test could bear on such a question. Yet everything about our realm, including our status as living and perceiving beings, depends on the flow of time. We must jump from moment to moment.

Thus one point that I want to emerge from this brief discussion is that as living beings and as investigators we take time for granted. It is very difficult to see in a time-flow rather than in an object-as-potent-agent manner. It is only recent and intensive investigations in the physical sciences that have shown the need for such a shift in perspective. However, these analyses, which deal entirely in law-like correlations of events, have not seriously considered the idea that 'objects', their states, and their interrelationships *may somehow be a function of 'time' itself*. Of course, we cannot push the law-like regularity point so far as to assert that everything *is* time, in the sense of time that is used in expressing these regularities. I would, however, say that the 'regularity' observation is suggestive in a way that I will return to later.

As either scientists or as living beings with a certain type of orientation, we do not tend to consider time as a factor that could be modulated or even stopped. On the ordinary level of experience, we still think very much in terms of 'object-with characteristic-power' orientation. Because we do not take time seriously, considering it only as an abstraction or an index, some facet of it has become a 'hidden variable' which, by being hidden, limits both the accuracy of our theories and our ability to realize maximum value during the *course* of life. Our lives are made up of typical law-like trends, but we have failed to perceive the real motive force and possibility for change and growth that is involved in such trends. Our 'self' or agent-oriented picture needs to be tempered by a greater appreciation of some subtle dimension of 'time'.

Rather than being considered both absolute and abstract, 'time' must be seen as variable and as intimately connected with both what happens and with our status as observers of what happens. In this century, physics has contributed to this desired reorientation by viewing a time-flow rate as a function of a particular space—where 'space' is understood as an active structuring medium rather than an abstract void. This time-flow rate is understood to include the observer-making-observations as an integral part of the variable flow of events. Thus there is a heightened appreciation of 'time' as being both 'space' or realm-specific and also as entering into the character of experience. There is an affinity between this last picture and the one I intend to introduce, although it fails to show how new possibilities and values (such as 'freedom') can have a place in a given 'realm'. That is the issue of principal concern to me, and to treat it we must now apply the observations that we have been making to a greater consideration of felt or lived time.

Lived serial-order time is a prerequisite for, and a dimension of, any ordinary experience. Lived time is a curious thing, because it preserves the abstract, index character of time as used in the physical sciences, while also appearing to us as compelling, inexorable, merciless—it carries us along from point to point. Our intuition, which is a poorly developed form of what I will later be calling 'knowledge$_2$', often takes the linear succession of time as an intimation that despite our 'self' or 'mind as free agent' picture, there is a dynamic at work which shapes the course of our lives and from which the 'potent-self' is merely an abstraction. Thinking of time in this latter way seems to be just a shorthand device for commenting on situations and trends that often are overwhelming; we abdicate from our position of responsibility by blaming everything on 'life' or 'time'. As in the case of physics, it is inappropriate to claim that ordinary time is actually an autonomous force that pushes us about. Moreover, I would agree that no external force is controlling us in a way that leaves us helpless pawns. But I maintain that the dissatisfaction we feel is a sign that some principle related to our being in the world has not yet been taken into account. We are controlled only to the degree that we allow ourselves to be so by failing to confront all factors relevant to our existence.

The case against a hidden force is based on the familiar notion of 'causal continuity', which urges that there are no events which cannot, in principle, be located in a causal nexus of a familiar kind. Thus, there is no need to invoke a 'hidden variable' or force, and certainly not one that is 'behind' the visible causal order. Furthermore, it is argued, even if there were such a force, it would be indetectible and therefore not an issue for scientific validation. Against this reasoning I would like to make the following points: It is quite true that this force would be indetectable to the familiar methods of science—but that is because such methods are dependent on ordinary cognitive and interpretive faculties. Despite the fact that the hidden factors which concern me are not accessible to an empirical investigation conducted with such ordinary faculties, they are nevertheless quite relevant to both the dynamic of our realm and to the limitations of our type of consciousness. Moreover, as we will see, the 'knowledge' which *does* apprehend these hidden factors is not a function of particular state or type of consciousness of either an ordinary or non-standard sort. The applicability of this 'knowledge' is more general than any state-specific point of view can be.

We should remember that while the 'causal continuity' picture can account for any specific event or series of events, it cannot explain the serial distribution of events in general. It can only account for a particular series within a perspective which assumes the fact of sequentiality and the validity of certain fundamental series of events. I do not mean to say that such a limitation is an intrasystematic defect, but only that I would not like this orientation to block other approaches to discovering why—and what it means that—we human beings exist in a world of situations and challenges. As a corollary of our consideration of the significance of such human engagements, an explanation of the 'unexplainable' linear and sequential character of time will emerge.

The ordinary picture of 'time' as an indexing device for arranging events and interactions between events has the effect of embedding all situations in a linear series. In lived time, the effect of this is that situations gain their meaning from their environment or location within the series of an orienting past and a confining future. Despite the alleged dynamism of the interaction between points in the series, our consciousness and knowledge are all in conformity to the series-character, and the net effect is somehow rather deadening.

However, instead of nailing each point down within this picture, we could also attend to any point in its *presence*—without locating it in a before-after causal nexus pattern. People have tried this in the past without much success, because although they were willing to let go of past and future connections, their attention to the present remained solidly structured in terms of fixating on the nominal elements or conventionally designated 'things' comprising the situation. Yet what makes a 'thing' be 'this or that' includes a certain characteristic movement; you cannot stop time by clinging to one of the conventional items which are given within time. It is possible with sufficient effort to carry such a fixation to the point of 'freezing' things for a while, but this only amounts to a postponement of ordinary time. As this process does not entail a new vision or alternative to the usual temporal order or to familiar things, you have to 'come back' to the 'order' which you know. By freezing things one has failed to learn what they and ordinary time are showing us. Time has just been wasted.

So, somehow we must learn to attend to the presence of both 'knowing subjects' and 'known objects' without clinging to the view of them *as* those things. It might then be possible for previously hidden dynamics to show themselves within and as the situation. In this way, dead facts and deadening trends can become living symbols, although such symbols do not have a content or referent, but are rather the first part of a path of discovery. Here the symbol or manifestation can give way to what is even more dynamic, namely, 'manifesting'.

Now this 'manifesting' character is interesting, in that it provisionally qualifies as a 'time-like' dynamic that 'does' the situations which comprise us and our lives. We will call this dynamic 'timing'. 'Timing' shows all features of a given situation to be interrelated, but not in a sense that reinforces the idea of separate items interacting. With the consideration of 'timing', situations acquire a kind of indivisibility, in which subject, object, surrounding space, thoughts, and things are all together. The independent-self-as-doer picture falls away, or more precisely, is itself a feature that can be seen to be 'timed-out'. Who or what sees this? That which I will call 'knowledge$_2$', a dimension of reality which is also carried by 'timing' and which is revealed precisely to the extent that the 'knowing self in an unknowing world of knowns' picture is dropped. Simply stated, we must stop taking knowledge to be a function of something in the tiny region of our heads. Everything within the scope of 'timing' is equally 'knowing'.

At this stage, this faculty of knowledge$_2$ is still not fully developed because many of our old biases concerning the primacy of the self, as well as many of our conventional perspectives, remain in force. One such bias involves the notion of 'here'. We believe that 'here' is a very solid and thoroughly known world, so that anything as nonstandard as 'timing' must be coming from elsewhere, from 'there'. But as we continue to work with the 'timing' insight, gradually, there emerges an appreciation of a kind of 'space', 'space$_2$'. When knowledge$_2$ can see the space$_2$ dimension, it also becomes possible to relate more fully to 'timing' as it acts within the infinite scope of space$_2$. Greater sense of 'timing' in turn exposes more of the character of space$_2$.

Time$_2$ emerges from this process when 'timing' is freed from its appearance of a 'doing' agent. It becomes clear that the apparent 'doing' in our familiar picture of reality is a reflection of 'timing' and this 'timing' in turn, is simply an imperfect view of time$_2$'s evocation of the undone, unbiased openness that is space$_2$. We see that the states of affairs, objects, actions, and events that have piled up through all time and seem to have prejudiced our freedom by nailing us down, cutting us off, walling us in, are, ultimately, nothing but manifestations of time$_2$ which serve to reveal the infinite, undiminishable capacity of space$_2$. At first we spoke of treating particular temporal points as manifestations. But now 'finite' manifestations can be seen to be not derivative of something else, not created within a particular slice of linear time, and not finite. Each manifestation is the timeless entirety of the intimacy of time$_2$ and space$_2$ and is uncreated.

The knowledge of the intimacy and mutually revealing character of space$_2$ and time$_2$ is precisely knowledge$_2$. By moving back and forth, feeding each level of understanding back into this illumining intimacy, space$_2$, time$_2$, and knowledge$_2$, become the complete fact of 'what is'. Manifestations *are* knowledge$_2$. At this point we have transcended the 'here-there', 'doing-done', 'familiar-unfamiliar' dichotomies, so the new view completely fuses with the old as being one reality. Thus, the space$_2$, time$_2$, knowledge$_2$ view does not set up an alternative world except in the sense of giving us a heightened appreciation of what the ordinary world is in its ordinariness.

It is quite essential to emphasize here that this heightened appreciation is not at all like what people now call a 'state', i.e. an 'altered state of consciousness'. Knowledge$_2$ is *not* a state specific output of some type of consciousness, nor is it an 'ultimate' known fact or secret. It is not someone's particular knowing act. Rather it is an insight by which reality remains clear to itself throughout all of its various state-specific configurations.

We might begin to unpack the significance of this last statement in the following manner: Every observation and manifestation can be seen either as K_2 or as the content of a given moment in ordinary linear time. Taken in this latter way, an observation amounts to a narrowing effect or filter that screens out the total impact of S_2T_2, reducing it to a level that the self finds manageable. Thus S_2T_2 becomes specific meanings, objects, felt realms or patterns. What is known or felt is a function of how S_2T_2 look from a certain position in an ordinary space-time grid. All ordinary knowledge works in this way, including the observations of the scientist as well as the mystical states sought by many meditative traditions. However, the K_2 dimension of each situation keeps abreast of the full significance of the 'playful' intimacy of S_2T_2. This is possible because the K_2 dimension is not confined to a location within ordinary time. It has not assumed a position. Thus, when seen in this perspective, every observation and position remains 'positionless'. All states remain 'stateless' and fully in touch with 'the reality of the situation'. Thus, we can say that K_2 is not a particular state because (1) the presuppositions governing 'states' do not apply to it, and (2) it nevertheless cannot be singled out and separated from these states.

It might be useful to draw out the consequences of the three main stages involved in the above-mentioned process of discovery. The first stage is the ordinary view shared by us all, in which there is only $time_1$. In this view conventional entities are separate but interact. In the case of the 'self', such interaction is pleasant at times and frustrating at other times. The obvious optimum strategy for the self would therefore be to control time, stopping, directing, and prolonging it, depending on the occasion. Such a strategy does not seem possible and so has been replaced by an emphasis on enhanced control of body, mind, and environment through technological means. (Technology derives from capitalizing on the law-like regularities observed by science). It is very doubtful that this approach has resulted in an increase of personal fulfillment or freedom. We seem to have adapted ourselves to seeking the things that technology can actually make or acquire, and such things are often very poor bearers of sustenance for our humanity. In trying to work within what we see as ordinary time, since our view is inaccurate, our efforts either bring little success or are frustratingly slow. We may even undertake a meditative discipline within this scheme, but since we maintain a rigid hold on the familiar character and logic of things, we do not get very far. We can implement a state of disorientation by feeding fantasies which are ungrounded in any real contact with the profound character of reality, or we can freeze things. Neither constitutes a significant change.

The second stage involves a change in perspective sufficient to enable us to apprehend 'the present' as a sheer presence rather than as an item in a series. We can discover 'timing' and through 'timing' can see $time_2$ as at least a possibility. Since 'timing' shows all features of a situation to be integrally related, with 'timing' itself being inseparable from our own consciousness, it becomes possible to exert some control over 'time'. This logic of 'control' falls far short of real insight, but it describes the fact that "things are getting better," that "things are going more my way." To understand such trends, consider that the apparent serial flow of ordinary time can be seen at this stage to be a summation of the output of 'timing', just as on the ordinary level 'objects' are convenient summations of time sequences. The flow of ordinary time is therefore fulfilling or satisfactory to the extent that the undiminishable freedom and variety offered by $space_2$ and the vitality of $time_2$ are preserved in the outputs of 'timing', i.e., to the extent that $knowledge_2$ is unobscured and can enjoy the intimacy of $space_2$ and $time_2$ in every particular manifestation. 'Control' is therefore a misunderstanding of a summation effect. A similar point can be made for the notion of 'power'. Nevertheless, 'control' of time and hence an increase in personal power do *appear* to obtain on this second level.

Meditation can also be much more precisely oriented at this stage, and progresses quickly. The meditative endeavor can also be grounded in greater confidence and expansiveness due to the deep sense that no state of affairs is irrevocably 'bad' or 'trapped' or 'insufficient'. There is an appreciation of a reversibility factor—anything can be traced back to the realization of perfection.

At the third and 'mature' level, $time_2$ is the same as $time_1$. Freedom and perfection are facts rather than goals; the ordinary is still present, but it is no longer ordinary in a problematic way. In fact, from this vantage point, it is clear that there has *never* been a departure from perfection in the first place, never an 'ordinary' time. Actually we cannot even say that 'freedom' or 'perfection' obtain here, because they are products of a lower-order logic that is no longer in force. However, we *can* say that $space_2$, $time_2$, and $knowledge_2$ constitute the ultimate refuge and preservation of our humanity. $Space_2$, $time_2$, and $knowledge_2$ are not the ultimate constituents of a building block universe in which humanness represents only a particular level of complexity, one which has the unusual feature of 'consciousness' associated with it. They are, instead, the fabric of a reality of which humanness and consciousness are central expressions. At this third level, everything serves to nourish us in our essential nature as human beings, a nature which *is* $space_2$, $time_2$, $knowledge_2$. From this viewpoint, we can participate with all existence in an unbounded intimacy which never levels off, but becomes ever more profound. Although I would not wish to claim that there is an exact correspondence, the Trikāya doctrine and the 'samsara-nirvana' equation tradition to Buddhism may be understood somewhat in terms of this $S_2T_2K_2$ orientation.

We can now review the issue of 'power' or 'being in control', an issue which assumes a different significance in each of the three stages just discussed. Although the 'control' picture gives way to the appreciation of perfection at the third stage, there is a sense in which infinitely more 'power' is available at that stage. $Time_2$'s total vitality is not damped down by a 'self' which feels threatened by it. $Time_2$ shows the uncontrived openness of $space_2$ and this perspective gives the 'self' no foothold, no basis for the 'control' and 'achievement' oriented struggles by which a 'self' is defined. To survive, the 'self' of the first two stages has apparently blocked out much of this vitality and freedom, and then set about to 'achieve' these for itself. This strategy is doomed to failure both on the level of $time_2$ and $time_1$—the self can never 'achieve' $time_2$ and $space_2$ while preserving *itself*, and it can never attain full satisfaction within $time_1$ because there it can only dabble with quantities of energy which are inadequate to the task of forcing $time_1$ to go a certain way. The remainder of the energy of $time_2$, though filtered out by the self, nevertheless reasserts itself within $time_1$ by being distributed linearly 'through time'. We cannot embrace $time_2$'s limitless energy directly and at once, so the finite structure we assemble as 'the present moment' is swept away in the face of $time_2$'s hitherto unexpressed power. That in turn is trimmed down to a manageable level as 'the next moment'. Hence we have the familiar facts of transitoriness and linear time. We can try to take advantage of the law-like trends of linear time. But the 'energy' and 'laws' are an inseparable part of the self-limiting achievement perspective of $time_1$, rather than the evocation of $space_2$'s perfection by $time_2$.

It is not possible to bring out the full character of the $S_2T_2K_2$ 'intimacy' here. However, we can elaborate a bit on the consequences of what I called the reversibility factor in stage two. The point of doing so is to draw out the $S_2T_2K_2$ perspective as it relates to the familiar elements and themes of our ordinary view. 'Reversibility' preserves the notion that we have 'strayed' from perfection, but indicates that the possibility of 'return' remains somehow available within the 'flawed' ordinary level. This has the following consequences:

1. The reversibility factor is based on the perception that a distortion of $S_2T_2K_2$ is what actually constitutes our realm. From this point of view, the character of each of $S_2T_2K_2$ is expressed in the internal logic and qualities of our level.

The openness of $S_2 \longrightarrow$ space as a 'container' of things and the notion of 'space' as 'freedom'.

The uncommitted 'anything can be' quality of $S_2 \longrightarrow$ infinite space wherein, as a matter of statistical likelihood, anything can happen.

The unity of $S_2 \longrightarrow$ space as a continuum, a unified field of units.

The 'no-thingness' of $S_2 \longrightarrow$ the object or content of all knowing acts.

S_2's open and fertile uncontrivedness $\longrightarrow$ the mind.

The vitality of pure 'Being' of $T_2 \longrightarrow$ existence, living.

$Time_2$'s timeless Being $\longrightarrow$ law-like regularities of linear time.

T_2's vitality $\longrightarrow$ energy as the basis for technology and the moving force in our realm linking one moment to the next.

T_2's power to make S_2 known in $K_2 \longrightarrow$ relations between subject and object.

T_2's expressiveness or ability to evoke S_2's openness $\longrightarrow$ speech.

$K_2 \longrightarrow$ thinking and knowing acts, cast in a 'x knows y' fashion, along with events of 'not knowing', and unknowing 'things'.

$K_2 \longrightarrow$ states of consciousness that reveal particular 'knowns'.
$K_2 \longrightarrow$ the subject.

K_2 as the stalwart 'witness' of the intimacy between S_2 and $T_2 \longrightarrow$ the 'body' as the embodiment, the expression of a mind.

2. Although $S_2T_2K_2$ have left their mark here as indicated above, these distortions are not deceptive in any final sense. They can be taken as symbols which point back to the higher order. (Myths, poetry, religion, and philosophy seek to do this, but it is difficult to succeed without a knowledge of how and where the symbols point.) Even a cursory examination of the $S_2T_2K_2$ perspective can therefore help very much to orient the proper reading of riddles on our level.

3. A consideration of 1 above shows that not only are qualities of $S_2T_2K_2$ reflected in ordinary items, but also that the $S_2T_2K_2$ intimacy is partially preserved in the internal logic of relationships between conventional items. Obvious examples include the mind-speech-body trio, the subject-object relationship, and the gravitational field-time flow-observer interrelation discovered by physics.

Although it would be possible to continue mapping correlations between these two views, seen from the transitional standpoint of the second stage, the important thing is to make the journey from the first through the third as directly as possible. Our status as human beings involves a tremendous heritage, one that can either be infinitely repressed, frozen, obscured, and subverted, or one that can expand and enrich itself infinitely, supported by everything, 'that is'. Much depends on our view.

Svalpākṣarā Prajñāpāramitā

Akira Yuyama

INTRODUCTION

1.1. The Sanskrit version of the *Svalpākṣarā Prajñāpāramitā* was edited for the first time by Edward Conze, see P. Beautrix, *Bibliographie de la littérature Prajñāpāramitā*, Bruxelles: 1971, No. 315, p. 49. This reference, hereafter abbreviated K, is: E. Conze, "Tāntric Prajñāpāramitā Texts," *Sino-Indian Studies*, Vol. 5, No. 2. Santiniketan: 1956, pp. 113-115: "Svalpākṣarā Prajñāpāramitā." (cf. also pp. 102f., 112). This *editio princeps* is based on a single MS kept in the Asiatic Society at Calcutta (cf. 1.3 below); Conze reconstructed the missing portion of the MS with the help of the Tibetan version. Subsequently, the existence of several other MSS, preserved in a better condition, has become known. One would therefore expect a critically-edited text based upon comparison of those MSS with the Tibetan and Chinese versions.

1.2 The text edited by P. L. Vaidya is not based on manuscript readings. This reference, hereafter abbreviated V, is: P. L. Vaidya, *Mahāyāna-Sūtra-Saṃgraha*, Part 1 (=*Buddhist Sanskrit Texts*, Vol. 17, Darbhanga: 1961), p. 93f. Text No. 4 ((Svalpākṣarā Prajñāpāramitā." Vaidya's text was "taken from Dr. E. Conze's edition as it appeared in the *Sino-Indian Studies*" (Vaidya, p. ix-xix). As a matter of fact, however, he has made a number of alterations without giving notes. This edition is to be found unequal to the text-critical and philological task.

1.3. The following six Sanskrit MSS are now known to us:

A = No. 419-III-150 (folios 289bl-292a5).
B = No. 420-XI-4 (folios 8a4-10b5).
C = No. 418-3 (folios 43a6-46bl)
The above three are kept in the University of Tokyo Library (cf. Matsunami's Catalogue, p. 212, also 148f).
D = No. 62-45 (folios 95b4-97a8), Bibliothèque Nationale de Paris, (cf. Filliozat's Catalogue, 1, p. 40).
E = No. 10757B (folios 2-4, missing folio 1), Asiatic Society, Calcutta. (Cf. Śāstrī's Catalogue, 1, p. 15f, No. 16), used by Conze for his edition. Śāstrī's readings in his Catalogue are quoted in my edition—Abbr. Ś.
F = Packet No. 30 (folios 1-4), Hem Raj Collection, Katmandu. (Cf. Nagao's Report, p. 19.) No further information is available.

I have been able to consult the first four MSS in photocopies. Variant readings are also noted from the texts edited by Conze (=K) and Vaidya (=V) and the text given by Śāstrī in his Catalogue (=Ś). In my edition I have added somewhat detailed footnotes explaining how I have adopted the readings.

2.1. The Tibetan version, *Śes-rab-kyi pha-rol-tu phyin-pa yi-ge ñuṅ-ṅu*, is to be found both in the *Śer-phyin* and the *Rgyud* sections of the Kanjur division of the Tibetan Tripiṭaka. This is indispensable for the study of the original Sanskrit text:

(a) *Śer-phyin* section:
D = Sde-dge Edition (Tōhoku Catalogue No. 22), KA 146a3-147b3.
L = Lha-sa Edition (Takasaki's Catalogue No. 24), KA 255a5-257b5
[=Bonner Xerox edition, Vol. 34, pp. 128.4.5-131.2.5 (Eimer's Catalogue, pp. 12/37)].
N = Snar-thaṅ Edition (Feer's *Analyse*, p. 202: 6.12.): KA 258bl-261a1.

(b) *Rgyud* section:
C′ = Co-ne Edition (Mibu's Catalogue No. 164), NA 41b7-43b6.

D′ = Sde-dge Edition (Tōhoku Catalogue No. 530), NA 92b6–94a7.
L′ = Lha-sa Edition (Takasaki's Catalogue No. 498), THA 42a5–45a1.
[=Bonner Xerox Edition, Vol. 88, pp. 22.3.5–24.2.1 (Eimer's Catalogue, pp. 20, 44)].
N′ = Snar-thaṅ Edition (Feer's *Analyse*, p. 312, 11.12), DA 89b1–92a3.
P′ = Peking Edition (Ōtani Catalogue No. 159), NA 38a2–39b7.
[=Reprint Edition, Vol. 6, pp. 165.3.2–166.1.7].

In my edition the Kanjur texts L, L′, N, N′, and P′, and a Tunhuang fragment (cf. 2.2 below) have been collated. As for the Narthang edition (*i.e.*, N and N′), I have been able to consult the copy kept in the Bibliothèque Nationale of Paris.

2.2. A single Tibetan MS from Tunhuang is fragmentary and contains only the last few lines of the text, which are identical with the Kanjur version: No. 101–1, *Fonds Pelliot Tibétain*, Bibliothèque Nationale de Paris. Cf. Lalou's *Inventaire*, Vol. 1, p. 34.

2.3. No Tibetan text records its translator's name or translators' names. The Tibetan version is, however, listed in the *Śer-phyin* section of the so-called Denkarma Catalogue. Cf. M. Lalou, "Les textes bouddhiques au temps du Roi Khri-sroṅ lde-bcan," *Journal Asiatique*, Vol. 241, 1953, p. 16, 1.16: *yi-ge ñuṅ-du* [!] (30 Śloka). See also S. Yoshimura, *The Denkar-Ma*, Kyoto: 1950, p. 4 [= Yoshimura's *Collected Works*, Kyoto: 1974, p. 1203, No. 16: *'phags-pa yi-ge ñaṅ-ṅu* (30 Śloka).

3.1. The Chinese version, *Fo-shou Sheng-fo-mu Hsiao-tzu pan-jo po-lo-mi to-ching* (Nanjio Catalogue No. 797), was translated by T'ien-hsi-tsai (alias Fa-hsien / Dharmabhadra), probably in the year 982 A.D., according to the most reliable source. This is *Ta-chung Hsiang-fu fa-pao-lu*, compiled by Yang I, etc. (1011–15 A.D.) = *Chung-hua Ta-tsang-ching*, First Series, Vol. 10, Fasc. 80, Taipei: 1966, p. 34566b18–27. Conze has given an approximate date of the translation as 980 A.D. without further reference. See Conze, *The Prajñāpāramitā Literature*, The Hague: 1960, p. 80. This is the year in which T'ien-hsi-tsai came from Kashmir to China. For further details, see Yuyama, *Prajñā-pāramitā-ratna-guṇa-saṃcaya-gāthā*, Cambridge: 1976, pp. xl–xlii.

3.2. T'ien-hsi-tsai is said to have brought no MS from India into China. (See P. Demiéville, *L'Inde Classique*, Vol. 2, Paris-Hanoi: 1953, p. 426, para. 2097. In translating the text, however, he must have consulted the original Indic version at his disposal, since it is believed that a great number of Buddhist texts written in various languages, including Sanskrit, were brought into China in the Northern Sung period (960–1127 A.D.). See Z. Tsukamoto, "Bukkyō-Shiryō to shite no Kinkoku Daizōkyō," *Tsukamoto Zenryū Chosakushū*, Vol. 5, Tokyo: 1975, p. 93. [Orig. published in the *Tōhō Gakuhō*, Vol. 6, Kyoto: 1934].

3.3. In this case, too, T'ien-hsi-tsai seems to have made a very free translation. At this stage it is safer to say that the Chinese version represents a recension different from the existing Indo-Tibetan tradition of the text. A more careful study is needed in regard to his translations.

3.4. I have consulted the following three editions:

(a) *Taishō Shinshū Daizōkyō*, [abbr. T or Taishō], No. 258, Vol. 8, pp. 852c22–853c26.

(b) *Dainippon Kōtei Shukusatsu Daizōkyō*, [abbr. Shuku], *Ch'êng*-8, pp. 29b–30b. Note that this edition is well known for its accurate collation. See A. Hirakawa and E. B. Ceadel, "Japanese Research on Buddhism since the Meiji Period," *Monumenta Nipponica*, Vol. 11, No. 3, Tokyo: 1955, p. 225.

(c) Chi-sha Edition, reprinted in the *Chung-hua Ta-tsang-ching*, First Series, Vol. 8, Fasc. 64, Taipei: 1965, pp. 28005b4–6b4. [Abbr. Chi-sha]. Note that this edition was discovered after the publication of the Taishō Edition. See J. W. de Jong, *Buddha's Word in China*, Canberra: 1968, p. 17, 25f. (n. 57). It is also carefully collated.

4.1. My translation had to be omitted in the first instance, for consideration of space. It also seemed somewhat superfluous to present another translation, as Conze's annotated translation has recently been published in full, although it is true that the text on which his translation is based is slightly different from mine. In the footnotes I have, therefore, added some grammatical, syntactical, and semantic explanations, whenever necessary (cf. also 7.1-4 below).

4.2. Two English translations have been published by E. Conze:

(a) *Selected Sayings from the Perfection of Wisdom*, London: 1955, reprinted 1968, pp. 122-124, Text No. 128, cf. also p. 15. —Abridged.
(b) *The Short Prajñāpāramitā Texts*, London: 1973, pp. 144-147, (cf. also p. iii).—Unabridged, annotated.

5.1. According to the tradition described by Bu-ston (1290-1364 A.D.) in his *Chos-'byuṅ*, Nāgārjuna on his visit to the abode of the Nāgas (*Klu-yul*) wanted to take with him a large quantity of clay to build *caitya*s and *stūpa*s (*mchod-rten*), and the *Śatasāhasrikā*. In addition, he obtained the *Svalpaksara*: *'dam man-po dan 'bum dan yi-ge nun-nu-yan gdan-drans-te* . . . See Lokesh Chandra, ed., *Bu-ston's History of Buddhism* (*Tibetan Text*), New Delhi: 1971.—Offprint. Fol. 830, line 4 (=orig. fol. 99B4). See E. Obermiller, *History of Buddhism by Bu-ston*, Vol. 2, Heidelberg: 1932, reprinted Tokyo: 1964, p. 124.

5.2. This legend may help us to understand the colophon which is found in the Sanskrit MSS A, B, and D (= Sanskrit text paragraph 9): *ārya-nāgārjuna-pādaiḥ pātālād uddhṛtā* / *iti* // "(The *Svalpākṣarā Prajñāpāramitā* has been) drawn up from the Pātāla [*i.e.* the abode of the Nāgas. Cf. Tib. *Klu-yul*] by His Holiness the Venerable Nāgārjuna." (Cf. Skt. text n. 124 below.) This does not by any means confirm the authorship of the text by Nāgārjuna. See J. Filliozat, *Catalogue du fonds sanscrit*, Vol. 1. Bibliothèque Nationale de Paris: 1941, p. 40: "Svalpākṣarā Bhagavatī Prajñāpāramitā attribuée à Nāgārjuna."

6.1. Bibliographical information with reference to the *Svalpākṣarā Prajñāpāramitā* can be obtained from the following works: works:

(a) Kōun Kajiyoshi, "Shō Butsumo Shōji Hannya Haramittakyō," *Bussho Kaisetsu Daijiten*, edited by G. Ono, Vol. 5, Tokyo: 1933. Reprinted 1964, 1967, p. 386b.

(b) Ryūjō Yamada, *Bongo Butten no Shobunken*, Kyoto: 1959, p. 191f. The English version by Shōyū Hanayama, "A Summary of Various Research on the Prajñāpāramitā Literature by Japanese Scholars," *Acta Asiatica*, No. 10, Tokyo: 1966, p. 37f.

(c) E. Conze, *The Prajñāpāramitā Literature*, 's-Gravenhage: 1960. pp. 80–82, No. 18, "Perfection of Wisdom in a Few Words."

6.2. For catalogue references to the Sanskrit MSS and Tibetan Kanjur editions see A. Yuyama, *Indic Manuscripts and Chinese Blockprints (Non-Chinese Texts) of the Oriental Collection of the A.N.U. Library*, Canberra: 1967, pp. 1–9.

7.1. The Indic version of the *Svalpākṣarā Prajñāpāramitā* belongs to the Buddhist Sanskrit tradition from the glossarial point of view rather than the grammatical. Here are some remarks:

7.2. GLOSSARIAL: *koṭī-* (so MSS often, instead of *koṭi-*) may be the true reading. (See Edgerton, *Buddhist Hybrid Sanskrit Grammar*, 10.162). In IV, *samādhi-* is clearly feminine with°*-pramocanā* and *yayā samāhitayā* (cf. Skt. text n. 36, also 7.4 below). In IV° *-pāda-mūla*, 'at, by, under . . .' (cf. Skt. text n. 45, also 124). In Vf, *pustaka-likhita-*, "book, text" (=*pustaka-gata-*) may be noteworthy. In KV *parṣan maṇḍalâbhiṣikta-* in VH is not possible; the true reading is simply *maṇḍalâbhiṣikta-*, which is used in a Tāntric sense, (cf. Skt. text n. 98).

7.3. GRAMMATICAL: MSS ABCD have *kṣepayiṣyanti* in IIIab (for *kṣap°*) which seems to have been corrupted in the course of transmission, (cf. Skt. text n. 19). In IIIab (end), *sidheran*, 3 pl. opt., has not been recorded elsewhere, (cf. Skt. text n. 24).

7.4. SYNTACTICAL: In IV *yayā samāhitayā*, instr. absol., "when he had entered the *samādhi*. . ." (cf. Skt. text n. 36–37). In Ve *buddhatve*, "with regard to the Buddhahood," (see A. A. Macdonell, *Skt. Gramm. f. Stud.*, para. 204a). In Vh *anayā paṭhita-mātrayā*, "no sooner than this is recited. . . ." (instr. absol. with *mātra-*), is syntactically interesting. (See Edgerton BHSGr. 7.34; also Macdonell, *op. cit.*, 205.1d; also Speyer, *Skt. Syntax*, 229.4); Conze trsl. "when it is merely being recited. . ." In KV, *-mātreṇa* is not acceptable. Phrases denoting the time are placed at the ends of two sentences, *i.e.* . . . *hy anāgate 'dhvani* in Vf and . . . *kalpa-koṭi-śatair api* in Vh.

Sv-alpâkṣarā Prajñā-pāramitā *

I. (A289b) oṃ namo bhagavatyai[1] ārya-prajñā-pāramitāyai //[2]

IIa. evaṃ mayā śrutaṃ[3] ekasmin samaye[4] bhagavān rāja-gṛhe viha(C43b)rati sma, gṛdhra-kūṭe parvate mahatā bhikṣu-saṃghena sārdham ardha-trayodaśabhir bhikṣu-śatair, anekaiś ca[5] bodhisattva-koṭi-niyuta-śata-sahasraiḥ,[6] śakra-brahma-loka-pāla-pramukhair anekaiś ca[7] deva-koṭi-niyuta-śata-sahasraiḥ[8] parivṛtaḥ puras-kṛtaḥ, śrī-ratna-garbha-siṃhâsane[9] ni(B8b)ṣaṇṇo[10] bhagavān dharmaṃ deśayati sma[11] //

IIb. ādau kalyāṇaṃ madhye kalyāṇaṃ paryavasāne kalyāṇaṃ sv-arthaṃ su-vyañjanaṃ kevalaṃ paripūrṇaṃ pariśuddhaṃ paryavadātaṃ brahma-caryaṃ saṃprakāśayati sma //[12]

IIIa. athâryâvalokiteśvaro bodhisattvo mahā-sattva[13] utthāyâsanād ekâṃsam[14] uttarâsaṅgaṃ kṛtvā dakṣiṇaṃ[15] jānu-maṇḍalaṃ pṛthivyāṃ pratiṣṭhāpya[16] yena bhagavāṃs tenâñjaliṃ praṇamya prahasita-vadano bhūtvā bhagavantam etad avocat / deśayatu me[17] bhagavān prajñā-pāramitāṃ sv-alpâkṣarāṃ mahā-puṇyāṃ (A290a) yasyāḥ śravaṇa-mātre(D96a)ṇa sarva-sattvāḥ[18] sarva-karmâvaraṇāni kṣapayiṣyanti[19] niya(C44a)taṃ ca bodhi-parāyaṇā bhaviṣyanti[20] ye ca sattvā[21] mantra-sādhana[22] udyuktās [23] teṣāṃ câvighnena mantrāḥ sidherann[24] iti //

IIIb. atha khalu bhagavān āryâvalokiteśvarāya bodhisattvāya mahā-sattvāya mahā-kāruṇikāya sādhu-kāram adāt / sādhu sādhu[25] kula-putra yas tvaṃ sarva-sattva-hitāya[26] sukhāya pratipannaḥ[27] sarva-sattvârthaṃ[28] dīrgha-rātram abhiyuktas[29], tena hi tvaṃ kula-putra śṛṇu sādhu ca (B9a) suṣṭhu ca manasi-kuru bhāṣiṣye 'haṃ te prajñā-pāramitāṃ sv-alpâkṣarāṃ mahā-puṇyāṃ yasyāḥ śravaṇa-mātreṇa sarva-sattvāḥ sarva-karmâvaraṇāni kṣapayiṣyanti[30] niyataṃ ca bodhi-parāyaṇā bhaviṣyanti / ye ca sattvā[31] mantra-sādhana[32] udyuktās teṣāṃ câvighnena mantrāḥ sidherann[33] iti //

IIIc. atha khalv āryâvalokiteśvaro bodhisattvo mahā-sattvo bhagavantam etad avocat / tena hi sugato[34] bhāṣatu sarva-sattva-hitāya[35] sukhāya ca //

IV. (A290b, C44b) atha khalu bhagavāṃs tasyāṃ velāyāṃ sarva-sattva-pramocanāṃ[36] nāma samādhiṃ samāpadyate sma / yayā samāhitayā[37] ūrṇa-kośād bhrū-vivarântarād[38] anekāni raśmi-koṭi-niyuta-śata-sahasrāṇi niścerus,[39] taiś ca raśmibhiḥ sarva-buddha-kṣetrāṇi sphuṭāny [40] abhūvan / ye ca sattvās tayā prabhayā spṛṣṭās te sarve niyatā abhūvann anuttarāyāṃ samyak-saṃbodhau / yāvan nārakāḥ sarva-sattvāḥ[41] sarve sukha-samarpitā abhūvan[42] / sarvāṇi[43] ca buddha-kṣetrāṇi ṣaḍ-vikāraṃ pravicelur,[44] divyāni candana-cūrṇa-varṣāṇi tathāgata-pāda-mūle[45] prāvarṣanta[46] //

Va. atha (B9b) khalu bhagavāṃs tasyāṃ velāyām imāṃ[47] prajñā-pāramitāṃ bhāṣate sma //

Vb. tad-yathā / bodhi(D96b)sattvena mahā-sattvena sarva-sattveṣu[48] sama-cittena bhavitavyaṃ maitra-cittena bhavitavyaṃ kṛta-jñena bhavitavyaṃ kṛta-vedinā ca bhavitavyaṃ sarva-pāpa-viratena[49] bha(C45a)vitavyaṃ // idaṃ ca prajñā-pāramitā-hṛdayaṃ āvartayitavyam[50] //

Vc. namo ratna-trayāya // na(A291a)maḥ śākya-munaye tathāgatāyârhate samyak-saṃbuddhāya //[51]

Vd. tad-yathā / oṃ mune mune mahā-munaye svāhā //[52]

Ve. asyāḥ[53] prajñā-pāramitāyā lābhān[54] mayânuttarā samyak-saṃbodhiḥ prāptā /[55] sarva-buddhāś câto[56] niryātāḥ[57] / tvayâpîyam[58] eva prajñā-pāramitā śrutā bhagavataḥ[59] śākya-munes tathāgatasya sakāśāt,[60] tena hi mayā[61] tvaṃ sarva-buddha-bodhisattvānām agrato buddhatve ca vyākṛto bhaviṣyasi māṇavânāgate[62] 'dhvani samanta-raśmy-udgata-śrī-kūṭa-rā(D96b)jo[63] nāma[64] tathāgato 'rhan samyak-saṃbuddho vidyā-caraṇa-saṃpannaḥ sugato loka-vid anuttaraḥ puruṣa-damya-sārathiḥ[65] śāstā devānāṃ ca manuṣyāṇāṃ ca buddho bhagavān //

Vf. tadīyaṃ ca ye[66] nāma-dheyaṃ śroṣyanti (B10a) dhārayiṣyanti vācayiṣyanti likhiṣyanti[67] likhāpayiṣyanti[68] bhāvayiṣyanti paryavāpsyanti (C45b) parebhyaś ca vistareṇa saṃprakāśayiṣyanti pustaka-likhitaṃ ca[69] kṛtvā sva-gṛhe[70] dhārayiṣyanti vācayiṣyanti[71] te 'pi sarve tathāgatā[72] bhavi(A291b)ṣyanti hy anāgate 'dhvani[73] //

Vg. tad-yathā / oṃ jaya jaya[74] padmāhe[75] avame[76] sara saraṇi[77] dhiri dhiri[78] dhirā dhiri[79] khiri khiri khirā khiri[80] devatânupālani[81] buddhottāraṇi[82] pūraya pūraya[83] bhagavati sarvāśāṃ[84] mama[85] pūraya[86] sa-parivāraya[87] sarva-sattvānāṃ ca sarva-karmâvaraṇāni[88] viśodhaya viśodhaya[89] buddhâdhiṣṭhānena[90] svāhā //

Vh. iyaṃ sā [91] paramârtha-prajñā-pāramitā sarva-buddhānāṃ jananī bodhi-sattva-mātā sadya-(D97a)pāpa-harī[92] bodhisattva-nāyikā,[93] sarva-buddhair api na śakyate[94] 'syā[95] anuśaṃsā vaktuṃ[96] kalpa-koṭi-śatair api, anayā paṭhita-mātrayā[97] sarva-[98]maṇḍalâbhiṣikto bhavati,[99] sarve ca mantrā[100] abhimukhā bhavanti //

VIa. atha khalv[101] āryâvalokiteśvaro bodhisattvo mahā-sattvo bhagavantam etad avocat / kena kāraṇena bhagavann i(C46a)yaṃ[102] prajñā-pāramitā sv-alpâkṣarā[103] //

VIb. bhagavān āha / alpopāyatvād,[104] ye 'pi sattvā mandotsā(B10b)hās[105] te 'pîmāṃ prajñā-pāramitāṃ[106] dhārayiṣyanti vācayiṣyanti likhiṣyanti likhāpayiṣyanti[107] sarve te[108] 'lpopā(A292a)yena[109] bodhi-parāyaṇā bhaviṣyanti / anena kāraṇena kula-putra[110] saṃkṣiptā[111] prajñā-pāramitā //

VIIa. evam ukte[112] āryâvalokiteśvaro bodhisattvo mahā-sattvo bhagavantam etad avocat / āścaryaṃ bhagavann āścaryaṃ[113] sugata yāvad eva bhagavatā[114] sarva-sattva-hitāya sukhāya[115] dharma-paryāyo deśitaḥ[116], manda-puṇyānāṃ sattvānāṃ[117] hitāya sukhāya cêti //

VIIb. idam avocad bhagavān / ātta-manā āryâvalokiteśvaro bodhisattvo mahā-sattvaḥ,[118] te ca bhikṣavas, te ca bodhisattvā[119] mahā-sattvāḥ, sā ca sarvāvatī[120] parṣat, sa-deva-mānuṣâsura-gandharvaś ca loko[121] bhagavato bhāṣitam abhyanandann iti // //

VIII. ārya-sv-alpâkṣarā bhagavatī prajñā-pāramitā[122] sa(C46b)māptā[123] // //

IX. ārya-nāgārjuna-pādaiḥ pātālād uddhṛtā / iti // //[124]

N O T E S (Sanskrit text)

* Minor variants are neglected in the footnotes. For abbreviations see my "Prefatory Notes" above.

1 So remains hiatus.

2 Conze instead has (*namaḥ sarva-buddha-bodhisattvebhyaḥ!*, reconstructed with the help of Tib. *saṅs-rgyas daṅ / byaṅ-chub-sems-dpa' thams-cad-la phyag-'tshal-lo*. No homage is paid in Chin. Conze does not close the parenthesis. However, he must have reconstructed the text ~~until~~ *pratiṣṭhāpya* in IIIa, since MS. E has far as begins folio 2 with *yena bhagavāṃs...*, according to Śāstrī's Catalogue, p. 15 (cf. n. 16 below).

3 V here daṇḍa (cf. n. 4 below).

4 K here full-stop. For this cliché see A. von Staël-Holstein, *A Commentary to the Kāśyapaparivarta* (Peking 1933), p. IV (with n. 7 on p. XIII); J. Brough, "Thus Have I Heard ...", *BSOAS*, XIII, 2 (1950), pp. 416-426; also H. Nakamura, *Hannyashingyō / Kongō Hannyagyō* (Tokyo 1960), p. 182f.

5 KV ... *sārdhaṃ dvādaśa-sāhasra-pañca-śatair* ... (K °-*śataiḥ*, ...); cf. Tib. *khri-ñis-stoṅ-lṅa-brgya'i dge-sloṅ-gi dge-'dun chen-po*. One would perhaps expect ... *dvādaśa-sahasra-pañca-śatair bhikṣubhir anekaiś ca* ... Our text counts 1250 bhikṣus (so trsl. Conze!). Cf. Chin. "1250 bhikṣus" (T. VIII 852c29).

6 KV here add *sārdhaṃ viharati sma*, ... (with Tib.?).

7 K *loka-pāla-ādi*, V °-*pālādi*-° for *śakra-brahma-loka*-° (so Tib. *brgya-byin daṅ, tshaṅs-pa daṅ*, ...).

8 C *deva-manuṣyâsura*-°! (for *deva*-°, so Tib. *lha*, Chin. *t'ien*); T. VIII 853a2 *ta-chung* (so Shuku!) should be emended to *t'ien-chung* (cf. T. 853 n. 1; so also Chi-sha).

9 C om. *ratna-* (so Tib. *dpal-gyi sñiṅ-po*, i.e. *śrī-garbha-*); K supposes *śrī-maṇḍa-* with question-mark (p. 113 n. 1); cf. Chin. *pao-tsang* (T. VIII 853a3), i.e. *ratna-garbha-* (cf. Mvy 665).

10 KV *viharati sma*, as Tib. ends the sentence here with *bźugs-so*, and Chin. with *chieh-chia fu-tso* (T. VIII 853a3), i.e. *paryaṅkaṃ baddhaḥ* (?); AB °*ṇṇā*, C °*ṇṇāḥ*, D *ni⟨ṣa⟩ṇṇo*.

11 In KV, Tib. and Chin. lack *bhagavān* ... *sma*.

12 IIb lacking in KV, Tib. and Chin. This cliché is found for example SP (ed. Kern-Nanjio) 17.12-13, 18.9-10 (here ... *saṃprakāśitavān*).

13 C *akha* (for *atha*) *khalv āryā*°; KV *atha khalu bodhisattvo mahāsattvo āryāvalokiteśvaro* ...

14 ABC *ekāsam*, D *ekāśam*, K *eka-aṃsam*, V *ekam aṃsam*; cf. Mvy 6276 *ekāṃsam uttara-saṅgaṃ kṛtvā*.

15 BC *dakṣiṇa*-°; cf. Mvy 6277 *dakṣiṇaṃ* ... *pratiṣṭhāpya*.

16 E begins fol. 2 with *yena bhagavāṃs* ... (cf. Śāstrī's Catalogue, p. 15).

17 Not in KVŚ (nor in Tib.); but cf. IIIb *bhāṣiṣye 'haṃ te* ... / *ṅas khyod-la bśad-do.*

18 K °*-sattvā!*; C °*-sattvānāṃ.*

19 So KVŚ: Tib. *byaṅ-bar 'gyur-ba*; ABCD *kṣep*° must simply be a mistake; cf. e.g. Vajracchedikā (ed. Max Müller 34.18-19) *tāni paurva-janmikāny aśubhāni karmāṇi kṣapayiṣyanti*; cf. T. Kagawa, "Kongō Hannyagyō Shohon Goi no Kenkyū", *Bukkyō Daigaku Jinbungaku Ronshū*, No. 3 (Kyoto 1968), p. 18/19; this passage is referred to by Śāntideva in his Śikṣāsamuccaya (ed. C. Bendall 171.11-13); Wogihara's reference seems to be confused in this regard (Wogihara's Sanskrit-Japanese Dict., p. 396b, *kṣip-*, caus. *kṣepayati*, s.v.); cf. also Sukhāvatīvyūha (ed. A. Ashikaga 60.8; Wogihara, *Jōdo Sanbukyō*, p. 188 ad ed. Max Müller 138.13-14, orig. 68.13-14) *paurvâparādhaṃ kṣapayitvā.*

20 AD *bhavanti*; one would expect a fut. in the context (so KV, BC).

21 K *sattvāḥ!*

22 ABCD °*ne* (so KVŚ); but cf. n. 32 below.

23 B *prayuktās*, C *bhyuktā* (for *udyuktās*, AD = KVŚ).

24 ABCD *siddhe*°, KVŚ *sidhyanti*; *sidheran* (for Skt. *sidhyeran*, 3 pl.opt.) seems to be the right reading; *siddheran* must simply be a mistake (possibly confused with *siddhi-*) rather than a semi-Skt. form of MInd. *sijjhati*, Skt. *sidhyati*. Cf. n. 33 below.

25 K mispr. *sadhu sadhu.*

26 KV °*-sattvānām arthāya hitāya* (cf. K p. 113 n. 8); cf. n. 35 below.

27 K *pradhānāya* (mispr. for *prah*°), V *pradhānāya*! Conze thinks it a copyist's gloss (cf. *Short Prajñāpāramitā Texts*, p. 144 n. 1). Our text is certainly better, but is missing in Tib.

28 So Tib., but missing in KV. Add here perhaps *ca.*

29 KV *niyuktas*!; cf. Tib. *brtson-pa*, i.e. *abhiyukta-*; ABC °*tās*, D °*tā·s.*

30 AC *kṣep*° (for *kṣap*°, BD = KV; cf. n. 19 above).

31 K °*āḥ!*

32 BC °*-sādhane* (so KV); cf. n. 22 above.

33 ABCD *siddherann*, KV *sidhyanti*; cf. n. 24 above.

34 C °*ta* (so em. K p. 113 n. 4 = V!).

35 KV °*-sattvānām arthāya hitāya*; cf. n. 26 above.

36 B °*no*, CD °*nī*; KV *sarva-duḥkha-pramocano* (cf. K p. 114 n. 6); Tib. *sems-can thams-cad dgrol-ba*, Chin. *chieh-t'o i-ch'ieh chung-shêng* (T. VIII 853a21-22), i.e. *sarva-sattva-pramocanā*. Also to be noted that *samādhi-* is here used as fem.; cf. Yuyama, *A Grammar of the Rgs* (Canberra 1973), 6.4-5.

37 KV *yasya ca samādhiṃ samāpannasya bhagavata(ḥ)*; our text corresp. to Tib. *mñam-par bźag-pa des*; cf. Edgerton BHSGrammar 7.34 for instr.absolute.

38 So Tib. *smin-mtshams-kyi mdzod-spu'i phrag-nas*; K *ūrṇa-kośa(jñā)vivarān lavād*, V *ūrṇā-kośa-vivarāl lavād!*

39 C *niścaranti sma* (so KV), B *niścaryas.*

40 KV *parisphuṭany.*

41 So Chin. (T. VIII 853a25); but ACD om. *sarva-* (so KV); cf. n. 42 below.

42 For *sarve* ... *abhūvan* K reports the defective E *(sa dhva sū ga sa ma + + +)*; V *(+ + +)*; this is missing in Tib.

43 KV *sarve!*

44 A °*celu* (so K!; V °*celuḥ/*...), B °*ceyūḥ.*

45 KV °*-mūlaṃ*, "on the ground at the feet of the Lord" (Conze), so trsl. Tib.

verbatim *de-bźin-gśegs-pa'i źabs-kyi druḥ-du*; but Chin. simply *vu chu-fo shang*
(T. VIII 853a26), "onto the Buddhas"; cf. Böhtlingk-Roth, *Sanskrit-Wörterbuch*,
IV, Sp. 652, *pāda-mūla-*, 1, s.v., for the expression of reverence; cf. also
n. 124 below.

46 KV *vavarṣuḥ*.

47 Only C *imāṃ*, supported by Chin. *tz'u* (T. VIII 853a28).

48 KV °*-sattveṣu* after *sama-cittena bhavitavyaṃ*; Tib. and Chin. om. °*-sattveṣu*.

49 KV °*-virata-cittena*; B °*-virahitena*, C °*-virahitā ca*.

50 E *ā(...)tavyam*, Ś only + + + + + + + + +; K suggests (p. 114 n. 8) *āpattitavyaṃ*
(with question-mark) with the help of Tib. *gdon-par bya'o*; V *āgrahītavyam*.

51 Tib. and Chin. om. *namo ratna-trayāya*. Otherwise, Chin. transliterates Vc,
while Tib. translates it.

52 Both Tib. and Chin. transliterate Vd.

53 C *asyā* (so K!).

54 KVŚ °*āt*!

55 KV °*-saṃbodhir anuprāptā*.

56 So DV, Tib. *'di-las*; A *cātā*, B *ca*, C *cato*, K *ca ato*, Ś *cāgrato*!

57 KŚ °*tā*!

58 KŚ *mayā*°!; our text corresponds to Tib. *khyod-kyis*.

59 K *mahā-* (for *bhagavataḥ*) is supported by Tib. *śākya thub-pa chen-po-las*.

60 KV *sākṣāt*.

61 C om. *mayā* (so KV).

62 So KV; MSS corrupt - AD *māṇakān*°, B *mānavakān*°, C *tvaṃ manāgate*! *māṇava* is
missing in Tib. and Chin.

63 So BD (D °*-kūṭa-*°); A *samamanta-raśmy-udgata-śrī-ku-rājo*, C *samanta-raśm⟨y⟩-
abhyudgata-śrī-kuṭa-*°; K (p. 114 n. 10) *sam(anta-raśmi-samu)dgata-śrī-kuṭa-rāja*;
V *sam(anta-raśmi-samu)dgataḥ śrī-kūṭa-rājā*! Taishō divides it like V (T. VIII
853b19); cf. Tib. *'od-zer kun-nas 'phags-pa dpal brtsegs rgyal-po*, i.e. *samanta-
raśmy-⟨ ⟩udgata-⟨̂⟩śrī-kūṭa-rāja-*; cf. also Tib. text n. 29.

64 K *nāmās*!

65 K °*-sārathī*!

66 So D; MSS corrupt - A *adīyaṃ ca ye*, B *tadiyaṃ ca ya*, C *tadīyam ami* (for *api?*)
yedaṃ; K *tvad iyam api ye idan*!, V [*badīyam api?*] *ye idaṃ*!; Tib. *khyod-kyi* ...
suggests *tvadīyaṃ ca ye*, which may be possible. In the context, however, our
reading seems better, as Chin. suggests: *shih miao-fa*, "this true law" (T. VIII
853b20).

67 KV (and Tib.) om. *likhiṣyanti*.

68 KV *likhayayiṣyanti*; Tib. om. *likhāpayiṣyanti*.

69 KV °*-likhitam api*.

70 K *gṛddhe*!; V *gṛhe*; cf. Chin. *wu chi shê-chê* (T. VIII 853b22; cf. n. 8!),
i.e. *sva-gṛhe*, which is missing in Tib.

71 KV *pūjayiṣyanti* (so Tib. *mchod-pa byed-pa*)(for *vācay*°).

72 ABCD *sarva-*°!; KV *te sarve alpopāyena alpa-śravaṇena ca tathā*°!; our reading is supported by Tib. *de-dag thams-cad ... de-bźin-gśegs-par 'gyur-ro*.

73 So Tib. *ma 'oṅs-pa'i dus-na*; but KV om. *hy anāgate 'dhvani*.

74 So Tib. and Chin.; but KV *jeya jeya*!

75 So Chin.; but KV *padmābhe* (so Tib.).

76 KV repeat *avame*.

77 So KV (*saras*°) and Tib.; Chin. *sara sariṇi* (?); AD *śara śaraṇa*, B *sara
sara*, C *sara saraṇe*.

78 Chin. *bhiri bhiri* (?).

79 Tib. *dhiri dhiri* (N adds further *dhirā dhiri*), Chin. *bhirā bhiri* (?).

80 KV om. *dhirā dhiri khiri khiri khirā khiri*; Tib. om. *khiri khiri khirā khiri*; Chin. om. *khirā khiri*.

81 KV *devatā anu°*; Tib. and Chin. *devatānupālane*.

82 So Tib.; Chin. *buddhotar°*; D *buddhāttar°*, K *yuddhāt-tāriṇi*, V *yuddhottāriṇi*!; KV here add *para-cakra-nivāriṇi*, which is not supported by Tib. or Chin.

83 So repeat KV (= Tib.L'); Chin. *puraya puraya* (?)(cf. n. 86 end).

84 So Chin.; [redacted] KV *sarva āśā ca*; cf. Tib. text n. 40.

85 So Chin.; Tib. *śama*.

86 C om. *pūraya* (so KV); Tib.L' *paripūraya*; Chin. *puraya* (cf. n. 82 above).

87 Cf. Tib. L'N' *sa-pa-ri-bā-*(L' *-bă-*)*ra-sya*; C om. *sa-parivārasya* (so KV, Chin. Tib. LP').

88 So Chin. (but Taishō mispr. *°-varmâv°*?:cf. Chin. version n. 5 below); so also Tib. (but cf. Tib. text n. 44).

89 So repeat Tib. and Chin.; A om. one *viśodhaya* (so KV).

90 So AD, Tib., Chin. (Chin. with *°enā*); BC corrupt; K *buddha-adhiṣṭhite*, V *buddhādhiṣṭhite*

91 B adds *kula-putra* (so KV), which is not supported by Tib. or Chin.

92 Emend possibly to *sadyaḥ-°*; cf. Tib. *'phral-du sdig-pa 'phrog-pa*; B *°-hārī*.

93 A *°-nāyitā*, C *°-nāyikāṃ*; E om. *sadya(ḥ)-pāpa-harī bodhisattva-nāyikā* (cf. K p. 115 n.12); K reconstr. *(bodhi-dadātṛī pāpa-hāra)kā*!, V *(bodhi-dātrī) pāpa-hārakā*; cf. Tib. *byaṅ-chub sbyin-par byed-pa*, i.e. *bodhi-dātrī*! Tib. adds here *'di-lta-ste* (a translator's gloss?)!

94 E *śakṛta* (?)(cf. K p. 115 n. 13); K em. *śaknoti* (so V)!

95 K *asyā*; V *asyânu°*!; one would expect *(a)syā(ḥ)*, gen.fem.!

96 So KV; ABCD *vaktraṃ*!; K adds *yāvad*, V *yāvat*!.

97 KV *°-mātreṇa*!

98 KV *sarva-parṣan-°* (K mispr. *°-parṣaṇ-°*?), which is not supported by Tib. *dkyil-'khor thams-cad-du dbaṅ-bskur-bar 'gyur-ro*. In this case *parṣan-maṇḍala-* is not acceptable. *maṇḍalābhiṣikta-* is without doubt used in a Tāntric sense; cf. e.g. G. Tucci, *The Theory and Practice of the Mandala* (London 1969), p. 44.

99 KV *°ṣiktā bhavanti*!

100 KV *°āḥ*!

101 So C, Tib. *de-nas*; KV om. *khalv*; ABD *evam ukte*.

102 A *°van iyaṃ* (so V!); B *°vatīyaṃ*.

103 C *saṃkṣiptā* (for *svalpākṣarā*); KV *svalpākṣarā prajñāpāramitā*; Tib. om. *svalpākṣarā*; Chin. instead *prajñā-pāramitā-dhāraṇī* repeatedly in the context.

104 K *°tvāt*!, V *°tvāt* (with daṇḍa).

105 So AD: Tib. *spro-ba chuṅ-ba*; other MSS corrupt; K *mandās mādas*! (cf. K p. 115 n. 14), V *mandasvādāḥ*, ...!

106 KV add *svalpākṣarāṃ* (so C *°rā*), which is missing in Tib.

107 KV *likhāyayiṣ°* (V mispr. *likhāyiṣ°*?).

108 C *te sarvo*, KV *te sarve*.

109 KV *alp°*.

110 K *°-putreyaṃ*, V *°-putra iyaṃ*; Tib. om. *kula-putra*.

111 KV add here *svalpākṣarā*; Tib. om. *saṃkṣiptā svalpākṣarā*.

112 So ABCD and KV (with hiatus).

113 KV *bhagavan* (K *°aṃ*) *paramāścaryaṃ*; Tib. does not support *parama-*.

114 KV *bhagavān*!.

[115] Tib. adds here *'di*, i.e. *ayaṃ*; K *ayan*, V *ayaṃ* (for *sukhāya*)!

[116] KV *bhāṣito* : Tib. *bka'-stsol-ba*.

[117] So BCD: Tib. *sems-can bsod-nams chuṅ-ṅu-rnams-kyi*; A om. *sattvānāṃ*; KV *manda-pudgalānāṃ*.

[118] K °-*sattvo*.

[119] K °*āḥ*, omitting the following *mahā-sattvāḥ* (so Tib.).

[120] BC °*vati* (so K!).

[121] K *loka*!

[122] C °-*pāramitā nāma dhāraṇī*; B *śrī-prajñā-pāramitā-śata-nāma-dhāraṇī*.

[123] C *parisamāptā*; K om. colophon; V *sv-alpâkṣarā prajñā-pāramitā samāptā*; cf. Tib. *'phags-pa śes-rab-kyi pha-rol-tu phyin-pa yi-ge ñuṅ-ṅu źes bya-ba theg-pa chen-po'i mdo rdzogs-so*.

[124] C om. IX (so KV, Tib., Chin.); *pādaiḥ* is used as an expression of reverence (cf. Böhtlingk-Roth, *Sanskrit-Wörterbuch*, IV Sp. 648, q.v. 1) and at the same time as the so-called "pluralis majestatis" (cf. Speyer, *Sanskrit-Syntax*, § 23 Rem.); cf. also n. 45 above.

Tibetan Text*

rgya-gar-skad-du / ā-rya-sva-lpā-kṣa-ra-[1]pra-dzñā-pā-ra-mi-tā nā-ma ma-hā-yā-na-sū-tra / bod-skad-du / 'phags-pa śes-rab-kyi pha-rol-tu phyin-pa yi-ge ñuṅ-ṅu źes bya-ba theg-pa chen-po'i mdo //

I. saṅs-rgyas daṅ / byaṅ-chub-sems-dpa' thams-cad-la phyag-'tshal-lo //[2]

IIa. 'di-skad bdag-gis thos-pa dus gcig-na /[3] bcom-ldan-'das rgyal-po'i khab-na bya-rgod phuṅ-po'i ri-la dge-sloṅ khri-ñis-stoṅ-lṅa-(L255b)brgya'i dge-sloṅ-gi dge-'dun chen-po[4] daṅ / (L'42b) byaṅ-chub-sems-dpa' bya-ba khrag-khrig 'bum-phrag du-ma daṅ thabs gcig-tu bźugs-te / brgya-byin daṅ / tshaṅs-pa daṅ / 'jig-rten skyoṅ-ba-la sogs-pa lha bye-ba khrag-khrig 'bum-gyis yoṅs-su bskor-ciṅ mdun-gyis bltas-te / dpal-gyi sñiṅ-po'i seṅge'i khri-la[5] bźugs-so //

IIb.[6]

IIIa. de-nas byaṅ-chub-sems-dpa' sems-dpa' chen-po 'phags-pa spyan-ras-gzigs dbaṅ-phyug[7] stan-las laṅs-te / bla-gos phrag-pa gcig-tu gzar-nas pus-mo gYas-pa'i lha-ṅa sa-la btsugs-te / bcom-ldan-'das ga-la-ba de logs-su thal-mo sbyar-ba btud-nas 'dzum mul-te bcom-ldan-'das-la 'di-skad ces gsol-to // bcom-ldan-'das / śes-rab-kyi pha-rol-tu phyin-pa yi-ge ñuṅ-ṅu-la bsod-nams che-ba[8] / gaṅ thos-pa tsam-gyis sems-can thams-cad-(N'90A) kyi las-kyi sgrib-pa thams-cad byaṅ-bar 'gyur-ba daṅ / byaṅ-(N259A)chub-la ṅes-par gźol-bar 'gyur-ba daṅ / gaṅ-dag sṅags[9] sgrub-par brtson-pa de-dag bgegs ma mchis-par[10] gsaṅ-sṅags 'grub-par 'gyur-ba bśad-du gsol //

IIIb. de-nas bcom-ldan-'das-kyis byaṅ-chub-sems-dpa' sems-dpa' chen-po 'phags-(P'38b)pa syan-ras-gzigs dbaṅ-phyug-la legs-so źes bya-ba byin-te / rigs-kyi bu / khyod yun riṅ-por sems-can thams-cad-la (L'43a) phan-pa'i phyir brtson-pa legs-so / legs-so /[11] de'i phyir rigs-(L256a)kyi bu / legs-par rab-tu ñon-la yid-la zuṅs-śig daṅ / śes-rab-kyi pha-rol-tu phyin-pa yi-ge ñuṅ-ṅu-la bsod-nams che-ba[8] /[12] gaṅ thos-pa tsam-gyis sems-can thams-cad-kyi las-kyi sgrib-pa thams-cad byaṅ-bar 'gyur-ba daṅ / byaṅ-chub-la ṅes-par gźol-bar 'gyur-ba daṅ / gaṅ-dag gsaṅ-sṅags sgrub-par brtson-pa de-dag bgegs med-par[13] sṅags 'grub-par 'gyur-ba ṅas khyod-la bśad-do //

IIIc. de-nas byaṅ-chub-sems-dpa' sems-dpa' chen-po 'phags-pa spyan-ras-gzigs dbaṅ-phyug-gis bcom-ldan-'das-la 'di-skad ces gsol-to // sems-can thams-cad-la sman-pa'i slad-du bśad-du gsol[14] //

IV. de-nas bcom-ldan-'das-kyis de'i tshe sems-can thams-cad dgrol-ba[15] (N'90b) źes bya-ba'i tiṅ-ṅe-'dzin-la sñoms-par źugs-so // mñam-par bźag-pa des[16] smin-mtshams-kyi mdzod-(N259b)spu'i phrag-nas 'od-zer 'bum-phrag du-ma[17] byuṅ-ste / 'od-zer de-dag-gis saṅs-rgyas-kyi źiṅ thams-cad khyab-par gyur-to // sems-can gaṅ-dag 'od-zer des reg-pa[18] sems-can dmyal-ba-pa[19] yan-chad sems-can de-dag thams-cad bla-na med-pa yaṅ-dag-par rdzogs-(L'43b) pa'i byaṅ-chub-tu ṅes-par gyur-to[20] // saṅs-rgyas-kyi źiṅ thams-cad-kyaṅ[21] rnam-pa drug-tu gYos-so // de-bźin-gśegs-pa'i źabs-kyi druṅ-du[22] lha'i tsandan-gyi phye-ma'i char-yaṅ bab-bo //

Va. de-nas bcom-ldan-'das-(L256b)kyis de'i tshe śes-rab-kyi pha-rol-tu phyin-pa gsuṅs-pa //

Vb. 'di-lta-ste / byaṅ-chub-sems-dpa'[23] mñam-pa'i sems daṅ / byams-pa'i sems daṅ / byas-pa gzo-ba daṅ /[24] sdig-pa thams-cad daṅ bral-ba'i sems-su bya'o // śes-rab-kyi pha-rol-tu phyin-pa'i sñiṅ-po 'di-yaṅ gdon-(P'39a)par bya'o //

Vc. de-bźin-gśegs-pa dgra-bcom-pa yaṅ-dag-par rdzogs-pa'i saṅs-rgyas śākya thub-pa-la phyag-'tshal-lo[25] //

Vd. tadya-thā / oṃ mu-ne mu-ne[26] / ma-hā-mu-na-ye[27] svā-hā //

Ve. ṅas śes-rab-kyi pha-rol-tu phyin-pa 'di rñed-pas bla-na med-pa yaṅ-dag-par rdzogs-pa'i byaṅ-chub thob-bo // saṅs-rgyas thams-cad-kyaṅ 'di-las byuṅ-ṅo // de-bźin-gśegs-(N'91a)pa śākya thub-pa chen-po-las khyod-kyis 'di-ñid[28] thob-pas / de'i phyir byaṅ-chub-sems-dpa' sems-dpa' chen-po-rnams-kyi mchog-tu gyur-to // khyod de-bźin-gśegs-pa dgra-bcom-pa yaṅ-(N260a)dag-par rdzogs-pa'i saṅs-rgyas 'od-zer kun-nas 'phags-pa dpal brtsegs rgyal-po[29] źes bya-bar 'gyur-ro // źes saṅs-rgyas-ñid-du luṅ-yaṅ bstan-to //

Vf. gaṅ-dag (L'44a) khyod-kyi miṅ ñan-pa daṅ / 'dzin-pa daṅ / klog-pa daṅ /[30] gźan-dag-la-yaṅ rgya-cher bstan-pa daṅ / glegs-bam-du bris-nas[31] mchod-pa byed-pa[32] de-dag thams-cad ma 'oṅs-pa'i dus-na de-bźin-gśegs-par 'gyur-ro //

Vg. tadya-thā / oṃ[33] dza-ya dza-ya / padmā-bhe[34] / a-ba-me[35] / sa-ra sa-ra-ṇi / dhi-ri dhi-ri / dhi-ri dhi-ri[36] / de-ba-tā-nu-pā-la-ne[37] / bud-dhot-tā-(L257a)ra-ṇi[38] / pū-ra-ya / pū-ra-ya[39] / bha-ga-ba-ti / sarbā-śāṃ[40] ma-ma[41] pa-ri-pū-ra-ya[42] sa-pa-ri-bā-ra-sya[43] sarba-sa-tvā-nā-ñtsa / sarba-karmā-ba-ra-ṇā-ni[44] bi-śo-dha-ya bi-śo-dha-ya[45] buddha-a-dhi-ṣṭhā-ne-na[46] svā-hā //

Vh. don dam-pa śes-rab-kyi pha-rol-tu phyin-pa 'di-ni saṅs-rgyas thams-cad skyed-pa / byaṅ-chub-sems-dpa'i yum / 'phral-du sdig-pa 'phrog-pa / byaṅ-chub sbyin-par byed-pa-ste[47] / 'di-lta-ste[48] / bskal-pa bye-ba brgyar-yaṅ saṅs-rgyas thams-(N'91b)ca-kyi phan-yon brjod-par mi nus-so // 'di bklags-pas dkyil-'khor thams-cad-du dbaṅ-bskur-bar 'gyur-ro[49] // gsaṅ-sṅags thams-cad-kyaṅ mṅon-du 'gyur-ro //

VIa. de-nas byaṅ-chub-sems-dpa' sems-dpa' chen-po 'phags-pa spyan-ras-gzigs dbaṅ-phyug-gis bcom-ldan-(N260b)'das-la 'di-skad ces gsol-to // bcom-(P'39b)ldan-'das / ci'i slad-du 'di śes-rab-kyi pha-rol-tu phyin-pa[50] źes bgyi //

VIb. (L'44b) bcom-ldan-'das-kyis bka'-stsal-pa / thabs sla-ba'i phyir-te / sems-can gaṅ-dag spro-ba chuṅ-ba[51] de-dag śes-rab-kyi pha-rol-tu phyin-pa[52] 'dzin-pa daṅ / klog-pa daṅ / yi-ger 'bri-ba[53] daṅ / yi-ger 'brir[53] 'jug-pa de-dag thams-cad thabs sla-bas byaṅ-chub-la gźol-bar 'gyur-te / de'i phyir śes-rab-kyi pha-rol-tu phyin-pa[54] źes bya'o //

VIIa. de-skad ces bka'-stsal-pa daṅ / byaṅ-chub-sems-dpa' sems-dpa' chen-po 'phags-pa spyan-ras-gzigs dbaṅ-phyug-gis bcom-ldan-'das-(L257b)la 'di-skad ces gsol-to // bcom-ldan-'das-kyis[55] ji-tsam-du sems-can thams-cad-la sman-pa[56] daṅ / sems-can bsod-nams chuṅ-ṅu-rnams-kyi don daṅ / sman-pa daṅ / bde-ba'i slad-du[57] chos-kyi rnam-graṅs 'di[58] bka'-stsal-pa / bcom-ldan-'das / ṅo-mtshar-to // bde-bar gśegs-pa / ṅo-mtshar-to //

VIIb. (N'92a) bcom-ldan-'das-kyis de-skad ces bka'-stsal-nas byaṅ-chub-sems-dpa' sems-dpa' chen-po 'phags-pa spyan-ras-gzigs dbaṅ-phyug daṅ / dge-sloṅ de-dag daṅ / byaṅ-chub-sems-dpa'[59] de-dag daṅ / lha daṅ / mi daṅ / lha ma yin daṅ / dri-zar bcas-pa'i 'jig-rten yi-raṅs-te bcom-ldan-'das-kyis gsuṅs-pa-la mṅon-par bstod-do // //

VIII. 'phags-pa śes-rab-kyi pha-rol-tu phyin-pa yi-ge (N261a) ñuṅ-ṅu źes (L'45a) bya-ba theg-pa chen-po'i mdo rdzogs-so // //[60].

N O T E S (Tibetan text)

* Minor variants are neglected in the footnotes. For abbreviations see my "Prefatory Notes" above.

1 L *sā-lpā-kṣa-ra-*˙, L' *svā-lpā-a-kṣa-ra-*˙, N *sā-lpa / akṣa-ra-*˙, N' *svāl-pa-a-kṣa-ra-*˙, P' *sal-pa-* (damaged).
2 Cf. Skt. text n. 2.
3 Cf. Skt. text n. 4.
4 Cf. Skt. text n. 5.
5 Cf. Skt. text n. 9.
6 Cf. Skt. text n. 12.
7 *Spyan-ras-gzigs dbaṅ-phyug* = *Avalokiteśvara.*
8 Cf. Skt. *Prajñā-pāramitāṃ sv-alpākṣarāṃ mahā-puṇyāṃ.*
9 L'N' *gsaṅ-sṅags*; both *gsaṅ-sṅags* and *sṅags* are used in IIIa/b, and Vh.
10 Cf. IIIb *bgegs med-par* : Skt. *a-vighnena.*
11 L'N' om. one *legs-so.*
12 L'N' om. *thams-cad.*

13 Cf. IIIa *bgegs ma mchis-par* : Skt. *a-vighnena*.
14 Cf. Skt. *tena hi sugato bhāṣatu sarva-sattva-hitāya sukhāya ca*.
15 Cf. Skt. text n. 36.
16 L *daṅ*, N *de*; cf. Skt. text n. 37.
17 Cf. Skt. *raśmi-koṭi-niyuta-śata-sahasrais*.
18 N om. *reg-pa*.
19 L'N' *dmyal-ba*.
20 Cf. Skt. text n. 42.
21 L'N' om. *kyaṅ*.
22 Cf. Skt. text n. 45.
23 Skt. adds *mahā-sattva-*.
24 Skt. repeats synonymous *kṛta-jña-* and *kṛta-vedin-*.
25 Cf. Skt. text n. 51.
26 L *mu-ni mu-ni*.
27 N'P' °*-ne-ye*.
28 Skt. adds *prajñā-pāramitā*.
29 N adds *gśegs-pa* (? Skt. *udgata-*) superfluously after *'phags-pa*; cf. Skt. text n. 63.
30 Skt. adds *likhiṣyanti likhāpayiṣyanti*.
31 Skt. adds *sva-gṛhe*.
32 Cf. Skt. text n. 71.
33 LNP' om. *oṃ*.
34 LL' *padmā-*°; cf. Skt. text n. 75.
35 P °*-mo*.
36 N *dhi-ri dhi-ri / dhi-ri dhi-ri /* (260a4) *dhi-rā dhi-ri /*; cf. Skt. text n. 79-80.
37 L' °*-ta-a-nu-*°, NN' °*-tā / a-nu-*°, P' °*-tā-a-nu-*°; cf. Skt. text n. 81.
38 L *bu-ddho-tta-*°, N *bu-dhod-*(?)*ta-ri-ṇi*, P' *buddha-u-* (damaged); cf. Skt. text n. 82.
39 N' *pū-*° *pū-*°; LNP' om. one *pū-ra-ya*; cf. Skt. text n. 83.
40 So only N'; L *sarba-śa-ma*, N *sarbā-*(?)*ā-śā-*°, P' *sarba-a-śa-*°; cf. Skt. text n. 84.
41 So only N'; N om. *ma-ma*; LL'P' *śa-ma!*; cf. Skt. text n. 85.
42 LNP' om. *pa-ri-pū-ra-ya*; cf. Skt. text n. 86.
43 So L'N' (but L' *-bă-*); LNP' om. *sa-pa-ri-bă-ra-sya*; cf. Skt. text n. 87.
44 N' °*-karma-ā-*°, N °*-karmā / ā-ba-ra-ṇa*, P' °*-karma-a-pa-ra-ṇa*, LL' °*-karmā-pa-ra-ṇa*; cf. Skt. text n. 88.
45 L *bi-śo-ddha-ya bi-śo-ddha-ya*; P' om. one *bi-śo-dha-ya*; cf. Skt. text 89.
46 Cf. Skt. text n. 90.
47 N' *byed-pa* (without daṇḍa); cf. also Skt. text n. 93.
48 Cf. Skt. text n. 93 end.
49 Cf. Skt. text n. 98.
50 Cf. Skt. text n. 103.
51 Cf. Skt. text n. 105.

[52] Skt. adds *imaṃ*.

[53] N' *'dri-* (instead of *'bri-*: cf. Skt. *likh-*; also Jäschke's Tib.-Eng.Dict. p. 283a *'dri-ba* 2, s.v.).

[54] Cf. Skt. text n. 110-111.

[55] LN om. *kyis*.

[56] Cf. Skt. °*-hitāya sukhāya*.

[57] Cf. Skt. *hitāya sukhāya ca*.

[58] Cf. Skt. text n. 115.

[59] Cf. Skt. text n. 119.

[60] Cf. Skt. text n. 123, also 124.

(*My thanks are due to the Bibliothèque Nationale de Paris and the University of Tokyo Library for having sent me photocopies of Sanskrit and/or Tibetan materials in their possession.*)

English Translation of the Chinese Text

I. . . .

IIa. (T. 8, 852c28) Thus have I heard once upon a time. The Bhagavat stayed in Rājagṛha on the Mountain Gṛdhrakūṭa together with a great *bhikṣu-saṃgha* 1250 strong, and with many hundreds of thousands of *koṭis* of *nayutas* of Bodhisattvas, (and) was also worshipped and surrounded by hundreds of thousands of *koṭis* of *nayutas* of gods[1] (including) Brahman, Śakra, (and) World-Guardians. (853a3) Thereupon, The Bhagavat sat cross-legged on the glorious Lion's Seat of Treasury (*śrī-ratna-garbha-siṃhāsana*).

IIb. . . .

IIIa. (853a4) At this time, Āryāvalokiteśvara Bodhisattva Mahāsattva arose from his seat, put his garment over the right shoulder, fell on his right knee to the earth, gazed upon the (Buddha's) face with respect[2] and did not turn away his eyes for some time, worshipped with folded hands, danced with joy, bowed down at the (Buddha's) feet with his forehead, and then said to the Buddha: "Pray, O Bhagavat, expound this *Svalpākṣarā Prajñāpāramitā-sūtra* for my sake! Let beings hear this law, attain great merits, completely extinguish every hindrance of deeds, and attain the utmost enlightenment swiftly! If beings were to produce the thought of whole-heartedness and hold and recite this *mantra*, they would definitely reach the goal in accordance with their wishes."

IIIb. (853a12) Thereupon, the Bhagavat said to Āryāvalokiteśvara Bodhisattva Mahāsattva: "Well done! You have explained this very well! Well done, well done, O Kulaputra! You are able to produce the thought of whole-heartedness in such a way, as to make beings attain contentment and longevity. Listen carefully, O you, Kulaputra! Listen attentively! I shall expound this *Svalpākṣarā Prajñāpāramitā-sūtra*. If beings hear (me) expound this law, (they will attain great merits, completely extinguish every hindrance of deeds, and swiftly attain the supreme, righteous enlightenment. If a being produces the thought of accepting this *mantra*, (he will) meet no calamity of the Māras and in every case reaches the goal."

IIIc. (853a19) At this time Āryāvalokiteśvara Bodhisattva Mahāsattva said to the Bhagavat: "O Bhagavat, O Sugata, expound now so that beings may attain contentment!"

IV. (853a21) Thereupon, the Bhagavat entered for a moment into the *samādhi* called the Emancipation of All Beings (*Sarva-sattva-pramocanā*), and arose from his concentration. The hair-tuft between his eyebrows then emitted hundreds of thousands of *koṭi*s of *nayuta*s of rays of light. Thesc great rays of light illuminated every Buddha-Land. Innumerable beings were touched by the rays of illumination. All attained the *anuttara-samyak-sambodhi* definitely and swiftly. Every infernal being attained contentment. The Buddha-Lands trembled in six ways. Upon the Buddhas rained heavenly sandalwood powder showers. Delicate incense was offered.

Va. (853a28) Thereupon the Bhagavat expounded this *Prajñāpāramitā-sūtra*.

Vb. At this time each one of all the Bodhisattva Mahāsattvas produced calm thought, produced compassion, produced a mindful and altruistic thought, produced a mind devoid of every hindrance of evil deeds, produced various thoughts for the common good, and produced a mind of the *Prajñāpāramitā*. At this time the Bhagavat said to Āryāvalokiteśvara Bodhisattva Mahāsattva: "You people, listen carefully! I shall expound the sacred *Bhagavatī-Svalpākṣarā Prajñāpāramitā-mantra* for your sake."

Vc. (853b6) *namaḥ śākya-munaye tathāgatāyârhate samyak-saṃbuddhāya /*

Vd. (853b8) *tad-yathā / mune mune mahā-munaye svāhā / /*

Ve. (853b10) The Buddha said to Āryāvalokiteśvara Bodhisattva Mahāsattva: "This is the sacred *Bhagavatī*-Svalpākṣarā-Prajñāpāramitā-mantra. All the Buddhas have by means of this attained the *anuttara-samyak-saṃbodhi*. By menas of this *Svapākṣarā-Prajñāpāramitā-mantra* I shall also attain the supreme, righteous enlightenment. Once upon a time there was a Buddha, Śākya-muni Tathāgata by name. Under this Buddha, (You/I)[3] heard (him) expound this law. That Buddha explains: 'In this way all the Buddhas in the three worlds will certainly become enlightened on account of this law!' " (853b17) Furthermore, the Buddha said to Āryāvalokiteśvara Bodhisattva Mahāsattva: "I now bestow the prediction for your sake. You will in the future world of human beings attain the *buddha-mārga* under the name of King (Possessed of) the Glorious Peak [Heap] of Wealth (risen from) the Rays of Light Emitted Universally (*Samanta-rasmy-udgata-śrī-ratna-kūṭa-rāja*), Tathāgata Samyak-saṃbuddha."[4]

Vf. (853b19) "You will be able to hear the true law in this way. You should hold, recite, copy by yourself, or teach to others, consider and understand the book. Moreover, for the sake of all the other beings, (you should) expound its significance in detail. Let them copy, hold, and recite this *Sūtra* in their houses. (And they will) swiftly attain the supreme, righteous enlightenment in the future world. At this time all the Tathāgatas will approve you people in the same way. I now furthermore expound the *Prajñāpāramitā-dhāraṇī* for your sake:"

Vg. (853b26) *tad-yathā / oṃ jaya jaya padmāhe avame sara sariṇi bhiri bhiri bhirā bhiri khiri khiri devatānupālane buddhotāraṇi puraṇi puraya bhagavati sarvāśāṃ mama puraya sarva-satvānāṃ ca sarva-karmāvaraṇāni*[5] *viśodhaya viśodhaya buddhādhiṣṭhānenā svāhā / /*[6]

Vh. (853c6) The Buddha said to Āryāvalokiteśvara Bodhisattva Mahāsattva: "This is the supreme *Saddharma-Prajñāpāramitā-dhāraṇī*. This is the generator, the mother of all the Buddhas and Bodhisattvas. As soon as beings hear this law, all the hindrances of deeds will disappear completely. All the Buddhas and Bodhisattvas will not be able to complete expounding the merits of this law even after hundreds of thousands of *koṭi*s of *kalpa*s. If (they) hold and recite this *dhāraṇī*, (they) will enter together into the entire *maṇḍala* and be able to be consecrated. Moreover, accepting all the *mantra*s, (they) will attain the goal."

VIa. (853c12) At this time Āryāvalokiteśvara Bodhisattva Mahāsattva said to the Buddha: "O Bhagavat, for what reason do you further expound this *Prajñāpāramitā-dhāranī*?"

VIb. The Bhagavat said: "I am concerned about all those beings with little skillful means and with laziness. For this reason (I) expound this *Prajñāpāramitā-dhāraṇī*. Let them hold, recite, copy, or teach the book to others! All these beings will immediately attain the utmost enlightenment." Like this, like this, the Bhagavat expounded well this *Prajñāpāramitā-dhāraṇī*.

VIIa. (853c18) At this time Āryavalokiteśvara Bodhisattva Mahāsattva said to the Buddha: "O Bhagavat, this law is indeed marvelous! O Bhagavat, this law is indeed marvelous! The Sugata Bhagavat of great compassion (*mahā-kāruṇika*), in his desire to save all the beings of little skillful means and with laziness, lets them attain the common good and contentment, (and) expounds this true law."

VIIb. (853c22) At this time the Bhagavat completed expounding this *sūtra*. Great Śrāvakas and Bodhisattva Mahāsattvas, the entire world of gods, men, Asuras, and Gandharvas, heard the Buddha expound (it); all rejoiced greatly, believed, practiced, made obeisance, and retired.

VIII. . . The *Buddha-vacana-Ārya-Bhagavatī-Svalpākṣarā-Prajñāpāramitā*.

NOTES ON THE CHINESE TEXT

Owing to limited space, detailed notes had to be omitted.

1. Cf. Skt. text n. 8.
2. *yen*, 'face' (cf. T. 8, 853 n. 2. See also Chi-sha) should be the true reading for T. 853a3, *t'ou*, 'head' (= Shuku!)
3. Cf. Skt. text n. 58.
4. Cf. Skt. text n. 63.
5. T. 8, 853c3-4 °*-varmāvaraṇāni* (without note) should be a misprint for °*-karmāv*° (so Chi-sha, Shuku) (cf. Skt. text n. 88).
6. Cf. Skt. text. n. 74-90.

Contributors

Harold G. Coward is Professor and Head of the Religious Studies Department, University of Calgary. He holds a Ph.D. in Indian philosophy and religion from McMaster University, where he studied under Professor T. R. V. Murti. He has been a visiting research scholar at the Center for Advanced Studies in Philosophy, Benares Hindu University. He is the author of *Sphoṭa Theory* (Motilal Banarsidass, 1976) and *Bhartṛhari* (Twayne, 1976).

Eva Dargyay is a Reader in Tibetology at the University of Munich, where she obtained her doctorate degree. She did research with various Tibetan groups in India and Switzerland. She is the author of *The Rise of Esoteric Buddhism in Tibet* (1976), *Struktur und Wandel des Tibetischen Dorfes* (1976), and several articles on the history of Tibetan religion and thought.

J. W. de Jong was Professor of Tibetan and Buddhist Studies, University of Leiden, from 1956 to 1965; since 1965 he has been Professor of South Asian and Buddhist Studies at the Australian National University, Canberra. His many publications include *Cinq chapitres de la Prasannapadā* (Paris, 1949) and *Mi la ras pa'i rnam thar: texte tibétain de la vie de Milarepa* (The Hague, 1959).

Lama Anagarika Govinda was born in Germany in 1898 and describes himself as "an Indian national of European descent and Buddhist faith, belonging to a Tibetan order and believing in the Brotherhood of Man." In his early life, he studied philosophy, art, and archaeology at three European universities and the International Buddhist Union. Later he settled in India and achieved distinction not only for his writings on Buddhism but also for his teaching at various Indian universities and for his paintings, which were exhibited in Calcutta, Bombay, New Delhi, Lucknow, and Allahabad. His published works include *Foundations of Tibetan Mysticism*, *The Way of the White Clouds* and *Creative Meditation and Multidimensional Consciousness.*

MASAAKI HATTORI is Professor of Indian Philosophy at Kyoto University. He holds a Ph.D. from Calcutta University; studied in Kyoto, Calcutta, and Harvard; and has taught at the University of Toronto. He is the author of *Dignāga, On Perception* (Harvard Oriental Series, No. 47, 1968), and several articles on Indian philosophy.

LEON HURVITZ was successively educated at the Boston Latin School and the University of Chicago, in the U.S. Army, at Columbia University, and in Kyoto, where he did "my *real* work under the tutelage of Tsukamoto Zenryū (with a little bit of help from his friends)." He has taught at the University of Washington, Seattle (1955 to 1971) and at the University of British Columbia (since 1971). His scholarly interest is mainly focussed upon Sino-Indian Buddhist contacts in the fourth and fifth centuries.

SHŌJUN INABA is Professor of Tibetan Studies at Ōtani University. He holds a Ph.D. from Ōtani, and also studied at IsMeo in Rome. He is the author of *Chibetto Koten Bunpō Gaku* (An outline of classical Tibetan grammar, rev. ed., 1966), and the translator of various works on the history of Tibetan Buddhism.

HISAO INAGAKI is Lecturer in Far Eastern Buddhism at the School of Oriental and African Studies, University of London. He holds an M.A. from Ryukoku University, Kyoto, and a Ph.D. from the University of London. He is a co-editor and co-translator of several editions of Pure Land texts published by the Ryukoku Translation Center, Ryukoku University.

YUICHI KAJIYAMA is Professor of Buddhist Studies at Kyoto University. He holds a Ph.D. from Kyoto and has studied and taught in the Universities of Nālandā, London, Vienna, Wisconsin, and California. He is the author and/or translator of numerous books and articles in Japanese, English, and German on Indian and Tibetan Buddhism. Among them are: *An Introduction to Buddhist Philosophy* (an annotated translation of the *Tarkabhāṣā* of Moksākaragupta), *Hassenju Hannya Kyō* (*Aṣṭasāhasrikā-prajñāpāramitā- sūtra*), and *Kū no Ronri* (The logic of emptiness).

LEWIS R. LANCASTER holds a Ph.D. in Buddhist Studies from the University of Wisconsin. He is Head of the Department of Oriental Languages, University of California, Berkeley, where he is currently an Associate Professor and Chairman of the Group in Buddhist Studies.

MAN-KAM LEUNG has been a colleague of H. V. Guenther in the Department of Far Eastern Studies at the University of Saskatchewan since 1965. A specialist in modern Chinese intellectual history, he has written several papers on different aspects of this subject, and is at present completing a major study of the career of the Ch'ing scholar-official Juan Yuan. He holds a Ph.D. from the University of Hawaii.

YUKEI MATSUNAGA is Professor of Buddhist Studies at Koyasan University. He is the author of *A History of Tantric and Esoteric Buddhism*, *Biography of the Successors of Esoteric Buddhism*, and *The Guhyasamāja Tantra: a New Critical Edition*.

HOJUN NAGASAKI was born in 1934 in Niigata, Japan and received his M.A. in Buddhist Studies from Ōtani University. From 1959 to 1964 he did postgraduate work in Buddhist thought and Indian philosophy under Dr. Satkari Mookerjee at Nalanda Pali Institute, India. Since 1970 he has been Associate Professor of Buddhism and Indian Studies at Ōtani University, specializing in early Indian Buddhism, Buddhist logic, and Jaina logic. His publications include *The Pramāṇavārttikam of Dharmakīrti—an English Translation of the First Chapter with the Autocommentary and with Elaborate Comments* (*Karikas I-LI*) [with Dr. S. Mookerjee], 1964, and numerous contributions to Japanese Buddhist journals.

JULIAN F. PAS is Associate Professor of Far Eastern Studies at the University of Saskatchewan where he teaches East Asian religions and philosophy. He holds degrees from the University of Louvain and a Ph.D. from McMaster University. He is presently engaged in work on a monograph on the Chinese Pure Land Master Shan-tao (613-681), about whose method of Amita meditation he published an article in *History of Religions*, November, 1974.

HUGH E. RICHARDSON was educated at Keble College, Oxford, and served in the Indian Civil Service from 1929 to 1950. His appointments as an officer of the Indian Foreign and Political Service included nine years in charge of the British and Indian Mission at Lhasa (1936–40, 1944, 1946–50), and two years in Chungking (1942–44). He has been a Visiting Professor at the University of California, Berkeley, and the University of Washington, Seattle. He is the author of *Ancient Historical Edicts at Lhasa* (*1952*), *Tibet and its History* (*1962*), and (with D. L. Snellgrove) *A Cultural History of Tibet* (*1968*).

R. MORTON SMITH holds M.A. degrees from the Universities of St. Andrews and Oxford, and was Lecturer in Sanskrit at Cambridge University from 1948 to 1955. Since 1955 he has been a member of the Department of Sanskrit and Indian Studies at the University of Toronto. He has written on various aspects of the Indian tradition and its historical development; on the history and early philosophy of the Brahmanas and the Upanisads, for which he has developed a rational chronology; on Indian art; and on the relation of the Indian tradition to contemporary life.

MERVYN SPRUNG is Head of the Department of Philosophy at Brock University, St. Catherine, Ontario.

SHŌKŌ TAKEUCHI is Professor of Buddhism at Ryukoku University. He is the author of the Japanese translation of Vasubandhu's commentary on the *Mahāyāna-saṃgraha*, *Chapter II* (*1952*) and of thirty articles on various aspects of Vijñaptimātra thought.

TARTHANG TULKU, RINPOCHE is a highly accomplished lama of the Tarthang Monastery in Eastern Tibet. In 1959 he journeyed to Sikkim and then to India with many other Tibetan refugees. Rinpoche served as professor of Buddhist philosophy at the Sanskrit University in Benares for six and one-half years. In 1968 he left India and traveled through Europe and America. On arrival in Berkeley in 1969 he established the Tibetan Nyingma Meditation Center, the Nyingma Institute, Dharma Press and Publishing, and Odiyan—Center of Nyingma Culture. He is the author and editor of many books in English and in Tibetan, including *Gesture of Balance* and five volumes of *Crystal Mirror*.

AKIRA YUYAMA studied at Osaka University of Foreign Studies and the Universities of Tokyo and Leiden, and obtained his Ph.D. from the Australian National University, Canberra, where he held research and teaching positions in South Asian and Buddhist Studies from 1965 to 1973. He then